TWENTY
ISRAELI
COMPOSERS

TWENTY
ISRAELI
COMPOSERS

Voices of a Culture

ROBERT FLEISHER

Foreword by Shulamit Ran

WAYNE STATE UNIVERSITY PRESS   DETROIT

Library of Congress Cataloging-in-Publication Data

Fleisher, Robert Jay, 1953–
    Twenty Israeli composers : voices of a culture / Robert Fleisher; foreword
by Shulamit Ran.
        p.   cm.
    Includes bibliographical references and index.
    ISBN 0-8143-2648-X (alk. paper)
    1. Composers—Israel—Interviews.   2. Music—Israel—20th century—
History and criticism.
    ML390.F59   1997
    780'.95694'09049—dc21   96-52284
                                                                            MN

Grateful acknowledgment is made for permission
to reproduce the musical examples that appear in this volume:
Examples 1 and 2: Jacoby, *Mutatio No. 1*
(Tel Aviv: Israel Music Institute, 1975),
courtesy of the composer.
Example 3: Ehrlich, *Bashrav*
(Jerusalem: Israeli Music Publications, 1959),
used with permission of Israeli Music Publications.
Examples 4 and 5: Seter, *Jerusalem*
(Tel Aviv: Israel Music Institute, 1970),
used with permission of the Israel Music Institute.
Examples 6–10: Avni, *Epitaph*
(Tel Aviv: Israel Music Institute, 1984),
used with permission of the Israel Music Institute.
Examples 11 and 12: Shapira, *Missa Viva*
(Tel Aviv: Israel Music Institute, 1982),
used with permission of the Israel Music Institute.
Example 13: Shapira, *Off Piano*, 1984,
used with permission of the composer.
Examples 14–18: Galay, *Tzu Singen un Tzu Sogen*
(Holon: Israel Brass-Woodwind Publications, 1983),
used with permission of Israel Brass-Woodwind Publications.
Example 19: Olivero, *Cantes Amargos*
(Tel Aviv: Israel Music Institute, 1983),
used with permission of the Israel Music Institute.

FOR MY PARENTS

CONTENTS

MUSICAL EXAMPLES

9

FOREWORD

It is an uncommon pleasure for me to contribute this foreword to Robert Fleisher's *Twenty Israeli Composers: Voices of a Culture*. Let me start by saying that the subject of this important study is near and dear to my heart, and one with which I can claim more than a passing familiarity, for the following reasons: I am a composer, I was born and raised in Israel, and I have maintained steady contact with Israeli music and Israeli composers over the years. For me, the participants—the cast of characters—who occupy the book's landscape range the full gamut from early mentors, to colleagues past and present, to younger friends and professional acquaintances. I know and recognize their voices as they emerge from its pages. Moreover, I have also had the pleasure of reading and hearing excerpts from these interviews at earlier stages.

The idea of this book is an excellent and timely one. Though various reference sources on Israeli composers have been published, I believe none has attempted to do what has been achieved in *Twenty Israeli Composers*. As will quickly become apparent to the reader, the book's subjects are people who have a great deal to say about a wide variety of topics. Their observations, diverse as they are, form a stimulating view of life in Israel, and of some of the immensely complicated issues, concerns, and challenges confronting Israeli society—seen

11

through the unique lens of the artist. The interviews in this book are both thoughtful and thought-provoking, encouraging at times, sad at others, and always very real. Moreover, they are presented in an ideal context: much important information and perspective is provided in the introduction and in the essays that introduce each generation of composers. The discography and bibliography are also valuable resources for further study.

Living as we do in the late twentieth century, ours is a small world—or so, at least, it seems. Thanks to the miracles of modern technology and communication and the easy accessibility of jet travel, television, satellite, and the Internet, we can be anywhere, anytime, literally at the push of a button. We certainly have the means and the capacity to experience the artistic expressions of peoples from around the globe without ever having to leave our own homes, if we so choose. In this day and age, Israeli music, Australian sculpture, or Sri Lankan dance should not be unfamiliar oddities. Yet in reality we are, for the most part, not only ignorant but also parochial when it comes to our knowledge of art and culture, especially contemporary art, in distant lands.

My own guess is that this situation is in no small measure a reflection of the general apathy to art created today, even close to home. Only a fraction of the vast majority of musical performing organizations' efforts in the United States is directed to the presentation and encouragement of contemporary music. Small wonder, then, that the part of the pie that is allotted (often by way of a token gesture) to new music is, for the most part, earmarked for American music. I am not suggesting that this is unfair. Quite to the contrary, one could readily argue that every society has an obligation to nurture and foster its own culture. But I am suggesting that in a better world newly created music, whatever its origin, would occupy a much more privileged position in the average concertgoer's musical priorities.

Which brings me back to *Twenty Israeli Composers*. The contemporary art-music scene in Israel is an extraordinarily vibrant and vital one, equaling in both quality and intensity that of countries many times Israel's size. This activity is all the more impressive when one considers that during its almost fifty years of statehood, Israel has enjoyed but the briefest periods of relative calm, politically speaking. Yet in spite of their exceptional creative achievements, Israeli composers are, as Professor Fleisher asserts, almost totally unknown in this country, even to specialists in the field of new music.

Foreword

Twenty Israeli Composers is a significant step in the right direction. The idea of opening a window into another culture by way of interviews with composers is far superior to the usual biographical entries included in the major reference books presently available to the music student or scholar. This book promises to be of interest to the scholar and to the nonspecialist alike. With his background in composition and ethnomusicology, Professor Fleisher has contributed something both unique and exciting. These interviews, spanning three generations of Israeli composers, are focused yet wide-ranged, thoughtful, and insightful. They reveal a broad panorama of views and provide an unprecedented glimpse into Israeli culture and society. There is a strong voice that emerges out of all of this—a voice that deserves to be heard. I say this not just as an Israeli, but also as a composer and as a citizen of the world.

I wonder whether, when he began doing his research some ten years ago, Professor Fleisher could have anticipated the degree to which the fruit of his labor would underline the broad notion that art and life are ultimately inseparable. Though it might not have been written with this objective in mind, this book is a must-read for all those who would imagine music to be nothing more than a form of comfortable, relaxing activity, something to soothe the day's travails at the office—a point of view that, regrettably, is gaining more and more ground even among those who would consider themselves faithful devotees of art music.

Looking from the outside at the field of ethnomusicology, I should think that one major goal of the discipline would be to turn "world music" into something other than a euphemism for "other people's music." This outstanding book is a welcome and significant contribution to this end.

Shulamit Ran
William H. Colvin Professor
in the Department of Music,
The University of Chicago

13

ACKNOWLEDGMENTS

This book and its author have received generous individual and institutional support, without which this publication would surely never have been possible. These acknowledgments can only begin to reflect the extent of these contributions and my gratitude.

First and foremost, I am indebted to twenty Israeli composers, who permitted a visitor whom they never met before 1986 to ask them many questions about their lives, their thoughts, and their music. It has been my privilege to be entrusted with each of their contributions to this volume, which together provide a rare view of Israeli culture and society. If in our first meetings these composers more than satisfied my interest to become better acquainted with contemporary Israeli music, their correspondence, and gifts of recordings, as well as of published and unpublished scores have further enhanced my appreciation of its breadth and variety. In addition, it has been possible to continue this process through subsequent meetings in the United States, including the visits of several composers to Northern Illinois University (NIU). I am also grateful for the kind assistance of Alice Jacoby and Dina Seter.

Among those whose contributions to the study of Israeli art music are cited in this book, two individuals, whom I have been privileged to know for many years, figure prominently. Alexander L. Ringer is Professor Emeritus of musicology at the University of Illinois, where

15

University of Chicago ethnomusicologist Philip V. Bohlman and I were graduate student colleagues. The writings of these two scholars concerning Israeli music evince great insight, and as critical, "outsider" perspectives, their objectivity lends these contributions special value. I am indebted to them both, not only for their important scholarship in this area, but also for their generous assistance, encouragement, and advice. Indeed, perhaps more than any other, Philip Bohlman has influenced the evolution of this book, from the initial project proposal stages to its publication. One stream of this influence has been the elegance and breadth of his own prolific scholarship; the other, his unwavering faith in the potential contribution of this book to an area of study that has been immeasurably enriched by his own eloquent writings.

Many others have provided valuable assistance, information, and suggestions. The helpful staff and many stimulating guests at Mishkenot Sha'ananim in Jerusalem, where I spent nearly seven weeks, made it an ideal base for my activities while in Israel. For several days I also enjoyed the hospitality of the nearby St. Andrew's Hospice, affiliated with the Church of Scotland. Yehudit (Jackie) Rudolph and Helena Flusfeder were two of the most amiable and helpful companions one could hope to encounter far from one's home. Professor Amnon Shiloah, of the Hebrew University, was a very gracious host, consultant, and an informative tour guide in and around Jerusalem.

David Beveridge read portions of an early draft and offered incisive and helpful criticism. Judith McCulloh at the University of Illinois Press provided much useful information and advice concerning copyrights and authorizations. Daniel Kazez subsequently provided many worthwhile suggestions which have strengthened the book in innumerable ways. Tzvi Avni and Noa Guy, two composers included in this volume, were uniquely qualified and kind enough to identify many details requiring modification or correction. Ari Ben-Shabetai and Yinam Leef, also in this book, provided information concerning other composers and the new Israeli Music Center. Alex Wasserman, a gifted young Israeli composer who once studied with Abel Ehrlich and was later my student at NIU, has been a very helpful consultant whose input I have sought on a number of occasions. Amnon Wolman at Northwestern University provided information concerning performances of Israeli works that he arranged in Chicago. Angela Cline translated an article about composer Tsippi Fleischer by Amnon Shiloah, from the original French. My cousin David

Leland and his wife Amira Joelson provided much useful information both before and after my visit to Israel. I am also indebted to Lee M. Floersheimer, formerly of the Elaine Kaufman Cultural Center's Birnbaum Music Library in New York City, and to the Performing Arts Research Collection at Lincoln Center and the Jewish Division of the New York Public Library. Several NIU colleagues also provided valuable assistance: Peter Middleton, Stephen Kern, Ted Hatmaker, William Baker, David Shavit, and Robert Green.

The Israel Music Institute, Israeli Music Publications, and Israel Brass-Wind Publications all kindly provided copies of scores and permission to reprint musical excerpts from various compositions. For the use of Else Lasker-Schüler's poem "Klein Sterbelied" I am grateful for the kind assistance of the previous copyright holder, Kösel Verlag (München), and to Suhrkamp Verlag (Frankfurt am Main) for permission to reprint it in the original German; to Eked Publishing House (Tel Aviv) and to the estate of Else Lasker-Schüler (P. A. Alsberg, administrator) for permission to reprint Yehuda Amichai's Hebrew translation, set to music by Tsippi Fleischer; and to Gila Abrahamson, for permission to use her English translation.

The Israel Music Institute has provided a great wealth of information and assistance, including the informative *IMI News,* issued quarterly. Former director William Y. Elias furnished a number of scores published by the IMI during my visit to Israel in 1986. While this book was being prepared for publication, director Paul Landau, *IMI News* editor Yuval Shaked, and Miriam Morgan—to whom I owe a special debt of gratitude—all responded generously to my seemingly endless inquiries and requests. In addition, the IMI, the Israel Composers' League, and the Jerusalem Rubin Academy of Music and Dance have provided copies of their publications.

Ephraim Mittelmann, archivist for the Israel Philharmonic Orchestra (IPO), provided permission to include Hanoch Jacoby's photograph and program note, as well as other valuable information and assistance. Avi Shoshani, general secretary of the IPO, granted permission to reprint passages of a previously published interview that Mr. Jacoby gave to Uri Toeplitz. Dr. Toeplitz, a chronicler and former member of the IPO, generously provided articles concerning several composers, previously included in IPO program booklets, and authorized the use of excerpts from the aforementioned interview. Dr. Gila Flam, Director of the National Music Library and National Sound Archives of the Jewish National and University Library, provided detailed information concerning the Israeli Music Center's recorded anthology of Israeli piano music, of which she is the producer. The photographs of each composer are used with the kind permission of the photographers acknowledged, as well as with the courtesy of other named individuals and organizations. Peggy Woznicki-Doherty at the Pittsburgh Symphony kindly relayed the photo of Ari Ben-Shabetai.

Shulamit Ran is among the most acclaimed living composers today. Trained as a pianist in her native Israel, she premiered her own *Capriccio* for piano and orchestra with the New York Philharmonic, conducted by Leonard Bernstein, at the age of fourteen. After attending the Mannes College of Music in New York, Ran studied with Ralph Shapey at the University of Chicago, where she has been a member of the music faculty since 1973. A recipient of many honors, including the Pulitzer Prize and Kennedy Center Friedheim Award, Professor Ran has also served as composer-in-residence with both the Chicago Symphony Orchestra and the Lyric Opera of Chicago. A vigorous proponent of contemporary Israeli music and arts, it was Shulamit Ran who first urged publication of these interviews in the present form. Her eloquent foreword to this volume is deeply appreciated.

This project would have remained merely an idea were it not for support received from the Northern Illinois University Graduate School (Jerrold H. Zar, Dean) and its Research and Artistry Committee. The first of several Graduate School grants, combined with a commission from the David C. and Sarajean Ruttenberg Arts Foundation, helped to support my stay in Israel during the summer of 1986. A concert and exhibition of "New Music from Israel," produced at NIU in April 1987 and featuring works by several of the composers represented in this book, was made possible by the generous support of the university and the Newman Fund of the National Foundation for Jewish Culture. In 1988, grants from the NIU Deans' Fund for Humanities Research facilitated transcription of the recorded interviews. For many months, Kelly Bowers spent countless hours accomplishing this arduous task, overcoming background noises, a variety of accents, and mechanical difficulties with good humor, and a growing interest in what these composers had to say.

Additional NIU support for research related to this project was provided by the Graduate School, Office of Faculty Development (Edwin L. Simpson, Director), the School of Music (Paul Bauer, Chair), and the College of Visual and Performing Arts (Harold A. Kafer, Dean). I am also indebted, for a variety of assistance, to the

NIU Office of Sponsored Projects (Linda Schwarz, Director). At NIU Art/Photo, Robert Banke produced prints of some photographs and of all musical examples. Considerable assistance was also provided by NIU music librarian H. Stephen Wright and library technical assistant Lynne M. Smith, as well as by the reference librarians at the Founders Memorial Library.

For *Twenty Israeli Composers* to have found a home at the Wayne State University Press is truly felicitous. I deeply appreciate the enthusiastic support, encouragement, and assistance of its director, Arthur B. Evans; the endorsement of the editorial board in welcoming this volume to its distinguished and diverse catalog; the meticulous scrutiny and many welcome enhancements furnished by copyeditor Jonathan Lawrence; and the understanding, wise counsel, and many forms of assistance generously provided by its managing editor, Kathryn Wildfong.

This book is dedicated to my mother, Doris, and to the memory of my father, Maurice Fleisher. Doris Fleisher has actively supported this effort in innumerable ways, and served in a variety of roles, including research assistant, editor, host, and, always, as a much valued advisor.

Finally, I am truly thankful for the encouragement, interest, patience, and assistance of my wife, Darsha Primich, throughout the many stages of this book's evolution.

INTRODUCTION

THE CULTURE OF ART MUSIC IN ISRAEL

In the mid-1960s, Alexander L. Ringer described the inspirations, influences, and stylistic elements associated with art music written by Israeli composers of the established "first generation" and by those of an emerging "second generation."[1] Ami Maayani, a prominent second-generation composer, a few years later celebrated "the breakthrough of Israeli music to countries overseas."[2] Though the increasingly active and eclectic contemporary art music of Israel[3] has been documented and disseminated through published scores, recordings, and international performances, most musicians, critics, and scholars outside of Israel remain unaware of this vibrant musical culture. The subject of contemporary Israeli music has been treated in depth by few writers. Though information concerning a small number of Israeli composers appears in standard music reference sources, few books on twentieth-century music mention Israeli composers or acknowledge the art-music tradition represented by those interviewed and cited in this volume. Books about Jewish music have emphasized traditional and liturgical genres, while most that have examined the art music of Israel and its creators, due to their vintage, have afforded greater attention to the era of the British Mandate than to the several decades of Israeli statehood that have ensued. Though more than a half-century of art music has been created in modern Israel, this

21

book is the first collection of interviews with any of this nation's many composers.[4]

Other deficiencies have also been noted in the literature concerning the arts of Israel. Peter Gradenwitz, a prolific chronicler of music and musicians in Israel since his immigration to Palestine in 1936, observed that "sympathy or lack of understanding" characterized most scholarship by "foreign" writers, while Israelis themselves were viewed as either "chauvinistic" or "over-critical" when treating the subject.[5] Indeed, much of the discourse, both past and present, concerning contemporary Israeli music has informed us more about its authors than its subject. A recent review by such a foreign observer, of a full-evening work by a composer in this book, lamented the "alien" influence of Ravel and the absence of Israel's "harsh topography and tough-minded mentality." Though acknowledging the "coherence" of the composition, the reviewer closed as follows: "One day, someone (and perhaps it will be he) is going to find the visceral center of modern Israel and turn it into important music."[6] The importance of musical composition is both a central assumption upon which this book rests and its raison d'être—a belief in the value of human creativity as a mirror of the individual artist and of his or her culture. This writer believes the past several decades have produced many important works by Israeli composers, some outstanding, all of which deserve a much wider audience. Perhaps as this repertoire becomes more familiar, fruitful discussion concerning the import of individual works will be more readily achieved.

During the past decade, several important new titles, by both "insiders" and "outsiders," have signaled the continuing development and growing recognition of Israel's contemporary art music.[7] The most recent is an informative social history of musical culture in the *Yishuv* by Jehoash Hirshberg, also the biographer of Israel's arguably best-known composer, Paul Ben-Haim.[8] Among Philip V. Bohlman's writings on Israel's musical history and culture are his studies of its German-Jewish community and, more recently, of the World Centre for Jewish Music in Palestine, one of the many cultural institutions established by members of that community.[9] Alice Tischler's bibliography of works by sixty-three Israeli art-music composers is the first reference source of its kind.[10] These publications have significantly advanced the state of knowledge concerning the art-music culture of Israel.

The present book of interviews with Israeli composers seeks to complement these important contributions to the study of Israeli musical culture, while also addressing a dimension that has until now been virtually neglected. As Mark Slobin recently stated, "We have not yet fully tapped into the rich resources of Jewish musical *consciousness,* as opposed to repertories."[11] During the 1978 World Congress on Jewish Music, held in Jerusalem, the distinguished ethnomusicologist Bruno Nettl explained why ideas about music need to be documented and preserved as much as the music itself:

> Of the various components of musical culture, the music itself, the sound, changes least rapidly; behaviour changes more, and the conceptions of music, the idea of what music is, what it does, what power it has, how it is defined, in the various cultures of the world, is something which changes perhaps most rapidly, or at least before the other components. If we are indeed to preserve something about music, we must find ways of preserving and recording the conceptions of music and musical behaviour; this seems to me to be in fact more urgent ethnomusicology than the continuing preservation of the musical artifact alone.[12]

It is in the spirit of preservation that this book presents twenty Israeli composers, discussing their lives, works, and ideas. In documenting a musical repertory, culture, and history, the interviews in this volume reflect the time and place of modern Israel.

Artists' first-person narratives provide a unique perspective concerning the interaction of inspiration, aesthetics, method, and cultural context. The study of contemporary music has been increasingly documented through collected interviews with composers of various national, ethnic, and aesthetic orientations.[13] This book is neither a definitive nor encyclopedic study of Israeli art music or its many composers. Rather, it is an unprecedented compilation of autobiographical texts that can contribute to our knowledge and understanding of contemporary Israeli music and culture. Book work and fieldwork have played mutually supporting roles in its formation, though its principal focus and contribution are unquestionably in the latter area. The dynamics of both cultural change and continuity are seen through the eyes and heard through the voices of these Israeli composers. At the same time, their accounts and recollections are corroborated by one another, and by written sources from past and present, from observers "inside" and "outside." The value of these interviews rests in the capacity of their unique perspective and considerable detail, neither found anywhere else, to balance and complement the growing scholarship in this area.

A number of additional considerations support the timeliness of this volume. Recent events signal a new stage in the ongoing development of Israel's musical culture: since 1990, the quarterly *Israel Music Institute News* has chronicled the activities of Israeli composers; orchestras have appointed their first composers-in-residence; the Israel Philharmonic Orchestra and New Israeli Opera have promoted the creation of new works through competitions; new graduate music programs, including those in composition, have been established at educational institutions; the Israel Composers' League created its own publishing firm (the Israeli Music Center) and is producing compact disk anthologies of Israeli piano music and art songs. Many important events have also occurred in the lives of those artists represented here: one was the first composer of art music in a quarter century to receive the coveted Israel Prize; several others received the prestigious Prime Minister's Prize; still others have received major international awards and commissions; and all have had works published, performed, or recorded both in Israel and abroad. On a sad note that also underscores the timeliness of this publication, two first-generation composers, Hanoch Jacoby and Mordecai Seter, are no longer living.

This book presents a broad and representative spectrum of Israeli composers, many of whom have earned places of special distinction in Israel and abroad. The remarkably diverse group includes all generations, sabras (native Israelis)[14] and immigrants, men and women, progressives and conservatives, those trained in Israel and those schooled abroad, those looking back on long, distinguished careers and those still establishing their own. This diversity reflects the pluralism not only of Israeli art music but also of Israeli culture and society as a whole. About a third of the composers included in this book are sabras, but their varied backgrounds also find expression in their work—as, for example, in Betty Olivero's settings of Ladino (Judeo-Spanish) poetry reflecting her Sephardic ancestry.[15] Like many of their fellow Israelis, the immigrant composers in this book (represented in all three generational groups) hail from a host of regions, including North and South America and Eastern and Central Europe. Entries concerning all composers included in Parts I and II appear in *The New Grove Dictionary of Music and Musicians* (1980) and in Alice Tischler's recent *Bibliography*. Most of the younger composers, presented in Part III, have experienced rapidly advancing careers and recognition in recent years, including performances, recordings, awards, and professional appointments.

Since the focus of this volume is the tradition and repertory of Israeli art music, which owes its existence to the sociocultural infrastructure established by European immigrants in the decades prior to independence, the region's popular, folk, religious, and ethnic musical traditions, both Arabic and Jewish, lie beyond its central scope. These traditions, which have received scholarly attention and certainly merit ongoing study, are among the many diverse influences on Israeli art-music composers. In applying an essentially ethnomusicological model of inquiry to the study of an art-music repertory and culture, this book takes its place in a steadily growing volume of scholarship that, since the 1960s, has demonstrated the compatibility of art music and ethnomusicology, the latter defined by Alan P. Merriam as "the study of music in culture."[16]

When these interviews were conducted in the summer of 1986, Israel was experiencing a nervous calm before the storm—in the aftermath of the Lebanon crises, the uneasy honeymoon of Labor and Likud parties in a "national unity" caused by stalemated election, and on the eve of the Palestinian *intifada* and the approaching Gulf War. Although fears of terrorism drastically diminished tourism, Israelis and other visitors still vacationed on the beaches of Eilat and visited Masada, the Dead Sea, the Holocaust memorial Yad Vashem, and the Old City of Jerusalem. Established cultural traditions proceeded as usual, including the biennial International Jerusalem Book Fair and the annual Israel Festival, featuring local productions and renowned performers from around the world. There were also special events: an outdoor rally in Jerusalem supporting the immigration of Soviet Jewry attracted a crowd estimated at ten thousand for a program featuring a variety of popular music and dance and speeches by government leaders Yitzhak Shamir and Shimon Peres, the late actor-singer Yves Montand, and Soviet dissident Natan Sharansky.

These interviews occurred during a seven-week residency at Mishkenot Sha'ananim ("Peaceful Dwelling"), a center for visiting artists and scholars near the Old City of Jerusalem. Between May 25 and July 15, conversations were recorded with twenty-four composers, both native and immigrant, ranging from distinguished representatives of the first generation to recent graduates of the Jerusalem Rubin Academy of Music and Dance.[17] A collective oral history based on

25

this multigenerational group of composers would, I thought, permit an important chapter of Israel's cultural history to be distilled and understood in an unprecedented way. My objective was to learn about Israel's art-music tradition at the midpoint of its first century, through the perspectives of its creative artists. The resulting collection of interviews offers a unique view of Israel's still developing but already distinctive culture—at once ancient and modern, Western and non-Western, religious and secular, traditional and progressive. Meetings with some composers were contemplated in advance, while others were suggested following my arrival in Israel. Most composers whom I contacted agreed to schedule an interview, and these took place in a variety of venues, including Mishkenot Sha'ananim, composers' homes, institutions with which they were affiliated, and in public places. In an effort to familiarize myself with the music of each composer, I attended concerts and rehearsals, studied scores, and listened to recordings, a process that has been ongoing.

Beginning with some of the composers whose music was discussed by Alexander Ringer two decades earlier, meetings were arranged with Josef Tal, Mordecai Seter, Abel Ehrlich, and Ben-Zion Orgad. Tal, Seter, and Ehrlich are highly individualistic representatives of Israel's first generation, a group numbering five immigrant composers in this book, including Hanoch Jacoby and Haim Alexander. Orgad, together with Tzvi Avni and Ami Maayani, are prominent composers of the second generation. While Avni and Orgad immigrated as children, Maayani is a sabra. The youngest and largest group of composers in this volume, designated the third generation, is the first to have been born and raised in the independent state of Israel. Like their fellow citizens, the composers of this generation have also experienced one or more wars in their midst, occurring every decade since 1948.[18] The oldest members of this group—Aharon Harlap, Arik Shapira, Daniel Galay, Tsippi Fleischer, Gabriel Iranyi, and Stephen Horenstein—were born between 1941 and 1948, a period that saw the end of World War II and the establishment of the state of Israel. Of these six composers, Shapira and Fleischer are sabras, while the other four are immigrants, all from different countries. The youngest composers of this group are sabras, with the exception only of Haim Permont, who immigrated from Eastern Europe. However defined, the experiences of these generational groups of composers reflect those of Israeli society at large.[19] The oral documentation presented here of Israel's art-music tradition thus forms an important chapter in its history and culture.

My approach to this project no doubt differs from that which another might have chosen. In these directed conversations, a core group of questions provided a narrative axis that served to unify the interviews. My background in composition prompted inquiries concerning musical training, influences, methods, and materials, while my ethnomusicological studies prompted questions concerning personal background, identity and nationalism, the motivation and ideas behind particular works, and composers' views of their own work in the broader context of contemporary Israeli music.[20] Specifically, subjects were asked to comment on when and where they were born; on their musical training and influential teachers or educational experiences; on the meaning of being an Israeli composer; on the role of, or relationship between, Western and non-Western influences in their music; and on their perspective concerning their music in relation to that of other contemporary Israeli composers.[21] Answers to these questions often prompted further queries, which elicited more specific or detailed recollections, or related information, insights, or opinions.

The responses to follow-up questions or those concerning individual compositions account for some of the differences among the interviews. While the reader will discern the expression of many common interests and concerns, the diversity of backgrounds, experiences, and points of view are also revealed. Other differences among the interviews reflect the broad range of personalities involved. In conversation, some composers were expansive, others succinct; some specific, others more general; some guarded, others revealing. In telling their own stories, they address a gap in the existing documentation of twentieth-century music, Israeli culture, and world cultural history. The autobiographical narratives presented in this volume enable the reader to step inside the creative process of Israeli art music, to better understand some of the infinite number of ways in which life becomes art, in Israel and elsewhere.

Each of the interviews, which ranged between forty-five and ninety-minutes in length, was conducted in English, a first language for only one of the twenty composers included in this volume. Since the preservation of the personal voice of each composer was considered as important as ensuring the clarity and comprehensibility of his or her remarks, the editing process was accomplished in several cautious and deliberate stages. After the interviews were transcribed, in 1988, each subject was sent a verbatim transcript and invited to make corrections, clarify meanings where needed, and fill in spaces left blank where utterances could not be clearly understood.[22] The resulting modifications to the interviews thus included minor changes, additions, and deletions. In the interest of coherence, my original questions and comments were ultimately removed from each interview, resulting in the present first-person narratives. Though further editorial adjustments then became necessary for continuity, changes to the original texts were purposefully limited in order to retain the meaning and expressive character of each speaker.

A recent book that includes interviews with five noted Israeli writers bears the title *Voices of Israel*.[23] Through the medium of first-person narratives, the twenty composers in the present volume also give voice to their experiences as creative artists within the contexts of Jewish and Israeli culture.[24] At the same time, the shared Jewish heritage and Israeli citizenship of the composers profiled here provides a framework that underscores their many individual differences—of generation, national origin, education, gender, and experience. The voices of Israeli culture in this book link the past, present, and future, and the music of local and global communities. Most of these interviews contain information about other artists (including composers, painters, filmmakers, writers, and sculptors), musical institutions, aesthetic influences, and the international framework in which Israeli art music has played an ever increasing role. Numerous twentieth-century personages whom these composers knew or found influential also appear, as do many significant historical events that have left their mark on this momentous era. Thus the social, political, and historical contexts that have helped to form these creative artists and their works are important dimensions throughout.

Issues of identity and nationalism are recurrent themes throughout this book, as they have been during the past two centuries and in the emergence and development of modern Israel. Jehoash Hirshberg has observed that British-mandate Palestine "presented a direct continuation of the history of the European national schools with their inherent tension between the vision of individuality and the urge to preserve links with mainstream world music."[25] Philip Bohlman has written that "Israel has an enormous repertory of national music."[26] The relationship between individual and communal imperatives has been a defining dialectic of Israeli culture. In the decades surrounding Israel's independence in 1948, when nationalistic impulses were intensely felt and expressed, much publicly debated criticism concerned the proper orientation and expression of the arts in the emerging nation. As in earlier and contemporary efforts elsewhere to forge a national art music, the use of folk and religious music was emphasized as a basis. But artists' individual priorities and materials are not always compatible with such collective aims, and many of the immigrant composers resisted the pressures and polemics of that period.

Each generation of Israeli composers has experienced different degrees of nationalistic fervor and influence. In the current day, the stated interests of many Israeli artists, like those elsewhere, have more to do with international developments than with the expression of a regional or nationalistic aesthetic. Among those represented in this book, the range of replies elicited to the question concerning what it means to be an Israeli composer offers ample evidence of the dangers of oversimplifying such complex issues. While evincing seemingly little interest in satisfying or perpetuating earlier notions of what Israeli music should be, contemporary composers have nonetheless created and continually expanded a body of literature that—as Josef Tal suggests in his interview—would not likely exist had the composers not lived and worked in Israel.

The culture of modern Israel in the broadest sense, with its native sabras and immigrants from the world over, is an intricate fabric of national and ethnic origins, languages and dialects, customs and traditions—a heterogeneous culture of cultures. A corresponding wealth of genres and styles coexists in Israeli musical life, including the classical music of Western and Middle Eastern traditions; musical genres associated with Jewish, Islamic, and Christian religious observance; and popular, rock, jazz, and "cassette" music.[27]

The language of Western art music exists in a material, written form, whereas even the most sophisticated and enduring music traditions of the non-Western world are orally transmitted. The tradition and repertory of art music in Israel in this sense is clearly Western, while its range of influences is extraordinarily diverse. Like the notational tradition of Western art music, the revived ancient language of Hebrew has proven adaptable to life in the twentieth century. So too has the development of contemporary art music in Israel, which, in reflecting the myriad influences elsewhere evident in Israeli culture, can be viewed as an expression of pluralism and unity.

The sphere of reference for Israeli art-music composers is reflected in the broad aesthetic palette of their works. Unlike their American and European counterparts, whose works have increasingly reflected the influence of non-Western aesthetics and musical traditions, composers in Israel do not view the East from afar.[28] As inhabitants of the Middle East, their sonic and cultural environment is a rich amalgam of influences from different times and places. The admixture found in contemporary Israeli music combines the old and the new—from the biblical cantillation of the synagogue and the modal and improvisational techniques of the Arabic *maqām* and *taqsīm,* to the twelve-tone compositional method of Arnold Schoenberg and his followers, to works employing electronic sound synthesis, digital processing, and multimedia.[29]

As in other cultures, the spectrum in contemporary Israeli art music includes conservative and progressive stylistic tendencies, programmatic and absolute music, the derivative and the iconoclastic. Classicism, romanticism, impressionism, serialism, and structuralist experimentation commingle with speech-rhythms of Hebrew, "Oriental-gestalt" and "mosaic" techniques of motivic organization.[30] Much contemporary art music in Israel concerns biblical subjects, Holocaust remembrance, or reflections of local landscape, historical events, or the sounds of Jerusalem's Old City. The choral tradition has played an important role in modern Israel, particularly in connection with life in the communal kibbutzim, and the "unusual interest in compositions for solo string instruments" has also been noted.[31] In these and other genres of Israeli music, in the abundant settings of biblical and modern secular Hebrew texts, as well as of poetry in other languages (Yiddish, Ladino, English, Arabic), the human voice and its instrumental extensions figure prominently.[32] Certain instruments, including trumpet and harp, appear to have favored status and symbolic value due to their association with biblical passages. Others, including violin, clarinet, cello, double bass, and percussion, are often used to evoke the *klezmers,* the musical ensembles born in the Eastern European shtetls.[33]

A much discussed element that has influenced the music of Israeli composers is the use of heterophonic textures. This approach can be described as combining simultaneous variations of a melody, rather than presenting these in the discrete succession typical of Western variation forms. While heterophony is common in ensemble traditions of Eastern Europe and the Near and Far East, its use in Western music is limited to jazz, experimental genres, and certain choral traditions.[34] The prevalence of fiorature (It., "flowerings"), ornamental melodic figurations, may derive from oriental musical traditions as well as from the influence of Hebrew cantillation.[35] The awareness of music by European and, to a lesser extent, American composers accounts for the presence in some Israeli works of serialism and other techniques or approaches found in the contemporary art music of these cultures.

Though the extramusical inspirations and influences, as well as the compositional techniques and materials, of Israeli art music have been discussed by various writers, little emphasis has so far been given to analysis of individual works, and neither is it a focus of this book. Such intentions and efforts have perhaps been complicated by the telescoped stylistic development of Israeli art music, as well as by the diversity of approaches and musical dialects coexisting within the works of each generation, even of individual composers. In this book, musical analysis is limited to the discussion by composers of their own works.[36] Zecharia Plavin, a pianist and doctoral student at the Hebrew University, identified a compositional feature that may characterize much Israeli art music: "It is interesting to note how deeply rooted is our practice of beginning with an introduction. It would seem, that in a post-tonal age, when harmonically based tensions are a thing of the past, introductions (designed to prepare the musical happening based on tonality) should have become obsolete by now. Quite to the contrary. In the works of many of our composers, introduction is indispensable. And perhaps that's a sign of our national character?"[37]

The objective of this book is to introduce readers to the world of contemporary Israeli music, and to illuminate its animating sources through the creative artists of its past, present, and future. As Israel's heterogeneous population is rooted in multiple and diverse immigrant societies, its broad spectrum of cultural expression in the arts defies facile or definitive reductions. Readers of these interviews will discern the extent to which the interests, concerns, and sources of inspiration of Israeli composers are distinctly colored by the time and place in which they live. The persistence of the arts in Israel, and particularly the tradition of contemporary art music, reflects the powers of collective humanism and of creative individual will that have formed the nation. The resonance of these voices of Israeli culture, through performances and recordings, has the same potential as does all music: to have meaning and to affect.

There are many more active composers in Israel than are presented here.[38] Among them are some whose names appear throughout this book: Yehezkel Braun (b. 1922, Germany; imm. 1924), Jacob Gilboa (b. 1920, Czechoslovakia; imm. from Vienna 1938), André Hajdu (b. 1932, Hungary; imm. from France 1966), Mark Kopytman (b. 1929, Ukraine; imm. 1972), Yehoshua Lakner (b. 1924, Czechoslovakia; imm. 1941), Meir Mindel (b. 1946, Russia; imm. 1958), Sergiu Natra (b. 1924, Romania; imm. 1961), Yizhak Sadai (b. 1935, Bulgaria; imm. 1949), León Schidlowsky (b. 1931, Chile; imm. 1969), Ruben Seroussi (b. 1959, Uruguay; imm. 1974), Noam Sheriff (b. 1935, Israel), Ron Weidberg (b. 1953, Israel), Joan Franks Williams (b. 1930, Brooklyn, New York; imm. 1971), Moshe Zorman (b. 1952, Israel), and Menachem Zur (b. 1942, Israel).[39] The music of these and other Israeli composers is deserving of greater attention, and it is hoped that this volume will stimulate further efforts in this direction.

It is the aim of this book to provide interviews in context so they can be situated in the broader framework of contemporary Israeli culture. This objective has been addressed in several different ways. The next section of this introduction presents a brief survey of musical institutions, organizations, and ensembles that figure prominently in Israel and which are important in the lives and careers of its several generations of composers. The final section provides a different kind of survey, that of definitions, perceptions, and attitudes concerning Jewish and Israeli music. The interviews that form the core of this volume are arranged in three generational groups, each preceded by a brief essay. Each composer's interview is preceded by an introduction and followed by an update section. Each of these individual composer introductions briefly describes the artist whose interview follows, noting significant professional achievements occurring before 1986. The section that follows each interview brings the reader up to date concerning each composer's more recent activities and achievements. These updates are of particular importance considering the many significant changes that have occurred during the past decade, in Israel's musical life generally, and in the lives of these composers.[40]

In several of the interviews, excerpts from specific works discussed by the composer help to illustrate their remarks and permit a better sense of the music being discussed. Some of these were works I heard performed prior to our meeting, while others were provided by composers as representative examples during the interview. A brief appendix lists several of the most important organizations that publish, promote, and distribute the music of Israeli composers. The selected discography will enable interested readers to become better acquainted with the music of these composers. Finally, a selected bibliography lists works consulted in the preparation of this book.

COMPOSING A MUSICAL CULTURE

The modern Israeli cultural history of which the composers in this volume are a part resulted from individual and collective efforts to compose a society through both the importation and invention of traditions.[41] Even while still under Ottoman rule, Jewish immigrants to Palestine from Eastern and Central Europe established schools, ensembles, organizations, and other institutions.[42] Though not all have survived, many of Israel's important musical institutions were established long before independence in 1948. Those central to the development of a modern musical culture in Israel include organizations in the areas of publishing, licensing and copyright, broadcasting and recording, promotion and dissemination, and research and education. These organizations, which play an important role in the lives of Israeli composers, are frequently cited throughout this book. In 1936 all of the following came into existence: the Society of Authors, Composers, and Music Publishers (ACUM),[43] the Palestine Orchestra (conducted in its inaugural performances by Arturo Toscanini, and later renamed the Israel Philharmonic Orchestra), the World Centre for Jewish Music in Palestine, and the Palestine Broadcasting Service (later the Israel Broadcasting Authority, also known as Kol Israel—the "Voice of Israel"),[44] which developed its own chorus and orchestra (the Kol Israel Orchestra was renamed the Jerusalem Symphony Orchestra).[45]

The Israel Composers' League (ICL), founded in 1953, is devoted to the promotion of contemporary Israeli music and serves as the Israel section of the International Society for Contemporary Music (ISCM). In addition to publishing a catalog of members' works, commissions, and performances, the ICL also organizes programs of Israeli contemporary music. According to composer Benjamin Bar-Am, the League also contributed to the creation of other organizations, such as the Israel Music Institute and the Israel Music Information Centre, which share its aim.[46] In 1993 the ICL announced the creation of its own publishing house, the Israeli Music Center (IMC), established to produce and distribute camera-ready scores by its members "upon demand and payment in advance" and "without applying any artistic criteria to the repertoire."[47]

Founded in 1961, the Israel Music Institute (IMI) publishes music by Israeli composers and a quarterly newsletter detailing their professional activities and achievements.[48] The IMI is jointly housed with the Israel Music Information Centre (IMIC), founded in 1968, which serves as a repository of scores and recordings and supplies information to music reference publications and individuals.[49] Israeli Music Publications (IMP), founded by Peter Gradenwitz in 1949, publishes books and scores, and distributes recordings through its affiliated Jerusalem Records.[50] Other music publishers include Or-Tav, Israel Brass-Woodwind Publications, and Merkaz LeTarbut (MLT), the cultural center of the General Federation of Labor.[51] While undeniably important to the careers of composers, publishing has also served as a substitute for performances and recordings of Israeli music.[52] Many Israeli composers continue to feel that there are inadequate opportunities to have their works heard in their own country. Those who have visited European cultural centers are dismayed by the conditions they are familiar with at home compared with those they find, for example, in Germany, France, or Italy.

Commercial recordings of music by Israeli composers have been produced periodically under various auspices, but generally they lag far behind music publications. In 1982 the Music in Israel (MII) Association was established by the Ministry of Education and Culture, Israel Broadcasting Authority (IBA), Jerusalem Music Centre, ACUM, and the Tel Aviv Foundation for Literature and the Arts. The MII and the IMI have jointly produced recordings of Israeli music.[53] The recently established IMC, affiliated with the ICL, has initiated a number of recording projects, including anthologies of Israeli piano music and art songs. Recordings of contemporary Israeli music have also been issued by American and European labels.

A variety of awards, prizes, competitions, fellowships, and commissions have helped advance the careers and encourage the work of Israeli composers. Some of these resources have come and gone, while others that have existed over long periods of time have only sporadically made such contributions. The most prestigious and most rarely granted is the Israel Prize, awarded for outstanding achievements in different fields. Israeli art-music composers who have received this award are Oedoen Partos, Paul Ben-Haim, Menahem Avidom, Mordecai Seter, Josef Tal, and Arik Shapira, of whom the latter three are represented in this volume.[54] The Prime Minister's Prize for Composers, intended to support creative work for a year, was established by the Ministry of Education and Culture in 1983.[55] Six of the composers included in this volume have received this prestigious award: Arik Shapira (1986), Abel Ehrlich (1989), Yinam Leef (1993), Haim Permont and Oded Zehavi (1995), and Ari Ben-Shabetai (1996). In 1994, Shapira was the first art-music composer in nearly a quarter century to receive the Israel Prize. Other awards include the Lieberson Prize, ACUM prizes, the Yoel Engel Prize given by the Tel Aviv municipality, and the Marc Lavry Award given by the Haifa municipality. The late Recha Freier was the force behind the Israel Composers' Fund and the Testimonium commissions.[56] Other commissions have been given by private individuals (including Chicago patrons Fanny and Max Targ), various music ensembles, and such organizations as the National Council of Culture and Arts, the Israel Writers and Artists Club, the IMI, and the America-Israel Cultural Foundation. In addition, new Israeli works are invited, by competition or commission, for the annual Israel Festival, the Zimriya World Assembly of Choirs, and the International Harp Contest.[57]

Perhaps the most important sources of commissions and performance opportunities for music by Israeli composers have been the ensembles, conductors, and soloists who have demonstrated their commitment to the creation and promotion of new Israeli music. The Batsheva, Bat-Dor, and Inbal dance companies have commissioned and performed many contemporary Israeli works. Two renowned choirs, the Cameran Singers and the National Choir Rinat, have performed and recorded many Israeli works, and their dissolution in the early 1990s is a profound loss.[58] Chamber ensembles that regularly perform contemporary Israeli works are the Israel Sinfonietta Beer Sheva, the Kibbutz Chamber Orchestra, the Ramat Gan Chamber Orchestra, Musica Nova, and Music Now.[59] In its first three years, the Israel Chamber Ensemble, led by Gary Bertini, premiered twenty-three new works by Israeli composers, many of which were repeated on tour abroad. Established in 1965 with the "declared intention" of performing Israeli music, this ensemble, since renamed the Israel Chamber Orchestra, has shown, according to Gideon Lefen, an "almost complete lack of interest in Israeli art music."[60]

Symphony orchestras that perform Israeli compositions include the Jerusalem Symphony Orchestra, the Haifa Symphony Orchestra, and the Rishon LeZion Symphony Orchestra.[61] According to Yaacov Mishori, writing in 1991, the Israel Philharmonic Orchestra (IPO) had performed 220 works by 51 Israeli composers.[62] The IPO has nonetheless been criticized for devoting too little attention to this repertoire.[63] On its fiftieth-anniversary tour in 1986, the IPO performed only one Israeli work, *To the Chief Musician,* by Paul Ben-Haim.[64] On subsequent tours, the IPO has performed Josef Tal's Second Symphony and Ari Ben-Shabetai's *Sinfonia Chromatica.*[65] In 1993 two Israeli orchestras created composer-in-residence positions. The New Israeli Opera, established in 1986, has since announced a competition designed to promote the composition of new Israeli works in this medium.[66]

Many factors support the perception that contemporary music in Israel has continued to intensify in activity and to broaden both its audience and base of support since these interviews were conducted. There has been a noticeable increase in the frequency with which works by Israeli composers are being performed, broadcast, and recorded. New scores and recordings of works by Israeli composers of all generations have been issued in recent years, and many more are forthcoming. In view of the geographic and demographic dimensions of the state of Israel, the activities and accomplishments of its many composers give evidence of a vital musical culture in progress.

DEFINITIONS, PERCEPTIONS, AND ATTITUDES

The terms "Israeli composer" and "Israeli music" have both engendered a broad range of conceptualizations, as is evident in the remarks of the twenty composers whose interviews follow this introduction, as well as those encountered in the related literature. The terms "Jewish composer" and "Jewish music" are equally problematic and inseparable from the ongoing debate concerning who is considered a Jew.[67] Even in the well-known figure of Ernest Bloch (1860–1959), a composer whose *Sacred Service, Three Jewish Poems,* and *Schelomo* have caused him to be strongly associated with Jewish music, one readily sees the attendant difficulties. Eric Salzman, an American composer and historian of twentieth-century music, has suggested that "in spite of the fact that Bloch wrote an 'epic rhapsody' for chorus and orchestra, *America* (1926), employing American folk songs, hymns, and even jazz, he can hardly be considered an American composer, and indeed, in spite of his well-known works on Hebrew motifs, he cannot be accurately or meaningfully classified as a Jewish composer."[68]

The fervent nationalism that has motivated Israel since the pre-state period has fueled ongoing efforts to identify and define the nature of all things Israeli. Numerous attempts have been made to describe both Jewish and Israeli music, though many Israeli composers regard such efforts as largely unnecessary distractions. Conflicting views concerning the identity of Jewish, Israeli, and "Hebrew" music have also surfaced in music criticism and journals. Appearing briefly in the 1930s, *Halel* promoted the views of Mordecai Sandberg, a composer who championed microtonality and insisted that "Hebrew music can be created only in the Land of Israel."[69] In contrast, *Musica Hebraica,* issued by the World Centre for Jewish Music in Palestine in 1938, was intended to provide "a forum from which many philosophies of Jewish music could be presented and argued."[70]

At least one of the difficulties of achieving such a definition is the broad diversity of styles and genres that are a part of Israeli music. Notes Philip Bohlman: "Historical musicologists already speak of 'schools' of Israeli composition (e.g., the Eastern Mediterranean School), ethnomusicologists analyze and computerize Israeli folk song (e.g., Cohen and Katz 1977), and popular-music scholars speculate why no other 'European' country wins the annual Eurovision Song Contest as frequently as Israel. That a national music is extraordinarily important to Israel almost goes without saying. But, in fact, one pauses before saying it, because it would be impossible to say exactly what Israeli music is."[71]

Bohlman and Mark Slobin have summarized three perspectives concerning Jewish music that are prevalent in the Jewish community and in Israeli society. One view holds that "the essence of Jewish music is an ancient melos embedded in both language and religion."[72] Another view rejects the possibility of identifying "canons of Jewish or Israeli music" because of the influence of other cultures "with which Jewish communities were historically in contact."[73] Finally, the role of such "external influence" in shaping Jewish and Israeli music has given rise to two related perspectives: to "pluralistic interpretations," which tend to be "inclusive" rather than "exclusive," and to "the notion of Israeli music at a crossroads between East and West, where 'Oriental' and 'Occidental' music come into intense contact with each other."[74] The latter conception is indeed a central theme of Israeli society and culture, encountered frequently both in writing and in conversation. All three of these perspectives are reflected, in a variety of ways, in the written and oral sources surveyed below.

Historically, the existence of a Jewish music was denied in some circles, even among assimilated Jews.[75] Kurt List rejected the presence of specific characteristics, but agreed that art reflects the experience of the individual in society: "To me there are no textual criteria, no snatches of melody or harmony that contribute to a body of Jewish music. For Jewish music as a successful historical and logical compound is non-existent. If there is anything that deserves the name of Jewish music it is a cultural attitude, partly an historical residue and partly the result of a specific situation in which the Jewish composer found and finds himself since his western emancipation began."[76] The Romanian-immigrant composer A. U. Boskovitch defined Jewish music as "the expression of the Jewish spirit and mentality in sound."[77]

In his 1951 book *Die Musik Israels,* the Czech-immigrant composer, writer, librettist, and dramaturge Max Brod (1894–1968) expressed a pluralistic view of Jewish music: "Any music composed by a Jew may be classified as Jewish. But if we attempt to find a more precise definition, we would have to say that only such music can be called Jewish as shows a specifically Jewish character, or, better, specifically Jewish attributes; for it cannot be maintained that there is but one type of Jewish music or that it is possible to discern one common archetype behind the various shapes and forms."[78] Brod described Israeli music as a cultural unity rooted in the diverse sources of its immigrant ethnic groups: "From every corner, very different stones are brought in, stones which today constitute the structure of our music."[79]

Writers in the area of Jewish music have increasingly emphasized the characteristics of diversity, multiplicity, and change. Mark Slobin, who notes the need to speak of Jewish "musics" in the plural, observes "how hard it is to work on the music of an extraordinarily mobile, widely-dispersed and frequently persecuted 'people' who cannot easily be defined by 'homeland,' 'race,' 'ethnicity,' 'nationality,' or 'religion.'"[80] Kay Kaufman Shelemay remarks that "Jewish music, like all topics having to do with Jewish history and culture, is virtually without boundaries in time or space." However, the "strong personal commitment" of scholars studying this tradition, and their desire "to establish beyond all doubt its authenticity and antiquity," according to Shelemay, has led to a "mythology of a Jewish music tradition made of whole cloth, rather than the patchwork one actually encounters."[81] Though she regards the diversity that characterizes Jewish music to be "the hallmark of a powerful and vital cultural tradition," Shelemay notes that such a pluralistic conception is viewed by some as a "pessimistic or even negative view of the subject."[82]

The persistent will to define Jewish and Israeli music has prompted two related studies, conducted nearly a half-century apart, that surveyed the perceptions held by Israelis themselves. In the late 1930s the Palestine Broadcasting Service tried to determine whether its listeners could distinguish Jewish from non-Jewish compositions, with interesting results: the musical example thought to possess the most "Jewish" quality, according to Amnon Shiloah, was the "Drunkard Song" from Moussorgsky's *Boris Goudonov*. By contrast, a Hasidic dance composition by Russian-Jewish composer Joseph Achron (1886–1943) "did not do very well in the poll."[83] The more recent study, conducted in Jerusalem in 1976 by Jehoash Hirshberg, suggested that Israelis do have at least "a vague conception of what Israeli music is, or is expected to be."[84] While the subjects in this study were generally able to distinguish Israeli and non-Israeli works, they tended to identify those having "strong Jewish character" as Israeli, regardless of their actual origin.[85]

A national musical style, according to Artur Holde, is the product of many individuals, "to some extent unified by common emotional experiences and common, or related, attitudes toward life, all of which go into a basic style and its form."[86] In decades past, such nationalistic sentiments encouraged the creation of a characteristic musical language, which, like Hebrew, could help to identify, unify, and represent the new nation. Much of this music is associated with the "Eastern Mediterranean" style that came to represent the emerging nation beginning in the 1930s.[87] According to composer and music critic Yohanan Boehm (b. 1914, Germany; imm. 1936; d. 1986), its sources of inspiration included Jewish history, biblical figures, and elements related to local geography.[88] The pivotal figure identified with this movement, and the composer whose works are best known outside of Israel, is Paul Ben-Haim, "the first European immigrant composer who set forth in new directions to constitute a style uniquely Israeli."[89] Profoundly influential through the next two decades, the Eastern Mediterranean movement waned in the decades immediately following Israel's independence, as an increasingly heterogeneous and international musical culture developed. The steadily increasing diversity of medium, style, and aesthetic has further challenged narrower definitions of Jewish or Israeli music.

A wide range of contemporary attitudes prevails among Israelis concerning these distinctions. The views expressed by several Israeli and American composers during the 1978 World Congress on Jewish

Music parallel much of the existing literature. The American composer Robert Starer remarked: "There are many facile ways to answer the question of the Jewish content in my music, the shortest and most obvious being: since I am Jewish, my music is."[90] In contrast, Moshe Cotel argued that "if there is such a thing as Jewish music, you don't have to be Jewish to write it, because Jewish tradition is not parochial, it is universal."[91] First-generation composer Josef Tal answered the question regarding Jewish content in his music with another question: "Where do we draw the line between Jewish and Israeli?" He also remarked: "I have the suspicion that this question about the Jewishness in my music belongs to the frame of mind of a Jew breathing the air of the Diaspora and desperately seeking an identity. Being a healthy Israeli composer, I do not suffer from paranoia. I believe that this question will disappear entirely, provided that the generations to come in Israel will stop making the State of Israel an extension of the Diaspora."[92]

Another perspective concerning the issue of identity as it applies to Israeli arts and artists was articulated at the 1978 World Congress by second-generation composer Tzvi Avni:

> I think it is quite natural for us to look for our identity as people who live here, also in our music, by using elements which we think belong to us. We cannot forget, I think, that we live in a country whose parliament has for years debated the topic Who is a Jew? I think that as somebody has already said here, for Hitler it was quite clear who is a Jew. For us it is sometimes not so clear. And if we are looking for identity, I think it quite natural that we should do so also in our music. It can be done and is being done in various ways. And I fully agree with my friend Schidlowsky that the very fact that we are here, that we are living in these circumstances, moulds us into something which I think is different from anywhere else and I feel that there is something in common in a graphic piece by León Schidlowsky and a very richly melismatic piece by Oedoen Partos or a piece based on some traditional elements from the cantillations by Orgad. I find that there are things which are common to all those various manifestations.[93]

Much of the diversity of today's Israeli music reflects contact with other societies, and this may also account for the comparable range of attitudes concerning Jewish and Israeli music. Elie Yarden has suggested that the only way for a young Israeli musician to discover his or her own artistic identity "is to leave and find a creative relationship to his land from the outside."[94] Generally, Israeli composers have either been raised in Israel and received their most advanced musical training elsewhere, or they have immigrated to Israel from their countries of origin following their training. This diversity of experience has contributed to the broad spectrum of compositional aesthetics and approaches found in Israel. Few American immigrant composers are active in Israel, and as a group they appear to hold a lower status than those of the longer-established immigrant communities.[95] Different values are also attributed to the Eastern and Central European composers of Israeli music. Zvi Keren's study of stylistic influences and sources of Israeli music makes such a distinction between Eastern and Central European immigrant composers, based on the "divergent" response of these communities to "the general upsurge of nationalistic feeling in Europe" in the late nineteenth century. Consequently, he finds different levels of "Jewish spirit" in the music of these two groups.[96]

Michal Smoira-Cohn recently surveyed the views of some younger composers whose remarks indicate their unique historical position in Israel's cultural evolution. Yinam Leef offered a perspective that may reflect the views of many of his peers:

Until recently I firmly believed that I belonged to the generation of Israeli composers who could find a synthesis between local and universal elements. This may still hold, but I am much less preoccupied by the issue nowadays. I think the Jewishness or Israeliness of my music is relevant in so far as I am a Jew and an Israeli and relate to those values. More specifically, there are certain technical devices that I have used, devices which perhaps have their origin in what I believed then to be either Jewish or Israeli (or more precisely, "Mediterranean"), but over the past few years have been gradually refined and now I consider them my own. As such I can use them or not, according to the specific requirements of a piece. I do not feel the burden of musically representing a culture or being nationally identified. But at the same time I may feel closer to certain musical values, sonorities, and so on, which could disclose their origin. I must add that there are times when I have to break away from those elements, and to wander around and keep searching for something unfamiliar, which could in turn become my own. For that matter, I do not exclude the possibility of being drawn to other cultures as well.[97]

Concerning the impact of personal experience and indigenous musical influences on his creative work, Oded Zehavi, the youngest composer included in this volume, remarked: "These experiences, as well as feelings and knowledge, are of course tied to the complicated reality into which I was born and in which I live."[98] Providing specific examples of such personal and musical influences, Zehavi stated:

> I can say almost without doubt that my service in the army, my struggles to remain sensitive after taking part in a war, and being a member of a society that relies on strength to survive and cannot afford to fail, in certain ways shaped my "creative tools." Furthermore, I am a native of Jerusalem and, acoustically, the air of this city is full of sounds for me: Oriental sounds, the sounds from the Sephardic synagogues, Eastern European music—these are not exotic, they are not to be cited and analyzed as "sources," they are part of my very being.[99]

When asked what it meant to be an Israeli composer, the composers interviewed in this volume provided responses revealing a broad range of attitudes. Noa Guy (b. 1949) discovered as a young adult that the songs she learned in her childhood and assumed to be Israeli were as Russian as the wave of émigrés that brought her own ancestors to nineteenth-century Palestine. Though she is a seventh-generation Israeli, Guy sees herself as a Jewish rather than an Israeli composer.

Tzvi Avni has described the bond he perceives to be shared by most composers living and working in Israel:

> With all the dissimilarity between Israeli composers, there is nevertheless a common base which characterizes the majority: an inclination toward personal involvement, both individual and artistic, in everything to do with the time and place in question, as well as an ongoing search for what is implied by the concept of a "contemporary Israeli composer." In practical terms this is expressed by one composer in the form of "committed" music which relates directly to political or social events, by another in a wide-ranging use of musical motifs inspired by tradition and folklore—even if the adaptation removes the material far from its source—and by a third, in intellectual motivation based on biblical or historical themes. Of course, some composers reveal a capacity for all these elements together. The Holocaust is a subject no Jewish composer can ignore. A number of Israeli composers have found the spirit and courage to confront its magnitude.[100]

Peter Gradenwitz has claimed that music composed in Israel is "indivisible from the creative efforts of its builders in all the spheres

42

of civilization and culture." He acknowledges a diversity that allows for both conservative and progressive works, as well as those that do and do not happen to sound "Israeli."[101] Although traditionally and increasingly eclectic, the environment of contemporary Israeli music is still somewhat more conducive to conservative rather than to experimental aesthetics. Orthodox Judaism considers those without children to be dead. Though only a small fraction of Israelis are strictly religious, certain themes pervade Jewish and Israeli consciousness—remembering the past, preserving traditions, and ensuring survival of its people. Even for secular Israeli Jews, these concerns show the priority accorded continuity of culture, and they may contribute to the persistence of conventional tendencies among some of the youngest Israeli composers.

It may be futile or premature to argue the validity of a genre of musical artifacts that might generally be understood as Israeli. In the postnationalistic stage of Israel's developing culture, the increasingly diverse spectrum of musical composition reflects not only the personal and immediate, but also global influences and interests. In this rapidly developing and complex modern society, with a continuously active musical life at the start of its second century, the personal and professional perspectives of contemporary Israeli composers may tell us much about Israel, about music, and about life in the twentieth century and beyond.

I

THE FIRST GENERATION
ROOTS AND BRANCHES

The roots of Israel's contemporary art-music culture may be traced most directly to the immigrant communities that arrived from Eastern and Central Europe between the two world wars. Eastern European settlers came to British-mandate Palestine in the 1920s from countries where "Hebrew cantillation, ghetto folksong and Slavic folklore had combined to create a specific Jewish style."[1] These materials were used by composers associated with the Society for Jewish Folk Music, founded in St. Petersburg, Russia, in 1908, many of whom went to Palestine or the United States.[2] Though it was due to Eastern European immigrant composers in Palestine that "a regular and continuous creative activity commenced in the 1920s in the realm of folk song,"[3] it was the *aliyah germanit*—the wave of German-speaking Central European immigrants arriving between 1933 and 1939—that was primarily responsible for establishing Israel's cultural and political institutions. As Arieh Sachs has stated: "While musicians of Eastern-European extraction sowed the seeds of the Israeli music to come, it was the composers from Germany who caused them to germinate."[4] These roots, established by European immigrant musicians, gave rise to a broad spectrum of folk, religious, popular, and art-music traditions.

These two European immigrant cultures were locked in conflict during the 1930s. Whereas Yiddish folk song was the established tradition of the Eastern Europeans, absolute music was the focus

45

of their Central European counterparts.[5] Despite their differences, these two groups of composers shared many common experiences. According to Jehoash Hirshberg, the Eastern European composers in Palestine had "apprenticed mostly in Germany and in France" and were therefore already acquainted with the influences that would soon become a dominant force in the musical life of the emerging nation.[6] All of the immigrant composers faced the same social pressure to create "a set of unifying cultural symbols" that would on the one hand be "oriented to the past" sufficiently to serve "the vision of the return to and resettlement" of the biblical Eretz Israel, and would on the other hand respond to the "drive to build a new, better society."[7] Tzvi Avni notes that most of the "founding generation" composers were younger than forty years old when they arrived from Europe. All of these immigrants knew "the experience of being uprooted and readjusting to a new country in the throes of seeking its own cultural, social and national identity, a process which was bound to exert a long-term effect on their artistic activity."[8] Most of those regarded today as first-generation Israeli composers were either raised or educated in German-speaking regions of Central Europe.

Although Eastern European immigrant composers were soon eclipsed by their Central European counterparts, the musical traditions of the former group continued to influence the development of Israeli music. According to Amnon Shiloah, some critics charged that the use of such Eastern European songs "as a mark of national distinctiveness" symbolized the Diaspora, insisting that "the new national style" should be based on the regional music.[9] Composer Tzvi Avni notes that folklore was, at this time, "an integral concern" that influenced the creative style of many composers. The *debka,* the *hora,* and other traditional Israeli dances developed during the 1940s and 1950s exerted a dominant influence on the art music by Eastern Mediterranean composers Paul Ben-Haim, Marc Lavry, and Menahem Avidom.[10] Most immigrant composers working with oriental materials discovered these largely through A. Z. Idelsohn's *Thesaurus* or through musicians such as the Yemenite-Jewish singer Bracha Zephira.[11]

The appeal of Yemenite and Sephardic musical sources and styles has been linked to perceptions of their historical authenticity, and specifically to presumed affinities with ancient Jewish religious music.[12] These oriental styles evoked the visionary East, and the "highly acclaimed" Yemenite singing, according to Shiloah, "has come

46

to symbolize the magical, genuine, and exotic Orient, perhaps representing the 'other.' "[13] Cyclic aesthetic theories that predicted the inexorable return from modernism to ancient traditions only increased the allure of such resources.[14] Bracha Zephira popularized these materials and promoted their many new arrangements by immigrant composers with whom she collaborated. But as she was perceived to have strayed from authentic sources and performance practices, her great popularity was tempered by public criticism.[15] Years later, Zephira acknowledged that despite the "respect and love" with which these immigrant composers approached the traditional songs, the result was nonetheless "Western music endowed with a whiff of Oriental exoticism."[16]

Despite the importance of Jewish melodies and subjects as a basis for the Eastern Mediterranean composers, the orientation of these immigrants, unlike their Eastern European predecessors, was essentially secular. These composers were not Zionists, nor were they "sensitive to the aesthetic vocabulary" of the Jewish folk music developed by their Eastern European counterparts.[17] As Alexander Ringer has observed, "Their compositions were in no way specifically religious, let alone liturgically conceived."[18] Largely a tradition of the Central European immigrant community, contemporary Israeli art music owes more to the spirit of Israeli nationalism than to a nationalism of Jewish spirituality. As Ringer notes:

> The attitudes of Israeli composers, both old and young, reflect the conviction shared by the majority of their countrymen that Judaism represents in essence more of a civilization than a religion, since it has always dealt with the totality of social existence, not excluding aspects associated elsewhere with secular culture. Thus, the fact that few Israeli composers would admit to being religious in the traditional sense is by no means irreconcilable with their dedication to the monumental concepts of the Old Testament and the spiritual wisdom of post-biblical literature, or, for that matter, their fascination with musical motifs and procedures that survived the ages exclusively through prayer and scriptural cantillation. Nothing is more symptomatic of the very special cultural climate of modern Israel than this unique interpenetration of religious, socio-political, and artistic values.[19]

One of the two principal artistic problems faced by immigrant composers who came to Palestine in the 1930s, according to Hirshberg, was an aesthetic conflict between conservative and progressive tendencies. In this context, the dodecaphonic compositional approach of Stefan Wolpe, a pupil of Anton Webern, was rejected by those seeking an amalgamated Jewish-oriental style. To some, Wolpe's adherence to the twelve-tone method of composition associated with the Second Vienna School could be viewed as "betraying one's historical mission."[20] The other problem was attempting to develop a musical style based on the ideological premise "of expressing the optimistic, new spirit of Jewish society in Palestine and reflecting the impression of the new landscapes, climate, and everyday atmosphere in the new country."[21] Facing these conflicts and pressures was a diverse group of individuals who had not previously known one another, whose personal and professional backgrounds were extremely diverse, and who acknowledged no single spokesperson.[22]

The conflicts between Eastern and Central European perspectives, and between conservative and progressive tendencies, were not unique to composers. All those who immigrated to Palestine to create a new society faced a still broader challenge: "On the one hand, it would have to be solidly based within Jewish traditions and Hebrew language; on the other, it would have to relate to a universal context."[23] Still new problems and challenges resulted from the "almost total isolation from outside influences" caused by World War II, which began shortly after the largest group of Central European immigrant composers arrived.[24]

Through the 1930s and 1940s, the response of local critics and journalists to each premiere was based, aesthetically and politically, on the extent to which new works were felt to satisfy the still unclear goals of the new style. While composers responded differently to these challenges, they recognized both "a certain communal and national responsibility" and the mandate to fulfill a "historical mission of creating something new, which would express and suit the reality of life in a young, active and restless society, full of conflicts, desires and ideals."[25]

The German-immigrant composer Erich Walter Sternberg (1891–1974) clearly sought to achieve this in his own way, or so it would seem from the titles and texts chosen for his compositions following his immigration to British-mandate Palestine in 1931. Nonetheless, he was criticized for composing insufficiently nationalistic music. Sternberg's struggle for artistic freedom in this polemically-charged climate led him to publish a justification of his orchestral variations, *The Twelve Tribes of Israel*, which warned that "all our efforts in the direction of creating a Jewish national music are foredoomed to failure so long as there exists no possibility of a mutual musical approach on the part of composer and public—no common ground where both sides can meet." Noting the difficulty of satisfying the heterogeneous "musical tastes and standards" of his audience, Sternberg proposed that "Under these circumstances, so it seems to me, a composer has only one course to follow: to care nought for what is expected of him, be it Palestinian folklore, or synagogal music, or pieces in the Russian manner, but to go his own way, to speak his own tongue according to the dictates of his muse."[26] Though initially the subject of severe criticism by some writers at its premiere in 1942, *The Twelve Tribes of Israel*, Sternberg's compositional "declaration of independence," celebrated the independent state of Israel in a live-broadcast performance on May 15, 1948.[27]

Philip Bohlman notes that while the Central European immigrant composers encountered "very pointed nationalistic demands to which immediate response was expected," their varied responses promoted a broader aesthetic framework than was previously accepted: "It was, perhaps, the most important quality of this contribution that it could tolerate and then foster diversity, instead of clinging to shaky notions of which music was or was not Israeli."[28]

Even before Israel's War of Independence in 1948, the desire for a nationalistic music was a potent influence. The advent of statehood reinforced growing societal pressures to compose a culture unique to the time and place of modern Israel. According to Don Harrán, statehood "not only gave the composers the national identity they fervently sought, imbuing them with a new sense of responsibility and artistic conviction, but also led them deeper into the past in search of the roots of Jewish associations with Zion."[29] The new state, with its challenges and opportunities, monopolized the consciousness of its rapidly growing citizenry. Unification of the culturally and ethnically diverse population was the overriding social objective, and music played an important role. Zvi Keren contends that most Israeli composers "have felt obliged to take some sort of definite stand with regard to what may be called an Israeli style in art music," one inextricably bound to the idea of synthesis between Western and Eastern musical elements.[30]

In this time and place, the objective of developing a unified musical language was inevitable and resulted from internalized pressures felt by individual composers as well as those imposed by audiences and critics. Though diversity has been the hallmark of music composed by European immigrants and by native Israelis, the Eastern Mediterranean style, which flourished in the 1930s and 1940s, has received the most attention in Israel and abroad. An important focus of this repertory was on indigenous (Arabic and Jewish, religious and folkloristic) musical materials and influences of the region, combined with Western compositional methods. As such, the Eastern Mediterranean movement paralleled the contemporary efforts of American composers—Aaron Copland, Roy Harris, and others—who promulgated a musical expression of American identity through similar means. In addition to this affinity with the "American Wave" and with contemporary European musical expressions of nationalistic neoclassicism, with their emphasis upon folklore and borrowed melodies, there occurred also a predisposition, beginning around 1948, toward "forms, linearity and archaism of pre-classical music," specifically those associated with the Renaissance.[31] As Bohlman observes, "Fundamental to the aesthetic problem faced by the immigrants of the 1930s was how composers could isolate something specifically Eastern Mediterranean and Jewish and then express these qualities in their music."[32]

Despite the environment of a rapidly increasing process of urbanization, the character of the Eastern Mediterranean style was distinctly rural, evoking a pastoral atmosphere through instrumentation, especially in the use of oboe, clarinet, flute, and tambourine. Among the primary sources of this characteristic was the music of French impressionism, a repertory significantly affected by the imported art of Japan and the music of Indonesia. In addition to underscoring programmatic aspects, the elements of folklore, pastoral evocations, and dance "represented musical Zionism," according to Avni.[33] As he explains, all of Israel's early creative arts reflected similar influences:

> This blend of Western European background with elements of the East infused with a distinct touch of the exotic, this idealization of rural life, this search for ancient cultural roots coupled with a desire to revive them by integrating them into everyday cultural life, in the same way that the revived Hebrew language was integrating itself so impressively into the dynamics of Israel's reality—these were the starting points for artists who lived and created in this country. What writers like Hazaz, Ashman, Bourla and Shlonsky expressed in literature and poetry, and painters like Rubin, Mokady, Ardon and

Castel expressed in art, was echoed in music by composers such as Ben-Haim, Boscovich, Avidom, Lavry and Salmon, among others.[34]

Recalling that these qualities left the impression that Eastern Mediterranean composers "nourished us on music which was no longer truly European," Nathan Mishori described the environmental influences that were reflected in their works:

> The brightness and warmth of our sunshine seemed to erase the fine chromatic shades of European harmony and melodic lines. Recitative and dance-like snatches of Hebrew songs and of some ethnic and liturgical Jewish materials, as well as original melodic inventions in the style of the above-mentioned, replaced the European motives. These and their arrangements, variations and elaborations in quite lucid and homophonic structures, seemed successful in conveying the scenic atmosphere of the country, and in reflecting the emotional attitudes of the people.[35]

Alexander Ringer suggests that the rural emphasis of the Eastern Mediterranean idiom reflected an alienation from the past shared by its adherents:

> As if to seal their conscious rejection of an urban, for the most part German, past, the members of the "Mediterranean School" turned to French, post-Impressionist methods of composition. Their melodies reflected the modality of the prevailing folk idiom, and the harmonic style relied a good deal on parallel motion of perfect intervals, as well as combinations of fourth chords. Rhythmic patterns were often derived from Arabic dance and the modern Palestinian *Hora,* while texts and descriptive titles drew heavily upon the lyrical poetry of the Psalms. Freed of the tensions that had beset diaspora Jewry for centuries, the Mediterranean School turned to David, the "Sweet Psalmist of Israel" (to quote the title of one of Ben-Haim's best-known compositions), the shepherd-musician turned king, who danced in ecstasy before the Holy Ark, as its guiding spirit.[36]

Debussy's absorption of Asian and Spanish musical characteristics, his excavations of musical antiquity, and his rejection of Wagner and Germanic culture naturally exerted a magnetic appeal for the immigrant composers who fled from Nazism. Freed from contrapuntal obligations, the melodic line found an environment in which "recitative in the style of biblical cantillation" would replace the learned style of German polyphony.[37] The influence of French impressionism on immigrant composers paralleled the experience of immigrant artists at Jerusalem's Bezalel School for Arts and Crafts, who were attracted to "the new stimuli offered by the *École de Paris*."[38] Many characteristics of musical impressionism—modality and diatonicism, quartal harmony, asymmetry of phrase and meter, intervallic and chordal parallelism—became defining traits in the music of Ben-Haim and other Eastern Mediterranean composers.[39] Moreover, some composers perceived a close affinity between the exoticisms of French impressionism and the modal, monophonic, and heterophonic elements they observed in the traditional music of the Middle East.[40] Indeed, in their adoption of French impressionism, itself an amalgamation of diverse regional and global inspirations and influences, these mostly German immigrant composers imported to the region traits that in some cases had previously traveled from Spain to France. Elaine Brody has observed that, among various "exotic" influences that inspired composers and other artists of fin de siècle France, Spain was viewed as part of their broader conception of the "oriental" world, which implied "the Near East and North Africa as well as the Far East, Russia and Spain."[41] This perspective, suggests Brody, may be attributable to the influences of past Arab presence in Spain.

Consideration of the Eastern Mediterranean style is inseparable from the concept of "East-West synthesis." Robert Starer recalls that the musical education he received in British-mandate Jerusalem exposed him to Schoenberg and Béla Bartók, to strict counterpoint and biblical cantillation, to the Arabic scale system, and to performance practice on the oud, a lute common in Arabic musical traditions.[42] Writing in 1961, Herbert Fromm stated: "If a national style is what the Israeli composers are striving for, a synthesis between East and West presents itself as the central problem."[43] Fromm described the Eastern Mediterranean style as a mediating force between the conflicting aesthetic orientations of the Eastern and Central European immigrant composers, and a link between East and West.

Peter Gradenwitz recalls that the early attempts at East-West synthesis by Israeli composers began with primitive imitations of oriental ensembles, leading to more sophisticated evocations of oriental vocal or instrumental performance practice.[44] Many composers, including those not associated with the Eastern Mediterranean school, explored to a greater or lesser degree the musical traditions in their midst, including that of the Yemenite and Sephardic traditions. The treatment of these indigenous materials was subject to a variety of stylistic filters with which individual composers were more thoroughly acquainted, principally those rooted in their own musical training. As Bohlman notes, "By the early 1950s the compositional techniques of Western art music had acquired a firm position in the Middle Eastern cultural environment."[45] Indeed, much of the music by first-generation composers could be characterized as efforts to Westernize recently discovered oriental materials. As Fromm observed in 1961, "The initial step to elaborate Oriental folk material in European fashion has now been superseded by the writing of original music which absorbs the experience of Oriental music in more independent ways."[46] Although many Israeli composers have in some way been influenced by the oriental musical traditions in their midst, few have abandoned Western traditions.

Some composers rejected the idea of a musical language that would represent the new state, either holding firm to prior stylistic orientations or seeking new musical approaches unlikely to ensure public acceptance.[47] The broad spectrum of aesthetic responses among Israeli composers has extended from the nearly total resistance of indigenous influence to the demand for a completely non-Western style.[48] Another factor opposing nationalistic pressures was the search by individual artists for their own voices, influenced by growing internationalist impulses. Israeli artists in the 1940s and 1950s thus experienced a creative tension caused by the conflicting needs of self and society: "Those were years of uncompromising desire for self-determination of the artists, but the time was a time of inevitable compromise brought about by the phenomenon of social melting pot in the life of the nation, due to mass immigration from all parts of the world. The culture which emerged in Israel, was multi-faceted, rich in contradictions, eclectic and wildly creative."[49]

Pluralism has remained a hallmark of the contemporary arts in Israel, as it seems increasingly to be of the society as a whole. The social doctrine of achieving cultural unity in Israel was a direct response to the diversity of its immigrant population, formed by the "ingathering of exiles" from more than a hundred countries, with their own languages, cultures, and histories. But the underlying diversity of Israel's population has resisted social, political, or aesthetic homogeneity. The unifying forces of Judaism, Hebrew, and Zionist nationalism have also been responsible for ongoing dispute and division in Israeli society. Within the diversity of this aesthetic context, one nonetheless perceives commonalities that might reflect a national identity. Bohlman has suggested that the interrelated influences of biblical cantillation

53

and the Hebrew language have served in this role: "The emergence of modern Hebrew as the language of modern Israeli composition symbolizes the transition of its many styles from the amalgamation of the immigrant generation to the consolidation of a new ethnic community."[50]

Interviews with five first-generation immigrant composers are presented here. Bohlman has characterized Hanoch Jacoby (1909–90) and Josef Tal (b. 1910) as exemplifying two of the three broad groups representing Israel's immigrant composers: Paul Ben-Haim led those "who adapted their compositional approaches to the broad stylistic shifts" of Israeli music; the more conservative approach of Jacoby, a pupil of Paul Hindemith, permitted the treatment of themes derived from folk music or cantillation according to the rigorous precepts of his European training; Tal, as Israel's foremost composer of operas and electronic music, and one who has long employed dodecaphonic methods, exemplifies those more intrigued by "compositional developments abroad" than by the treatment of Jewish or Israeli themes.[51] Zvi Keren regards Tal and Abel Ehrlich (b. 1915) as "avant-gardists," the latter for his use of graphic notation, serialism, and proportionality.[52] The only Eastern European immigrant in this representative generational group, Russian-born Mordecai Seter (1916–94), employed serial procedures in a way, according to Avni, "which more closely resembles Messiaen than Schoenberg."[53] Haim Alexander (b. 1915) is the only first-generation composer represented here for whom jazz has been a significant inspiration and a lasting influence. Representative works by all five composers are listed in *A Descriptive Bibliography of Art Music by Israeli Composers,* by Alice Tischler.

Hanoch Jacoby, photographed by Allan D. Cisco. Courtesy of Mrs. Alice Jacoby and the Israel Philharmonic Orchestra.

1

HANOCH JACOBY

Hanoch (originally Heinrich) Jacoby, a German-immigrant composer, conductor, teacher, and music administrator, performed for many years as a violist with the Israel Philharmonic Orchestra.[1] Philip Bohlman contends that as a composer, Jacoby "never fully adapted the Central European framework to the Israeli musical culture."[2] The influence of Jacoby's training was so evident in his harmonic language and use of conventional musical forms that friends suggested sending his music to Germany "to show the Germans how an Israeli preserved the German spirit of music."[3] Still, Jacoby sought to integrate his European musical heritage with the new environment of Israel, employing melodic materials he learned through his brief association with Bracha Zephira and later evoked in his own writing. Like many other Israeli composers, he employed modal melodies and inflections, as well as rhythmic formulas of the *hora* and other dances. But like his teacher, the German composer and musical theorist Paul Hindemith, Jacoby remained a polyphonist. He regarded his contrapuntal treatment of oriental melodies to be unique, and felt that the polyphonic potential of these melodies justified their treatment "like the *Inventions* of Bach."[4]

I interviewed Hanoch Jacoby on July 1, 1986, at his home in Tel Aviv. He had ceased his activities as a composer nearly ten years earlier.[5] This decision, as is evident from his remarks, was tied to deeply felt emotions. I learned from Mrs. Alice Jacoby early in 1991 that the composer passed away on December 13, 1990.[6]

———

I was born in 1909 in a town that doesn't exist anymore. It was Königsberg in Prussia. It was once in East Prussia, in the northern part of Germany. Today it is Russia. In between is now Poland, then comes East Germany, West Germany—all has changed. Königsberg was destroyed in the Second World War. Today there is nobody there speaking German, no German people anymore—all in Siberia or fled to the West. It's a big town today, called Kaliningrad. It's a very important town from a strategic point of view. I left Germany in 1933 for Turkey. It was very nice there from the point of view of landscape. I liked Istanbul very much; it's one of the most beautiful cities I can imagine. But from the point of view of cultural life it was a disaster. One year in Turkey was absolutely enough. It was even too much. So when I came to Jerusalem, I felt at home. I came to Israel in 1934.

I became a member of the Jerusalem String Quartet, of which the first violinist was Emil Hauser. He was the first violinist of the first Budapest String Quartet, which he left in 1932. I heard his last concert in Frankfurt. I knew him only here in Israel; he was a very good musician. I was a member of the Jerusalem String Quartet for five years, until Hauser left for the States. I joined the Academy at the same time. In 1934 it was a very small institute, but there were some very important people on the staff.[7]

My early musical experience started at six years of age, when I started to play the violin. I composed already before this, but it was nothing worthwhile. I began composition lessons when I was fourteen or so. I studied with Hindemith for two and a half years at the Berlin Hochschule. I loved his music. In the last part of his life, he was very conservative, but I understood him very well. It was a reaction. Anyhow, I studied composition and viola. And for many years I was a violist, and played in different chamber music ensembles. When I left the Academy I went to the Philharmonic Orchestra, when I was fifty. It was really almost a wonder that they accepted me at this age.

First of all, I tried to find out the folklore. Then I started to write my own folklore, in the style of folklore. When I had found this style, it was not modern anymore. The *hora* and all these things were already forgotten in the fifties. I wrote still in this style, so I was always a little bit late. Afterwards, but even before, I searched for Eastern oriental material. I was very interested in religious music and dance music, but mostly religious, cantillation. Also Arabic music, but mostly Yemenite, Iraq, Kurdistan. And one of my compositions, *Mutatio,* is a model.[8] I'll tell you the whole story.

When I left the Philharmonic Orchestra, in retirement, I was engaged as a professor in the Haifa Technion. I was not really to teach, I was to compose a piece. I was artist-in-residence for the whole year. But that's not my style. I conducted the orchestra, I gave courses and played chamber music and did all things together. But the most important was to write a composition. Now the year before, I had a request from the Israel Music Institute to write music for three instruments—educational music, for violin pedagogy— on Jewish material. And I took this book from Haim Alexander, who did the research on that—two hundred different melodies in this book.[9]

So I took some ten or fifteen that I liked and I started to work them out for three instruments. You know, this music is all in principle for one voice, but I wanted to add Western ideas to this music. And I always work in a contrapuntal style. When I had all these melodies worked out, I looked them over and I was very disappointed that two of these melodies came out almost alike. I had not read the titles, because this was not important to me. When I looked over the book, I found that the two melodies had the same title. Now I compared them, and I found out that one was an Iraqi melody and the other Kurdistani, of the same prayer. I learned later that the words of the prayer were written in the thirteenth century. You see, Kurdistan, Iraq, Baghdad, are very close together. But the solution was absolutely different. One was a diatonic melody in major (ex. 1), and the other was a chromatic melody in minor (ex. 2). But the source was the same. And I was fascinated about the thing.

And when I came to Haifa, I had the idea in my head, I have to write a composition about these two melodies. All this was about twelve years ago. At the same time I conducted the orchestra in the *Art of the Fugue* of Bach. And when I played the chorale at the end, which doesn't belong to the *Art of the Fugue* but was added by his sons, suddenly I had the idea that these two melodies are based on a melody that doesn't exist anymore, but I had to find it. And I started my composition with a chorale prelude establishing this unknown melody. That was almost a musicological subject.

1.) Kurdistan - Version

Ex. 1

2.) Bagdad - Version.

Ex. 2

Hanoch Jacoby

It was written for the orchestra of the Technion, which was very special because it had one bassoon and four clarinets. I wrote it exactly for what I had. I'll read you a program note:

> *Mutatio* was commissioned by and dedicated to the Technion Symphony Orchestra, which performed it under the baton of its conductor, Dalia Atlas, on May 20, 1975. The dedication to a student orchestra meant, of course, that I had to take into account the limited technical standard of the players, and the fact that not all orchestral instruments were available, and certainly not in standard numbers. That is the reason for the odd orchestration I accepted, not as a limitation, but as a challenge.
>
> *Mutatio* is certainly a piece of music looking to the past for inspiration. First of all, to the Jewish past. It was a chance musical and musicological experience that led me to compare two different versions of a medieval prayer for the new year, as sung today by the Jews of Kurdistan and Baghdad. There exist more versions of the same prayer, all recorded in Israel from Persian, Moroccan, Spanish, and Greek sources.[10]
>
> By comparing the two aforementioned versions, I found out that they had the same melodic structure outline. This idea inspired me to the conception of a composition in three variation forms based on an unknown theme.
>
> But *Mutatio* is not only looking at the Jewish past; it is looking back also to sources in the history of European polyphonic writing. All Near Eastern music is essentially one-line music, pure homophony,[11] or heterophony, while all European music since about eight hundred years ago is essentially polyphonic. Israel is geographically and historically the ideal place to combine and unite the two contrasting principles in music. Polyphonic treatment, especially the use of free imitative counterpoint, adds new dimensions and depth to the expressive oriental, melodic line.
>
> First, I searched for the basic unknown theme of the medieval prayer, as an archetype synthesis of the two different versions, in the way a baroque composer paraphrases in a chorale prelude. Afterwards I introduced the Kurdistan version once using stylistic trends of medieval tenor counterpoint and the second time in a soprano-oriented arrangement in later imitative style. These two sections form the first part, Andante.
>
> Starting the second part is a variation of my own. It is constructed like the exposition of a sonata form Allegro, developing and contrasting different melodic and rhythmic motives of the basic theme, and

introducing free fugal counterpoint. As there is development in this variation, a sonata form development section is unnecessary. Instead appears the Baghdad variation, as a middle part in free imitative counterpoint.

The recapitulation of the sonata form variation follows, but in changed order, so that the fugal counterpoint section can be used as a countertheme to a fugato based on the Kurdistan version. To form the climax of the composition, a short exposition serves as a coda, corresponding to the coda of the first part. My own variation intends, of course, to express a synthesis of the style—elements of East and West—and serves as today's commentary on the different and contrasting sources. *Mutatio,* as a whole, shows certainly where I stand in relation to Jewish ethnic music, to music of today, and to the music of Israel.[12]

I think this was printed for the performances of the Israel Philharmonic Orchestra. The piece was very often performed. The first performance was by the Technion Orchestra. Afterwards, it was performed by the Kol Israel Orchestra, and later it was performed very often by the Philharmonic, and in Holland, different places.

In recent years, I have not written very much. I'm fed up with contemporary music. My reaction is: if I must not write, then I will not write. If I explode, I will write. But at the moment I am very satisfied in playing chamber music. I have no complaints about the performing of my pieces. Everything I have written was performed, very often and very successfully. I always had success with the public, with the orchestras, and with the conductors. I can't stand it, the music of today. I'm not interested anymore. I don't go to concerts, I'm satisfied with the music I make myself. I almost don't hear any music.

You see, first of all, I was already angry with this Schoenberg style that was absolutely against my taste. Everybody tried it. And, you see, the serial music and all this stuff is based highly on what Schoenberg did to the music. I can't accept it. {I compose tonally. I see dissonances as harmonic tensions that find their solution in relaxation, i.e., consonance. This effect of building tension through dissonance can occur only in tonal music, which in its planning provides for a direction of tension and subsequent relaxation. But this tension—and any tension, for that matter—quickly peters out, unless followed by planned relaxation. Anton Webern sensed the danger of quickly dwindling tension, and therefore wrote very brief works, lasting only as long as the shock effect holds, and before tension can dwindle they are over.

The tonal conception of a work is the basis for its formal structure. This factor is much stronger than the building of rhythm or melodic motifs. There are some basic types of form that depend on tonality as an acoustical fact in the same manner as architecture is based on the laws of gravity. Atonal music can be compared to architecture that dispenses with gravity.

I feel an inner need to express the tensions that exist inside me, and those that exist in relation to the world I live in. These tensions are simply human and should be reflected in my music. Intentionally writing "modern" seems to me as merely following a current "mode" or fashion. At a time as progressive as ours, there is only one way to be progressive: to appear to be reactionary, and not to follow any fashion.}[13]

Josef Tal went in a direction I never understood. I worked with Partos when he started to base his works on Jewish music. We even worked together. But I soon saw that what he did was absolutely different from my conception. I didn't follow. I accept it, I understand it, but my way always was to adopt the oriental style and to make it Western by counterpoint.

Partos started with Bartók, and then he was really good. He got into his illusions with the dodecaphonic system. I would say Ben-Haim, Avidom, that was the Mediterranean style—Boskovitch partly. I didn't feel a part of that at all, I was always alone. Maybe in the following generation, Yehezkel Braun is somebody who is going a little bit the way I tried. And then there was a kibbutz composer, [Theodor] Holdheim. He died two years ago. He was also going a little bit in my way, but that was the next generation. I was alone in my generation.

———

Jacoby's music is heard regularly in Israel and abroad. His composition for chamber orchestra, *King David's Lyre* (1948), was performed by the Jerusalem Symphony Orchestra in 1990 and by the Symphonette Orchestra Raanana in 1993. A memorial concert presented in 1991 by Jacoby's pupils and colleagues included the composer's *Little Suite* (1941), which received additional performances in 1993 by the

Yad Harif Orchestra and the Aviv Chamber Orchestra, and in 1994 by the Ashdod Chamber Orchestra. In 1992, Jacoby's *Seven Miniatures* for piano (1944) was performed during the 27th Brno, Czechoslovakia, International Music Festival. A performance of *King David's Lyre* was also given in September 1995 in Prague.[14]

Josef Tal, photographed by Herlinde Koelbl. Used with permission.

2

JOSEF TAL

Josef Tal's position as Israel's preeminent electronic composer, noted by Alexander Ringer in 1965, is a designation of continuing validity despite the increasing involvement of his younger Israeli composers in this medium. Tal (originally Gruenthal) employs electronic media as an integral facet in much of his compositional output, which includes numerous operas, symphonies, concerti, and oratorios as well as solo and chamber works. He began his lifelong association with the twelve-tone method of composition through his teacher Heinz Tiessen, who "belonged to the small but radical group at the Berlin Academy associated with Schoenberg."[1] Ringer observed that "Tal's numerous works for traditional media defy classification as part of any 'school,'" noting a variety of important influences, including dodecaphonic principles, oriental melodic sources, and biblical inspiration.[2] Elsewhere, Ringer provided a more detailed description of Tal's style:

> The characteristics features of Tal's music are broad dramatic gestures and driving bursts of energy generated, for example, by various types of ostinato or sustained textural accumulations. Complex rhythmic patterning is typical of the widely performed Second Symphony and of a number of notable dance scores. But Tal's marked dramatic and philosophical propensities find total expression only in opera, particularly in the large-scale 12-note opera *Ashmedai*, commissioned

and first performed by the Hamburg Opera. The libretto, originally in Hebrew, relates a post-biblical Jewish legend in the form of a morality play, with allusions to the perversion of power in Nazi Germany. It is a profoundly expressive work, drawing on a wide range of media and styles.[3]

Philip Bohlman has called Tal "the most individualistic composer of the immigrant generation from Central Europe," and one who exemplifies the progressive, pluralistic trend among Israeli immigrant composers: "Throughout his career he has maintained that the unique character of Israeli culture was not its unity but its diversity, its openness to numerous cultural streams. At times he has defended such a position against the onslaught of considerable criticism. Tal's position, nevertheless, has endured and persists as an acculturative response that embraces change in Israeli culture, rather than eschewing it."[4]

Tal has been awarded the Yoel Engel Prize three times, received the Israel Prize in 1971, and was awarded the Arts Prize of the City of Berlin in 1975. He is an honorary member of the American Academy of Arts and Letters, and in 1983 he shared the Wolff Prize with pianist Vladimir Horowitz and composer Olivier Messiaen.[5] Tal has received many awards and honorary distinctions in Germany, where his works are frequently performed. His music is also available on numerous recordings. In addition to his career as a composer, Tal is well known as an educator, pianist, and conductor. The composer's autobiography was published in Germany in 1985.[6]

I interviewed Josef Tal at his home in Jerusalem on June 20, 1986.

———

I was born in a small village that today is in Poland. At the time I was born there it was part of east[ern] Germany.[7] But I moved with my parents as a child of a few months to Berlin in 1910. I lived in Berlin, went to school and the Academy of Music, and finished my training there. I started to work on my own and then came Hitler, and I decided immediately to leave. I came to then Palestine in March 1934. I couldn't immigrate as a musician because according to the British-mandate rules this was regarded as a freelance profession, and in this country there was a danger of becoming a social case with such a profession. So they demanded a minimum of one thousand pounds sterling in the bank from which I could live comfortably on the interest. I hadn't any possibility to get this money, which at the time was a huge sum of money.

So I found out it was much easier to come here on a "certificate of craftsman." And just for this reason I decided to learn a craft, and as a hobby I always loved photography. So I saw nothing bad to learn that and to do it properly. I managed to get a sponsor, to let me learn. I did it in a quick, very concentrated course in Berlin. This school doesn't exist anymore, but at this time it was a famous art school with a department of photography. They behaved very nicely to me. The director understood the reason I did it. The normal course would take four years, but I told them that I had no more time than maximum one year, and they all agreed to it. But they told me it's at my own risk, and I did it. So I came to this country as a photographer and started as a photographer. You can't do everything in your life, but I love it still. I worked also on a lot of experiments in photography, I was also very much interested in the chemical side of photography. I made my own developers. All this fascinated me very much. And I was very much interested, always, in theater. There was even a time I wanted to become an actor. In Germany, in school already, I was known as an actor.

Photography was not regarded as an art but a useful craft for daily life. And they were right. Indeed, I was asked for by some man in Haifa who had the money to put up a studio, but he wasn't a professional photographer. So he took me in. But it was very difficult also at this time. I went to a kibbutz [Gesher] and in 1936 started with the Palestine Broadcasting Service in Jerusalem. And they needed, of course, a musician. So I came over to Jerusalem, and since then I lived in Jerusalem. As soon as I could express myself as a musician, I started as a pianist. I started to give concerts at the settlements, the kibbutzim, traveled a lot in this country. In 1936 or 1937, I was already an established musician. There were only a few professional musicians at this time in the country. Neither composers nor pianists. It started then in 1936, when the Philharmonic Orchestra started. There was a big influx of professional musicians of all kinds, and this changed the picture entirely. Then they started with the real education in music, and all this had been before but in a very improvised amateurish way, not really professional. But then it started seriously. At the beginning there was only a school for amateurs, a so-called conservatoire. And in Europe, Vienna for instance, a conservatoire was also the academy—it's the same. Here they named it like in Germany— a conservatory for the amateurs and academy for the professionals. These are just names.

The [Jerusalem] Academy started about 1936 or 1937; I immediately became a member of the staff. From 1948 to 1952 I was the
director. In 1951 I was appointed a lecturer at the Hebrew University
and since then was connected to this university. In about 1966 I started
with the Department of Musicology and was the first chairman of the
department, for six years. And now I'm an emeritus of the university.
I was also the director of the Centre for Electronic Music. In fact, I
was the first one who started with this activity here in the country. It
was not so easy to do that, but I did it. Today it's common for each
university to have its own electronic music studio. I started that here.
They make a fuss over it, but I don't do that exclusively. It's part of my
general music activity. In fact, I started with electronic music already
as a student in Berlin in 1927. As far as I know, they had the first
electronic music studio in Europe. There were wire recorders, they
had sound generators, amplifiers, this kind of thing. It started with
the play of overtones, to make combinations of harmonics and to
imitate an oboe or a clarinet. For us today, it was the most primitive
way, but at this time it was something sensational. It thrilled me from
the beginning. I was fascinated by the possibility of working with that
medium, playing with the different possibilities.

Well, that was a start, but I couldn't go on because of the political
circumstances. After our War of Independence I started to look around
in the world, learning what happened meantime in this field. I found
out that in order to really know what is going on in technology—it
developed so quickly during the world war—I couldn't follow up here
in this country. I had to go abroad to study, for which I didn't have the
financial means. I managed to get a UNESCO fellowship and twice I
went to Europe and the States, and came back and founded here the
first studio for electronic music with some equipment, which from
time to time developed but was always behind because of financial
reasons. But I went on and on and today I am very busy with a research
project on electronic notation for electronic music, and this is, of
course, in the computer field.

[Karlheinz] Stockhausen's scores were very primitive. From any of
those graphic notations and diagrams, you never could reconstruct a
piece, never. At best you could follow something. And this in my mind
is a great problem. Because the information is of such complexity that
it's impossible to remember all those details. For instance, imagine you
would like to write a symphony by Mahler and you wouldn't have had
the notation for it. I'm very doubtful if ever such a symphony would

have been written. So I think the artistic level of electronic music today has much to do with the lack of a proper notation. Because there are not enough criteria, not discipline, not references, and so on. I know how they work. You go to the studio, you tune up, and you are fascinated, rightly so, by the sound. But you go the next day and you forgot at least 50 percent of all that you've done, and I've done that myself. I don't blame anybody. This is the situation. But I forced myself to try to solve this problem—anyway, to make a contribution to this subject. And we've advanced quite far. I hope that next year, at the latest, I will come out with the first publications. And this will, in my mind, change basically the whole thing.

My idea is to write the score for electronic music at my desk, at home—and I don't need any equipment for that. I'm writing and I'm going the next day to the studio. And I realize it because everything is written down in an economical language, with still quite a lot of possibility of changing, improvising even. But a composer is his own interpreter, he has nobody who plays it. I know also from experience that equipment is developing quickly, also the quality of the sound. The quality of loudspeakers is still very backward, the other equipment advances much quicker. But I'm sure that one day the loudspeakers will be of a quite different acoustical level. And therefore it's quite possible, let's say in another hundred years, that a piece will be reconstructed that has been written down today and you will come much nearer to the reality as the composer imagined it. On this I am working right now.

I've written a number of operas. And the theatrical part of my operas is equal to the musical part, absolutely equal. So I saw to it—so far I've succeeded—always to have a stage director who understands that music and stage are not two different things but are going together and inspiring each other. This is a story in itself, and there are many very interesting stories from this chapter. I even wrote one opera that is entirely electronic—there was no orchestra. It's an opera on Masada. And right now there are negotiations. They want to make a film—not here, in Europe—and it might go onstage also in Europe. It was written for the twenty-fifth anniversary of the state of Israel and was commissioned by the state. It has been performed here in Jerusalem. I will have performances next year in Europe in the 750th-year festival of Berlin.

I am going on, as you see. I'll tell you frankly, the word "retire" is just a word for the administration, but not for me. I am much busier now than before. I never made a distinction between teaching and composing. I love to teach because I explain to myself what I don't know. Good students ask proper questions. Nothing is more fruitful than that. So I never regarded an hour of teaching as a lost hour of composing—never, never. It might be that I would have composed more in quantity with fewer hours of teaching, but that doesn't bother me. I'm busy composing, I'm still lecturing quite a lot, and so on. I don't draw lines between the past and present, it's just a continuation.

Now, the issue of being an Israeli composer—well, this is the very famous question about national music. You should know the answer from your point of view as an American composer. What does it mean to you? I just looked at some scores of yours, and I couldn't find any American expression in that. It could have been everywhere. It means you are, so to say, a cosmopolitan, yes? But now on the other hand, you know from your experience, you live in a society, you live in a certain environment, and it's impossible not to be influenced by it because you can't isolate yourself completely. It would be artificial to do so. So you listen and you speak, and you hear questions and you give answers. And, of course, you are interested that people could understand you, what you are speaking. And it's the same in music.

Music is a communication, and if you communicate you speak to somebody. If somebody can't make any sense of what you are speaking then you are speaking to the walls, right? But music is not a language with words in which every word has a determined content. This you can't have. You can't say in music: "Please sit down." So we call that abstract—which is not at all an abstraction because it's not an abstraction of a word's reality. It is a reality in itself, it's a different language. English is not an abstraction of Chinese, or vice versa. So music is not an abstraction of spoken language. It is a language in itself. It has its own grammar, its own rules, its own organization. It has its own feelings. It creates its own emotions as any language does. It has in itself both elements, the emotional and the discipline. The question is, how can you make yourself understandable to a listener who hasn't known music methodically, who isn't a professional? Because over the hundreds of years, in music, certain expressions have been accepted as general. Let's say, for instance, major and minor. To have a funeral march in major, although there are exceptions—or to write a wedding march in minor—would be grotesque, would be something for comedy. Why is that so? What's the logic in it? Only because the minor third makes me automatically sad?

72

Israel is a fact. The state of Israel is a fact since 1948. But the people of Israel are facts for thousands of years. So they are two different things. And, of course, the people of Israel remember their past and in the case of, let's say, an observant Jew, sings old traditional melodies. Sure, and there are some, they are formulated on the musical language of hundreds of years before our time. And then, this was a time when the Western music was consolidated into what we call classical music or romantic music or any other term for it. And, of course, this became a traditional music. So if you go to the synagogue to pray for Yom Kippur or Rosh Hashanah, then, of course, you sing the traditional melodies and they are near the major-minor scale, or the ecclesiastical modes. And quite understandably, when we started here with Israeli music in 1948, we started consciously to create Israeli music as a national expression. Then, of course, there were many people who said we have to write in the old scales—in Dorian, Phrygian, and so on. Because they were regarded as exotic things from ancient times, which they are not so much, certainly not from the biblical times. So unfortunately we don't know what King David really sang. As we don't have any notated music of this time, we don't know. So the Israeli music in Phrygian, or Dorian, or Lydian, or Aeolian modes is quite European, and anything else, but not Israeli.

Now, of course, the big problem was to start something which is the present and to disconnect it from the past, which in itself is an artificial process. You can't do that, it really doesn't succeed. Take today all the young composers, they don't have these problems anymore. They only attach themselves to what's going on in the world, as Japan did with regard to Western music. Now what is going on in Japan, is it Japanese music? They are writing like Stockhausen, [Iannis] Xenakis, [Pierre] Boulez, you find all that in ultra-extreme expressions in Japan. Still they are going on with their traditions, and why not? Well, this is what you have here too. You can take the old traditional tunes, let's say, and to quote them in your music and harmonize them modernly has always been done here. Yemenite songs have been harmonized in Western tradition. The question is, should you do that? I question it, but you can do it. There will come a day when you will give a blessing to it or you will say it destroys the melody. But to do those experiments is understandable, and I wouldn't just laugh at that. I myself didn't do that. I mean I'm not above all that, I tried to make my own experiments. I didn't think that I shouldn't try that, shouldn't participate in this struggle which was just a humanistic struggle, so to

73

say, in music. For instance, my Second Piano Concerto was written on an old Jewish-Persian lamentation that I found extremely interesting as a piece of music—not at all old-fashioned, quite modern. I took out of the piece certain motives, and I used them as the basis for this piano concerto. Of course, here and there you can recognize it, and if I analyze the piece I can easily show this. So I made my own experiments with that, but very few.

Actually, I don't think that a national expression ends with a quotation of old music. There are national elements and there is the behavior in the street, how the people behave. What's their morality? What is their degree of aggression? And so on. And this is a nationality. This should come out in the music, you see, because I live it and I'm confronted with it day by day. If you start now to translate those things, then already you are on the borderline between language and music, common language and music language. Because to speak about music in itself is principally an impossibility. But I did it for many, many, many, many years because I had students—I had to speak about music. And I tried hard not to speak only about music, but also to *speak* the music, which is difficult. But I think you can do it. At least you can manage to bring the student nearer to what you are meaning, to fire his imagination so he can participate in your own way of thinking. But if you put me down to examples, show me—"Here on page twenty-three and bar fifty-six, you have Israeli music"—that you cannot do.

Now look, I'll give you another example. About the same time were living three composers well known in Europe, and their names were Haydn, Mozart, and Beethoven. Not only about the same time, but even in the same region geographically. And they traveled quite a lot and they saw the same places, lived in the same places, came into contact with the same people. But what can you point to in any bar of those three composers? Only if they quote. If they quote the most popular behavior in Vienna—let's say there is a waltz—then, of course, you can recollect the Viennese waltz, or anything else. Or in the German dances by Mozart, or these kinds of things. But take a piece, I mean any string quartet by Mozart or Beethoven where there is no quotation. Even if you take the Russian quartet by Beethoven, the Razumovsky quartet—well, there is a quotation of a Russian song, but this poor song, what remains from it that is Russian in the piece? You just can't do that.

And this is what they always demand from you, because then you can write about it and you can speak about it. And it returns in each interview, every interview wants to nail me down to the Israeli motives in my music. And there is no question they are in it, no question. And if I wouldn't have decided to go to Palestine in the early 1930s, or would have gone to London or New York, I don't think I would have written the same music. I don't think so. Let's say, from the technical point of view, the interest in twelve-tone music would be the same, and from this point of view there would be the same elements of twelve-tone music in it, or electronic music, or any other thing. This would be common. But this is what we call today cosmopolitan. You can't change it because in your TV box you have the whole world every day, and you are not disconnected from it. So my environment is not only Israeli, my environment is absolutely international. You can't avoid it. Even if I don't want to do that, I have to do it. I listen to the radio, I look at the TV, and I read newspapers. I'm a normal human being, not a pathological artist, you see. So I am a member of the whole world, but I am living in a certain country which is called Israel and very near to all that interests us—our fight in life, our struggle in life. And this certainly comes out in the music, no matter if it is written for piano or for electronics, or for whatever you want.

I'm also of the opinion that the Jewishness in Mahler is in his symphonies, without mentioning sentimental things. And he quotes quite a lot of Austrian melodies, quite a lot. And it is part of his Jewishness in this work. But if you know where he had lived as a young boy and what education he got, I think it's not difficult to make the translation, or to make the bridge, from his traditional songs to his way of melodic thinking as, for instance, in the slow part of the Fifth Symphony, the famous part that became the film music for *Death in Venice,* which is built entirely on the Fifth Symphony by Mahler. And not so wrong, not at all. I don't know that they knew that consciously. But it's the same conflict, the same basic Jewish conflict in a different society, and all that comes out in this story in the struggle between two people. It was not so silly to take this music as movie music. It did a lot for the movie. And I have seen this movie several times, just to concentrate on the relation between the music and the picture. I did it just to study it. It's tremendous.

Now, you can analyze the music by Mahler in regards to his Jewishness quite easily, without any associations to his becoming a convert Jew or any other thing. Not just the programmatic things, which you can immediately translate. This is an approach, an amateurish approach, to tell stories—science fiction—but not the real thing. The real thing is really in his building of melodic motives, and to expand them. And you can see in that the Jewish quality, which is environment, of course. He learned his music in lessons, but he was injected with all Jewish liturgical music. And this is crossing of two cultures, and out came something that became Mahler's music.

Schoenberg too, certainly. No question about it, no question. The whole idea of twelve-tone method is a very Jewish idea, the big role that number plays in life. So the twelve-tone music is anything else, but not mathematical play around with numbers. And Schoenberg's music itself is the best proof because there is no twelve-tone music with so many licenses as in Schoenberg's twelve-tone music. And to study why does he make a deviation in this certain place, from the twelve-tone method—why does he do that? Here you can learn the real meaning of twelve-tone music, from his deviations and not from the words of systematization. This you can learn in ten minutes, no problem.

I met him, but I studied with Hindemith. Hindemith was at the Academy of Music, but Schoenberg was at the Academy of Arts. This is a different institute. The Academy of Arts is an institute like the Académie Française, or the Royal Society or the American Academy of Arts and Letters. In those academies, you don't teach. The Academy of Music was not called an academy, but in German, the Hochschule für Musik—"high school" of music. Even today they call it that. Academy is a different thing. Schoenberg only gave master classes. But this is in effect not a school, the Academy of Arts. In America—well, that was his destiny. He wanted to come here. He wouldn't have been very happy here because the situation was way too backward and too primitive for him. Today it's different. Today he would have the means to build up something. At this time, it was very, very primitive.

I was twenty-three when I left Berlin. When you're twenty-three you're already a human being. The first time I visited Berlin I escaped, I couldn't see it. Because it was still in the stage of havoc at this time, few things had been rebuilt. This was a nightmare to see. But then in the course of my musical doings I visited it again and again. And then, of course, today it is all very different from what it was.

There are always changes, always. I never go on with the same thing. I mean this is part of our century. We all went through so many different periods. I still remember my examination to enter the Academy of Music. I had to improvise on a given subject in sonata form, on the piano. Franz Schreker—you may know the name—was

76

the director then. So I played it. I was very strong in improvisation, so I did it with pleasure. And when I finished he said to me with a certain smile, "Well, my young man, it was somewhat like Beethoven." I was impertinent enough to reply to this remark, "Herr Professor, shall I take this as a compliment?"

———

Among Israel's most prolific and celebrated composers, Josef Tal remains extraordinarily active in his ninth decade. He wrote in 1990:

After the completion of my last larger scores, the opera *The Tower* and the Fourth Symphony, and the intense work on the iconographic notation for computer music, I am fully aware of the process of fundamental change in musical composition. The full length of the twentieth-century dealt with more or less radical changes of systematization in the world of sounds. With the introduction of the computer as a music-realizer, the entire pitch concept moves toward a different music perception. This point is now my main interest. In addition to smaller works, I am now working on the score for my Fifth Symphony, commissioned by the Berlin Philharmonic Orchestra.[8]

In 1991, Tal read a paper on "Iconographic Notation and Its Consequences" at a symposium sponsored by the Institute for New Music at the Academy of Arts in Berlin. He finished his Fifth Symphony, received a commission for his Sixth Symphony and completed a number of smaller chamber works.[9]

Tal's music is frequently and widely performed. Since 1991 his works have been heard in Romania, Hungary, and the Czech Republic, during International Festivals of Jewish Art Music held in Odessa (Ukraine) and Vilnius (Lithuania), as well as in Israel and throughout Germany (including the opening of the 1992 *Documenta* exhibition in Kassel). In 1994, Tal's Piano Quartet was performed by the Cantilena Piano Quartet in New York and Washington, D.C. His orchestral works have recently been performed by the Jerusalem Symphony Orchestra, the Israel Chamber Orchestra, the Israel Philharmonic Orchestra, the North German Radio Symphony Orchestra, the Berlin Philharmonic, the Berlin Radio Symphony Orchestra, and Niederrheinische Sinfoniker. Among the conductors leading these orchestras were Zubin Mehta, Daniel Barenboim, and David Shallon. In Israel, Tal's works have been performed during the Israel Festival, the Eleventh International Harp Contest, and at the opening concert of the 1992 Zimriya choral festival.

Tal's opera *Josef,* commissioned in 1993 by the New Israeli Opera, was premiered in 1995 under the baton of Gary Bertini.[10] Other 1995 performances included the composer's Sixth Symphony (1991), given by the Jerusalem Symphony under the direction of David Shallon. The same year, Tal was one of three recipients of the Johann Wenzel Stamitz Prize, awarded in Germany.[11]

Haim Alexander, photographed by Scoop 80 Photographers.
Used with permission.

3

HAIM ALEXANDER

Haim (originally Heinz) Alexander has composed more than seventy works for a wide variety of media, including many arrangements of folk songs. He also collected more than two hundred traditional Jewish melodies that have been the basis of many compositions by Israeli composers.[1] Stylistic diversity is a hallmark of Alexander's music, which draws on modes, the twelve-tone method, folklore, jazz, and improvisation, and combines elements of neoclassicism, expressionism, Eastern Mediterranean pastoralism, and polyphonic textures recalling the compositions of Bartók and Hindemith. Alexander has received awards from the Israel Music Institute, the Society of Authors, Composers, and Music Publishers (ACUM), and the Zimriya choral festival, as well as the Yoel Engel Prize (1951) for his *Six Israeli Dances,* one of the most often heard contemporary Israeli works. He is well known as a pianist, with a special interest in improvisation. Alexander taught at the Jerusalem Rubin Academy of Music and Dance from 1945 to 1981, and continued to teach part-time thereafter.

Michael Wolpe has described three stylistic phases in Alexander's work: from 1945 until 1958 he participated in the Eastern Mediterranean style dominant during the period, employing modal materials with elements of folklore and jazz; from 1958 until 1969 his work was freer, with a greater affinity to the avant-garde, specifically in employing the twelve-tone method; during the 1970s and 1980s still more freedom in the choice of form and material was evident.[2]

I first met Haim Alexander at a concert during the Israel Festival. Our interview took place at his home in Jerusalem on July 7, 1986.

———

I was born the ninth of August 1915, in Berlin, Germany. {I remember Berlin as a vibrant city, culturally as well as politically and socially. I personally had little share in its bustling life. My family was not well off. My father died when I was seven. I was sent to the Auerbach orphanage for several years. At the orphanage I made many friends, some of them musicians. They had a reform synagogue, with a big harmonium. I played regularly, at Friday evening and Sabbath-day prayers, and on festivals—works by Louis Lewandowski, Salomon Sulzer, and others.

Private lessons with various tutors, singing in the Berlin Boys Choir, one of the best children's choirs of the day—these were my initiation into the world of music. We sang in many places, mainly sacred music. I may have been the only Jew in the choir. I could not afford to go to concerts or the opera, yet I vividly recall attending concerts. I had the good fortune to hear Otto Klemperer and Bruno Walter, and to sing in a children's choir at a performance of Bach's *St. Matthew Passion,* conducted by [Wilhelm] Furtwängler. I was even at the premiere of [Kurt] Weill and [Bertolt] Brecht's *The Threepenny Opera* with the unforgettable Lotte Lenya. Before I was five I began improvising on the piano and composing little pieces with relative ease, and in this natural way I learned the basics of harmony and counterpoint.}[3] I now know my teachers in Germany were, I would say, quite mediocre. And I had one teacher for piano who was an accompanist of Willi Domgraf-Fassbaender, then a quite famous singer. But he didn't give me much. He was also my theory teacher, and I had some other teachers. But it was at the time the Nazis came.

I left Berlin when I was twenty-one, in 1936, for Palestine, as a student of music. Emil Hauser, the violinist, was then in charge. He was the director of the Palestine Conservatory and Academy. I would say he rescued me from the Nazis, at the time. I had been in Berlin from 1915 to 1936 going to school, then going to the Stern Conservatory. And I wanted to enter the Hochschule für Musik in Berlin but this was impossible because in the meantime everything was *Judenrein.* {In 1934 I was expelled from the Musicians Union, and then, together with the other Jewish students}, they also threw me out of the Stern Conservatory, and I found that I had nothing more to do there. Germany was now forbidden for Jews, and for artists as well, so I waited for my chance to leave the country.

{A wealthy uncle who later perished in the Holocaust knew I was desperate to leave Germany.} He told me that there was an advertisement in *Die jüdische Rundschau,* a newspaper for Jews in Berlin, that Emil Hauser comes later that week to Berlin to look for talented young students—boys and girls—to take them for two years to study at the Jerusalem Academy—Palestine Academy and Conservatory for Music. {This is how Yohanan Boehm, Herbert Brün and many others came to Jerusalem. It was a two-year course, but for many of us it became a lifetime—there was no way back.} He was the husband of the then quite well known children's physician, Dr. Helena Kagan, one of the founders of many things here, artistically. {He organized chamber music concerts at his and his wife's home. Through him I got to know the quartets of Mozart, Haydn, Beethoven, Mendelssohn, Brahms and others.} Emil Hauser could have done nothing without her. She gave the money. He went abroad and he listened to students. He was also, together with [Bronislaw] Huberman, one of the founders of the Philharmonic Orchestra, because Huberman alone could not listen to all of them. They were friends, and one went here, the other one there.

I don't know if my memory is so good now, but I think my main studies started when I was twenty-one. I was a student of Stefan Wolpe and his then second wife, Irma Schoenberg, who was not a relative of Schoenberg but a very good pianist and teacher. She died also a few years ago, I think, in New York, like Wolpe, who died much earlier. I've got here some material written by him, also some letters from him. He was at that time the most important person, and his teaching was like a shock to me, because my education was on the classical-romantic side. My compositions were like a continuation of Mendelssohn. When he saw this he said, "Now this is very good, throw it into the dustbox, throw it away—now we start making music!" And he meant, by music, certainly only serial music.

So my first acquaintance with dodecaphonic music came through Stefan Wolpe. {Wolpe was a powerful, acerbic extrovert who did not suffer detractors easily. He was energetic, temperamental and super-impulsive. He would leave a lesson in the middle if the muse called. Studying with him was a unique experience. As a pupil of

Arnold Schoenberg and an exponent of the dodecaphonic school, he considered it the only method for modern music. His wife was very different from him. She was reserved, a highly gifted pianist with a unique technical and musical approach. I think she was her husband's intellectual superior. Her playing and teaching method were carefully calculated.}

Wolpe was also a conductor, and I sang in his choir. He taught us conducting as well, not only composition. So I had all my experience here. But I must say that Wolpe left the country because he didn't feel well here. There were other reasons he went to the States. The general trend at that time was much more focused around the Mediterranean style of Marc Lavry and Ben-Haim. And the funny thing is that Wolpe was not completely unaware of this. He wrote several works, which I possess, mainly for a cappella chorus. They are also more or less Mediterranean, but his instrumental works were completely different and nobody wanted to listen to them. So he left the country, together with other musicians like [Wolf] Rosenberg and Peter Jona Korn. The latter is quite well known in Germany. Korn went afterwards to Schoenberg to study with him.

{My first years in the country were an intensive intellectual debate on all levels, including music. First, two schools dominated: Wolpe, and Lavry and Ben-Haim. I personally was torn between my modal, Mediterranean tendency and Wolpe's aesthetic-dodecaphonic demands. Then, like today, symposia were held to deal with questions concerning the nature of new music, whether there was a Jewish music, an Israeli music, and so on. Each school was totally dictatorial. The Wolpians heaped scorn on the Ben-Haimites in the most vitriolic terms, while the Lavryites waved the Zionist banner and believed fervently in the folkloristic approach. To Ben-Haim's credit, he granted legitimacy to everyone and stayed out of the fray. His works spoke for themselves, in a clear Mediterranean voice.

For Wolpe, Ben-Haim was anathema to his universal style. Wolpe rejected Hebrew as a language of expression and opposed the folkloristic, simplistic approach. His departure from the country was an act of despair; broken-hearted, he fled the recriminations and begrudged the recognition gained by his rivals and the damning judgment of his "Zionist" critics. Wolpe's departure left me and other young composers facing a stylistic dilemma: whether to assume the "burden" of the Mediterranean style, or to undertake a fervent examination of the European avant-garde. Lavry preached an "authentic" Israeli music while in effect perpetuating the Russian nationalist school. Many of the German composers were influenced by him and artificially grafted the Mediterranean style to their work, sometimes with grotesque results. The dodecaphonists turned to Schoenberg, Webern, and Berg. Hindemith was studied with fervor by the Mediterraneanists. Bartók became known in Israel later—largely thanks to Oedoen Partos, but he has, I think, become a very influential composer here.

There was a strong German clique, and we spoke German—even the Czechs among us. But we slowly learned Hebrew. This group was the standard bearer of music in the country. Later the Hungarians came, bringing with them new ideas and new material. Gradually new blood was added, from Eastern Europe, and the "Yekke mafia" blended into the new Israeli reality.[4] The composers who had come from Germany had no interest in nationalistic trends, even scorned them. I was searching for a personal way, far from the German culture which in the war years for me became the embodiment of evil. What some of the Yekkes could not apprehend in the Hebrew language found expression in music. No wonder Jacoby, Avidom and Ben-Haim were so avidly Mediterranean. Only in the sixties did I begin to listen to folk music, and I transcribed two hundred songs for adaptation. But actual quotation is very rare in my works.}

I listened to the Schoenberg school sometimes, but I always started laughing. I didn't understand; it didn't mean anything to me. {I was more familiar with Hindemith when I came from Germany. My initial relation to Wolpe was one of a pupil's respect for a teacher. In fact, it was much later that I began to implement some of Wolpe's ideas, after I had been to Darmstadt. While studying with Wolpe, I earned my living as a cocktail pianist in Jerusalem bars. This may account for lighter, more humorous elements that appear in my music.}

So from 1938 onwards I had no more teachers like Wolpe, and I went to somebody you've probably heard about, Hanoch Jacoby. I studied five years with him, and he gave me more insight and understanding of the work of Hindemith, because he was a Hindemith student. {Jacoby's influence was immediate and our friendship instantaneous, as between peers. He helped me publish my first compositions, which had strong intimations of Hindemith and modality. I eagerly adopted a personal modal style, with neo-modal leanings, and an occasional folkloristic bent. I composed a lot for choir, mainly in Hebrew, and piano.}Then I had some lessons from Partos, but I was not really studying with him. I had also some discussion with Josef

85

Tal, and after this I was on my own. I had three times a grant from the DAAD,[5] and I went to Freiburg.

{I returned to Germany in 1958.} I couldn't do it before. The first time I went back to Germany it was awful. I couldn't look at people because my whole family went into the gas chambers. And so it was for me an awful experience to see the old people who looked at me and said "we never did anything." So I said "I didn't ask you if you did anything." They started, they'd say "Are you from Israel? You have to know that we had nothing to do with it." Never mind, these are things I said so often, and it always hurts me. {The reason was an invitation to a conference in Darmstadt. I felt the time had come to see what was happening musically in the world. To this day I believe the time we were shut into the borders of our country created a kind of cultural ghetto that gave birth to the Mediterranean style that dominated in Israel in the forties and fifties. On the 1958 trip I could not yet face Berlin, but I did go there at the end of the sixties. The wall had already been erected, and I went to see my sole remaining kin—Jews who were saved thanks to Christians who had hidden them in the city's netherworld.}

I went three times to Darmstadt, and there I met Wolpe again, who taught there, and people like Stockhausen, Boulez, [Henri] Pousseur, and other avant-garde composers. By the way, Wolpe did not succeed there as well, could not get through. Stockhausen had two hundred or more students; to Wolpe came three or four, nothing. They were not interested in this style. He said his music was too old-fashioned for Darmstadt and too new in Israel. He was also a very individualistic man, and with all his extrovert appearance he couldn't make friends. I met Ligeti there, and other people. Then I went to Freiburg for further studies, and I learned the harpsichord with Neumeyer and I listened to lessons from Wolfgang Fortner. He wrote many operas. I went to Freiburg twice. And then I had a third opportunity to visit Germany as a guest. Many other Germans also had the opportunity. I was in Hannover, Essen, and Munich.

I met other musicians there, heard their students, and I started writing real dodecaphonic music after the second visit to Darmstadt. I like very much Alban Berg, he's my favorite. But I like Bartók as well. And I wanted to make some experiments with these two styles. I wrote four or five works, really completely dodecaphonic works. And later I became more or less a composer of post-serial music. I wrote one work which I liked very much. It's very short, a piano work called

Patterns (*Tavniyot*), which sounds really serial but it is not. But I never would have written that without going through the serial work. Now I'm very much interested, more or less, in styles like Messiaen. I wrote three pieces, songs, which were performed a few months ago by the Sinfonietta, with Lili Tune, a very good singer, and I think this will be on the radio this month. Whatever a composer writes, even if this is completely tonal or even if it is rubbish, it is certainly a part of his output. So, for better or for worse, you can say it is my work.

What it means to be an Israeli composer is a difficult question, but I'll try to answer it. Perhaps you don't know that I'm also a quite good, they say, a very good improviser. I wrote a book on improvisation, and just two weeks ago it came out in Germany, not yet in English.[6] So if you ask me what is Israeli music I would say, first of all, there comes my intuition as an improviser. So I have an idea—I don't care if this sounds Israeli or not, because I never heard a correct answer concerning what is really Israeli or not. I just care if it's good music or not.

I write really in many styles. In younger years I wrote many a cappella choruses for the Zimriya. I got first prize for the first Zimriya, I got the first prize for the second Zimriya, and then they said, "Please don't participate anymore," so I stopped. But the Bible text inspired me. The accent of the Hebrew words inspired me too, to write not only modal but also according to the Hebrew accent. And this inspired me also in the instrumental music. For instance, one of my works, called *Six Israeli Dances,* for piano, which is my best-known work, was inspired by these elements. I've made two orchestrations, the latest a year ago. Aaron Copland, who heard it in '45, said to me, "This is a good experiment to be called Israeli music." So this gave me a push to continue, but I did not continue that way.

We had a composers' session for one week. He came over from the States in 1945; Frank Pelleg invited him. Pelleg was an excellent musician, a very good man. He died too young.[7] So he called Copland to come here, and we sat and Copland listened the whole day to some of our music. And I was then quite a young man, thirty years old. He was very friendly to me. I sent to him later another work of mine that I thought was a good one, but he didn't like it. He said there was too much influence of Prokofiev. Now I know he was right, this was not my best work. It was a big orchestral work, forty minutes I think, done with the Philharmonic, and also here with the Symphony Orchestra of the Jerusalem Broadcasting Service.

{From 1945 to 1958 the Mediterranean style ruled, in the spirit of the Zionism that fired the young stage. Those were busy years for me: I began teaching at the Academy in Jerusalem. I loved it and made it an integral part of my life in music. Those were happy years, of personal and professional progress, of walking in the streets and hearing music—in harmony with the creative atmosphere that infused the country. Then I would go home to my room and compose. I used many of the techniques taught me by Jacoby. Some days were dull and expectant but later on the muse would return. My army reserve duty afforded my first practical work in light music, as composer and arranger for an army entertainment troupe. I set texts to music, taught them, and adapted my own and others' works. Some of my songs even reached the hit parade.}

You asked about the influence of Israeli music. I wrote not only on Bible texts but also a work called *Artza*—that means "homeland." This is a symphonic overture. And then I wrote another symphonic overture, and both of these have a connection to something I thought then to be Israeli music. If I look at it now, I would say it is a little Russian and a little Mediterranean. {I studied the Bible fairly intensively. That was at the time when the Song of Songs and Psalms were set to music. In *And I Gathered You In (Vekbatzti Etchem)* I was assisted by one of my pupils, who suggested integrating texts from Ezekiel and Psalms. The style of my choral works of that period is purely modal.

In *Let's Praise His Name in the Dance,* I encountered the conflict between traditional form (the sonata) and the quasi-Israeli melodic material. I think sonata form presents a problem for the composer using this kind of material, and this spurred me on to seek another form. I am particularly partial to variations. Already in 1947 I composed piano variations I am very proud of, using several chords in a style far from both the dodecaphonic and the Mediterranean styles. I wrote a number of works in the personal modal style, but in the fifties I gradually began to feel the need to learn new things and change in order to emerge from the ideological Mediterranean ghetto we had built in Israel.} But the real Israeli style, which perhaps you could find in some of Ben-Haim's work, is more or less absent. I didn't like that too much. I felt that if you do that too much it becomes a cliché. Then, anyway, I went to dodecaphonic works.

I met Wolpe again in Darmstadt twice. It took a long time to understand what he said to me in 1936. In 1936 I couldn't understand him, but in 1958 I understood him. I liked him more, I understood him. I started to think that maybe tonal music is over, which I don't think today. But then I thought so and I wrote four songs on Omar Khayyám's *Rubaiyat,* which is perhaps one of my better works. And I wrote a piano work that won the first prize from the Israel Music Institute for the best piano work of the year in 1964. This was all after two visits in Darmstadt. {Even though I was shocked by what went on there, and skeptical about its quality, I went regularly for years. I watched the deep ebb and flow of fashionable trends. Often the explanations were longer and more interesting than the works themselves. But there were also fine moments that gave me the inspiration for new creativity, beginning in 1958.}

Then I was much involved with all this. I mean I thought over which kind of music would suit me. I didn't care if it suited Israeli style. I didn't believe in that, I mean in the way, for instance, Ben-Haim believed in it. With every work I found myself thinking about how I could really overcome the first difficulties of writing it. It was always a new experience for me starting a work on a grand scale like a piano concerto. I had an idea that pushed me forward, but I didn't mind the dodecaphonic method, which I left later. I started serial composing about 1962, I think, and I stopped it about 1970. I did not stop it exactly, but little by little, going over to the scales of Messiaen. The three songs I mentioned earlier are based exactly on the Messiaen mode number two. {Modality and serialism are only techniques. My own personal expression—the strong connection to the text, the sometimes nearly jazz-like rhythms and the humor, things that cannot always be expressed in words—these are, I hope, constant throughout my work.}

I just finished, for four young musicians, a quartet for four trombones that is also a work in a modern folklore style, with lots of clusters in it. It is based on an Israeli song. I thought, if I write for young German people, then I will give them Israeli music. I dedicated it to them, it is called *At adamah (You Are the Earth),* and it is a song about the Negev desert. It starts with the song. I heard it's a Bedouin song really. Everybody knows it. What I did—I didn't even say variation or metamorphosis—I said *Betrachtungen,* it's *histaklut* in Hebrew. It means I look at it—it's an observation. I always use some of the motives, but it is through a way of meditation, I would say. It goes from one extreme to the other. But anyway, even then it remains folklore in a way, in a modern way.

I worked more than three years at the Hebrew University when Recha Freier asked me to collect songs in two books. These two hundred songs I collected were used by many composers who even now use the book. I heard thousands of songs, but I chose only the ones that I thought are possible for youngsters. I mean I didn't take, for instance, music of the Samaritans—this is a special sect who sing microtonally.

I teach improvisation on a serial basis, on whole-tone scale, on Messiaen scales, on Purcell style, on the Bach style, on Beethoven, Mozart, Schubert. It's called "Improvisation at the Piano." I even go now next month to teach improvisation at the Jeunesses Musicales, which is an international group, for young musicians and students who meet once a year in a summer course. This time it is near Haifa. There I also give improvisation courses for whole groups with different instruments, I don't mind if it's not only piano. So I'm flexible, you see. This comes perhaps out of my long experience as a piano teacher and harpsichord teacher. For the harpsichord I taught mostly baroque music. At the piano I taught also lots of modern music and the classical-romantic style. {Ever since I wrote songs for my sister, the singer Lili Alexander, when I worked the cafe circuit in Germany of the Thirties and Forties and went on to do jazz improvisation, and even recently in my *Teyko*, I have loved jazz and been intrigued by popular music. In my analysis course at the Academy we dissected Beatles songs. Clearly, some of this involvement is evinced in my works.}

Maybe it would be better if I would have a certain "narrow" way. And I know my friend [Ben-Zion] Orgad very well, he chooses such a way. He's a very clever man and he's a philosopher. He also writes lyrics. Orgad is a man with much thought, he thinks a lot how to develop. Orgad is much nearer to Seter, so he writes in a way modal. He is not a serialist. He is serious, and we like each other very much. But as much as I'm a man of humor, he's a man without humor. So sometimes I think it's quite strange if you listen to that too much. I mean it's just a little bit one-sided. I don't know his whole output, but anyway he's an interesting man.

Lavry, whom I knew very well, was a man with a special talent for melody. There was a joke that would explain everything about Lavry, that somebody called Lavry at his home on the telephone, and Mrs. Lavry lifted the receiver. The man said, "Could I speak to Marc Lavry?" and she answered, "How could you dare to telephone now, he's just started an opera!" So the man said, "Excuse me, I won't do it again." She said, "Now wait a little bit, if you wait a few minutes, he will finish it." So he had an amazing speed of writing. He could sit in the middle of an orchestra concert and write a cantata. I don't understand it, how he did it. His music was on the light side. I mean if Ben-Haim was a folklorist then Ben-Haim and Lavry perhaps had something in common. But Ben-Haim was a giant and Lavry was, in my opinion, inferior to him. Anyway, he has some memorable melodies that up to now are played. But funny as it is, after his death, almost everything stopped. Before that he had a great influence on other musicians.

Boskovitch was an excellent composer and teacher. His interest in serial music started toward the end of his life, so there are not many such works composed by him. Partos was a really serious, earnest musician, a very good viola player. He wrote much music for viola. And he was very much interested in Bible cantillation. We had many talks, and one day he said, "Haim, you know that there is a lot of common material between the Bible cantillation and the dodecaphonic method. I'm writing now a piece or two where I combine the cantillation with the method." It was very interesting. Maybe these talks influenced me to try this out by myself, because the Bible cantillation and some of Bartók's style are very much related. I mean in his string quartets, you have motives that are not far from cantillations. Later I met Partos again. We had another talk and I asked, "Do you still write Bible cantillations mixed with dodecaphonic method?" He said, "No, no, I left the twelve-tone method long ago." So, I think this was only a passing thing. He was very much interested in oriental cantillation, not in European—Hasidic—not at all. But only in oriental cantillation, which is, by the way, an influence for Seter and Orgad as well. Orgad told me that he very often went to the oriental synagogue in order to listen to the cantillations. Partos, in my opinion, was one of the best composers here. He was the first principal of the Academy in Tel Aviv, and he had a strong, if not always pleasant, personality. You didn't dare come to see him without a previous appointment.

{Things have improved enormously in the past twenty years. No more dictatorship of schools as in the fifties and sixties. Now there is a greater freedom of expression everywhere. If it will actually take root in Israel I cannot predict. I think the Israeli composer, in addition to his personal or national connection, must find universal expression. People everywhere should be able to enjoy and understand his music, while being ever aware that it is Israeli. How to achieve this is the question. With a text it is perhaps easier. Without a text the challenge is far more difficult.

I have a personal credo: war prevents artistic rootedness. I left Germany and came to Israel. I had high hopes and even moments of joy. But my elder son was killed in battle. And I wonder time and again—why? The world is marching towards the universal. In the arts, too, techniques are shared, and with the help of mass communication and mobility the world is becoming one unit. Against this background national expression may turn dissonant. Likeness of style began on the technical plane but is becoming quite natural: the same music is heard in Japan, Israel and Poland. Sometimes I think that what was a national Mediterranean expression now appears almost sinful. Almost fascist! The days are over, of the innocent Zionist idealism, that sincerely enabled the spontaneous growth of music drawn from the folk traditions and seeking national expression. It is hard to accept, and this is also the main reason why I do not write grand orchestral music. These are not the times for songs of praise. All this leads to my intimate style, my simple and modest approach. Biblical oratorios have been replaced by love songs for voice and piano.}

———

Haim Alexander continues to compose and receive performances of his music internationally. In 1990 his trio for piano, violin, and violoncello was premiered in a live broadcast, and the Vienna Madrigal Choir performed his composition for mixed choir a cappella, *And I Gathered You In,* at the Musikverein, conducted by Aharon Harlap. Alexander's *Mein blaues Klavier,* for eight women's voices and percussion, a setting of a poem by Else Lasker-Schüler, was performed by the Ensemble Bel Canto in Germany in 1990 and the Jerusalem Rubin Academy Chamber Choir in 1991. A 1991 premiere in Jerusalem of his *Metamorphoses on a Theme of Mozart,* for piano, was broadcast live. Performances in 1992 included his *Four Songs* for voice, flute, viola, two guitars, and percussion, performed by the Kaprisma Ensemble in Jerusalem; *And I Gathered You In,* performed by the National Choir Rinat; and *Shepherd's Round,* for flute and piano, performed in London at the B'nai B'rith Jewish Music Festival. In 1993, recitals of works by Israeli composers held at the Israel House in Chicago included Alexander's *Metamorphoses* for violin, performed by David Wolf, and his *Variations on a Bukharian Song* and *Variations on a Hassidic Niggun,* performed by oboist Kathryn Pisaro. In 1994, *De Profundis* for organ was heard in a live broadcast performance; a new work, *Questions and Answers* for soprano, flute, and piano, was premiered in a live concert broadcast in Jerusalem; and Allan Sternfield performed Alexander's *Six Israeli Dances* for piano in Banska Bystrica (Slovak Republic).[8] In 1996, Haim Alexander was awarded the ACUM Prize for Life's Work.

Abel Ehrlich, photographed in Moscow (1990) by Alexander Gofman. Courtesy of the composer.

4

ABEL EHRLICH

Abel Ehrlich, undoubtedly Israel's most prolific composer, has completed over twenty-five hundred works, of which his *Bashrav* for solo violin, written in 1953, is probably the best-known.[1] In this work, which evokes both the rhetorical style and formal conception of Turkish and Arabic musical traditions, Ehrlich employs microtones and rhythmic patterns derived from these models.[2] His later compositions combine the extremes of serial rationality with romantic irrationality. His musical language ranges from accessible, tonal, metric, and witty neoclassicism to pointillism, clusters, and dissonant atonality.

Yuval Shaked, a composer, essayist, and teacher who was once Ehrlich's pupil, has written that "Ehrlich the composer is still to be discovered," noting that he has perhaps been more influential as a teacher.[3] Of Ehrlich the teacher, Shaked has written:

As one, who was made to face his identity when quite young; as one who, all of a sudden, was forced to become self reliant—Ehrlich excelled in instructing his students in the inevitability of going ahead and discovering their own selves. His ability to encourage, to honestly desire another's personal good and his search for ways to ensure it, is extraordinary. Ehrlich has the most rare and individual gift of taking part yet not interfering. . . . As a teacher Ehrlich respected every artistic direction of his students, even such as he would not have taken himself.[4]

Shaked has also provided observations concerning Ehrlich the composer:

There is a balancing force in Ehrlich's works. At times he adopts a childlike approach out of choice. Amusement and spontaneity were always present in his pedagogical work and exist in his music. They originate in conceptual daring. The anxieties the audience projects through its expectations and judgements neither diminished Ehrlich's adventurousness nor harnessed it. This could explain his occasional Dadaistic tendencies. From time to time he touches the macabre, perversity and sarcasm, not in order to shock and not for their evocative potential, but only as a means of elucidation. In this speaks out a mature man, whom experience has freed of all fears. In the title of a little suite for guitar (1985/1986) Ehrlich wonders WILL IT WORK . . . ?—a doubt devoid of anxiety, a query secure in the absence of any concern whatsoever.[5]

I interviewed Abel Ehrlich at his home in Maoz Aviv (near Tel Aviv) on July 3, 1986.

I was born in Germany in 1915. I came here in the beginning of 1939 after being in Yugoslavia. I left Germany one year after Hitler, after making my matriculation at the school, and went to an uncle in Zagreb. And I studied violin there, which I left later, and came here through Albania in January 1939. I was thrown out of Yugoslavia as a German Jew during the time [Milan] Stojadinović was there, the prime minister. Hitler told him: "Throw out all German Jews." And then I went to Albania and waited for my certificate here for Israel, for Palestine then.

I was in Jerusalem at the beginning and studied there almost at once. I had a scholarship for Jewish music or something like that. My teacher was [Solomon] Rosowsky, who went later to the States. He was a very old-fashioned man, a pupil of Rimsky-Korsakov. He gave me, almost with the exact words, what he studied with Rimsky-Korsakov or [Sergei] Taneyev, in counterpoint and so on. And after several years I said to him, "Good-bye," and he wanted to teach me further, and I said, "No, thank you, that's it." And he said "But composition!"—because I had only studied the foundations. But I didn't want anything from him. That was long ago. I stopped in the forties, I think in 1944 I stopped with him. I studied since then to today, that is, going to summer courses in Germany, too, to Darmstadt several times, and being very much interested in new music, which was almost unknown here.

I started going to Darmstadt in 1959 and have been several times in Donaueschingen, and so on. And once I was invited by the German *Musikrat* to be there in the summertime. And since then I have been in Europe and Germany too, but not studying there. It was a very interesting time, and I think that even at the beginning there were already clefts and rifts between [Luigi] Nono and Stockhausen. It was really dramatic. And Stockhausen, I don't know about today, but he was very, very much influenced by [John] Cage. And Nono was very much anti-Cage, and this made some interesting, dramatic things there. But today I would say a lot of things spoken there—not only taught, but spoken—have been quite idiotic, including the words of all the famous men who exist now. But sometimes I heard very interesting compositions. Stockhausen—I didn't love so much his compositions, though I was impressed. But I think it was very adventurous even to listen to his explanations, which were very science fiction–like. It was really an adventure for a man coming from a closed place, and Israel was a very closed place. In 1959 we didn't know very much, so it started. It was very interesting for me to know, let's say, how they didn't take anything for granted that had been taken for granted during the last century or so.

In Germany I learned nothing, perhaps violin. And in Yugoslavia it was very simple-minded, very traditional-minded, teaching of harmony and counterpoint—very dry stuff. I taught myself, but I think I learned a lot from other composers, too, when I was young. Today I wouldn't be able to learn from other people, but then I was able to—a lot from Webern. I was most influenced by him, more than by Schoenberg, for instance, more than by Berg. And later, when I was a bit more adult, I learned a lot from classical composers, too, because as a young man I was very much for new things. I knew classical music by ear and I loved it, but I got so far away from it during that time when I started to try out how I would react to those new things.

With Webern—I can say it now only historically because my interest is not so strong as it was, but I felt it at the time—I didn't know him in the 1940s and I knew very little about him in the 1950s, but I learned a lot about him because I studied his works in the 1960s. I had the feeling he was one of the most honest composers I had ever known. He was the opposite, in a certain sense, of composers throwing around their emotions uncensored, almost improvising—like Schumann and so on, I would say today also like Berg sometimes. But I felt almost a religious feeling to the music: don't waste anything; you have to create music in other ways than go explode your emotions. This made a big impression with me, and I thought I wouldn't know whom to put into the same category, perhaps sometimes Bach, but not always. It sounds a bit exaggerated when I say it today, in my ears, but I felt this. You know it's very interesting to look back at it now, when one remembers he was a pupil of Schoenberg—and Schoenberg was a giant, and is a giant—and those were his pupils whom he criticized. And he said, "They don't understand what I mean." History will teach us something else perhaps. This influence is not very original because it influenced almost the whole of music in Europe, especially, and made very strange disciples—that love was very strange, because from this very economical stuff Webern did, they spread out, let's say, throwing around kilograms and kilograms of notes, Stockhausen for instance.

The last time I was asked what it means to be an Israeli composer was in Jerusalem, when I was invited to the Academy to talk about myself. It was the first of June, not so long ago. And I must say, I thought about it so much—sometimes I thought against it and sometimes for it. It's so far away from me that I can only construct an answer. I would say today, let's say as a general remark, the same that young people would say today: an Israeli composer is a composer in Israel, or an Israeli composing—including perhaps, an Arab, if he is an Israeli. I want to exaggerate what I mean by it, and I think that's the only natural way today to talk about it. Because even if I would have a credo, I wouldn't want to put my credo on other people. This is an awful thing, if one would do it, and it's certain that there are people who would answer in that way. And there have been always certain people who answered in that way—who use certain phrases, who use certain melodies, who are influenced by the oriental melos, or by the oriental rhythm or oriental color—but I would not say so.

I would say this: in the 1950s there was enormous weight given to that question, and it was not very helpful. You know, thirty years ago, in 1956, there was a composer, Yizhar Yaron, living in a kibbutz where there was to be a summer course. Partos was a composer and a violist, and he was a wonderful teacher for chamber music. And he invited me to teach during the seminar he intended to give at the kibbutz Ein Hashofet. He wanted me to teach a bit of theory, like writing exercises. And Yizhar Yaron, who knew me before, said, "Let's try an experiment: teach Israeli music," to which I said, "This doesn't

98

exist!" It was in the 1950s, it was 1953 or so. He meant "*try* to." He said, "Let's not wait twenty years more and then, again, weep we have no special music—teach it." I said "OK," and first of all I took this famous *Thesaurus* of Idelsohn's, where there are very interesting old melodies from Israeli communities, Eastern ones, and taught them. And I taught a lot of elements of Eastern music I studied years before. Since 1939 I studied Eastern music, not only Near Eastern, but Far Eastern too. And I taught elements of rhythm and rhythmic patterns and multirhythms, and *color* and *maqām*, and the principle of *maqām*, not only *maqām* itself.

When I arrived in Eretz Israel I went into the university and read every book they had about non-European music, and sometimes in languages I didn't understand, like Dutch. But I understood the examples. And I tried to listen to what it was possible to listen to, and I was very much interested in Indian music, and in African music, and so on. And I taught a bit of that. And I started a bit, in parallel, to teach—which I think now is almost stupid—I thought, in Europe they started with polyphony and organum style, so I'll teach a bit of organum. And that was my course, and there were sixty people and they were very interested. And I tried to teach them a bit of quarter tones and so on, and we invited an Arab group of players from Nazareth. It was a very important time I think for me and for those sixty young men, some of whom are living now and composing. And I wrote then a composition that was very much influenced, I would say, not by Eastern music but by the elements of Eastern music. I suffered a bit from *Bashrav,* because I was called "the composer of *Bashrav.*"[6] And after having written *Bashrav,* I left it. This is lots of years ago, thirty-three years ago.

I wouldn't make now any theory, and I think I'm not stupid, but I have now no intellectual skeleton for my composing. That means I wouldn't try to define what's my way. I know that certain things from Eastern music entered my blood, and I don't use them consciously, generally. And I would like to add that when I wrote *Bashrav* and some, let's say, spiritual children of *Bashrav,* it was not love for this Eastern music. It was something else, it was a bit of a fright. It was some strange thing for me, it was something outside my life. It was some inimical thing and not a friendly thing. I mean when I composed it I remember it was not a friend, it was an enemy. I remember exactly where I started to compose it. It was an old, dirty, Arab hotel in Akko [Acre]. The whole night there was, on the radio—I think from Egypt—

99

one motive. And it was the beginning motive of *Bashrav*. It was a dynamic motive. I felt it as something inimical (ex. 3). But I used in that composition, I would say, two things: I used the East and the West. And as the West I took a motive my daughter invented when she was maybe four years old, singing about some old story by the Grimm brothers, about the three bears or something. She invented it. She looked at the pictures and she couldn't read, but she saw the father bear, the mother bear, the little bear.

Ex. 3

I want to tell you something. As I taught those guests in that kibbutz in 1953, then I had really a credo. I said, "I don't think that it's right to photograph Eastern music, like folklore, and to bring us a quotation in your compositions." I said, "One should try to study Eastern music and to find out elements, and use the elements again yourself, as you see them." I hated so much the Mediterranean style when I lived through it. I didn't like what Ben-Haim wrote, and what Mr. Lavry wrote. To say it exactly, I hated it. I thought it was sweet, syrupy. With *Bashrav* I didn't photograph anything, I took the elements—though when I listen to it today I find it very oriental. I would never write this today. *Bashrav* means "rondo."[7] And this—for instance the individual player, if he is not a percussionist, he learns it, he learns those patterns. Let's say for a melody written in a very interesting rhythmic way, this means almost Western, and suddenly an eighth is left out, or it goes in triplets, and suddenly it goes in quarters or something like that. And let's say the rhythmic accompaniment follows that line and afterwards the melody changes or goes back to something normal, but the rhythm continues repeating what was before. Always some interesting stuff going on—I won't say always, sometimes it's very, very boring.

And I loved very much the idea that is perhaps not so, let's say, characteristic for this country, but farther east or farther south, and that's polyrhythm. That means there are a lot of streams going on at the same time. And I know [Luciano] Berio was influenced by the study of an Israeli man, Simha Arom,[8] who studied African music and recorded it a lot, and found the principle that everyone plays a very simple thing, but he knows when to play. Berio wrote his composition *Choro* exactly according to this principle.

At the beginning of the 1960s I wrote a composition that was some super-serial work that projected some mass of notes in all directions, and not only in intervals but in everything. It was overdone, because I tried to outdo them. It was years after I did that and tried to find my own way in serial music. I was very far away from that idea. This would apply much more to Mr. Seter in that time. But it was a part view.

Contemporary music here has developed in a rather organic and natural way. That is, a lot of young composers have been very interested in new music, and we have quite a lot in our young generation who are very gifted. And everyone goes more or less his own way, not too exactly following every trend in the world outside. And I think there are anti-elements too, because the whole establishment in

Israel tends to conservatism. It's not only political, it's culturally too. But it does not so much influence many individual artists. But, for instance, our section of new music is in the hands of our composers' organization.[9] And the composers' organization doesn't do anything especially for new music. But in the time of Orgad there were always concerts of Israeli composers, and what I see now as a special gift of Orgad. He stood up and explained a bit to the audience what they will hear. He did it in an interesting way, and he didn't think only to take very established composers. He took very young ones, who were pupils of mine who only started. And there was a time when they had a very interesting idea—it didn't remain so—to put together compositions around a certain poet, an Israeli poet, quite good. This was very successful, I think it was three times. And now it's in more conservative hands, it's Maayani and [Joseph] Dorfman. Dorfman is a composer of new music, but in his style of organizing he is very conservative. And Maayani is very much anti-new everything. Acoustic 7–11 is another organization. It's a bit one-sided because there is almost no evening without the music of the organizers, and this is a bit selfish. I certainly wouldn't be against it if there would be compositions by [Daniel] Galay and Dorfman and [Gabriel] Iranyi and [Lior] Shambadal, but not every time. But that's only an aesthetic point of view. I do the opposite thing, I don't do anything about self-promoting. It's even perhaps a greater thing than self-promoting, not to promote yourself.

If I would speak about strong influences, I could describe it in this way. First of all, influences were almost unconscious, when I heard classical music in Germany until my eighteenth year. I say unconscious, but I took it in and later I took in all music that was possible to hear. Then I was very influenced by Eastern music. It didn't start in Israel; it started in Yugoslavia, where I had been for four years, and in Albania, where I was for two months. Remember, I had no equipment. For example, I went to the best singer in Tirana and asked her to sing for me. And they had beautiful music, much more beautiful than Arab music, using microtones and so on—really lovely, lyrical music. This I worked on while I studied Petersburg harmony and counterpoint with my teacher Rosowsky. At the same time I studied this Eastern music and I broadened my knowledge. And then it was like, let's say, a pouring in of new music in the 1950s and 1960s, and I would say that was the time when I was very open, listening to outside influences. And my development is perhaps very

102

natural and very general and obvious. I tried more and more to, let's say, compose well. I tried more and more to use what I had, to become better, and this also not consciously. But I worked a lot, I composed a lot, I think almost more than all of them put together. I have now 850, something like that, that I've finished. And it's not a graphomania, because I like to compose. I don't like so much to write it down later. It's not always necessary to copy parts, because I have not a lot of occasions when I can listen to my work.

And I didn't leave off, let's say, the subject of my Israeliness or Jewishness coming through another door, and this was literature, poetry. I love very much Israeli poetry, and I went back and I started to know Hebrew poetry through the centuries, and this influenced me very much. And I composed a lot, without being a bit religious. I am a Jew, but I don't go to synagogue and I don't burn bus stations because of the legs of some nice girl.[10] But I've composed a lot of *Tanach* music, for instance, Bible music. So it's the Hebrew-language influence a bit, but I composed not only in the Hebrew language. I composed in Latin, I composed in German, I composed a lot in English, a language I love very much—to read, not to talk, because it is difficult for me.

If you would ask me, "How do you explain yourself today?"—I wouldn't know, would you? Not only that, but "What are you?"— "How did you develop?" It's very difficult because you explain yourself by writing this note or this high note, or you want this; I use everything and I try to use more. I had my graphic period from the 1960s onward, and later I had my verbal period, that was thirteen years ago. I mean I wrote compositions describing in words, even works for orchestra— with no score. And I tried combinations with explanations, and so on. And I tried combinations with different styles of writing the music, as an experiment—graphic and nongraphic, and aleatoric and verbal, and so on, all within one work. And I must say, there are two things I could say today, perhaps, about myself—which are not perhaps positive things, but to explain myself negatively. First of all, I can't, let's say biologically, care so much to do something that *looks* interesting—I'm too old for it, you know? It wouldn't help me. Let's say, in a dirty way to explain it, I try to write—if it's conventional, it's conventional; if it's not conventional, it's not conventional—it's writing. But I don't bother so much, that's one thing. The other thing is, my interest in new streams is less than it was in the middle of the century or the middle of my life, let's say, because when I went the first time to Darmstadt, I was crazy with delight that there were such and such theories—not even music, but theories—about time, and so on.

———

In April 1987, Abel Ehrlich was one of several composers represented in this book to participate in a concert and exhibition of "New Music from Israel" at Northern Illinois University.[11] For this program, Ehrlich offered the following, typically whimsical, biographical sketch: "Born 1915, Cranz (near Königsberg, Eastern Prussia), now Russia, came to Israel 1939, married 1947, 2 children, composed since age of 11, teaches composition (at Tel Aviv University, Academy of Music) STILL GOING STRONG."[12] In 1990, Ehrlich provided an update concerning his activities:

> So, what happened with me after [19]86: I got two further ACUM prizes, and this year the prize of the head of Israeli government (the last helped especially financially for one year). I happened to be invited to Moscow this year to participate at the premiere of a work of mine for female choir and string orchestra. The conductor, [Alexander] Gofman, a man of high musical and human ideals, and a genius—he'll give performances of that piece in Germany this winter. And I have been proud that they performed in Hebrew language (words of Amichai) and performed wonderfully.
>
> I have also been in Prague, where our children's choir ANKOR performed my ANI SHOMEAN ("I Hear," poem by Yair Horowitz) under the conductor Arnon Meroz, who—a shame—decided to leave this choir, which has been built solely by his hard and so fruitful work (got prizes in Europe and steady invitation to Wales choir festivals).
>
> I look into the list of my works and see, that since Autumn 86 I have written 685 further compositions—it sounds formidable, but together with your request it puts certain problems on the table: You ask very intimate questions about changes in my attitude, and so on, and I am totally unused now to answer. One of the reasons is that I stopped teaching about general ideas in music. My only teaching now is concerned with the products of my pupils and the wish to help [them] to develop themselves—as they are—or as they could be.
>
> The second reason is that I compose so much—like a chain-smoker one could say. And there is a certain difference in my doing it—if that is from experience or from age or from the "chain-smoking" urge I do not know: I do not anymore meet myself in concilium, walk and talk aloud about my ways of composing, about criticism of

my work (i.e., self-criticism), about new ideas, about how to renew myself, about how to approach the next composition—about trying out a new experiment, and so on, and so on.

And I am not ashamed to declare, that these have been the highlights of my life as a creator. I spoke with myself in fifty tongues—I have not been a schizo, one could say I have been a multi-schizo—and that made me into a harmonic, quiet being, always on the alert, my own watchdog. And now I am like a bulldozer—all ideas come the moment I start a new work—I am quasi-in the background now—not I am important, not my way, not my ideals, not my understanding, not my principles, not my renewals, not (certainly) my originality—not what I want to express, but *what this composition should be.*

If there is a text, the text composes almost without me (this is a meant overstatement). If it is abstract, an idea develops or a feeling develops—or I approach the ocean—which is not I. I would like to answer one of your questions about my Israeliness. Life, fate, hate from outside, love from inside, *Common fate,* family, past, made me so much into an Israeli, that I cannot analyze special features of mine (as dealing in music) in a rational way.

When I try to steal a chance view of myself from the side: What influenced me musically, so that I am now, that who I am: Some eastern melodic and rhythmical gestures (oh yes), some great men like Monteverdi, Purcell, Bach, and a thousand others and Shakespeare, and Rembrandt and a lot of painters of the 20th century—and Israeli and English poets—and the whole of literature and my fate as a little dirty Jew—thrown out of Europe (more than one presumes) and my fear that Jews are not better than other people about their reacting to minorities . . . and my love of nature—and my love of life.[13]

In response to an *IMI News* survey of composers' reactions to the 1991 Gulf War, Ehrlich wrote: "The strongest impact seems to have been on my productivity—I compose twice as much as I do in times of peace. Since January I feel that music is pouring out of me and I exist in two worlds—in the heaven of composing and in the hell of almost normal daily routine and the nights in which one may become 'just a victim.' "[14]

Although most of Ehrlich's compositions have yet to be heard, many of his works have been performed internationally in recent years. Since 1989, when he was awarded the Prime Minister's Prize, Ehrlich's music has been heard in Israel, Russia, England, Germany, Sweden, the United States, and the Czech Republic. Ensembles that have performed his music during this period include the Jerusalem Artists Chamber Orchestra, the Rishon LeZion Symphony Orchestra, the Kaprisma Ensemble, Musica Nova, the Ankor Children's Choir, the 21st-Century Ensemble, Ensemble Oriol, and the Keele New Music Ensemble.

In 1994, Ehrlich's *My Friend Ephraim* for violin and violoncello was performed during a ceremony in which the composer received the ACUM Prize for his life's work. In 1995, Musica Nova, conducted by Menahem Nebenhaus, presented a program honoring the composer's eightieth birthday, which included *The Speech of the Drowning One* (four songs for tenor and chamber ensemble), *Bashrav,* and *Gnihton and Gnihtemos* (text by Jean Arp).[15] Erlich is now included in the catalog *Komponisten der Gegenwart (Composers of Our Time),* published in Germany.

Mordecai Seter, photographed outside his home in Ramat Aviv (1986) by Robert Fleisher.

5

MORDECAI SETER

Mordecai Seter (originally Starominsky) is among the most respected composers and celebrated figures in Israeli music. Though Seter has received numerous awards and honors, his focus has always been on the process of composition.[1] His *Ricercar* won the Societé des Auteurs Prize in 1965 and the ACUM Prize in 1957. In 1962, the Prix d'Italia was awarded to the Jerusalem Broadcasting Service for its production of Seter's *Midnight Vigil*. Seter was awarded the Israel Prize in 1965, and composed nearly fifty works between 1970 and 1987.[2] He died on August 8, 1994.[3]

Alexander Ringer observed affinities between Ehrlich's *Bashrav* and the music of the Russian-born Seter. The latter's interest in chant and Renaissance polyphony, from his studies with Nadia Boulanger, caused him at first to focus on vocal music, and to value "purely melodic considerations" over the Eastern influences favored by some of his contemporaries. Ringer also noted, however, "the influence of oriental monophony and heterophony."[4] While one can hear the narrow melodies and "creeping chromaticism" described by Ringer in Seter's work, other recurring features are also present. A number of his works exhibit heavy, dark timbres, characterized by sustained, ominous sonorities in lower registers. Seter's melodies range from modal to atonal, and his textures often involve sustained dissonances, clusters, and open space. In a 1990 retrospective article, Israel Music Institute director Paul Landau summarized Seter's role in the evolution of Israeli music:

> Although he taught for almost five decades, he neither founded any school nor did he strive to have his students follow in his footsteps. He was deeply concerned with the ideological and creative movements in Israel from the end of the 30s onwards and even used materials from the Jewish-Oriental folklore. However, Seter was not a member of the group of composers working in the so-called "Mediterranean Style" affected by Ben-Haim, Boskovich and others, nor was he tempted to place his work at the service of a specific ideology or any other collective concept. True to his views that an artistic creation is essentially an act of an individual, Seter trod his own path with remarkable logic and consistency in search of a suitable mode of expression for his spiritual world.[5]

Seter provided a succinct summary of his own compositional work: "On the one hand, my music is conservative, that is to say it preserves the essence and is not affected by the innovations of contemporary music. On the other hand, it is not academic music, since it represents self-expression within the framework of a national situation, defined by the international present."[6] On the occasion of Seter's seventy-fifth birthday, Tzvi Avni provided the following praise for his former teacher: "As a man and as an artist he was guided, first and foremost, by his conscience and profound inner awareness of the meaning of his art. . . . He has always been for me both a symbol and an example: a man and artist of complete integrity, a profound thinker at once sensitive and sensible. His works, in my opinion, are solid evidence of a generation that knew despair and hopeful elation; suffered doubts and regained faith."[7]

I was informed of Mordecai Seter's reluctance to grant interviews, but was also urged to be persistent. Indeed, my first telephone call to him did not result in a meeting, as he was busy supervising the recording of a string quartet. Ultimately, I enjoyed an extended conversation with Seter at his home in Ramat Aviv (near Tel Aviv) on July 7, 1986. This was shortly after the composer's seventieth birthday, which was observed by an article in the Israeli newspaper *Keshet*.

I was born in Russia in 1916—not the Soviet Union, but czarist Russia—one year before the revolution. In 1926, when I was ten,

I came here with my family. I went to Paris when I was sixteen and worked for one year with Paul Dukas, the last year of his life, then with Nadia Boulanger for two years. And I studied piano with Lazare Levy for three years. Here I studied only the piano because we had no one to teach music theory—theory yes, but not harmony and counterpoint. Stefan Wolpe came here. There was Sternberg, who was born at the end of the last century, and he was here from the 1930s, I think. But he spoke only German and I couldn't speak German. Musically speaking my education was in Paris. I learned counterpoint and absorbed the spirit, as I could, of Paris in these years, musically.

The most important part of my training was the study with Boulanger, especially the first year. The second year it became stifling, I couldn't support it. You see, she was extraordinary, there is nothing else to say. But she had absolute truths, and this was not good. When I first came I accepted the absolute truth, but then I discovered that she moved from the truth—the truth became relative. But then I lost the contact with her, because if you are absolute and the pupil accepts it, he believes you. When he discovers that you are capricious, it doesn't work any longer. So I finished my second year, but I felt stifled. I felt, "I can stay here no more, because it grinds me up." I couldn't suffer it anymore, and it was because of her authority—"No more absolutes!" And she was capricious because she was a woman; she was a kind of mother figure for all the young generation. It's very impressive. But I learned a lot from her. First of all it was her culture, her musical culture. It was enormous. She really knew the history of music. She really knew everything from Greek music to Hindemith and Stravinsky—it's about two thousand years of music! And she knew it very basically. She lectured about Greek music and medieval music, and we learned about the motets of early Renaissance and fifteenth century and so on. And there was Monteverdi and Gesualdo, and we sang it. And she had a madrigal ensemble—they recorded it, with five soloists, and she accompanied them on the piano. It's a nice recording, maybe on His Master's Voice. They sang chansons with her, from the sixteenth century and Monteverdi madrigals. And she played a few instruments, she played the piano and the harpsichord.

Then I learned counterpoint, strict counterpoint. But she gave the essentials of counterpoint, such as you can use in any style, the concept of counterpoint. And we learned from the chorales by Bach, and she permitted us to harmonize it freely. So it was a kind of composition. She taught at the École Normale for twenty years, and she taught at the American Conservatory of Fontainebleau. Dukas was also at the École Normale. I studied with him from 1934 to 1935, it was really half a year. And then I began with her from the end of 1935 to the end of the school year in 1937. We learned the Gregorian chants, of course. You see, when I returned to Israel I first met with traditional chant in Idelsohn's *Thesaurus of Hebrew Oriental Melodies*. And I discovered that this is parallel to the Gregorian with Latin texts. Because it was a parallel situation—not in music, but in a sense. And it was quite a discovery for me. It was a traditional chant from I don't know how many centuries ago. And it was crystallized. It was a tradition with a Hebrew text, original Hebrew text, with an authentic Hebrew pronunciation. So it immediately talked to me directly. And it was not popular song, it was from the synagogue. It was a kind of recitative.

Stutschewsky introduced me to these chants. He came in 1938.[8] All of those musicians you heard about came when Hitler entered Prague. Then Max Brod came, and Frank Pelleg, because they had to escape. And when Hitler entered Vienna, then came Stutschewsky. And when it became a fascist government in Hungary, then Partos fled from there, and Boskovitch, who was from Transylvania. You see, when Hitler chased out the Jewish musicians from the orchestra, Huberman founded the Philharmonic Orchestra here. It's all Hitler, you see, because it begins in 1933 when he came to power. So when I came back, Boskovitch was not yet here and Partos was not yet here. They came a little later, in 1938. Stutschewsky came also in 1938, and Pelleg was already here. Pelleg was not a real composer. He was a composer of incidental music for theater. Stutschewsky was a composer and a cellist. He performed quite a lot. He made propaganda for Jewish music. He didn't know what it was yet because he thought of Jewish music as Hasidic music, Hasidic tunes. He was educated in that, he was from the Ukraine originally. Of course, he was a Russian Jew, but he lived most of his life in Western Europe. But he had a few volumes of Idelsohn. I didn't know Idelsohn, but I think he died in 1939 in South Africa.[9]

Here there was no original music, but folk songs and pseudo–folk songs. Songs by Amiran or by Zephira, it's another generation.[10] By Yedidya Admon [Gorochov].[11] They weren't what would be called popular songs. They had their roots in a different source. For instance, Amiran is a little bit Hasidic and Zephira is more oriental. And Admon

112

Gorochov is more Arabic. They were inspired by popular traditions. Earlier Israeli folk music was of Russian origin. That was before the First World War, because most of the people who came in the first *aliyah* and second *aliyah* were Russians. Afterwards they came from Poland, after the First World War.

The Hebrew and oriental chants in Idelsohn's book were closely related to the Gregorian. Not in a direct way, but as an analogy. There were tropes, for instance, as you have in the Hebrew text of the Torah, of the Bible. There are small symbols above and below. These are the tropes. You have to chant it. It's melodic and grammatical. It shows where the accent is and how is it to be pronounced, and how the phrase is divided. There were signs indicating that this is the end, or half-end—full cadence and half cadence. So it's grammatical. And this was very important for me, too, because these tropes were grammatical and they were in tones—they were musical, but not personal. It was traditional, it was not the interpretation of the words as meaning, you see. It's not a lied, where you put your own interpretation to the words. It's a traditional basis that is to be clear when you transmit it, and melodically and intonationally clear in acceptance with the grammar and the color of the words, but not the meaning of the words. So it's absolutely free. Expression of the words, but not interpretation of the words.

This gave me the analogy with the text of the motets or the Mass—the Latin text, or Gregorian chant—which is not personal, but it's very expressive and grammatical. This is the analogy that I understood. It's extraordinary, it's quite a treasure. I discovered a treasure, you see. And what is more, I was the one who discovered it, because I don't know who used Idelsohn—those who were here then didn't know Hebrew. I spoke the language and I knew exactly what it means. I knew a little Hebrew even in Russia, when I was six or seven. But it wasn't new for me, you see. That's why all of those who came here at the same time as I came or earlier, like Ben-Haim, began to study Hebrew. All of them began to study, and all of them were eager to get the folk songs because this was a melody and it was the oriental character. And it was measured—the Idelsohn one is not measured because it's a chant, like a Gregorian chant. Ben-Haim and Lavry could not read them. They couldn't appreciate them. They got a complete, already closed melody with such and such periods and so on. And they went to Bracha Zephira and she sang to them, and they notated it. They're from oriental sources.

Vocal music is the basis of my work. One of the examples from my music included in Ringer's article comes from chant. It's in my Sonata for Two Violins. It comes from chanting because it's vocal. But the root of it is vocal. And it's always melodic—not vertical, but linear, contrapuntal. I've also written for the dance. I worked with Inbal. I have written two ballets for Inbal, for Sara Levi-Tanai, the artistic director. One of these was the *Midnight Vigil*. It was a ballet of fourteen minutes, and it became an oratorio of forty-three. I absorbed the gesture of the dance of the Yemenites, the Yemenite dancing and the atmosphere, which is quite extraordinary. I don't use much heterophony. Yemenites sing it. In 1978, I revised my *Midnight Vigil*. I corrected some of the orchestration, that's all. Because it didn't satisfy me, because it was not what I wanted. I changed it several times. I also wrote two ballets for Martha Graham, and a ballet for Rina Sheinfeld, *The Daughter of Jephtah*. I went to the U.S. in 1979 when I had a sabbatical year. I visited music schools, I went to New York, Washington, and Boston. And then I went to Europe. But this visit had nothing to do with Martha Graham. This contact was in 1962, 1963. I wrote her two works, *The Legend of Judith* and then another ballet that she called *Part Dream, Part Real.*

There is always a change in my work, but oriental elements go inner, and less and less I may distinguish between something oriental and non-oriental. Because it became personal. Now it has become my personal style, you see, so I can't distinguish them already. It's all long ago. It began as a language, a kind of a language. It is between West and oriental, and between myself and traditional, you see? It's very mixed, I can't separate them because it's already—it's mixed, it's like a language. I can't say how it has evolved, because I am in evolution. I am involved. You see, it's like a flow of water. You can't separate water, it's a whole. You can't divide the flowing, because it's a unity. I can't separate it. I can't see myself evolved, because you are part of the evolution. You can't analyze it.

In 1937, when I returned, there was a conservatory that exists no more, and I taught theory there. And I met Stutschewsky, and he had organized a series of concerts of Jewish music in Tel Aviv in Beit Brenner. He didn't commission me, because he had no money, but I participated. I wasn't interested in the twelve-tone method, and I wasn't affected by the nationalism in music here in the 1930s and 1940s, not at all. Because they had a manner—it's superficial, a certain color. It's "Israel" Israeli music. I was not interested in color, I was interested in expression—not in songs, not in folk songs, but in tradition and in language, and so on. I wrote motets, for instance, on psalm texts, taking the cantus firmus from Idelsohn. I worked with cantus firmus. It's another thing I learned from Nadia Boulanger.

I used serial techniques freely in my string quartet. It's not a serial work, it's not a row. I looked for something basic and not a row, because a row is not basic—it's too organized, already too organized. What I looked for was something elementary, like a mode, like tonality. But today tonality is not acceptable for me. I was never tonal, always modal. So, all my life, all my compositional life, I worked with modes, with different aspects of modes—for instance, in the *Sabbath Cantata* composed in 1940. The modes are given. They are close to Gregorian chants, the modes—I mean, Dorian, or Phrygian, and so on. But even there, one of them is not such a single mode, but it's oriental and it gives some possibility of a kind of *maqāmāt*. It still has its tonic, but the mode does not have seven tones, but rather ten or eleven tones, like the Arabic. So it gives a special atmosphere, and it's not oriental in the cheap way. It's oriental in the inner way, like Indian ragas, and so on, but not songs. The songs make it cheap and vulgar. So there is the possibility of shade—shade and light modality. It gives a different illumination of things. I think I succeeded in bringing it out, harmonically. You can hear it.

As far as what it means to be an Israeli composer, I think that today the outsider sees better than those who are involved. He can tell you what the connecting links are between different personalities. The links that exist, if they do or do not, he can see them better, and he can say what makes it Israeli. Because if I speak of myself, I can't distinguish it or separate it. With all organic processes, you cannot disengage from the flowing of the process. The process is a flowing because when it stops flowing, it's dead. It must flow all the time you are living, and composing. You are in the flow, and you can't separate it. Because if you see the flow, you are there no more. You can't compose self-consciously. Being an Israeli composer is simply a fact. It's not political, it's not nationalist. All these things are exterior. You see, today you may be a nationalist, tomorrow you may be an internationalist—you can change it as you change your clothes. But I believe you can't change yourself.

Simply to be inspired by Hebrew-language rhythms, biblical stories, or Israeli sites like the Dead Sea—this is not characteristic of Israeli music, because this could be on every point of the world. It could be in Switzerland, with Bloch, who wrote psalms in Hebrew, I think. It could be in America. The biblical language and the Hebrew language, and the liturgical chants—you could live in Honolulu or in the South. But you would not be an Israeli composer. It's a composite of very many different things, not only musical things, but mentality and the general atmosphere and general fate. All of us Israelis have a general fate, which is one—which is not a general Jewish fate, it's another fate. It's political, that's the external expression of it. But it's an inner fate that is quite different from every other Jewish community elsewhere. And all these components, plus music and personal expression, the digestion of all this—then you become, in my opinion, an Israeli composer. You want to analyze—try, try to analyze. You can't separate all this—we are built of all this.

You can be everywhere you want. But where you live, you are not a tourist. And your emotional experience, and what happens here, and not in Honolulu—in Honolulu, you can follow with your television, but not emotionally. No, it's not real. You have to experience it really. Yes, and then you can judge with this experience comparatively. You can judge what happens to Honolulu from your point of view, because you have a separate point of view—a specific point of view of the land you live in. It's very complicated, but it's very simple too. I am the roots—I am sorry to express myself in such a vulgar way. Everyone looks for his roots, but I am my roots here. That is simple. I do not know how to express it, because I can't explain it.

It's all merged, you see. I came nearly fifty years ago, returned from Paris in 1937. So during these forty-nine years, all which boiled and happened here, it happened. These fifty years are at least—I don't know—for Jews it counts in centuries, not one century. Because you can't imagine the difference of the new country and new state. It's the unique experience of the last two thousand years, you see. It's not propaganda, it's a fact. I'm part of it. Maybe I don't like the government, this government. But it's your place, it's your people, so you have to suffer. You have no other choice. No other choice and an inner choice—not choice of possibilities, no technical choice.

I don't think about my work—I compose. Since 1966, I have discovered the idea of a mode—I can show you the mode in this symphony called *Jerusalem,* inspired by the Six-Day War.[12] It has augmented unisons—B-flat to B-sharp, and A-flat to A-sharp. There is a pentachord. It's arranged as a group of pentachords (ex. 4).

And you see, here it is used, that the mode is used—it begins with this note. It goes there to A. I write it simply here as A-sharp because

116

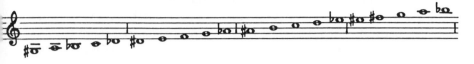

Ex. 4

it's easier for them to sing, but it goes to A. It's free, chanting is the idea (ex. 5):

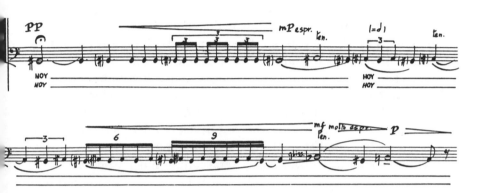

Ex. 5

Contemporary music in Israel—before I answer this one, I want to tell you I feel, I guess other Israelis feel—those who stay here—a little bit like the Englishmen in England. They complain about the weather all the time. They complain about the fog, and the rains, but they stay there. All the same, they don't go abroad. Contemporary music in Israel is in a way a simple question and really not so simple. Because what do you call contemporary, what is composed now? There are several trends, many trends, but I think—what generation? Because there is Tal—working hard, composing operas, and he's seventy-five, yes. He always was a dodecaphonic composer, from the beginning. When he came to Israel he was already writing twelve-tone music, and then he wrote electronic music. And there is the middle generation, like Avni, and Orgad—Avni more than Orgad, because Orgad belongs to the former.

And there is the young generation, men and women of about thirty. And generally, I think, they all look at what is done abroad. To learn the latest. And they are afraid to be late, to miss it—to miss the train and to miss the latest, what do you call it—the dernier cri [newest fashion]? And they don't understand that they are chronically late. Because when it comes here, it's already changed there. So they can't catch it, it's a train that always runs late. And when they catch the latest thing, it's already dead. But it's pretentious, it has pretensions to be modern and to be the latest fashion.

But there are musicians who are not impressed or influenced—I think Tal probably, because he developed his way as he developed, and now he enriches his work with new language or with new discoveries, and so on. Because he also stays in the mainstream. For myself, I never ran after anything. So I developed as I developed. I cannot see myself as a modern composer, because what I do is not classic, it's not romantic. I do what I feel, that's all. If I discover my way, like a way of working with different modes and material, and so on, it's my way.

There are even composers writing in a new Ben-Haim style, a renewed Ben-Haim style, and I don't know what for—what for? Maayani, he was a pupil of Ben-Haim. He still does this. I don't know why, I just don't know. Because you can't—you have to evolve, and evolution is personal. It is not that you learn different things. That's not evolution, it's the evolution of others or of general culture. But personal evolution is personal. I mean, what I write today, I could not write years ago. For instance, this one—today I would not write it.[13] I feel it, but I feel it as an old idea. You have to evolve. But you can't evolve consciously. This is the problem. You can't say "I must evolve." Very well, but how, how do you evolve? By using new tricks, by using tricks? It's not your evolution—evolution is personal. Composition is a personal thing. I didn't discover it—it's the truth. Absolute. You have to be yourself, and you have to evolve from yourself. There is no other who can do it for you. It's like love. Like life and like love.

———

The music of Mordecai Seter is frequently and widely performed. In April 1991, at a concert celebrating the composer's seventy-fifth birthday, Musica Nova performed the composer's *Partita* (1951) for violin and piano, *Yemenite Diwan* (1957) for nine players, *Epigrams* (1970) for flute and violoncello, and Piano Quartet No. 2 (1982), and gave premieres of *Events* (1974) for flute, clarinet, and bassoon, and *Episode* (1987) for piano. In recent years, Seter's works have been performed in Hungary, Germany, France, England, Lithuania, and the United States. Ensembles that have performed his music during this period include Musica Nova, the Israel Sinfonietta Beer Sheva, the Israel Chamber Orchestra, the Israel Philharmonic Orchestra (Zubin Mehta and Gary Bertini, conductors), and the National Choir Rinat. Ora Rotem has performed Seter's piano compositions on many occasions, and her interpretations of these works can be heard on two compact disk recordings issued in 1993 and 1995.

II

THE SECOND GENERATION
IMMIGRANTS AND SABRAS

"It is only from a native-born generation," wrote Artur Holde, "that a 'school' can arise, such as we find it in the Viennese classicists, the German Romantic or the Russian nationalist school."[1] Israeli composers of the second generation, a group that emerged in the early 1950s, found themselves in a time and place profoundly and permanently affected by regional and global events. The era during which this generation matured provided a scenario of numerous possibilities, but also momentous change and conflict. The result is a body of music literature still more diverse than that produced by their teachers. The second generation included, for the first time, native Israelis, or sabras, whose relationship to their society was felt by some to have special significance. Like the "New Wave" writers studied and interviewed by Joseph Cohen, Israeli composers of the second generation "came to maturity after the War of Independence, and in a sense, grew up with the nation."[2] Aron Marko Rothmüller claimed that "the composer, born and educated in Israel," was "part of the Jewish country, its life, its culture and civilisation—it is this that is expressed in all his work."[3] Arieh Sachs suggested that unlike their first-generation predecessors, these composers had "no need to search after a suitable expression for the reality of the State of Israel."[4] Elie Yarden compared the circumstances distinguishing the second-generation composers, especially sabras, from their immigrant teachers:

121

They do not overly concern themselves about problems of belonging—the country belongs to them. Hebrew is their native tongue, and they are fully in contact with the destruction and re-creation of new channels and patterns in literature and other arts. It would seem that the future is theirs but for the fact that their education has taken place in a society wherein the independent creative activity of the composer has little importance. Their teachers, who saw themselves as bearers of a great tradition, devoted themselves to transferring what they had learned as pupils rather than to conveying what they had discovered as composers. The peculiar result is that most of Israel's younger composers are far less adventurous than their mentors. It is in their work that one easily detects the dissipation of a derivative creative impulse and the ultimate devaluation of exhausted means.[5]

Nathan Mishori, similarly, observed that Israel's older, more established composers were the ones to "refresh the old nationalist atmosphere with more cosmopolitan ideas," such as serial techniques and proportional notation.[6]

Although most of the first-generation composers were educated and professionally active in Europe prior to their immigration, many younger composers, born or raised in Palestine and Israel, soon sought advanced training elsewhere. Intense interest concerning developments in other countries resulted from the isolation of British-mandate Palestine from most of the world during World War II, and of Israel from its neighbors following independence. Educational institutions in the nascent state of Israel had acquired few resources, such as scores and recordings, through which young composers might study current musical developments. Tzvi Avni notes that Israeli composers began to travel abroad after the 1950s, recognizing "that a revolution in the conception of musical sound and its potential was in progress all over the world."[7] Some, like Avni, studied at the Berkshire Music Center at Tanglewood, while others traveled to such European new-music centers as Darmstadt and Donaueschingen. According to Zvi Keren, "The invasion of new musical concepts from abroad was so irresistible that it affected every single Israeli composer to a greater or lesser degree."[8] In traveling abroad, principally to German and American centers of new music, Israeli composers of both first and second generations recalled the earlier migrations of American composers to their studies with Nadia Boulanger in France.[9]

The new experiences and perspectives of second-generation Israeli composers no doubt contributed to the gradual decline of the

122

Eastern Mediterranean style. According to Bohlman, "The Eastern Mediterranean movement never became more than the aesthetic gesture of immigrant composers, hence still wanting the total potency of an Israeli national school."[10] This movement nonetheless formed the influential context in which second-generation Israeli composers developed and became the focus of high expectations within their society:

> Eastern Mediterraneanism had formed a bridge to a younger generation of composers who had been born in Israel and had more intuitively internalized the sounds presumably unique to that region. Many critics believed that this generation could somehow acquire the techniques of the immigrant generation, but mold from them an aesthetic uniquely Middle Eastern. As this generation began to mature artistically soon after Israeli independence, it symbolized an optimism for an almost utopian cross-fertilization between Western and Middle Eastern musics. If Hindemith and Bartók had provided the underlying techniques for the previous generation, the Middle East and its musical traditions might theoretically yield new principles to the young Israelis; in the wildest throes of optimism some even believed that *maqām* could replace Western modes, and improvisational forms akin to *taqsīm* might supplant Western formal structures.[11]

After 1950, according to Keren, disenchanted with what they felt were the superficialities of the Eastern Mediterranean style, younger Israeli composers sought a more profound orientalism that would utilize methods similar to the Arabic *maqām*. Among the means employed were the abandonment of European harmony, the use of heterophony, and oriental rhythmic patterns and techniques of drumming.[12] Writing in 1961, Keren observed that "in the Israeli arts, Oriental aesthetic ideals have begun to replace those of the West."[13] His perspective just twelve years later was quite different, however, following a decade in which many Israeli composers had studied abroad: "The sharp rise of the influence of new Western musical thought among the composers in the early 1960's was, at the same time, accompanied by a similarly sharp decline in the degree to which Eastern music affected their works."[14]

The multicultural environment in which younger Israeli composers found themselves drew their attention to many diverse musical resources, including those associated with immigrants from countries such as Yemen, Iraq, Iran, and North Africa.[15] Beginning in the

1960s, one can hear older and newer elements combined in the music of second-generation composers, including Avni, Lakner, Maayani, Gilboa, Sheriff, and Orgad.[16] Keren noted the waning of modality and the increased use of dissonance in the music of this period, attributing such changes to the abandonment of earlier styles by some composers and the arrival of new composers.[17]

Ultimately, the innate pluralism of Israeli society affected both political and aesthetic viewpoints. Amnon Shiloah suggests that the opposition in the 1970s to Israel's "melting pot" ideology was less a rejection of cultural unification than of the Western emphasis of the new state, coupled with a demand for greater equality for and improved representation of its oriental community. This increased ethnic consciousness indicated that such unification "could not be achieved like a magical alchemic operation," and consequently the force of cultural pluralism eclipsed the ideology of the melting pot.[18]

Two conflicts of orientation challenged composers of Israel's second generation: one involved local and international influences; the other, individual and national interests. The first conflict became increasingly important as Israeli composers returned home from studies abroad. Max Brod distinguished between "national" and "universal" character in music, a source of creative tension for composers in Israel and elsewhere.[19] Keren noted that in the "struggle for supremacy between the two contradictory ideals of internationalism and regionalism," the predominantly regional outlook of Israeli composers before 1960 subsequently shifted toward internationalism.[20] Regionalism seems to have influenced attempts to express elements of Judaism and Jewish history, either through folklore or through biblical sources, whereas internationalism has largely assumed the form of incorporating Western compositional aesthetics. Israeli musicologist Don Harrán compared the motivations associated with these influences:

> The reasons for deeper immersion in Jewish traditions are easy to grasp. The legal debate in Israel over the question of what "Jewish" signifies (a race, a religion or a nationality) has affected artists, who are also concerned with self-definition. The Arab-Israeli hostilities have forced them to examine their history to explain their present position, and the threat of renewed strife, awakening the instinct of preservation, has led to cultural introversion. The reasons for increasing Westernization and subsequent internationalization of Israeli music are equally understandable: the initial period of nationalist fervour has ended; the challenge of crossing the boundaries

imposed by geography and culture, of opening new horizons in art, has stimulated many to adopt an international outlook; the younger generation of native Israelis is less concerned with the past than with the actual or ideal present.[21]

The cultural introversion noted by Harrán is perhaps reflected in the number of Israeli compositions that are about Israel—works "shaped by certain creative forces indigenous to the country and its people: the southern sky, the vegetation, the language, the poetry, the mores and customs and, of course, the religious impulse of the population."[22]

The conflict between the needs of the individual and those of society continues to affect Israeli composers and other artists. Avni has observed, however, that the consciousness of collectivism, a potent force during the period of Israel's independence, has steadily yielded in recent decades to a more intense focus on the individual:

> The sixties and seventies witnessed a general erosion of the collective ideologies which had held sway during the period immediately following Israel's birth. Urbanization of national priorities meant that even the kibbutzim shifted weight from agriculture to industry; estrangement from the values espoused by "the old Zionism" meant that manual labor, and work in general, was no longer perceived as a means to automatically restore the Jewish nation from the ills of the Diaspora; the all-important questions which began to exercise society after the establishment of the state (Who is a Jew? What is Zionism?)—all these developments left their mark on Israel's cultural life. Giant strides in communications meant that Israelis were able to keep in touch with cultural happenings far and wide and this, too, exerted an influence. Increasing individualism began to characterize the efforts of Israel's creative artists, including composers, and today it is hard to point to any typical stylistic common denominator among local music-makers.[23]

Presented here are interviews with perhaps the three most prominent second-generation composers, all of whom have been active and influential in promoting contemporary Israeli music internationally. Ben-Zion Orgad (b. 1926) and Tzvi Avni (b. 1927) came to British-mandate Palestine as children; Ami Maayani (b. 1936) is a sabra. Starting out as a composer, Avni was strongly influenced by the Eastern Mediterranean style, which seemed "like the natural language of a young person, a young musician, who grows up in a country and he comes to something which exists already."[24] Though all three men were at one time students of Paul Ben-Haim, only Maayani has remained loyal to the aesthetic outlook of Eastern Mediterraneanism. All three advanced their professional training in the United States: Orgad earned a degree at Brandeis University, Avni and Orgad were at Tanglewood, while both Avni and Maayani studied electronic music at Columbia University. Whereas Maayani continued in the tradition of his Israeli teachers, Avni's music took a modernistic turn following his American sojourn. Since Avni also studied with Abel Ehrlich and Mordecai Seter, and Orgad was once a pupil of Josef Tal's, these second-generation composers provide important links to the first-generation group presented in Part I of this book. Representative works by all three composers are listed in *A Descriptive Bibliography of Art Music by Israeli Composers,* by Alice Tischler.

*Ben-Zion Orgad, photographed in New York City
(1991) by Rebecca Rass. Used with permission.*

6

BEN-ZION ORGAD

Ben-Zion Orgad (originally Büschel) is among Israel's most prominent and frequently performed composers.[1] He has also lectured extensively on contemporary Israeli music, both in Israel and abroad. Orgad pursued his musical education both in his adopted country and in the United States, including studies with Aaron Copland at Tanglewood. In 1952 he won the International Koussevitsky Competition for his biblical cantata, *The Story of the Spies*. Orgad served in the Israel Ministry of Education and Culture for more than thirty years as Supervisor of Music Education, heading this division from 1975 until his retirement in 1988. In recent years he has published articles, pedagogical publications, poetry (including translations of poems by the late Paul Celan), and a book of prose.[2] In 1990 he was awarded the General Federation of Labor [Histadrut] Prize for Music.

Orgad's compositional palette is quite varied. Yohanan Boehm regarded him as a composer who "employed a modern technique without neglecting Israeli melos."[3] Much of Orgad's music is slow, lacking a perceivable meter, and employs both sustained dissonances and dense polyphonic textures. Repeated figures are frequently encountered, and other rhythmic treatments are reminiscent of Stravinsky. Many works emphasize soloistic passages in both unison and heterophonic textures, and Orgad's melodic lines often suggest the "creeping chromaticism" that Alexander Ringer has associated with the music of

Bartók. Another salient feature of Orgad's music is the accumulation of dense textures within which one may detect discrete, disparate, and sometimes discordant components. In a number of works, Orgad has also employed spatial relationships, positioning musicians in different locations within the performance space. The antiphonal-responsorial textures effected between groups of performers in such works are also related to Orgad's use of simultaneity, both of textures and texts.

Orgad's interest in "cantillation and prosody of the Hebrew language" as a compositional resource, observed by Ringer more than three decades ago, remains the central focus for this composer.[4] These influences are closely linked to the emphasis on soloistic and monophonic texture that Ringer observed to be a common trait among Israeli composers. Although raised in a "non-religious home," Orgad has long been preoccupied with biblical texts, and, even in compositions of purely instrumental music, the linguistic basis remains of fundamental importance. The composer provided a succinct explanation for this focus in the opening paragraph of an article published in 1975: "I have been asked why, although I am a secular composer, I make so much use of traditional religious texts and materials in my works. It seems to me that you cannot be born into a group of people who are fated to wage a continual battle for survival, without being very much a part of it, unless you deliberately set yourself apart. At times when our very existence is at stake, the sense of mutuality and belonging sweeps even those of us who in more tranquil times feel quite alienated from the great 'togetherness.' "[5]

I interviewed Ben-Zion Orgad at his home in Tel Aviv, where he introduced me to composer Arik Shapira, who also appears in this volume. Orgad expressed himself slowly and deliberately, taking care in choosing his words. Subsequent to the meeting documented in this interview, I returned for a further discussion of temporal and spatial relationships in music.

I was born in Germany in 1926. I came here to Tel Aviv in 1933 when the Nazis took over. I started to play the violin, and I just loved to play, sing, and listen to music, mainly classical. I think I started to compose very early, I must have been about nine years old. And then I took a course in the theory of music, and things connected. And then later on, I think it was when I was about fourteen, I became a pupil of Paul Ben-Haim. I stayed with him until almost 1945. If you know the years 1940 to 1945, these were very crucial years around the world. I went on studying violin with a very good teacher who was a concertmaster of the Israel Philharmonic Orchestra, Rudolf Bergman. And then in 1946 I went to Jerusalem, where I studied at the Jerusalem Academy with Josef Tal. And right after that, in 1947, I went to Europe and spent half a year helping Jewish refugees. I came back, right into the war. I was immediately mobilized, as a veteran of the Palmach, the special forces of the underground, the Hagganah. That was my extramusical career.

Then came the war. During the war I won a scholarship to go, in 1949, to Tanglewood, and I became a pupil of Aaron Copland. I think I was one of those lucky persons who got some private lessons. I stayed there about half a year and then I returned to Israel, where I got a position at the Ministry of Culture and Education as Supervisor of Music Education. In 1952 I won the UNESCO Koussevitsky Prize, and I went again to the United States to further my studies with Copland. Then in 1960 I went to Brandeis University, where I got my Master of Fine Arts degree. I was a student of Irving Fine and Harold Shapero.

My two earlier teachers, Ben-Haim and Josef Tal, represented two extremes: Ben-Haim, an impressionist; Tal, an expressionist. It seems that I have had a tendency toward pluralism, to which my studies in the U.S., exposing me to a variety of styles and musical thought, were a real asset. I must admit that I'm not conscious about my own stylistic changes. I'm not bothered with it at all. There is an enormous influence of cantillation in my music, in the *Vigil in Jerusalem,* too, I think. The biblical cantillation has an enormous influence, it's part of my musical language. It's mainly a melodic influence that can be traced in the harmonic textures, leaning on certain kinds of modal structures. This work is subtitled "The Third Watch," a reference to the night watches of the Old Temple, which were divided into four periods. It's part of a cycle that includes three "Watches," *Songs of an Early Morning,* and *Hallel.*

For me, being an Israeli composer enables a certain tendency. As one who intends to be part of the very definite Hebrew culture, I declare "I belong." Now, what's the meaning of belonging? It demands, first of all, an acknowledgment of a tradition, of collective memory, which manifests itself in behaviors. Belonging means the language, because the language is different from any other language, and as such it serves as a bridge to tradition and its origins. Not only as spoken, but as a "tonescape." And, of course, you have the panorama, the landscape, with all of the emotional layers and history that it bears. And then, the people, which, as you must have noticed, are enormously varied. It's a real heterogeneous society, whose real common denominator is the language, so strongly connected to the Bible, and to the book of prayers that all congregations use many times a day. This kind of spiritual common denominator serves like a territory. On these I did elaborate in my essay, which deals with the musical potentialities of the Hebrew language, as far as intonations and rhythmic structures are concerned, which are very specific to the Hebrew language.

My work is not as direct a translation of the Hebrew language into music as it is with a friend of mine, a composer by the name of François-Bernard Mâche, one of Messiaen's pupils, a wonderful composer who really tries to depict the sound qualities of language in music. But not only languages—he also does it with birdsongs.[6]

I draw rhythms from the essence of Hebrew. Yes, and some other qualities that must have been influenced, let's say, by the biblical cantillation of the different types that we have; they are different yet connected to the same words, the same language, to a similar way of pronunciation. It's not only microtones and ornamentation. It's also very definite melodic structures and very definite accentuations and stresses: phonemic structures that have a definite meaning. I can't hear it from the outside. I'm part of it.

I'm not sure whether entirely, but I think I did escape Western influence. I'm not writing Eastern music. I'm using the Western way of staging the music, Western instruments and notation. I deal with words too. In the last five years I've been writing poetry, so words for me—in their meanings and sounds—are part of my expression; it's a way I communicate, though I think I still prefer music. Yes, I do.

I use conventional notation even when I tend to simultaneity. There are pieces where I do what [Charles] Ives did. I place different groups in the hall to play from different corners. Yes, it started with *Mizmorim,* and later, in 1971, in my *Ballad* for orchestra, which was written for Lukas Foss: six of the brass players leave the stage, while the orchestra goes on playing, and move to the balconies, and then join in an antiphonal playing with the whole orchestra. I like this very much. In a more recent piece, *Individuations,* which is a concertante for chamber orchestra and clarinet solo, I have two wind trios on both sides and a trumpet in the back of the hall. That kind of interplaying, the kinetic experience of sounds moving around, interests me very much.

I used to be a reconnaissance man, so I used to be outside in the open a lot. I know this country intimately, know it with my feet. Sounds in nature don't come from one angle, they move from all around. It's the way the sounds are coming to you, relate to you moving toward them, that is important to me, especially now when I feel that most of the audiences tend to be very passive. They sit and wait for music to come to them without necessarily feeling a need toward it. I am trying to change that by provoking at least one question: "Where does the sound come from?" It's not obvious. And then the extra magic that you get, for example, when you have a trumpet in the back, and a trumpet onstage, and they're playing one against the other. Something happens, the sound waves, you can really feel them. And for me this is really magic. And in a way, it is as if I'm trying to resist the recordings, because these things you can't record—it's impossible—not yet.

I feel myself as if I'm always on a search. I came close to the poetry of Paul Celan, a Jewish poet from Chernowitz who went through the Holocaust and ended up as a professor in Paris. He is considered one of the great poets in German, at least in the second half of this century. He committed suicide in 1970. I was reading his poetry in German, and noticed how he succeeded in dealing with the time element. His poetry actually forms its own time. When I read poetry, I hear it in my ears. The awareness of the way he captures time and molds it with contents has not only been a guide and sensor to my translations of some of his poems into Hebrew, but has been serving me, quite consciously, in my composing.

I feel that one of the problems of what is done in contemporary music is the relation to what Susanne Langer calls "the articulated form," which enables you to relate simultaneously to the whole and to the particles in that whole—while achieving the right balance between the materials and duration. What happens to most music that has been, and is being, composed in our century is that the particles tend to be so strong that they stick out from the overall articulated form. The events—the moments—are more important than the captivity of time. My trying to find that kind of balance started with the poetry of Paul Celan, yes, and with his voice, too. I have a recording of a recital he gave in 1968 in Jerusalem. Listen to it, it's very interesting, the music of it. It has nothing to do with the understanding of the meaning of the words. It's the meaning of the sound that really prevails.

It's very strange. One evening I was reading this poetry. In the morning, when I woke up, I heard a whole poem of his as if it was conceived in Hebrew, and I wrote it down. It's the accentuations, you see, it's basically iambic meter, always with the stress toward the end. He uses the German in the same manner, and he combines words, too, to get a similar effect. And that line of that poem he has, which started like "Du sei wie du, immer"—for me, in Hebrew, is "Ha'yi asher tehi, tamid"—the very same. He knew Hebrew, he grew up with Hebrew. He was a multilinguist like many Jews in Chernowitz. The way he reads stresses it even more.

Now let me dwell a little on the captivity of time, which in our instance relates to volume of time, to intensity of time, to qualities of time and to the ability of sounding text to form them. Almost any start arouses expectations—it evokes many possibilities to be anticipated. And when slowly, slowly, the number of anticipations narrows until you are left with one only, that should be the end. This overall shape, as perceived, with the connection to its comprised moments, can be found in Bach's music, and the way he deals with these elements is an ideal I long for. I don't have to tell you how difficult it is to work on moments, and while you do it bear the overall shape in your mind.

Hindemith believed that one could perceive a symphony of Brahms the way he perceives a city's skyline in one second of lightning. But it is not the one second that counts to me. No, for me it's more the approach of Hume or the Hindu, for whom time is a succession of moments. This interests me; this and simultaneity.

I reached simultaneity long after knowing [Charles] Ives's music. I think it started with *Mizmorim,* in which I allowed different texts from different psalms to run together. They complemented or contradicted each other quite dramatically, thus enabling me to establish tensions and releases that suited my approach to the familiar, often-used chants. By joining various sound layers into one musical expression, I have tried to achieve a certain plenitude. That was my way to simultaneity in music.

A friend of mine guides tours in Jerusalem—"sound tours." On Friday they go to the Muslims, on Saturday to the Jews, on Sunday to the Christians, to listen to the various ethnic and liturgical musics. At the end of the tour, while still in the Old City—she takes them, before sunrise, at three in the morning—the "third watch"—onto a roof, where she plays a recording of my *Vigil in Jerusalem.* I receive reports that the sounds of my music intermingle quite naturally with cocks' crows, church bells, as well as with resoundings of previous experiences. A sensation quite gratifying for me.

————

Ben-Zion Orgad's music is widely performed. Since 1990 his works have been heard in Israel, Lithuania, Spain, Germany, and throughout the United States. Ensembles that have performed Orgad's music during this period include the Cameran Singers, the Jerusalem Symphony Orchestra, the Kibbutz Chamber Orchestra, the Rishon LeZion Symphony Orchestra, and the New York Debut and Premiere Orchestra. Orgad's music has been heard frequently in the United States, where he attended several performances in the early 1990s.[7] In 1993, Orgad's *Reshuyoth* for piano (1978), commissioned by the Tel Aviv Foundation for Literature and the Arts, was heard in Los Angeles and San Diego.[8] In 1994 the composer attended performances of his *Shaar, Shaar* (text: Abba Kovner) in New York and Washington, D.C., by the Cantilena Piano Quartet with vocalist Mira Zakai. Ms. Zakai also performed one of Orgad's Three Songs for alto solo, settings of poems by Paul Celan.[9]

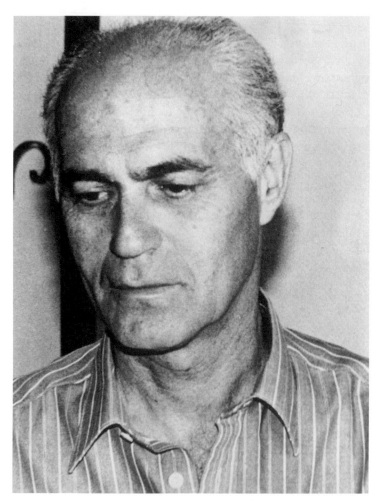

Tzvi Avni, photographed by Dina Guna (1989). Used with permission.

7

TZVI AVNI

Tzvi Avni (originally Steinke) is one of the most widely performed and recorded Israeli composers, and an eloquent proponent of contemporary Israeli music. Avni has written music for a wide variety of media, including ballets, films, and radio plays. A recipient of the Lieberson Prize (1970) and the Yoel Engel Prize (1973), Avni was awarded the ACUM Prize for Life's Work in 1986.[1]

Avni's study of electronic music in the United States caused a dramatic change, steering him away from the spirit of Eastern Mediterraneanism that had characterized his previous compositions. Consequently, Avni's earlier works are modal, neoclassical, and emphasize quartal harmonies, while later compositions are ametric and characterized by dissonant, sustained tone clusters. Typical of the folkloristic character of Avni's earlier music is the *Capriccio* for piano, composed in 1955. His later works also show an interest in exploring new notational means, including graphic approaches. Whereas the stylistic basis of his early works may be found in the music of Ben-Haim, Seter, and Bartók, Avni's later works suggest the stronger influence of Edgar(d) Varèse.

I interviewed Tzvi Avni at his home near Tel Aviv University.

I was born in Saarbrücken, Germany, in 1927 and immigrated in 1935. With our generation in general, when we studied composition here thirty years ago, it wasn't like now. Now you have composition lessons at the Music Academy with an individual teacher, lessons that have no relation, sometimes, to what you study in harmony and counterpoint, and so on. I had here quite a few students throughout the years, in the Academy, who studied harmony and counterpoint courses, which I don't teach now. Composition, free composition, they studied with me. At that time, actually, there was no such thing in the framework of the music academies, no such course as composition. You studied harmony and counterpoint and form, and you studied mostly with the same teacher. If you were a composer, you would show him also some of your works and hear some comments, and so on. If you were a conductor, you were working with somebody else on conducting. In my case, anyway, I really started as an autodidact, I would say, a self-taught composer, at the age of fourteen. Composing was, for me, something very natural, very basic.

I didn't have a piano at that time. I had an accordion, a mandolin, and a recorder. I didn't know how to write music, I didn't know how to read music—so I invented a special script to notate these melodies that I composed. I had one for the accordion, and then the other one I invented for the mandolin—a kind of tablature, as I would notate the number of the string and the position and so forth. Only at sixteen did I start playing the piano and learning to read music. So this was really a hard beginning, which was caused by my circumstances. My father was kidnapped here by Arabs in 1938 and was never found again. I started working to earn my living at fourteen, so I didn't have the conditions to learn music. I didn't have, also, any serious background from home, so I came to it, somehow, by myself.

I also painted a lot at that time, and I was sometimes vacillating between painting and music. There was a time when I was sure I was going to study painting. I think that's why I remain so much attached to tone painting, as in the *Five Pantomimes,* which is based upon five different paintings by Picasso, Klee, Kandinsky, Dalí, and Chagall. When I started my piano lessons, I was all the time composing. At eighteen or so, I composed a piano sonatina without actually having had one lesson in composition. I learned form from what I had read and played, and I found the harmonics just by ear. And when I started studying harmony and counterpoint, and so on, there was always a kind of parallelism. They were like two parallel lines, you know—I

138

was composing what I was composing, and I was studying what I was studying. I would write the fugues and motets and chorales and all these necessary things, with no connection whatsoever with the pieces I was composing at the time. But I knew these two parallel lines were going to meet someday, because I knew what I was learning was going to influence somehow my technique, my way of thinking—and to improve it.

My first serious theory teacher was Abel Ehrlich. Later I was very lucky to come to Mordecai Seter, because he was actually the person who opened my eyes and my ears to what is in that chorale that you are harmonizing, in a much wider sense than just to find the harmonies— to construct a composition from it. And this influenced very much my way of thinking later in music. I enjoyed also very much working with Ben-Haim, which we mostly did in orchestration. I studied with him, also, a bit of piano, and I showed him compositions and so on. Actually, I would say Mordecai Seter was the man who influenced me most in the way of thinking and the way of facing the problems of music. Ben-Haim was much more impressionistic, and my early works were influenced by more or less impressionistic music—let's say, somewhere between Bartók and Ravel and Debussy and Ben-Haim. And later I came under the influence of Seter. This was that group—Seter, Boskovitch, and Partos—who were more in the radical direction of Israeli music.

Today you say "Mediterranean" for everything that has some basic Middle Eastern elements like melodic elements, rhythm, and so on. But what we called at that time Mediterranean was more Ben-Haim's direction—Ben-Haim, Lavry, Avidom, and so on. But the trio— Partos, Boskovitch, Seter—looked for more radical ways of expressing these motives, these traditional elements of the Yemenites and other ethnic groups. And they too were influenced by the rhythm, and so on. But the way of thinking was more toward a radical texture, using dissonant combinations, in the Bartók direction, using also heterophonic elements. I mean the minor seconds and the smaller intervals, working with them vertically as "linear" harmonies. These were the elements that were more apparent in their music, whereas this other direction was more in the triadic tradition.

Later, Boskovitch and Partos also used Schoenberg's twelve-tone method. This was quite natural for them since they looked for a more radical texture. We had a lot of discussions, Partos and I. We were good friends. I didn't have any formal lessons with him, never. But we used to talk, and he liked to talk to me very much. I felt a kind of special relation between us, a young composer and an older one, more experienced. He told me: "Bartók is a very great composer, but it doesn't open for you a way—it's a closed circle. Whereas Schoenberg is an opening, it can lead to many things. With Bartók you can't get anywhere else, you can get just to Bartók. With Schoenberg you can get everywhere." That was his opinion. And I think it was interesting to see his development, from his early Bartókian works via Middle East *maqāmāt* and so on, to the techniques of twelve-tone music in his later works.

In a way, I think that Jews have a special need for melody, more than for harmony. Take, for instance, Schoenberg, who spoke about *Klangfarbenmelodie,* and he was the first to do it.[2] In my mind everything was going in the direction of Webern in Schoenberg's music. But then he came to a certain point where he saw that he needed melody. And that's why, I think, he had also this obsession of going on with the classical tradition and keeping the classical forms. I think melody was very important for him and he couldn't do away with it.

And, of course, speaking about the great violinists especially, being Jewish—yes, I think it's another aspect of that and many, many other things. Maybe one day I'll write an article about it when I have the time.

I studied in the States from 1962 to 1964. And that was a time when everything was boiling there—experiments, electronic music—and you had the concerts in Hunter College with Cage and Morton Feldman. Everybody came there. Stockhausen was there at the time, he came for a concert of his works. And I was at Tanglewood in 1963 in the summer; Copland gave me a scholarship. And there were Xenakis and Gunther Schuller and Lukas Foss. By the way, I admire Lukas Foss very much, he's also a friend, and he conducted a few of my pieces. And with all those things together, I came into electronic music, advised by Varèse to do so. I actually wanted to study with him and he said, "No, you don't need any studies. If you want me to teach you new tricks, I wouldn't teach you anyway. I want to keep my tricks for myself, you find your own tricks." But he said, "I would advise very much you should go to electronic music," and he called up Otto Luening and spoke with him and said, "I have here a young man . . ."

Luening didn't teach at that time, but he was still around. They gave me a scholarship there for a year in the Columbia-Princeton Electronic Music Center. And these two things, electronic music with [Vladimir] Ussachevsky and that interesting summer in Tanglewood, were very stimulating. We heard quite crazy things there, and "happenings," and everything was going on. I got so confused. Copland told me, "You are going to get mixed up here," and I did. And you know, you start thinking, "Where is the world, where am I, what am I doing?" I had that problem when I came back, really—"Where am I going?" I did the *Vocalise* in New York, an electronic piece that is on a Turnabout record. And there already I tried to find my own world in the new sound environment. And then, when I came back here it took quite a few years, somehow, to adjust and to choose what I felt was right and good for me, and sincere. And to remain myself, although I wanted very much to use new sound elements like, of course, tone clusters and tone rows and sonoristic elements and electronics and so on.

It took me a few years in which I composed works that were kind of experimental. But I reassessed myself into some way of thinking, like, perhaps the most representative piece at that time and some say still my most representative—my warhorse, *Meditations on a Drama*. It was issued on a record and performed by many, many conductors here in Israel and abroad, many times. It's for chamber orchestra. Other new developments, I think, were here and there, neotonal elements. And I would say my music became more Jewish, if you can say so, in the late 1960s and 1970s. Especially in the melodic area and perhaps some kind of nostalgic elements, I cannot define it exactly. But I feel that now it's much more important to me to know what it means to be a Jew. Let's say in the 1950s and the 1960s I was very busy, like many others, trying to understand what it meant to be an Israeli. But now, you know, we have a kind of national identity here, and you look for the wider cultural identity much more than local nationalism, which is now perhaps already established.

In my score of *Meditations on a Drama,* you see textures, and various kinds of clusters. Here in the middle, it comes to a kind of aleatoric section where you get clashes of happenings and various elements are almost falling apart, but then begins a reassessment. I have the same development in that *Vocalise* that I did in New York—it's the same thing, in the middle section. You have a kind of dramatic disintegration of what was before, and then there's a kind of reassessment looking for a new sort of buildup of positive solutions.

My *Five Pantomimes* uses proportional notation and gives freedom to conductor and performer—choices in terms of durations, tempi, and ordering of sections. I would say what would pertain here to my earlier life would be the connection to painting, because at that time, in the sixties, I was very much interested also in visual aspects. Like this piece that was performed in Boston at the ISCM [International Society for Contemporary Music] festival, which has a strong visual dimension to it—a kind of symmetrical structure. It's for four clarinets, *Three Aspects of Janus*. So you have the visual element of parallelism or symmetry in the score itself. Here it is also that way, from the middle, kind of three variations on the same element. And the other one is also a graphic idea, namely, a main section and two interpolations, a kind of rondo form.

And these things were very much in my mind when I was experimenting, around the 1960s. From the beginning of the 1970s, 1971 or 1972, I was looking already for a kind of synthesis of various elements. So, you can find it in more recent works. Let's say you can find—and that's what interests me, by the way—this kind of confrontation of elements—not to be on one side of the bar, you know? And in this piece, *Programme Music 1980*, "The Machine Game" is a kind of minimalistic movement of various rhythmic elements that later develops into a rich texture. This is on the record of the Israel Philharmonic Orchestra. And here and there, you see, the machines get somehow astray and everybody plays his own rhythm. Usually you will find in my music clearly defined elements along with some more "open" ideas. The second movement is called "The Dream of the Broken Mirror"—a kind of surrealistic image. You have the background for that—you see, for instance, strings going in microtextures. And in the third movement, "Magritte—A Dilemma," there is a quotation from Beethoven's Seventh Symphony, in a kind of stream of consciousness. Here, at the end, you have again the section that is "open," where they have slowly to fade out. The last movement, "It's a Busy Day in the Beehive," was never performed yet. Since the movements are independent, I didn't refuse to have only the first three performed. This was composed in 1980, and it was performed also in the World Music Days here in Israel that year, that was the premiere. And then Gary Bertini conducted it on tour for Kol Israel, and the Philharmonic did it on the record with Zubin Mehta and on a tour in the United States in 1985.

I think that I'm now mature enough to find what goes with what, and what I'm really looking for, and I'm not afraid of mixing various elements. I'm not trying to be a purist, I use various things together, including sometimes neotonal elements. More abstract ideas with

142

more, let's say, conventional ways of thinking doesn't disturb me. I find it's a kind of integration, this whole era now. It's maybe kind of a fin de siècle, I don't know. You know, I think I can accept myself now much more than I did in the 1960s, let's say—after Tanglewood, after America. When I came back and worked on electronic music, for instance, my earlier works—I despised them, I couldn't stand them. Now I accept everything I did in its own way. I think I did some things I like very much in my early work. As Schoenberg says, I loved that work when I wrote it, and that's why I love it still now. Because, and I think I agree fully with that, I feel that I did a good job there, and I like what I did. Now I'm not committed to anything that is one-sided. And here and there, if I feel a melody comes to me that belongs, perhaps, to an earlier time of myself, I say it's still here—so it can go with my new ways of thinking because it's still me. As long as it can be worked out in the way I feel now, it is OK with me.

And as I said, together with that, I feel in a wider sense a kind of Jewishness that influences the meaning of music to me in general. This also led me to the legends of Rabbi Nachman of Bratzlav.[3] This piano sonata, *Epitaph,* has some Jewish elements.[4] Here too, you have various types of textures and so on, which are mainly sonorous, but these have a specific meaning. Even that starting on one tone, you know, and so on. Kind of really transcendental, like a psalm tone (ex. 6):

Ex. 6

But later on, for instance, you have this, which grew out of the same thing (ex. 7):

Ex. 7

For me it's Jewish, it says something very Jewish. It's not a quotation at all. It's kind of a "speaking" melody, you know. That's what I mean when I say Jewish melody—it has a nature of a confession or speaking, a kind of rhetoric quality. Not necessarily biblical. It can be mixed with that, too. But I mean it's not conditioned by that.

These short chordal attacks, with a "sound tail," are a more sonoristic thing. I was very much fascinated by the piano being able to sound like something that is not a piano. This tone that remains after the attack, it sounds not like a piano. The attack is kind of a percussive effect (ex. 8):

Ex. 8

This repeating melody is like a cantillation (ex. 9):

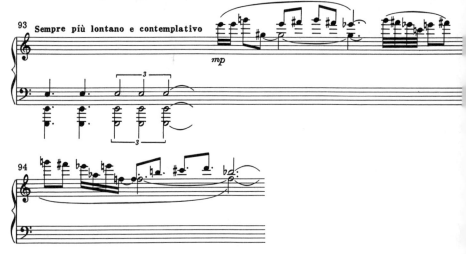

Ex. 9

The ending of the piece is fading out into something very lofty, I would say, standing alone, I don't know how to describe it. It should always be very far away—disappearing, let's say—somewhere in space (ex. 10):

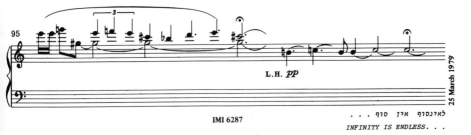

L.H. _pp_

IMI 6287

25 March 1979

. . . ‏אינסוף אין סוף‏ . . .

INFINITY IS ENDLESS. . .

Ex. 10

To me, it is a very important—this piece especially—a very important landmark as a proof of possibilities, you see, of getting something that is an amalgamation of elements. Because I have here tone clusters, and I have melodic elements at the same time. It's free and, as you have seen, mostly without bar lines—though there are some. It's also a kind of inner development of conception that is trying to give the feeling of freedom in time. And I mean, after all, the values are not undefined. They are defined and they are relatively clear. And it has also something to do with that legend of Rabbi Nachman that speaks about time. As you see here, in the introduction, I quoted a part of that legend.

Yes, it's a work about time—perhaps about God, about the meaning of life, I don't know—about everything. I think, actually, I would say it is my most personal work, this sonata. It was composed between 1974 and 1979 after a very hard personal experience. My first wife died from cancer two months after the death of my mother, and it was a very hard period of life. And, of course, it is also significant of a way of thinking that may be present in other works of mine. I think, in general, that both naturally and also consciously I am changing. I would not like to repeat the same piece for thirty years in other ways, in other variants. So whenever I see a kind of change in direction, for me it's a sign of vitality.

And the bigger joy I have is when I find also the connection with the other things I did, you see? When you find you are changing, but you are still the same. There is that growth, slow change and continuity. I think Thomas Mann wrote something about it once. I think that's very important, after all—like a tree, you know. It grows out of one kernel but changes shape. So that's what is so interesting.

And after all, a person is a process, we are not a static thing. Some composers grab one thing and they stop there, and I think, after all, it's boring. At least it's sad to become a mass producer of the same idea.

Being an Israeli composer, it's a basic existential situation. To live here means to be a person who made a certain choice, yes? Of course, everyone who lives anywhere makes a choice, but I think it's a more passive choice. Because it's still a country here in a state of formation, and many keep coming here by choice. If I would like very much to go away from here, I could. I could go to America, I could go to Europe, I could return to Germany—because actually I can have German citizenship. So, I chose to be here. If you choose something, you also ask yourself sometimes the reason—why do you choose something, and what does it mean to you, after all?

I'm not a religious man, but I believe in the tradition of the Jewish nation, it means a lot to me. When I read the Bible sometimes I cry. Certain chapters—when I read the story of Joseph, or Abraham when he was going down in the Negev in Beer Sheva—I start crying. Maybe this could happen to someone who never was here. But still I feel that these are my brothers, my fathers, my ancestors—I feel differently. I feel that this is my inner world, somewhere it is there.

In general I think that Israeli composers are more committed socially and culturally, in many ways, than in other places. I mean, if you are living here, in some way you have some kind of involvement in things that are going on around you. You may not be using any kind of folkloristic or traditional elements, and so on, but still. Let's speak about Josef Tal, who is kind of a more universal composer. He doesn't consider himself—he doesn't look for Israeli elements. But he is living in an old Arab house in Jerusalem with many, many Middle Eastern elements—furniture, and so on, pictures. Take his oeuvre— it's all historical. Take his operas, everything is based on some kind of tradition. Now maybe musically he's not using certain elements, although I think here and there you find even such elements in his music, too. But still, he's committed in some way to his historical tradition. That's what I claim, that everybody here is committed in some way—more, less. One is doing it in a simplistic way by using Hasidic or Middle Eastern melodies and reshaping them or arranging them. Another absorbs such elements more "inner-ly," in a more integrated way, or feels them subconsciously.

I feel that I have them somewhere in myself, like in the way Ernest Bloch said—I feel it comes from somewhere, I don't know from where. Wagner spoke about a child sucking the elements of the national traditions with his mother's milk. And you know, he said the Jews did not have that because they were all the time nomadic. They came from one place to another, so they were busy, not with having the basic elements, because they were busy learning new things. And that's why they are so good in catching the "how," catching the mannerism of how to do things, but not the inner meaning of them. That's what he accused Jews of. To a certain extent there is something in that. I don't disagree totally with it, because it manifests itself in the Jewish interrogative mind in the drive to ask questions and look for new ways. However, I disagree with his conclusions. Being occupied with the "how" does not necessarily mean that you neglect the "what"—the contents. Throughout the generations Jews have proved themselves to be profound thinkers and, both emotionally and mentally, they have experienced some of the highest human spiritual achievements.

Summing up, I believe that there is something really intrinsic, basically Jewish, in compositions of many people who are of Jewish origin. Maybe it can be learned, maybe it can be also "reproduced," like Shostakovich took Jewish elements and motives and so on. Speaking about myself, I've always felt this kind of Jewish rhetoric in the music I compose. Maybe it's in the melody and in some general "gestures" in which I express myself. You "speak" with your music sometimes. I think I have in my music outbursts of elements that are also a kind of rhetoric, as if the whole orchestra is becoming a story, a confession, or a lament.

———

In recent years Tzvi Avni's music has been performed in Denmark, Germany, the Netherlands, Russia, Switzerland, France, Germany, Austria, Poland, Slovakia, the Czech Republic, Greece, Japan, and the United States.[5] Ensembles that have performed his music during this period include the Israel Philharmonic Orchestra,[6] the Jerusalem Symphony Orchestra, the Israel Sinfonietta Beer Sheva, the Jerusalem Rubin Academy String Quartet, the Bochum Symphony Orchestra, the National Choir Rinat, the Israel Kibbutz Choir, the Herzliya Chamber Orchestra, the Israel Chamber Orchestra, the Warsaw Sinfonia, the Austrian Women's Chamber Orchestra, the Philadelphia Youth Orchestra, and the New York Concert Singers.

In 1991, Avni was awarded the Küstermeier Prize by the Israeli-German Friendship Association "for his contribution to the understanding between the people of both countries in the field of culture." In 1993 he was elected chairman of the Israel Jeunesses Musicales. Avni's *Beyond the Curtain* (text: Abba Kovner), which received performances in Israel and Russia in 1993, was performed in New York and Washington, D.C., in 1994 by the Cantilena Piano Quartet in a program that also included "The Whitest of Doves," one of his *Three Lyrical Songs* (texts: Paul Celan), performed by Mira Zakai.[7]

Tzvi Avni and his family returned to Israel in the summer of 1995, after living in the New York area for two years. During this period, many of his works received performances in the United States and abroad.[8] Avni has now retired from his position at the Jerusalem Rubin Academy, but he resumed teaching there on a part-time basis in the fall of 1995.

Ami Maayani, photographed by Ran Shaviv (1995). Used with permission.

8

A M I   M A A Y A N I

Among Israel's second-generation composers, Maayani has been most
indebted to the Eastern Mediterranean style of his teacher Paul Ben-
Haim. He has received the Engel Prize (1963) and commissions from
the Israel Philharmonic Orchestra, the Jerusalem Symphony Orchestra, and the Tel Aviv Foundation for Literature and the Arts. Consistent
with the influence of French impressionism on Ben-Haim, Maayani
once identified himself "as part of the French school."[1] Maayani's
Symphony No. 3 (Hebrew Requiem), composed in 1977, prompted
one reviewer to note: "The essence of the Middle East is clearly there
but the work also engenders a more universal language."[2] According
to Laya Harbater Silber, who has studied Maayani's vocal music:

> He makes use of Near Eastern elements such as the formal, modal,
> and rhythmic aspects of Arabic music, coupled with classical Eu-
> ropean forms and French impressionistic orchestration. His use of
> variation, ornamentation, and short passages or fragments of melody,
> clearly associates him with the composers of the East. He often
> develops a recurring rhythmic unit, employing occasional alterations
> according to the Arab folk tradition. Although he does not clearly
> state Arabic *maqāmāt* in this song cycle, he creates sound which
> may be closely associated with their tetrachordal structure. Other
> progressions of semitones create the microtonal impressions so often
> heard in Oriental music.[3]

151

Maayani cites, in addition to himself, Noam Sheriff, Tzvi Avni, Ben-Zion Orgad, and André Hajdu as having "striven for a synthesis of such diverging and yet related elements," and he identifies some of the features characterizing the work of these composers: "Liturgical chant and freely elaborated cantillations, open forms of Near-Eastern music, and interwoven rhythms and sounds heard in the East echo in their music. Florid ornamentation is abundant in order to underline the improvisatory character of the melodic invention."[4]

I interviewed Ami Maayani at the Samuel Rubin Israel Academy of Music in Tel Aviv on July 9, 1986.

I was born in Israel in 1936. I'm second generation in this country. Incidentally, *Ami* means "my people," and *Maayani* means "my fountain" or "my spring." It's a very pretentious name. My family is Russian-descended, from white Russia. My mother was born here, and my father came here quite young. He graduated from the Technion, which I also graduated from. He was a civil engineer, construction. I was born into the Hebrew language. The time was quite something. I had my courses in architecture here at the Technion and then took my master's degree at Columbia University. I also had some courses in electronic music with Ussachevsky at the time, as extra credit for my program in the School of Architecture. I did both since I started with architecture, and for ten years after that I was practicing architecture and doing composition.

My major training in music was done in Israel, I would say all of it. And I started as an instrumentalist—I played violin, viola, and then I added trumpet and percussion. I played all of them in professional orchestras, I was a very good musician at the time. I gave up because of the army, and then I went into conducting. Finally I went into composition, but that was some sort of joint project while I was a student at the Technion. I studied, and then my first work actually came when I graduated. I got into the School of Music before I went to the army, at the age of seventeen. So the army was a crucial point for me to make up my mind as to whether I would keep on with music and be a performing artist. This created a problem, because during the time of the army I stopped playing, I could not. So going back into playing was a difficult thing to do. While I'm not sorry about that, at the time I also realized that to be a performing artist I had to practice so many hours every day, and I had so many other things in life that I wanted to do. So I gave it up, which actually was not conscious.

After the army, I worked as a professional architect. I had my own office. I wrote music, and further on I started my graduate studies in philosophy. It's not finished, but I went to be an M.A. and I'm lecturing on philosophy as well. I'm quite involved with that. My project now is a book on Wagner in Hebrew that would deal with his prose work, the influence he got from other philosophers at the time, talking about symbolism, melos, myths, and music symbols. Maybe some kind of psychological analysis of his character, and his images, and the art he created.

I didn't have many opportunities for the first building at the Rubin Academy in Jerusalem—there are two buildings there. But we just renovated the main building, so I didn't have too much to do with the spaces that are there. That's a building that exists twenty years, and I just sort of adjusted it as far as I could to the facilities that we would need for studying mainly, not for performing. But the other building, the performing building, has materialized to be very nice, this new building—with facilities like an opera hall, offices, stage, recital hall, and dance studios.

I teach at both Tel Aviv and Jerusalem academies, I was appointed by both of them. This is a very peculiar year. We had many people at Tel Aviv University who went for sabbatical, and one of our teachers died. So I had to take that course even without getting paid for it. I teach theoretical courses such as harmony and counterpoint to instrumentalists, not to theory majors. And I like to work with the instrumentalists. After all, they play. I've found them more attuned to music. Their knowledge is far wider than the theory majors, and each of them at least knows the repertoire for their instrument, which is already an advantage these days. I teach orchestration and music notation. And in Jerusalem I teach in the dance department, which I like very much. I work with choreographers and give lectures in music and music theory and form, analysis, and so on—so a dancer may be able to use some sheet music and do something out of it.

I teach Israeli music one semester, a course consisting of twelve lectures. There are three assignments: to attend the lectures, to perform an Israeli work with my instruction, and to write a paper on one of the subjects that I would deal with in my lectures—to enlarge it and go a little deeper than I would be able to go in the lecture itself. Some people would write on the Israeli folk songs. We go through the history also. I give some kind of background in the history of the Jews and Jewish music, so that goes back to the Bible. We touch on certain periods like the Renaissance, Jewish music of the synagogue and out of the synagogue, then in the fifteenth and sixteenth century. Then the Hasidic music, cantillations of the Bible, the different tribes, and the nationalist movement, the Petersburg school that was formed by a few Jewish composers, mainly to find out the origin of Jewish music. They went back and investigated the communities, mainly in Caucasia, and they saw that those are the most traditional and most preserved. One of them, the top one, was Yoel Engel, who you might know from the music of *The Dybbuk,* this most impressive work of Jewish theater.

It's a shame that you don't have in America the Jewish theater you used to have. It's not the factor it used to be. Anyhow, Achron belonged to that school—he went to the United States. Milner and Rosowsky and some others, Gnessin. So they were the first composers that trained properly under the Russian school, with great Russian composers at the time. With the transnationalism, they decided to do something with Jewish music. And it was the beginning, part of which we sort of continued here in Israel.[5] So the course continues up to date. We have in the class some performers who do their own music, student composers. I focus mainly on the Near Eastern kind of music, the Mediterranean school that was formed here and includes the majority of composers. It's a very interesting trend, I think the most interesting one we have. But this is my personal opinion, not everybody will agree with me. It was very prominent here in the thirties and forties, but it went right up to the beginning of the sixties, and there are some composers who are still writing like this, from the old days. They developed it, they became more sophisticated with the material. They got more involved with that clash of Eastern and Western ideas. But they suggested some solution to the kind of difficulties and problems raised out of different kinds of mentalities.

If we talk about East and West, we don't mean Russia or America. I mean for us, West is Central Europe—including the United States. It's a major school these days, but not fifty years ago. I'm talking about East as being the Russian school, Eastern Europe. What we call East is the music of the Orient, not the Far East but the Mediterranean. For Jews here, we have a sort of European-Western culture, and when we say East we mean Near East, the Jews who came from

Muslim countries, that's the difference. In the States when you say "oriental," it means the Far East, because they are not aware of the Near Eastern culture, which is also oriental. The Orient Express goes up to Turkey.

But anyhow, the most interesting thing is the different mentality. The Western culture really maintained the individuality of the great composers. They have the traditional and strong use of forms, harmony, very rigid. You can work as an individual and then break away from it, you build your own solid style. What we call Eastern is a culture that goes from generation to generation. It is more a static kind, there is not much development. The individual is not important, it's more oriented toward a folklore that goes with the people. They don't use the rigid forms of the Western school—sonata form or lied form—everything is more improvisational and fantasy-like. They have flexible things, and they don't use harmonic functions, the major aspects of the Western school. They work in modes and there is no leading tone, it's not minor and major. There is no traditional school. The music is of the primitive tribes, it's not that much developed. There are beautiful tunes, beautiful rhythmic patterns. But there is nothing like what we would call a classical tradition developed, mainly because of lacking the individual focus, where the individual creates something. Take Wagner, for example. You can like his music or not like his music, but he is an individual who creates something that influenced or did not influence others.

The Arabic *maqām,* even the ancient modes or the scales that we use in our music, is completely different from anything we can compare to the Western approach. So this is a real clash, and as a composer you can do it or you don't. Many people say that you cannot bring those things in, and I'm not talking about the colors of microtones or oriental color, or what we call the European color. Some people tried to imitate it. You take a work like *Islamey* by [Mily] Balakirev, where he tried to imitate Islamic music. Or the arabesque to a certain extent. So it is a great problem because it's a clash between completely different mentalities. I don't know if I resolve it. The problem is—and I represented it in a few of my works—if someone can actually take an oriental theme, for example, and treat it in sonata form. It's against the structure or the essence of the Eastern tune, it cannot function with the harmonic tradition. Well, it might go better with a modal theme, or there are many other things to do, maybe in a contrapuntal way using pure fourths and fifths.

Another major problem here is the Hebrew language. It's a revival of an archaic language that is a thing by itself, yet it brings some problems. I myself could not write anything in Hebrew, because of these problematic things—I mean, where you infuse the Hebrew language into all this mixture of Eastern and Western mentalities. My song cycles are in the Yiddish language, two song cycles in Yiddish, and why? Because where I'm standing is a mixture of the very strong traditional school of Central Europe, which is concerned with musical form. I write in the big forms—symphonies, operas, song cycles, concerti—all these kinds of monumental things. It reminds me of the romantic era as well. My orchestrations and colors go to the French school, impressionism. And the music material is mainly Jewish, in which I refer to all different kinds of tribes and traditions.

In my last symphony each movement is based on a different folklore—the first movement on the Yemenite, the second on the Sephardic, the third is Eastern European—like the klezmer tunes, and the last one is a Persian Jewish style. And I tried to use Western musical forms like sonata form in the first movement, variation form in the second, scherzo in the third, and a sonata rondo, something like that, in the fourth movement. It's a very difficult thing to do. There is a little difference, a little gap between what I would think in a philosophical and very rationalistic way, and when it comes to practice. I mean, it's necessarily like fitting a glove to a hand. And sometimes you become more aware of your feeling and sensitivity in order to solve certain problems that cannot be done by thinking with our way of thinking. So my other works represented that exactly, the combinations.

As an Israeli composer, of course, I do believe that music that comes from Israel has to represent something special and unique that comes from this zone. It should reflect the culture. It should not reflect the problem, it should reflect the culture. It should show something, that it's a different heritage, that there is something that is tied to our chain of being, our history. I strongly believe in history, not only in the philosophical way. I hate the word "roots," but I use the tradition, and I think that we have to—since I believe we do have a different mentality as Jews. Our music or what we do in the arts should be different.

I'm not saying that we should use religious elements or certain things or symbols, but the most important thing is that I get what I want, also in the reactions of people from all over the world. I did a lecture tour all over the United States, and in Madison, Wisconsin, someone said, "Well, I cannot exactly define where this school belongs, but it's completely different, there is something different in it." You know, I might think it's a German lied or I might think it's French—it's not that. There is something in the air of that kind of thing that all evaporates when you realize that there is a state like Israel and that particular state should represent that particular culture, a particular type of man or, as I'm saying, a different mentality. It doesn't mean that we are inferior. I mean most of my music was written in the United States, and every piece of mine is different.

I wrote a lot of music in the United States because I stayed there for a long time, altogether about seven years. I started in 1961 for one year and then 1963 or 1964 I came for another year, and after that I was coming and going. Nothing there changed my approach, I believe. I never even tried any different kind of styles then, or ideas. I feel so strongly about that, and I became stronger and stronger while I listened to a lot of people's works. I mean I could care less if a piece that came from Japan sounds like it is from the West Coast of the United States. I would like to be able to identify the Japanese piece immediately.

You might live all your life long somewhere else far away, but your mentality and your tradition, if there is something like that, this is important. There is only one way that you expose it, in your own language. I believe that was the reason that nationalistic music became so strong and is still so strong. For example, I think there is a very strong American school. I'm not talking about academic music these days, I am talking about American style. I love the music that accompanies the western—I used to look at that and enjoy it tremendously, from all different composers. I think it's the country's music, and some people used that—like Barber and Copland. Well, some American music these days does go back to the style of those composers. Like the idea of trying to build what I would call American music in our time. The old generation did a marvelous job, with Leonard Bernstein to a certain extent, George Gershwin and the others, all great composers. And in what's going on today, you lose your identity. I don't believe in the international style.

It's hard to predict what the future will be, but the problem with the present is that it's very fast becoming a part of the past already—you cannot even talk about it. You know, Israel has this spectrum of composers, which might be true with many nations. Although I don't see a possibility that much in the Far East, because there it is sort of a combination with Japanese music of traditional music and the Western culture. What I mean is you take some kind that is very problematic, it's more problematic—what we call the Mediterranean Orient. It's complicated because first of all with the pentatonic system and the tradition of the instruments, it's very hard to transfer this sound into the European orchestra. If you take the traditional oboe from any tribe here, you can use it—it's a huge sound. But what can you do with the koto or shamisen in the orchestra?[6] It's a very problematic thing. They try to imitate the sound, or they use the instruments with amplification as I did in my guitar concerto. It cannot work otherwise, so it's a major problem.

I think we have different trends in Israel. And it's becoming very difficult to define it exactly. My major concern, and it's a part of our civilization in general, is what I do believe is a lack of talent in the arts. There is a lack of technical facility in writing. There is a lack of patience needed to work on a piece of artwork—it's ready and it's done—to perfect it. There is a lack of understanding exactly for what you write or for whom you write—when you write a piece for clarinet and it could be very easily good for the flute, or it does not use the instrument as it should. There is a lack of professionalism. So it's very hard to predict what will happen. I have the feeling that there is a tremendous decline in arts projects. I cannot tell you—I mean it's very hard. I am almost in the process of quitting music. I am not going to write anymore. I have written enough, I believe.

I just have the feeling that if they are not considering seriously the use of Jewish music or Jewish history whatsoever, that might cause us problems—to assimilate completely. I don't want to see myself assimilated. Assimilation is once you lose your own mentality and you start things without controls. All the world is sort of drowned by this kind of influence. I cannot think that way, I am part of an Eastern mentality or civilization. I would keep on very strongly the idea of the individual and what he has to do in combining all of this in art—or to mentalities, some way of thinking. So I'm not that pleased. We have lots of problems in Israel. Our students start composing quite late. First of all they have to go to the army, and once they are out it takes them a while to get into something. And then they finish education at the age of twenty-six or twenty-seven. Our young composers are past thirty already a long time. I guess our youngest composer in the League of Composers is now thirty-three years old. So that's a problem.

My major resistance for teaching composition is that I think you should start composing once you are at the end of your studies. In other words, you study, you have your instruments, you've gone to school, you've earned your B.A., your M.A., and then—when you've played in an orchestra, played music a lot, played chamber music, conducted—then you compose. That's the most important thing. People start composing when they have absolutely no idea about music. I can show you immediately when I look at a score if the person has absolutely no idea about music, never heard Beethoven's symphonies. I'm sure about what I am saying, I've examined them. And it's complicated. I wouldn't dare to predict what's going to happen. But the scenery, as it is, is very depressing as far as I'm concerned. Even major composers don't spend enough time for a piece. They just get a commission, they write fast, and they don't spend the time to go over and over it again.

You know, the process of revising is because you didn't work carefully in the first place or you don't have enough talent to work it out. I never revise a piece of mine. I work very carefully on each note, each bar, each page—to make sure I know what I am writing. I have nothing against revisions or revised editions. I did do revised editions because I wanted to change the publisher. We had some problems with publishers, but that's the only reason I did some revised editions of my music. But most of the composers don't even know what a piece is going to sound like, and everybody wants to be a composer. I think there is something glamorous about it. They don't know what a big mistake they have made. Well, everybody learns from his own experience, I believe.

My process and development in the arts was very careful, very consistent, starting from an early age through playing music and playing chamber music, playing band in the School of Music. And going to the Academy and finishing that, and going into conducting and playing with the orchestra, playing in the opera and playing and playing and playing. And listening to music and trying to learn scores by heart, to learn some other people's music, before I even touched paper to write music. Because people have no respect for what other people are doing. How often do they go to concerts? Do you see your students at concerts? Rarely you see them. And they couldn't care less about what their teachers are doing. I don't understand that, no respect for other people's work. They only think of themselves, that's terrible.

159

Wagner was such an egocentric, there is nothing to compare to it. He knew only one thing in life, and all the rest, whether it could be in his orbit or not, he'd throw out. He denied everyone who would not agree with him. Schoenberg was another person like that. But Wagner conducted lots of music, and he knew lots of music he performed himself. He was a lousy pianist. Take Schoenberg, how much this man knew about it. What's going on these days? They know nothing, just want to get their music played. They want to be considered composers, and the rest is not important. And you cannot produce any good piece of music or piece of art unless you know what happened before you and may be able to predict what will be in the future.

I present one idea, I'm not obsessed by it. I wouldn't press or strongly maintain my ideas. Joseph Dorfman, his perspective is wider than mine. He thinks when we have a competition, it's only for very avant-garde music. I don't impose my opinion, even on our concerts. But you can see right away, we have about three or four concerts a year that our League of Composers sponsors, and we usually try to program music that was written during that period.[7] But very few composers come to listen to their colleagues to begin with. And then the public makes right away the selections. There's no other way to close this competition—what the public thinks of your music. And if you don't care about that, if you think you write—I don't know for who—for God and his angels, you are in trouble. And there are some who couldn't care less. Art is supposed to be a tool of communication, and if you are not taking this into consideration, then what is the reason of your wasting time?

I don't know how much Ives was involved in music in general. I guess he knew music and he heard music. He was kind of a unique person. At least he wrote the music for the pleasure of writing. He said he did not think what he was doing was important. It's almost like the story with Kafka, who asked Max Brod to burn all his writings. Once he read it, of course, he could not, because he saw it was a tremendous body of literature, what this man did in his life. I mean, you can say Ives wasn't sure of what he was doing, he didn't have to make a living out of it, but he was a very worthy man. I know the story that Bernstein invited him to come to the New York Philharmonic, to play for him, and he refused. Maybe he didn't appreciate his own music. There are still people who don't like his music, but I had an opportunity to play sonatas for a while on the piano, and I thought it was good work. You cannot judge on geniuses. Our century is full of idiots, mediocrity is

160

all over. I don't understand how someone wakes up in the morning and says to himself, "I'd like to be a composer," and he starts. Think of that—I mean, what kind of music is that? Hegel said it already in 1820, when he gave his lecture on aesthetics.

———

Maayani's works have been heard both in Israel and abroad, with the composer conducting some orchestral performances. Performances of Maayani's music have taken place in Hungary, Poland, Russia, Lithuania, Germany, and the United States.[8] In 1992, Maayani's *Sinfonietta on Popular Hebraic Themes* for chamber orchestra (1982) was performed in Israel by the Symphonette Orchestra Raanana, and in Vilnius, Lithuania, by the Latvian National Symphony Orchestra, the latter performance during the First International Festival of Jewish Art Music. Maayani conducted the Jerusalem Symphony Orchestra in live broadcast performances of the Interlude from *The Legend of Three and Four* (1978) and his *Yiddische Lieder* (Song Cycle No. 2) for alto and orchestra (1974). His Concerto No. 1 for Harp and Orchestra (1960) was also performed in a live concert broadcast by the Jerusalem Symphony Orchestra.[9]

Since 1993, Maayani has served as head of the Samuel Rubin Israel Academy of Music at Tel Aviv University. His study of Richard Wagner was published in 1995.[10] The same year, he announced that he had ceased his activities as a composer.[11]

III

THE THIRD GENERATION
INDEPENDENCE AND INTEGRATION

The immigrant composers of the first generation imported formed aesthetics and compositional methods that they continued to employ in Palestine, tempered by varying degrees of new regional influence. The native and immigrant Israeli composers of the second generation emerged in a Hebrew-speaking society with strong nationalistic sentiments born of emerging statehood. Whereas their immigrant forebears responded to the new environment of Palestine with a variety of aesthetic directions, composers of the second generation reflected in their music the experience of their travel and study abroad. The orientation of the third-generation composers, the first group dominated by sabras, has been increasingly international and individualistic in approach. This group includes composers such as Shulamit Ran, born in the independent state of Israel, whose experience and outlook has differed significantly from that of their teachers.

From the mid-1960s, according to Tzvi Avni, influential stylistic elements from the West included "sonorism, serialism, aleatorics, and graphic or proportional notation."[1] Like their predecessors, younger Israeli composers have sought advanced study in the United States and Europe. Some third-generation composers have, however, remained abroad longer, earning doctoral degrees, unlike their forebears, for whom this was not yet considered the terminal degree.[2] Consequently, Israel's youngest composers have also experienced the greatest exposure to, and influence of, contemporary musical developments abroad. It is perhaps not surprising that such a generation of artists who have integrated diverse materials within their own work also includes several composers who have themselves been integrated into the life of contemporary musical cultures outside of Israel.[3]

Though the third generation has been characterized by cosmopolitan and international perspectives, the distance from nationalistic pressures that earlier generations of Israeli composers encountered has also led to new and fresh approaches to integrate regional and global musical dialects. Michal Smoira-Cohn has observed that some of Israel's younger composers have returned to a preoccupation with musical origins. The syncopated rhythms and oriental modes of the *hora,* which formed the "stylistic trademark" among many composers in the 1930s, were abandoned three decades later when Israeli composers "cut the umbilical cord and went out into the musical world at large." Beginning in the 1970s, however, such features returned "in the form of a Jewish flavor, an identification with universal Jewish roots, and the search for expression of the Holocaust trauma."[4]

Though parallels between the Eastern Mediterranean movement and the music of the "American Wave" have been cited previously, it is worthy of note here that both of these musical dialects declined during the decade following World War II and Israel's War of Independence. For Israeli composers and other artists, the post-independence era loosened the grip of collectivism that was such a powerful force in the period leading to statehood. Many of Israel's third-generation composers, consequently, have required adjustment neither to immigration nor to the shock of new compositional approaches discovered following the country's isolation during the era culminating in Israel's independence. The younger professionally active Israeli composers today, according to Haim Permont, are "free from all 'isms.' "[5] Perhaps exemplifying this perspective, composer Smadar Handelsman (b. 1954) remarked:

> "Israeliness" is a changing thing. Israel of the thirties and the sixties is not Israel of today. The generation of composers born and raised here is not the generation who came here with their European cultural heritage at a time when the country was in its nascent years. They absorbed the Israeli reality as it was then, which is a different story. That was when the synthesis of East and West was formed that exists to this day, mainly in light music (Yemenite songs—in pop and jazz,

Mediterranean jazz) and this is a symptom of saturation of American and European influences and the search for indigenous models.

As a "sabra" (which means a native-born Israeli) I see my musical environment and identity entirely differently. In my early years I also looked for the foreign and the different, and this was expressed as a European influence.

Today, after an initial gestation stage, I feel I have reached a balance between absorption from within more than from external sources. My work is very different from that of the older generation of Israeli composers. Jewishness—which is irrelevant to my work— and Israeliness are notably absent from my music, and I think this applies to the entire generation creating in Israel today.[6]

Ami Maayani notes the absence in present-day Israeli music of the nationalism that characterized the Eastern Mediterranean movement, but suggests that "the unique and singular East-West synthesis, attempted by most of the country's serious composers, gives an unmistakable flavour of its own to Israeli music." He regards the search for this synthesis as "the compelling aspect of the new Israeli music" and as an effort "to accomplish what might seem to be the impossible."[7] Zvi Keren suggested that the notion of East-West synthesis would of necessity change as Israelis themselves changed: "The new young Israeli composer is—or will soon be—a natural unselfconscious amalgamation of East and West in one and the same person."[8] While some Israeli composers express only an interest in writing the best music they can, and many claim only an allegiance to the contemporary international milieu, others continue to seek a musical dialect that can speak universally while bearing imprints of their personal and musical experience. For Yinam Leef, this challenge takes the following form: "The deeper the roots of my musical tree, the more secure I feel to fly away off its branches, and the further I reach, the more I long for the roots. If that is what it means to be a composer in Israel, so be it."[9] For this young composer, the aim of integrating disparate elements into a personal dialect involves a mediation between different musical traditions and the eras they represent:

Actually, I feel part of two traditions, an older and younger one, each pulling me in a different direction; and much of the music that I have written (although not all), bear the marks of my attempts to reconcile between these two opposing forces. The older tradition, namely the nature of the development of Western music throughout

165

the centuries, involves the gradual rejection and replacement of past values in favor of new ones. The younger tradition, namely the development of Israeli music during the last few decades, involves quite the opposite—the possible preservation of certain particular elements, ingrained in what we believe is our musical heritage and its various sources, and their incorporation within aspects of the older tradition.[10]

Leef's views reflect the prevailing pluralism of contemporary attitudes, which may enable Israel's younger composers to achieve, rather than the mythic synthesis of East and West, an integration of aesthetic and stylistic components, dictated by individual voice rather than collective sensibility, and by a clear vision of the realization that each compositional idea requires. Leef also acknowledges that the present environment for Israeli composers is freer and more flexible than those of earlier times:

> Curiously, I find myself doing something similar to what the composers . . . of that generation, had done, and that is to incorporate materials of "local" character into a seemingly unrelated harmonic scheme. The difference may be that technical vocabulary available to me is perhaps more varied and expanse [sic], and common denominators may be found to bridge over different materials without having to sacrifice one for the other. I may also do away with "locality" altogether, as today's pluralistic scene frees me from being overly conscious of "stylistic consistency." This sacred cow seems to have been slaughtered long ago.[11]

Perhaps another indication of both the need for and the possibility of integration is the perspective younger Israeli composers have concerning their native musical environment, such as Oded Zehavi's earlier-cited description of the musical elements of Jerusalem as part of his "very being."[12] American-born Israeli composer Max Stern (b. 1947) offered the following view of the context in which he and his peers work, a view that articulates goals and possibilities beyond the need to link East and West:

> One of the prerogatives of our time and place (Israel) has been a protracted search to integrate Western artistic aspiration within a context of Jewish identification—a quest for ancient sources of inspiration against a backdrop of 20th century horror and despair. Some of those who have undertaken the journey are rebels against the presumptions of tradition; others are prodigal sons returning to the

166

fold after the cold of alienation proved too great to bear; still others illumine trodden paths with new insights and approaches. Shared is an awareness of the tension between tradition and innovation, stasis and initiative. In common also is the motivation to bring to bear a timeless perspective on the fractured state of human consciousness— mirrored in styles of complexity and contradiction.[13]

Even two generations removed, the influence of Eastern Mediterraneanism has been a force with which younger composers have had to reckon, and it seems likely that future generations of Israeli composers will continue to do so. Whereas the Eastern Mediterranean composers added Eastern hues to essentially Western music, recent works by younger Israeli composers have explored the music of their region in new and different ways. Unlike their predecessors, who were content to evoke Middle Eastern musical traditions and textures, younger Israeli composers have incorporated oriental instruments in some of their works. The first-generation immigrant composers Oedoen Partos and A. U. Boskovitch, once associated with Eastern Mediterraneanism, later sought to integrate the twelve-tone method of composition with traditional Jewish or Arabic musical materials and techniques.[14] The efforts of these composers may provide a path for yet another branch of Israel's contemporary music.

Immigration of composers from other countries has continued to influence contemporary music in Israel. Keren estimated that about a third of the composers professionally active between 1960 and 1973 were immigrants, mostly from communist satellite countries in Eastern Europe or from the Americas, of which the latter are associated more strongly with "avant-garde leanings."[15] The youngest group of composers in this book is also the most broadly diverse, including three women, seven sabras, and immigrants from Eastern and Central Europe and North and South America. This variety reflects the ever-widening demographic spectrum of Israeli culture and society. Several composers in this youngest group include among their teachers composers previously introduced—including Josef Tal, Haim Alexander, Abel Ehrlich, Mordecai Seter, and Tzvi Avni.

Though aesthetic pluralism and stylistic diversity have always exemplified Israeli art music, this characteristic has become progressively pronounced among Israel's third-generation composers, resulting in a repertory more individualistic and varied than at any time before. At the same time, a half-century after the era of Israeli independence, with its attendant pressures, imperatives, and polemics, the present stage of Israeli music seems one of greater aesthetic freedom and equilibrium than at any time before. In the recent literature, and in conversation, many different perspectives still obtain. The musical dialects that have historically competed for the attention of Israeli composers, described by some as "local" and "universal," now correspond to an exponential proliferation of influential musical styles, traditions, techniques, technologies, and aesthetics—as numerous as the many languages and dialects spoken by the citizens of Israel's heterogeneous population. Other historical and social dualities of modern Israel continue to color the context in which its artists work: ancient and modern, conservative and progressive, religious and secular, sabra and immigrant, immigrant and émigré, Arab and Jew, Labor and Likud, the full range of social and cultural stratifications, and other factors conceptualized as representing East and West.

Aharon Harlap, photographed by Wim Bronkhorst. Used with permission.

9

AHARON HARLAP

Aharon Harlap (originally Aaron Charloff) is active as a composer, conductor, and accompanist, and is the only Canadian immigrant among the composers in this volume.[1] Harlap was awarded the Reuben Hecht Foundation Award for his cantata *The Fire and the Mountains* in 1978, and the ACUM Prize in Composition in 1983 for his Three Songs (texts: Yehuda Amichai, Lea Goldberg). As a conductor of choirs, Harlap also has a special interest in composing for this medium. I attended a performance of his Two Choral Settings (1983–84) by the Ankor Children's Choir in Jerusalem at the Israel Museum.

Since 1976, Harlap has served as music director of the Opera Workshop at the Rubin Academy of Music and Dance in Jerusalem, where he was appointed principal conductor of the Academy Chamber Choir in 1985. He became music director and conductor of the Kibbutz Artzi Choir in 1980.

I interviewed Aharon Harlap on June 22, 1986, at Mishkenot Sha'ananim.

I was born in a little place called Chatham [Ontario] in 1941, and came to Israel twenty-two years ago, in 1964. My family remained in Canada and the States. I studied music in Canada since I was five— playing the piano, theory, harmony, the whole business. I learned

171

privately through different teachers, and then I started composition at a much later stage, of course. I did a Bachelor of Science degree in mathematics, I went into medicine and dropped out, then I went back to complete my Bachelor of Science. And then my elementary training was from a teacher in Winnipeg. After attending the Royal College [of Music] in London, I went straight to Israel.

I lived on a kibbutz [Ein Hashofet] for a couple of years and started composing—serious composing, let's say. Then I left and decided to study at the Rubin Academy in Tel Aviv, where one of my teachers was Partos. I conducted the Israel National Opera for two years and then went to Vienna to study conducting with Hans Swarovsky at the Vienna Academy. I went to South Africa and conducted there a year—opera, ballet, concerts—and I came back in 1971. I've been here ever since. At that time I had almost no work. I've been at the Rubin Academy for ten years now, since 1976. I was in charge of the Opera Workshop, and every year we did a production. Only recently I started teaching choral conducting. I took over the Jerusalem Rubin Academy chorus last year, and that's what I'm doing next year, the chorus and choral conducting. And I conduct the Kibbutz Artzi Choir, I've been with them for six years.

And I have the Youth Symphony Orchestra of the kibbutz, which is my pride and joy because I love working with kids that age, from sixteen up to army age, around nineteen. I've been doing that for twelve years. Three or four times a year we get together for a week at a time, we perform in whatever area we happen to be in at the time. So as far as my experience and repertoire, I gained it from that. And I do guest conducting for different orchestras here and there. I've never composed an opera; it's one of my dreams to write an opera. You can't find a text anywhere. It's difficult to find a good libretto, any kind of libretto, to find somebody who is good and who would be willing to sit down with me and write a libretto. You would have to adapt a biblical text for opera. I mean, the choral pieces use the texts exactly as written, with no variations.

I think I feel it more when I'm outside the country, how much of an Israeli I am, and have become in many ways. The mentality is different, it's a certain kind of mentality. Things that bothered me when I first came don't bother me anymore—little things like the outwardness and straightforwardness of Israelis, the pushiness and all. Sometimes it really gets you down, but you get used to anything. As far as being an Israeli composer, I think I'm a Jewish composer, not only because I use Hebrew texts—you can be a Gentile and use Hebrew texts, it's not that—but I have a feeling for it. My father was a cantor, my mother until today still sings in a choir at the age of eighty, and her whole life is devoted to liturgical music.

I think it's more of a subconscious thing that's within me. The song, and the liturgy—all that has influenced me, and I feel very much Jewish in a sense that every Friday I go to synagogue and I enjoy the customs of being a Jew. So I'm very close to that side of Judaism. I'm not particularly religious, but I feel closeness as far as tradition. I'm not even orthodox; I'm not a *shomer Shabbat,*[2] for instance—I write on the Sabbath. I suppose I'm not a complete Jew in that sense, but what's important to me is the tradition. So I think that if I lived somewhere in the States, I would still continue that, because it's very close to me. Here, we've got it all. I'm somewhere in the middle of the spectrum. I do what's good for me. I don't think of criticism, what other people think. It's important for me to light the candles on Sabbath. And maybe I became much closer to it even since my father passed away, which was three years ago, in November of 1982. That hit me pretty hard. Since then I became much closer, I think, to the religion. But to say what is an Israeli composer—looking around me at different Israeli composers, it's hard to put a stamp on it and say this is an Israeli composition. Especially when you're talking about avant-garde music, or concrete music, or whatever it is. I mean, how can you identify this as Israeli? You can hear it in Europe today, the same kind of music.

Obviously, my choice of texts has a lot to do with the identification as a Jew, not as an Israeli especially. When you talk about biblical text or the work I've written, the cantata, *The Fire and the Mountains,* which is a text on the Holocaust and rebirth—that's identification as a Jew. Although rebirth is Israeli, the Holocaust is also rebirth—but more as a Jew, and the tragedies that we've had to overcome. These texts have been the inspiration for what I've written. There is an Israeli music, it's called Mediterranean—*yam tichoni*—Mediterranean-type music. It's oriental, I guess you would say—Yemenite influence, Sephardic. I stay away from it, as a matter of fact, because of the danger of quotation, which I'm very much against. I have always had this feeling. You do a rhapsody on oriental themes—I have never done anything like that, and I don't intend to. It's kind of cheating in a way, it's been done successfully by people like Boskovitch and Partos. They've done it very well. I think anything that might sound traditional or Eastern in my work is purely coincidental or subconscious—except, for example, in *The Fire and the Mountains,* where the text says, "It sounds like an ancient melody of King David." I used an ancient melody that is my own. Or in the flute thing that you heard today in the Old City where I used the quarter tones and it sounds kind of Moorish, I used that programmatically, and that was in the context of a very Western suite of character pieces.

I do use a lot of modes, my music is very modal in many ways, but not specifically Middle Eastern modes. And I write very much in a serial style also, and based on motives, on all kinds of variations. But that's technical. I can't pinpoint it—I know I'm influenced by jazz, and by jazz rhythm. I know I'm influenced by Bernstein and Gershwin and Mahler, and it's all one big mumbo jumbo. For instance, I have three songs that sound like Mahler when I think about it. So here, again, although Mahler was a very Jewish composer in many ways and subconsciously there is a lot of Jewishness or Eastern European Jewishness in the music—in a sense I have that identification with him also. Perhaps because of that I have that identification, and maybe that's why it sounds like Mahler in a sense, or even in the orchestration.

The first one of the songs you heard the Ankor Choir perform is "Beterem," which means "before," and it describes all the things that happen before death—before the gate is closed, before the holes of the flute are cut off, before the melody stops, before the concrete hardens. In other words, "Do what you can now, before it's too late" is what the song is about. Yehuda Amichai, who is one of the major poets in Israel today, wrote it; it's very strong. And the second one [text: Nathan Yonathan] is about a little girl who's selling flowers. She hasn't enough money to buy herself shoes, or even to keep some flowers for herself, she's so poor. That's very much more painting a picture, rather than the first one, which is much stronger.

It doesn't bother me, but I'm considered not avant-garde at all. Modern in a sense, but I cannot identify, and never could, with the avant-garde kind of music. Some of the works that I've heard I find some identification with—but for me to write, I can't. That whole style is strange, foreign to me. I listen to it, I can identify with Nami Leef's music.[3] But compared to mine it is pretty far out. Look, it's a very small percentage of people that listen to it anyway, even in the States or Europe. It's very limited, to an intellectual stratum. But it's true, in Israel, the average audience would not go to a concert of modern music, whereas in Vienna, for instance, quite a few people would go to a special program set aside for modern music.

All I really want to do is write, that's all. I think I'm very lucky in that I have the opportunity to have my works played, and I've gotten a lot of feedback, which I think is important for every composer, good feedback. People do like my work, and it's a nice feeling to walk down the street and someone like Raanan Eylon, a well-known flutist and flute teacher in Israel, says "*Nu?* When are you going to write the next piece?" Or Arnon Meroz, who wants me to write a piece for his choir. Or Stanley Sperber, who wants me to write for the Haifa Symphony Orchestra next year.

So, I don't think I can ask for any more than that. All I have to do is sit and write, that's all. I think I'm affected intellectually, let's say, by avant-garde music. I don't know if it does affect me—I'm a romantic at heart, I'm a sentimental slob. I cry at *Little House on the Prairie,* that's how I am. I've never been a great intellectual anyway. I think one has to know more or less what he is. I just don't think about it. Brahms is both emotional and intellectual—I think he's the continuation of Bach in that sense. That's what I always try to think of. You can't say that he is completely emotional. If it was completely emotional there would be anarchy, but there's construction, there's something going on.

The horn is important as a biblical reference, it has been mentioned many times in the Bible. To me, it's a very noble instrument, and the only instrument I could think of for the text of *Jephtha's Daughter.* It has everything. There's also an International Harp Contest here that spurs people to write for harp. I don't know if it's completely biblical or not. Ami Maayani, for instance, writes a lot for harp—his sister Ruth is a harpist. And so everything that he's written has been played, automatically. I attempted once to write for it, it's not easy. You really have to know a lot about harp technique.

I think Israeli composers are not satisfied with opportunities here. It's very limited, in the sense that most orchestras are not going to stick their necks out promoting Israeli music. I must say that [Yehuda] Fickler, the manager of the Jerusalem Symphony, has been very good to me. And the guy who's been my salvation is Stanley Sperber. He only got the Haifa Orchestra last year, he is the conductor of the Rinat National Choir, situated in Tel Aviv. They're very good, he's been with them for almost ten years. He originally began as a choral man and then branched out into orchestral-choral, and last year he got the Haifa Symphony Orchestra, which is going very well for him. He's very charismatic and a very excellent musician. And we became friends, real friends, in 1976.

I had just come back to Israel from conducting a piece of mine in Winnipeg, with the Winnipeg Symphony—*If I forget thee, O Jerusalem.* They loved it in Winnipeg. My parents were in the audience, three thousand people were there from the Jewish community—it was a happening. I listened to it the other night. I couldn't believe that I had written that, but that's all part of growing up.

Anyway, he was walking through the Academy, and I stopped him in the hall. He was an Academy staff member, situated here in Rehavia. And I had never met him before, although he knew of me and I knew of him. I said, "Stanley Sperber," and he said, "Yeah, but I'm very busy now." So I said, "Busy, busy, very busy." He says "Who are you?" So I told him, and he said "OK, for you, I've got five minutes." That's how it started, and since then, everything that I've written, most of the music I've written—it's a double combination of being a good friend of mine and liking my music. And he's pushed everything that I've written. He's opening the Zimriya, the international choral festival, with another choral work that I wrote two years ago. He premiered *The Sacrifice of Isaac,* he conducted this big work of mine, all this orchestra music, with the Jerusalem Symphony, and broadcasted it on the radio. Look, he's the guy—I was very lucky—there aren't many. You know, when I look around at the other composers, they don't have the chance that I have, that I was lucky enough to gain his friendship and, at the same time, that he liked my music and was willing to push it. Fortunately, because of Stanley, I am getting my compositions played.

Stanley was supposed to do my Three Songs last year, and I think he's doing a work by Mary Even-Or—she's in Haifa. She's become a little bit known out of a competition they did with the Philharmonic, and her work was played with the Israel Philharmonic.[4] But these things are so few and far between. The more people you know, the better it is. This is only Stanley's second year there, so I guess you could say he's playing it safe. You have to take that into account. What you could do is have a special series just for contemporary music.

I don't even know how I got to know Raanan Eylon at the Academy, but he's done everything I've written for flute—four pieces already, and two on a record. I didn't write those two pieces for him. They were published by Israeli Music Publications, and he saw them and liked them. So I was lucky, it's really a lot of luck. It's really, really difficult, I think, for anyone—not only in Israel. It's difficult for anybody anywhere to break through.

I am lucky also in the added sense that I'm a conductor. So I conduct some of my pieces too, why not? That's the only way. With the choir, it depends. The choral works, OK, but I don't think it's up to me to push my music too much, up to a limited amount. I have a feeling that if I do it, it's not the same, credit-wise, as when someone else thinks that my music is good enough. So that's one of the reasons I kind of shy away from it.

I try to promote others, too. With the Youth Orchestra, for instance, I try to do a lot of Israeli works by young composers, for instance, that are playing in my orchestra. I have two or three who have written works for the orchestra—sixteen, seventeen years old, very talented. One of them just writes—it's unbelievable—and I did some of his compositions. I did some of my own works when I first had the Youth Orchestra, but today I don't.

Audiences are not tolerant, let's put it that way. It's up to the conductors, I think, to educate the audience.

In 1987, Aharon Harlap founded the Chamber Opera Theater, Jerusalem, which he continues to direct. He served as music director and conductor of the Kibbutz Artzi Choir until 1990, when he was appointed music director of the Tel Aviv Philharmonic Choir.

Harlap's music has been performed in Israel, Austria, France, Tbilisi (Georgia), Hungary, Norway, Spain, Germany, Banska Bystrica (Slovak Republic), and the United States. Ensembles that have performed his works include the Vienna Madrigal Choir, the Cameran Singers, the National Choir Rinat, the Jerusalem Symphony Orchestra, the Lithuanian State Symphony Orchestra, the Tivon Chamber Choir, the Illinois Symphony Orchestra (formerly Springfield Symphony Orchestra), the Haifa Symphony Orchestra, and the Jerusalem Duo.

In 1990, Harlap conducted the premiere of his *Cain and Abel* (1989) for soprano, tenor, mixed choir, and orchestra, which received additional performances the following year in Israel and elsewhere, including a live television broadcast in Hungary. Harlap's *For Dust You Are, and to Dust You Shall Return* (1991) was performed during a 1992 American tour by the National Choir Rinat, conducted by Stanley Sperber. Harlap received the Marc Lavry Award for this composition in 1993. In 1994 his *Scenes of Jerusalem* was performed in Germany, and his Symphony No. 2 (*L'Oiseau de la guerre*) for soprano and symphony orchestra was premiered in Israel by the Haifa Symphony Orchestra, Stanley Sperber conducting. Composed in 1992, this thirty-five-minute work featuring settings of texts from the Old Testament books of Genesis and Isaiah was inspired by the work of Dutch artist Hans Hogendoorn, who completed a painting of the same title at the outbreak of the Gulf War in 1991.[5] In 1995 Harlap completed an opera, *Thérèse Raquin*, based on the play by Émile Zola (libretto by Dana Gur), that was awarded a prize by the New Israeli Opera in 1996.

Arik Shapira, photographed by Daniel Chakim. Used with permission.

10

ARIK SHAPIRA

Arik Shapira studied at the Samuel Rubin Israel Academy of Music in Tel Aviv from 1963 to 1968, where his teachers were Abel Ehrlich, Mordecai Seter, Oedoen Partos, and Yizhak Sadai. A composer of chamber music, symphonic, electronic, and multimedia works, Shapira is more of a modernist than many of his colleagues. The sonic spectrum of his typically static, nondevelopmental compositions ranges from quiet, transparent textures to clangorous, dense, multilayered blasts. He seems to regard each new work as an opportunity both for experimentation and for making political statements.

I interviewed Arik (also known as Arie) Shapira at the home of Ben-Zion Orgad, who introduced me to the younger composer.

I was born in November 1943, here in a kibbutz. My parents came from Russia, and they were members of the kibbutz Affikim, in the Jordan Valley. It's a very big kibbutz now, very old. My parents left the kibbutz in 1947, when I was four years old. I remember a few things, a big *hamsin*—an especially hot day, it was unbelievable heat. It was the record, forty-eight Celsius degrees, and I remember it. It was near the Lake of Galilee, on the Jordan. My father was a physician, and he got a job in a hospital here, and then we moved.

I went to the Academy. Before that I studied the piano and listened to a lot of records. My father collected records, he was a heavy collector. And he bought, let's say, early baroque, starting with early Italian baroque, up to Mahler, everything—classical, romantic, Wagner, Strauss, anything like that, Debussy, Mahler. And I heard modern music—twenty, twenty-five years ago, at home—records.

But the most meaningful place, most importantly, was the Music Academy in Tel Aviv. And I graduated in 1968, when it was still small and intimate. It was not part of the university at that time. And we were three students in the composition class. Now they have twenty students. My composition teacher was Partos. He was associated with the Mediterranean school—quite awful music—but he was a great musician. He studied with Bartók and [Zoltán] Kodály in Hungary. He had a Bartók complex, the famous Bartók complex. He was not compulsive. He told me, "You write anything you like, as long as it's interesting." And he wanted quantity, by the kilo. Partos wouldn't take you seriously with just a few bars. And it was a threat—if you don't write, don't come. Now, I write periodically, I'd say. As a student, it's important to write regularly. Now, when I have an idea, then I sit—or a sound or something. And you need to rest, relax, waste your time. And it will come.

Partos was my only real composition teacher, but I don't accept the Mediterranean music. It's a group, it's a tradition in my eyes: Avidom, Partos, Boskovitch, Orgad in a way. But his teacher, Ben-Haim. Tal is different. Tal is much older than Orgad. The Mediterranean music—I can't stand it. First of all, it's not Israeli.

We live in the Mediterranean. Paul Ben-Haim—he didn't, I think, know a word in Arabic. He never experienced anything Arabic—let's say, food. It's the generation. It's awful music. I mean this kind of combination, European technique combined with oriental local material, melodic lines—awful, I can't stand it. I know Bartók very well, but it's far away from this. I like it as a listener, as an art consumer, but not as a composer. It's different. Partos and Ben-Haim, they were exiles. They were exiles in Europe and exiles here. Actually, I don't feel committed to any cultural tradition or—in other words, as we say today, no roots. No roots, and I'm happy with it. I don't have roots, I don't belong. Ben-Zion Orgad was born in Germany, I was born here. I have roots here in a rootless country, in a rootless generation, my generation. I don't have roots. Only—let's say, immediate, handy—day to day. I'm not a sociologist, I really don't know. I feel it, I mean I don't have roots and I'm happy with it. I try to take advantage of it, being uncommitted. Being an Israeli composer for me is only a label. I compose for myself. I use Western notation, but it's only technique, notation is only technique. I'm interested in disintegration, not building up. That's aesthetics to me, modern aesthetics. Climax mentality is not mine. My *Missa Viva* is very Jewish. It's a transformation of a "Messiaenic" complex, of Messiaen's way of thinking.[1] It's very Jewish. I don't know, I mean I can detect it. I say it's Jewish. Historically, in a wide sense of it—not religious. I'm antireligious. It's a tradition.

The beginnings of pieces are not so important. The beginning is meaningless. The end, that's the most important. Silence is technique, I mean, it's effect. It's not music, silence. It's music inside the piece, someplace. But it doesn't matter where you start. I mean, it's not like chess. I mean the first move or sentence in a nineteenth-century Russian novel, the meaningful first sentence—it's shit. When it comes to good players, professional players, every move is significant, very important. But not in art and music, I can start here or I can start here. I'm very careful about it. The attack—I like all the instruments to attack at the same time. I need the noise, as it is, simply noise. And then a note is kept—played, and then you listen to the end of the sound. It's not noise anymore. It's a sound, it's an acoustic way to find sound, flute sound, or something like that. The attack is a mess, a chaos.

The *Missa Viva* has several different ensembles at once—a rock group, a brass group, four percussionists, keyboard stuff (ex. 11).[2] It's a story of disintegration that starts at a certain point when the rock group starts playing and all the extra instruments. It's not climactic thinking. The disintegration is all. That's the music—single notes, simple line—two well-defined notes, that will do, nothing more. No meaning, no message, nothing big, great, important, meaningful (ex. 12).

I'm an Israeli composer, let's say a Tel Avivian composer. My music is Tel Avivian, that's all. That's the finest definition I can find. It's not good, but—we call Tel Aviv "Hebrew City." Jerusalem is too old, ancient. This is a new city. It's very ugly, but very alive, high speed. Tel Avivian composer, that's the best definition, if you need one. *Missa Viva* means Tel Aviv. *Missa Viva* is "going around," Tel Aviv is "Aviv". It's a missa for Tel Aviv, it's a mass for Tel Aviv. Why not rock? It's part of Tel Aviv, it's a subculture. Rock is American or English, it's not really Israeli. It's imported, but it's part of Tel Aviv. We have a rock culture.

Ex. 11

Arik Shapira

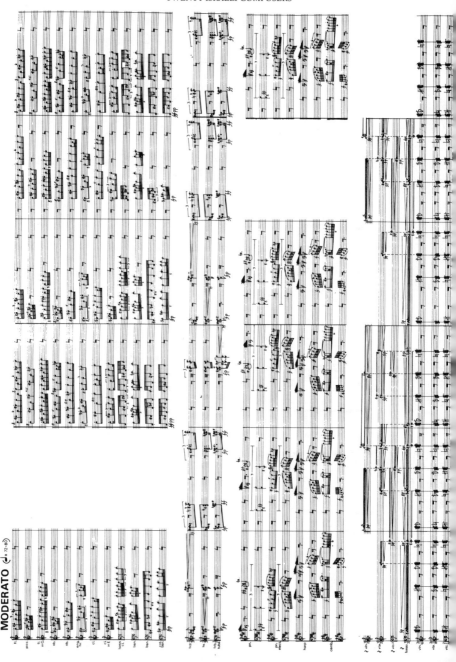

Ex. 12

Philip Glass writes awful music. I can't stand it, I'm sorry. It's bad music, that's all. I heard it two weeks ago on the radio, a new piece of his. Shame, shame. And it's money. There is always the big, green dollar behind it. I can't stand it. Steve Reich is more sophisticated. It's not enough. I heard his *Tehillim,* of course. I don't like it.

My piece *Off Piano*—it's not really music.[3] It's written, but it's meaningless notes. I could have written E-flat instead of D, and so on. I want to make an atmosphere of noncommitment. Let's say, "Don't take me seriously." It's like mumbling. You know, it's piano, piano, piano. I chose the notes; I was looking for the right nuance, let's say, that's all. It could have been a different nuance. I like a lot of notes— meaningless, just sound. Like, let's say, when you're waiting in an airport, and something is suddenly defined. And you listen to a word. I'm looking for the small things in music. A single note will do (ex. 13).

Ex. 13

We are all part—the Israel, the other—of the European tradition. Let's say of the modern European tradition. And we know all the tricks. You probably have met academic avant-garde composers in Israel. The middle way of the avant-garde, the mainstream. It's not real avant-garde. Do you know Tod Machover? I met him in Paris. That's international academic avant-garde, Well, being an Israeli, I mean being born here, I'm not like Ben-Zion, I was born in a kibbutz. I was raised here and my language is only Hebrew, and I don't give a damn about Germany or about German. I don't have roots. I have roots only here. It's not culture, it's daily. And we belong to the Middle East, and we're part of the Orient, no doubt about it. Oded Assaf claims that I write oriental music. Even not writing Western music, then I write oriental, OK. Maybe in time, yes. It's oriental, I'm part of the Orient. And it's good enough for me, I like it. Music written here in Western style sounds awful. It's not real.

I'm uncommitted to European tradition, and I don't respect European tradition. And I don't have any complexes concerning Europe like Partos or Ben-Haim. If you don't really feel the Orient then you take the oriental melodies, and so on. But if you feel the Orient you don't need those melodies, it's part of you. I'm part of the Orient, I don't think about it. It's my native country. I mean, it's my language, it's oriental.

I'm trying—I do my best to present a process in which a single note is looked for, or the subject of which is disintegration, falling apart of the pieces. Not building, not hooking them together. But I don't have the right verb in English.

You know, I met composers in Graz, young composers like me. I've met young Israeli composers. We meet, we drink beer together and we talk about music, and we all have the same ideas. I mean the same generation, being born here, educated here, and if lucky enough, avoiding Juilliard and America—if lucky enough. And I was lucky enough. And it's not surprising if you tell me of another work of this nature. On the contrary, I expect it. I need the allies, and I have met many.

———

Shapira wrote in the summer of 1989:

I have never been so frustrated in my life. I can't bear the political situation here. The country is moving towards quasi-fascism—ultra-nationalistic, immoral and repulsive place to live in. Electronic piece of mine was performed last week in Bourges, France. I didn't attend the occasion. Another electronic work is due to be performed in September in Stockholm. I will not attend it either. I can't stand the idea of being introduced as an "Israeli Composer." Writing music nowadays seems so ugly when ten miles east Palestinian boys are shot. If I were younger and bolder I would have left the pencil and bought a pistol. There are plenty of mad dogs barking here.

I am sending you a cassette with a new piece of mine—*We Are Heading Hiroshima Towards the Rising Sun.* It is for an actor/singer, flute, oboe, clarinet, piano, trumpet, trombone, violin, viola, double-bass, recorder, congas and electronic gear. It is based on the poem "New Dawn" by Robert Penn Warren, and was performed last November in Tel Aviv. Most of the piece is in Hebrew of course. There are a few quotations which are "Israeli." The idea is simple: the next war will be the last. You can count on the mad dogs who are running Israeli government: they will push the sweet button. The Iraqis will launch gas missiles and Israel will retaliate with H-bombs. Hiroshima/Baghdad/Tel Aviv/Damascus/Givatayim/Amman. As I told you—the last war at last. The concert was great. The hall was crowded. The audience was dead silent. The message was clear and hard. It's a pity you weren't here to witness the occasion. I don't believe that an American performance will have that impact.[4]

In 1991, Shapira provided the following update concerning his compositional activities:

In 1988 I wrote a piece called *Left Over* for oriental instruments (oud, sass, geitar, jimbush, congas, tablas, darbukka) and Western instruments (harpsichord, viola, violin and cello). The piece was performed live and on tape. The idea was to show that Western or oriental, all instruments can serve the modern composer.

In 1989 I wrote a trio for clarinet, piano and viola, which I named *Clip*. It was performed three times but, alas, I can't send you a recording—the viola player hated his part and played accordingly.

Then I made an electronic piece *On Thy Ruins Ophra*. It takes an Israeli to understand it fully. Anyway, Ophra is a settlement on the West Bank, famous for its extremism.[5]

In 1990 an old piece of mine (1983) was performed twice, a concerto for flute and orchestra.[6]

Two weeks ago a new piece was performed at the Tel Aviv Museum. It's for soprano, flute, oboe, trumpet, and two amplified classical guitars, and is titled *The Prophet is a Fool*. The text is from Jeremiah.[7]

Arik Shapira's music has recently been performed in Israel, France, Sweden, Germany, and the United States. Ensembles that have performed his music include Musica Nova and the Rishon LeZion Symphony Orchestra. Shapira is becoming much better known in Israel, due in particular to two recent distinctions. Shortly after our meeting, in 1986, Shapira received the Prime Minister's Prize in Composition. But the Israeli musical community virtually erupted in late January 1994 when the composer was awarded the coveted Israel Prize. Only a handful of art-music composers have received this award, the most recent having been Josef Tal, nearly a quarter century earlier, in 1970. In the chain reaction of published responses, which continued for months after the award was announced, musicians and critics attacked one another, as well as praising or deriding the composer, jury, and governmental bureaucracy that administers the award. So contentious was the public reaction to this announcement that the same issue of the *IMI News* that acknowledged Shapira's distinction with a featured interview devoted twice the space to some of the vehement responses, on both sides of the issue, that appeared in the printed media in the weeks immediately following the announcement.[8]

In view of the rarity of the Israel Prize and the extraordinary public debate concerning its most recent recipient, it seems appropriate here to devote some attention to these events. The statement excerpted below, provided by the jury that awarded Shapira the prize, reveals several significant elements of change in the first half-century of Israeli culture:

> Arie Shapira's diversified works bear his distinct personal mark: an economical, almost minimalist style; innovative spirit curious to explore the limits of voice and instrument, provocative and fascinating at all times.
>
> On the one hand Shapira's musical language is international, universal in spirit, so that his works have always found an eager ear among listeners abroad, as well as among many musicians who spared no effort in performing and promoting his music. On the other hand, Shapira's music is very Jewish and Israeli in its themes and content. As an involved composer he takes a stand in his works regarding the temporal and local, as suggested by the titles of his works: *We Are Heading Hiroshima Towards the Rising Sun, The Kastner Trial, Upon Thy Ruins Ophra, Illabi-Illabi* (a translation into Arabic of a poem by Tchernichovsky), and many more.
>
> This musical individualism, unaffected by transient fashions, is part of Shapira's teaching to his many composition students. He teaches them to be true to their inner creative truth and not serve as a mere reflection of their teachers.[9]

However consistent the ideals of individualism and innovation might seem to be with the aesthetic outlook of a nation that achieved independence only in 1948, many Israeli artists in this first half-century of statehood were enveloped by cultural ideologies of collectivism and attitudes of traditionalism. Similarly, the "provocative" and "fascinating" qualities praised by the jury in Shapira's music would have been considered in past decades subordinate, if not contrary, to the priority of expressing the ineffable qualities of the new nation. The jury's recognition of both the "international, universal" dimension and "Jewish and Israeli" traits likewise signals changes in Israeli culture. Though international influences have always affected the arts in Israel, concerns about appealing to international listeners represent more recent developments. Israeli composers have felt the need to speak an international language, in part because of the less-than-rewarding response their music has received at home. Though "temporal and local" characteristics have traditionally been sought and praised by Israeli critics, the time and place evoked in Shapira's titles (nuclear threat, Israeli settlements, Lebanon war, relations with Palestinians) reflect a qualitatively different "here and now" than the new homeland that inspired many of his predecessors. Indeed, Shapira's compositions are expressions of a profound personal concern with matters of life and death in modern Israel and the Middle East.[10]

One of the first writers to respond to the announcement of Shapira's award proclaimed: "A severe blow was dealt this week to the highest, most important of Israeli prizes—a blow that could bring about its withering and abasement."[11] This view was evidently shared by Ami Maayani, director of the Samuel Rubin Israel Academy of Music in Tel Aviv, where Shapira had been teaching:

> The fact that Mr. Shapira won the Israel Prize causes a great amount of mystification and many objections among a large number of musicians and the people responsible for music education and composers in Israel. The award to Mr. Shapira is a political act in the fullest sense of the word. His compositions (which are of marginal value from the point of their creative and technical achievements) do more than hint at this fact. Therefore, it is no wonder that serious musicians are not of the opinion that Mr. Shapira is worthy of a prize, which is the most prestigious awarded to a musician in Israel.[12]

But Shapira also had his supporters:

> Shapira belongs to the third generation. He is not committed to his predecessors' artificial "Mediterranean" style, which strived to compress the hummus and tehina, the cholent and the "gefilte fish" into artistic expression in music. He has developed an independent language, a personal syntax. Isn't the development of a new, independent musical language worthy of the Israel Prize? . . . Shapira

191

has lit the fire of creation, which is a purely personal truth, in Israeli music. . . . Shapira has no part in the consensus of Israeli mediocrity; but since when is it worthy of prizes? Since when is the Israel Prize granted to "splendid" mediocrity?

There is no one who deserves more than Shapira to be called a committed composer.[13]

As one writer observed: "The parties to this controversy argue about two different things: the supporters talk of Shapira's quality as a composer, whereas the opponents . . . are concerned . . . with the essence and purpose of the Israel prize."[14] Some aspects of the award's administration have been questioned, including its recent transfer from the Ministry of Education to the Ministry of Arts, Science, and Communications; the rotation schedule of award disciplines, which precludes the possibility of another composer being selected for at least seven years; the qualifications, selection, and preparation of jury members; and the stated criteria underlying the award. Many agree with the sentiment expressed by Oded Assaf: "What's needed, in fact, is more prizes, to many composers, all the time."[15]

When asked to respond to a list of questions provided by Yuval Shaked, to appear in the *IMI News,* Shapira admitted that the Israel Prize "came as a surprise," as he observed that it "is usually awarded to composers who are part of the consensus, 'solid' composers." Shapira added, "I have never written anything to please anyone. I never wished for my works to be liked. I asked to be understood."[16] Responding to a question concerning the controversy surrounding his award, Shapira provided the following statement:

> The public uproar which followed the Israel Prize decision is telling. It is not the upshot of bad upbringing, Hottentot manners or ill-will. Neither is it a personal assault directed at me. By no means: my colleagues would never stoop that low. This is a cry of despair, a frustrated howl coming from the depth of the soul of an entire generation, who has lost its way; its endeavor a sham, a mere murmur of leaves on a stormy night. I am referring to disciples of Ben-Haim and Boskovich—not a small group of composers— who keep treading the path laid by these two men. It's a road born out of an artificial and false synthesis which, in its prime, may have nurtured some wan flowers (that soon withered), but never bore any fruit. This is a school without a trace of skepticism, criticism, defiance or rebellion. A school interested not in art, but in arabesques. They swear by the pursuit of glory, respectability, solidity

192

and mediocrity, not the artistic truth. It is a school which slowly expired a generation ago, but its death certificate has only now arrived.[17]

Some months later, two prominent Israeli musical figures responded to Shapira's remarks, viewing these as a summary dismissal of Ben-Haim and Boskovitch rather than of the music of their "disciples." In letters written months apart, composer Shabtai Petrushka (b. 1903, Germany; imm. 1938) and musicologist Jehoash Hirshberg (b. 1938, Israel) both defended the reputations of these composers whose music, they felt, Shapira had inaccurately and unfairly characterized. Petrushka noted that Boskovitch "abruptly abandoned the Mediterranean style" (a term originally coined by the late composer) following the orchestration of his *Semitic Suite,* and later employed new compositional approaches, including serialism. Recalling Arnold Schoenberg's 1946 essay "New Music, Outmoded Music, Style and Idea," Petrushka added: "I was privileged to hear all of Boskovich's works, most of them in premiere performance, and quite a few of Ben-Haim's. Sound musical ideas prevailed in all those compositions, never mind the style."[18]

Hirshberg rejected Shapira's recognition of a "Mediterranean" school, insisting that "compositional activity in the 1930s and '40s was that of a highly pluralistic group of immigrant composers with no leader and no consensus whatsoever." He added that Ben-Haim "continuously composed in several simultaneous tracks, responding to his sincere inner call to find ways to the new reality of life in Palestine while retaining the great heritage in which he was educated." In closing, Hirshberg's direct appeal to Shapira sought equally to accommodate his independence and that of his predecessors: "My advice to Arik Shapira: continue in your own way, and we would all respect your commitment, but do not depreciate the 'founding fathers' of Israeli music, who, may I assure you, were sincere, inquisitive and committed. Moreover, please remember Arnold Schoenberg— probably the most honest and uncompromising of twentieth century innovators—and his deep respect and commitment to tradition (as distinct from convention). Progress does not necessarily imply destruction of past achievements."[19]

A letter from Arik Shapira accompanying a copy of his electroacoustic opera, *The Kastner Trial* (which the Israel Prize enabled him to issue on compact disk), included a statement of his intention to

193

leave the Samuel Rubin Israel Academy of Music at Tel Aviv University, where he had taught for four years.[20]

Shapira began teaching in the newly established music department at the University of Haifa in the fall of 1995. The same year, he composed two "electronic lieder" (on texts by Nathan Zach and Oded Sverdlick) for soprano and alto, and was at work on a composition for thirteen instruments, and another for ballet.[21] Shapira's *Ear Drum* for percussion and tape, also composed in 1995, was performed in Israel by Karen Phenpimon, and his *Letzte Briefe aus Stalingrad* for baritone and five keyboards was performed in Berlin, conducted by Jeffrey Burns.[22]

Daniel Galay, photographed by the composer. Used with permission.

11

DANIEL GALAY

Daniel Galay (originally Goldwasser) is the only composer in this volume to have immigrated to Israel from South America. Other Israeli composers from this region include León Schidlowsky (Chile) and Ruben Seroussi (Uruguay). Galay's music reflects elements of his varied cultural backgrounds and experiences, which includes graduate study in the United States. Also a pianist, Galay principally composes chamber music.

My meeting with Daniel Galay, the first composer to be interviewed, took place in his home in Ramat Aviv (near Tel Aviv) on June 8, 1986.

———

I was born April 17, 1945, in Argentina. In 1965 I came to Israel. I studied music at a conservatory in Buenos Aires, and at the Academy in Tel Aviv. There I studied with Schidlowsky, he's from Chile. Later, in the States, from 1977 to 1979, I did my master's in composition with Ralph Shapey at the University of Chicago. I had studied privately with Josef Tal, and they knew each other, and Tal recommended very strongly that I go to Ralph Shapey. I had two very intensive years of study.

Being an Israeli composer means a lot of things. First of all, it means also to be a citizen of the world. And it means to be aware about Jewish history, Jewish people, and the specific area where we are living, about Arabic countries and neighbors, about the history of this place. When I was studying Jewish history, I was learning the Jewish past of the whole world, different countries, different centuries. These are different sources of consciousness. Of course, a composer doesn't have to work with every source all the time, but he's very aware of landscape. The composer has to choose from all these, what he has learned, and say it in a contemporary language. You have to choose what you want to say, something very particular or something very abstract. Sometimes you can try to put things together, and all this is what it means to be a Jewish composer living in Israel.

There are some particular problems with Jewish, Israeli music. We did not have a tradition of music here because, as a land, we became independent only in 1948. And when Jews were dispersed for over two thousand years, they did not have unified customs and musical life. We have here a lack of tradition in music. It's not the same situation in literature.

I wrote a composition, a duet for flute and clarinet titled *Tzu Singen un Tzu Sogen*.[1] In English, the title means "to be sung and to be said." It is very much connected to a saying in Yiddish. The piece is in four sections, played without interruption. The first section is very much like oriental landscape and atmosphere, but very contrapuntal (ex. 14):

Ex. 14

The second section does something Jewish, but most of all it has a lot of violence. It is built from a fermata sound and a sforzando sound, throughout—this is the motive. It is very abstract, and it's a very violent and concentrated section (ex. 15):

Ex. 15

198

The third section starts very much improvisatory and also a little bit oriental (ex. 16):

Ex. 16

But it becomes an ostinato through an accelerando, and it's very intense, violent, aggressive (ex. 17):

Ex. 17

And at the climax, suddenly you are in a Jewish mood of the shtetl. The shtetl is where the Jews lived in Europe, in Poland, and Russia. This is the fourth section, and there is also a small coda.

You have, in one piece, four different movements that become one fresco—that is, representing different and contrasting fundamentals that are part of my life, and part of the life of this people. If I would do only one part of it, the piece would not be complete. All of them are different things related to places, but these are also parts of your mind, of your feeling, of your internal moods.

In this particular piece, the problem was melody and tonality. I'm very much interested in abstract languages and methods and techniques of writing music, but it also bothers me—that is, how not to negate melody, but to use it as part of my language. There are more abstract languages and techniques that, in my conception, are related to an eye capturing reality or behavior. Melody is related to the verbal and conscious part. We can very easily understand why it was pulled apart in the last twenty, thirty years. But composers, in a natural way, are looking and trying to understand what it means.

The shtetl is very clear melodically, and in a very pure sense. It's not a quotation, but is in the style of the music—not with sentimentality or with longing to the past. It touches your heart more than the other parts, and I feel this when I hear it—I feel suddenly so happy and released. But I feel it because this part is very fast, even cool, and very strong and forward (ex. 18):

Ex. 18

If the same idea would be too relaxed, it would kill the piece. The melodic language, the part of the heart—of romanticism—you have to be very aware of it and use it in the amount that you need.

We are living in a new century, developing always forward, but we can keep some things from the past and combine them with other things. It's not easy, and you have to choose each time how to do it—what this means, and what this means—and what the connection is. Each piece is another world. The question is sometimes one of interpretation. It's very important, because there are things that are not written—you cannot write each note out with interpretation. And if you have a performer who is aware of a lot of things, he will be able to interpret the content, to create communication—and not to create things through overemphasizing some parts at the cost of others. But these are more specific kinds of problems.

The Jewish language, Yiddish, was created through hundreds of years of wandering of Jewish people in Europe, putting together German and a lot of Hebrew, and some Latin and French. They created a language that is the face, and a lot of expressions, of the Jewish faith—this sad and intelligent faith. Here we don't speak Yiddish, we speak Hebrew. Hebrew, in its rhythms and as a Semitic language, is another world. At the beginning, my technique was to take the rhythms of this saying—"tzu singen un tzu sogen"— that are characteristic rhythms of Yiddish. But I make a rhythmic transformation, and I put it in an oriental atmosphere, related to the area where I live today.

One of the most interesting things in music is to try to analyze a modulation. What does it mean? We usually talk about that from the technical point of view and we are fascinated, but we are not always aware of the structural significance of modulation, and its connotations. It is the same thing in contemporary music. You create some conditions in a first section, you go to a new section—sometimes in two or three measures. It is an insight that's very important, because it is showing a secret link between the one and the other. These things may be understood on an analytic level. Any musicologist can follow this phenomenon—discover it, describe it, understand it. But for me as a composer, I can put it on paper only if I am living through it. You have to accept one vital experience, then another one—and to be able to put them together, and later, to understand the passing from one to the other—that explains modulations. It's very important to try to understand people, life, connections—in order to communicate with society. And after that, there is the pure compositional, professional world that autonomously exists.

The idea is to make connections between life and art. I will give you another example. I was talking about Jewishness, history—but let's leave it for a moment. I am also a citizen of the world. In a contemporary society, we are very often thinking about violence and pressure and tension. If I want to describe life in New York or Tel Aviv, or another urban center—with all the differences—there are things that are common to big cities. This problem interests me, without any direct connection to Jews, religion, or anything else. In 1984 I decided to write some etudes for piano solo, which I later performed. In one of them I was very much concerned to create an atmosphere of great pressure and violence, but my intention was to present it like a positive kind of pressure.

There is a borderline in our society between positive energy that attracts—with industries and creations and advances and new things—and pressure that is bad for the health. Where is the borderline? Sometimes the same thing, the same industry, the same situation may be good, but at some moment it's bad for people, for their health. My interest in this particular piece was to make something with a great, but constructive, pressure. This is a problem, because of this world we are in. We cannot throw it away; it's ours. The question is how to stress forces and answers that are on the side of the people, and that may be good for them. This particular piece was an attempt to deal with this problem of power—not negative, but positive power—and in this piece and other pieces, I have been dealing with this for about two or three years.

Let's say you are living in the United States, but you are conscious about Japan, and about what happened to the Indians two hundred years ago—and you are living with these feelings, atmospheres, associations, and ways of life and tradition. But you are also living in a contemporary society with violence and progress, and all these are influences. People are very disoriented by them, and the task of the artist is to face reality, outside and inside—to try to put things together, and to try to reorient things. Because there is a big mess in the world, and there is a lot of fear about the future, insecurity, nuclear war, and violence. One of the tasks of the composer, of the artist, is to try to be a citizen of the world, to try to put things together on the level of feelings, on the level of—in a pure ethical and moral point of view— what is good and what is bad. He has to deal with this. The task of the composer—the artist—is a very complex one, a challenging one. Each of us is living in a particular society and has to understand his society and his point of view, his interests, but also to understand wider processes. And I'm trying to do it from here, from Israel.

The future of society does not depend only on politicians or military people or economists. The physical future of society depends on civility, on the capacity to listen to each other, to show the inside of society—and to create alternatives to the destructive forces that are operating today. I am talking to you as another composer—we have to be very active, with a lot of initiative in our effort to put our concerns at the center of society. Artistic personalities have something to say that no other people have. Musicians are not discriminated against, but they don't have good positions that people writing for the theater sometimes have, and it doesn't have to be this way. I think that composers in particular have to be a lot more conscious about society, and about their own power. It's not easy to do that, but I think it is very important to do our job as composers better and to stay more in communication with the society in which we are living. In each society there are also more specific problems that each composer can respond to, and try to understand, and I'm trying to do it from here. But as a parallel, I'm very much open and interested to know what is going on in Argentina, in Japan, and the United States. And the collaboration that Acoustic 7–11 is doing is very important. It's very important that composers try to understand what other composers are doing, and have the personal contact.

Acoustic 7–11 is a group of composers, including Joseph Dorfman, Gabriel Iranyi, and myself. We have been active since 1980, and each year we have a series of concerts. We do them in cooperation with embassies and cultural institutions like the Goethe Institute, the Canadian Embassy, Istituto Italiano, and others. And in our programs, we try to include international music, or the music of a particular country, and Israeli music. Each time, one of us is the music director of the particular program. We use musicians—the best that we have in Israel—from the philharmonic orchestras, and also freelance. We are gaining experience in making concerts, and have a lot of dealings with audiences. Trying to create an audience for contemporary music is hard. One of the weakest points—not only for us, but in a lot of places—is the problem of how to attract more and more audiences, and not only professional people who are already coming to our concerts. We have had concerts with a lot of people, but we haven't had enough success to make our audiences wider, so that we could repeat them.

My conclusions about this are related to things I was talking about earlier. We have not only to do our job as composers and music directors, but we have to look to society face-to-face, as a whole. We have to go into a lot of sociological politics, institutional politics, in order to understand the level of consciousness—where society is—and try to catch them, bring them to our concerts, and convince them that these contemporary music concerts are about their society and about the possibility or impossibility of communication. That you have to listen to our complicated world, not only at the level that you read newspapers. A very sophisticated and concentrated level comes from listening to contemporary music. And it's not important which composer—maybe a bad composer, maybe a fantastic composer—but through a lot of pieces that are well performed, you can get closer to where you are living.

We have to fight, because it's a question of finances and forces. We have to take some energies from other places—and create forces directed to meet people and institutions, at a very high level—in order to create audiences. Because these audiences will give us a sense of history, that we are able to change feelings, to create something new. If not, our music certainly does not have any future. You cannot know if your music is working, or which music is working, or what some particular music means to a public, if you don't have a broad and varied kind of public. And it's very good to appeal to a nonprofessional public—it's open. There you can really feel what happens. I think that things will become better. I am optimistic. But it has to start from this, that composers understand they have to fight. This is not a question of public relations, having a manager—it is very good for public relations if you can have a manager. We have organizations that are doing some of this work, and all of it is important. But the composer has a particular spiritual force to do it.

Many people don't understand music as something by itself. It's a big problem, but we have to find a solution. I have spoken on occasion with Hans Ulrich Engelmann, a very well known composer who teaches at Darmstadt and Frankfurt. He was talking about why he writes music, and he said, "I wrote so many operas; they paid me lots of money, but they were not performed." And he was talking about the hard part of writing music, that people hate contemporary music. He said, "Why do I write music? Because I have a strong need to write music." This approach that we write because we have a strong need, or something tells us to, or we cannot stop—I understand it. But from some moment I started to develop a new philosophy that is openly contrasting with this one. I write music because I want to change; I want to have new experiences, and I want to bring to society these new and exciting experiences. I understand that each one of us has his irrational reasons for writing, and it has to be this way. But it's very important to stress the other part, the intentional part, the part looking forward. Because this is a creative approach. This is the approach of liberty, of choosing what you are doing—for what, and to what, you want to write. It's interesting that I spent twenty years in Argentina and twenty years in Israel. Now, as more years pass by, I am becoming more conscious about these elements. And it's also logical, because the first years when you arrive here, there is a big change. You have to get used to a new language, new and strange people.

The mind of man can accumulate a lot of things, but sometimes it has to be concentrated in one thing. So today I'm feeling more and more my capability to choose parts of my past from Argentina, and to develop it. I will give you one example. I wrote in the last few years a piece called *España—Spain*. This was created in the category of pieces about Spain, written by different composers, for different instruments. And it seems not to be contemporary music, because one of the characteristics of contemporary music in general is the universality of technique, and mood. And Spain is so much connected with the particular experience of one nation, and something like this looks to be very narrow. What I tried to do in this piece is something like this: there are some melodic designs that are very Hispanic, and each person will identify it like that. But the technique itself is very plastic, and open to different directions. Sometimes composing is like chemistry. Music is also a chemistry, like I was talking about how it works in *Tzu Singen un Tzu Sogen*. In this particular piece, I am totally aware that I'm emphasizing the Spanish moment, even too much. But this piece may be played for a lot of people, it could create some communication with them and bring them a little closer to contemporary music. My intention was to touch some very particular spirit, to touch the Spanish soul. And it's very hard to do it, because the soul is the sound that exists there. You cannot change it—it is. You can describe it, you can present it—that's it. Each piece has its history, its raison d'être.

Another problem that bothers me is how to create continuity without boredom. That is, how to create one thematic idea that develops constantly and can keep one particular feeling—how to extend it for a long time without boredom—and create a new thing that comes out from the first one. It's an interesting problem. As you can see in classical music, they had the technical development, taking the motive and changing it this or that way, or a part of it. We can take this as an antecedent, but we have to develop our own personal techniques according to the particular themes that we are dealing with. Since our themes are not like then, the way of development may not be exactly the same.

It's very hard to describe my work in the context of Israeli music, because it brings together a lot of parameters—generational, stylistic, and national parameters. There are a lot of composers here from Russia, from Germany, and Israeli-born—but I will try to give you one answer to this complicated question. It is to be understood as a process, because what I am today is a result of the last decades of work.

My point of departure is one that stresses spontaneity, a kind of expressionism, romanticism, and a lot of humanity—a lot of things neglected by contemporary music. Contemporary music stresses intellectual approaches, structure, a lot of things, but not spontaneity. I am talking about the dominating forces over the last ten to fifteen years. Now trends are again changing a lot. You cannot exist in this world only being sensible, or only being romantic. Society pushes you to develop arms, weapons, to defend your humanity. If you only develop weapons, you will be very strong, but cold, and the question is if you can have both of these things together. A man is a complicated machine—sometimes strong, sometimes weak, sometimes it loves, sometimes hates—and it's a great challenge to integrate all this. I cannot say that I am not the same person I was fifteen years ago. But some ideas crystallize—the process of presentation of ideas, how to present it and how to stress it—that defines my way of writing. In general, I'm trying to put together expressionistic and romantic approaches.

Local and universal elements affect my work, but it's happening with a lot of composers, in a lot of places. It's because each one is speaking the language of his nation but is also aware of what is going on outside. The question is what to stress from each, what to stress in the techniques and in the content of your work. In some sense, composing means putting the world in motion again and again.

———

In 1990, Galay's *Ritorno* for flute and violin was premiered in Israel. In 1991 several of his works were performed: *Hassidic Suite* for solo violin; *Rabbi of Israel* for violoncello and piano; *When the Ship Sails,* four songs for voice and piano based on poetry by Oded Sverdlick; *Chazunish* for piano; and a premiere of "Twilight" and "Beneath My Tent," two songs for voice and violoncello based on poetry by Yona Berkman. The composer participated in some of

206

these performances and gave a recital of his own works for piano in Buenos Aires, Argentina. In 1993, Galay presented his works in Israel in a series called "Open Stage," and in 1994 he participated in the premiere of his *Wish* for soprano, clarinet, and piano, a setting of poetry by Miriam Lindberg.[2] Galay writes that he is composing solo, chamber, and orchestral works devoted to Jewish themes and Yiddish language. He has performed his piano music in Israel and abroad, and he has lectured on improvisation and his system of "comprehensive piano performance." He is currently director of the educational music center Beit Frankfurt in Tel Aviv, and of the Acoustic 7–11 Forum for Contemporary Music.[3]

Tsippi Fleischer, photographed by Jörg Lantelmé (1995). Used with permission of "Archiv Frau und Musik Kassel."

12

TSIPPI FLEISCHER

Tsippi (Zipporah) Fleischer resides in Haifa, where she was born and raised by Polish-immigrant parents. She is a prolific composer whose works, performed in Israel and abroad, focus on the interaction of Western and oriental elements, languages, and styles. While a student of musicology at Bar-Ilan University, Fleischer also compiled a two-volume history of Hebrew song.[1]

Ora Binur-Schmit has written that Fleischer "may be considered the current reincarnation of a generation of composers who created the Mediterranean style."[2] Jehoash Hirshberg has written that "Tsippi Fleischer represents the boldest attempt so far to integrate Arabic culture into a musician's personal world as composer, not as scholar or explorer, but as a sensitive and motivated artist." He called her song cycle *Girl-Butterfly-Girl* (1977/1987) "one of the most original and fresh musical products of the past decade in Israel" and "a faithful reflection of a direct encounter between east and west."[3] Fleischer composed Arabic and Hebrew versions of this work, which is recorded with two different (oriental and Western) groups of instruments, musicians, and tuning systems.

I recorded my interview with Tsippi Fleischer in the Tel Aviv train station on the morning of July 3, 1986, following a performance the previous evening in Old Jaffa (near Tel Aviv) of her *Lamentation* for soprano, women's choir, two harps, and percussion.[4] This work is a setting of the poem "Klein Sterbelied" ("Little Song of Death") by Else Lasker-Schüler—in a Hebrew translation by Israeli poet Yehuda Amichai. Much of our discussion, consequently, concerned this composition.

———

I was born in 1946 in Israel. I finished the Academy of Music in Jerusalem, composition and conducting and theory. My most important teachers were Noam Sheriff, Yizhak Sadai, and Mendi Rodan— also Haim Alexander, and I studied a little bit with Tzvi Avni. And all the other things I learned by myself from the best composers from the beginning of the century. Then I did a master's degree in music education at New York University. This is a very important field with me, music education. I have many students, some of them are well-known conductors and composers. And now I am working on my Ph.D. in musicology at Bar-Ilan University with Professor Bathia Churgin. She was at Columbia University for many years. My research topic is the opera *Medée* of Cherubini, some comparisons with his other works and those of contemporaries. Also comparison with some French music written at the same time, revolutionary opera, and, more importantly, with the great operas written in the classic epoch by Gluck, Mozart, Beethoven, Spontini—to see what place this work can gain. Because it seems that it is a very important work that hasn't yet been looked at. Most important romantic composers admired this opera and admitted it was a great lesson for them.

Maybe I chose musicology because I feel that I need the credential of a doctorate. I want to know more, and this is the way to do it. You learn a lot, you see many scores, and if you are talented you can analyze it better. If you are not such a good musician you do less important work in analysis. Most of my thesis is music analysis. But composition for me is something that I don't relate to a degree. I suppose this is because I'm already so well rooted in the musical life as a composer. Also, my works are starting to be performed outside of Israel, so I don't need that degree. In the coming years I would like to meet again some of my colleagues, some of the composers that I like, for example, György Kurtág from Budapest. IRCAM [Institut de Recherche et Coordination Acoustique/Musique, Paris] recently did a very good recording of some of his works with Boulez. He is one of the best composers today in Europe. I met him in Hungary. I love his music. We feel somehow the same toward the combination of musical expressionism and folkloric flavor. On my record there is a piece dedicated to him. Ravel and Stravinsky are also important teachers, although I did not meet them personally. I suppose that many of the younger composers who learn composition, they start to imitate their teachers if they are not talented enough or don't have their own way of expression, their own fight; it doesn't start in the right way. It starts not with a special struggle for building something, but with some imitation. This is related to my negative feeling concerning degrees in composition.

I chose a music education degree also because it's a way of life, to teach people, to teach young musicians. I teach here in the College for Music Teachers, which is a part of the Levinsky Pedagogical Institute, near Tel Aviv. Then I also teach part-time at the University of Tel Aviv and at Bar-Ilan University. They invite me on special topics. I give yearly courses in harmony and harmonization of songs, methods of music analysis, jazz, light and pop music, and the research of Israeli folk songs from the end of the last century to today. I am very interested also in the popular music that comes out of today, and the teachers like to know about it so I work with them, in harmony and research.

I decided for the idea of the opening ceremony for the women's festival to use the medium of the women's choir with other components. Then I got the idea of the *Lamentation,* for soprano, women's choir, two harps, and percussion. The poem is by Else Lasker-Schüler, who is a well-known Jewish-German poet. She was born in the second half of the last century and she came to Palestine. She lived here for a while and died here.[5] She wrote almost nothing in Hebrew. She wrote in German, and she's very well known as a very lyric poet. And among all the women poets from whom I could find something in Hebrew that also had some very strong connection with death—for example, the loss of a baby, or a son, I picked those connected to death in such ways—at last, I chose this song. So I knew simultaneously that the idea is a lament and that this would be my medium, this special ensemble of women, with the soloist—a good soprano, one of our most brilliant ones. This women's choir is located in a special institute in Petach-Tikva. These are young women training to be music teachers. I knew this choir from when they performed my composition *The Clock Wants to Sleep,* which was scored for children's or women's choir.

Then, for the rest of it, I decided it would be very nice to take percussion, but something—well, very modern but not so harsh—not so noisy as contemporary composers do today in music for solo

211

percussion. So I used the marimba and the vibraphone as the body of the harmony orchestra, let's say, instead of strings and winds. And many ways of combining with the two harps that will become, in all, a soft and homogeneous timbre together, a very special ensemble. That was the sound I wanted. I wanted a sound that would gain some depth because of this, because the women and the soprano are very high all the time, and thin. I wanted to make it broader with these instruments. I was satisfied that I should get quite a full sound out of all this very special combination—it doesn't exist anywhere. I examined many, many scores that have those instruments, but I saw such a combination never was before. I was very happy, because it's not that I wanted to do something new, but I came to this idea and saw that nobody yet touched such a special ensemble.

And then I wrote it, I turned this little poem into the *Lamentation*. The poem is only a way to inspire me. Because it's very quiet, it really just grabs you, it lies very low. It's a quiet song, a quiet poem. It was so impressive, that it pushed me to the music of twenty minutes of, let's say, a theatric poem, or even a little opera with movement possibilities, about death and life altogether, that would be very surrealistic. Every word became a world, and every few words of the poem, which are very whole, became a bigger world—that's how I made twenty minutes' music for a little poem. So this is the poem. Here it's translated into English by Gila Abrahamson:

"Klein Sterbelied" (Else Lasker-Schüler)	"Shir Mavet Katan" (tr. Y. Amichai)	"Little Song of Death" (tr. G. Abrahamson)
So still ich bin, All Blut rinnt hin.	Shketá 'ani, Nigár kól dami.	So still am I, My blood runs dry.
Wie weich umher. Nichts weiû ich mehr.	Misaviv kó rákh. Lo 'edá shúv 'al kákh.	How soft everywhere. No more to bear.
Mein Herz noch klein, Starb leis an Pein.	Katán 'od halév, Mét shakét bikh'év.	Small yet, heart of mine, Dies gently in pain.
War blau und fromm! O Himmel, komm.	Kakhól hayá vetám! Shamáy bó'u mishám.	It was pure and true! O come, heaven in blue.
Ein tiefer Schall— Nacht überall.[6]	'Amók héd kól— Láyla bakól.[7]	Deep echoes call— Night over all.[8]

So as I developed it, I took like five pictures, or scenes out of an act of an opera. "So still am I, / My blood runs dry"—it was the beginning. It takes us into the atmosphere of death, the room in which the dead lie—very cold. Like you could see maybe the picture of some piercing snow and something very cold that leaves you in a very bad mood, melancholy. And then "How soft everywhere. / No more to bear." And that's where the more contrapuntal ideas come in a fugue of the girls, the harps, and the soloist. And there is much more movement.

The way I read the poem, at the last moment, you are angry that you are going to lose life, and in any case, it is not the end of the poem. Then: "Small yet, heart of mine, / Dies gently in pain." Here, before these words comes the instrumental part, which is like a dance of death. It is a concertino, like the giants or very bad creatures— the powers of hell, or of death, that are going to come and conquer the whole area, and they dance. Then it's safe, when the girls start to shout "Katán 'od halév! Katán 'od halév!"—"The heart is still small, the heart is still small." In Hebrew it doesn't say that she speaks about herself, but here, and also in the German—"Mein Herz"—as you saw yesterday, it is very obvious that she said it about herself. Anyhow, this is to signify the fight, the fight for the last moments before somebody dies. It's very tragic. It is a very cruel fight, you know—"Katán 'od halév!" They ask it in forte, but then when it's "Mét" ("dead"), it's the biggest shout and everything stops. That means somewhere the act of dying already happened.

And then immediately the soloist starts with the two harps—"Dies gently in pain" statements. She starts to do a lament. After the lament starts the connection with the heavens, and the spirit that says that we still believe there is some life after this physical act. So that's how it starts to be with echoes, very colorful vocal effects. It starts to be very physical, the heavens start to call the soul to come, and at last it ends like a requiem with a chorale.

"Deep echoes call— / Night over all." This is the night that has some sound in it, and not the night that says everything is black and dead and empty. No, there is life, some little life, some movement in the night. So that's how it ends. I don't know if it's optimistic. It sounds very full and soft and quiet about the life after death.

If you want to say there is some connection between the poem and this big work, then that's the way to explain it. Because the work also stands for itself, and this is something that inspired me to write it. It is not the conception of the lied, [which is] to go word by word for a few minutes. It's something much more demanding of myself, to do something big out of this little, very impressive song. It was very natural to me to use "passages of undetermined pitch, old modes and the 'Mediterranean' elements, and more."[9] I thought it is very dramatic. It's true. That's the way to express things still in music. I chose it, I was very anxious to use it. Nothing disturbs me to take such techniques into my compositions. The local flavor that gets its expression in my works is very, very obvious. And it's prominent also. But I would not say that I'm the one to make the perfect analysis of it. I suppose that Eli Karev can hear things that I did unconsciously, or subconsciously. So he found some influences of Mediterranean and old modes. But I used some on purpose, I used some Indian scales. This is explained in the notes. So this is something that I know about. I took these origins and I dealt with them.

For example, that melody, it's like some little party is taking place in the heavens, of the little *malachim,* the little angels, before the motive that leads into the chorale-requiem. Something that comes, surrealistically. Then it starts to be like a big *neshef,* a festival of the night, the Queen of the Night—the soloist brings us into the kingdom of the night or "La La La Layla." I picked the combination of tones out of the Indian scales and I made my own melody. This was the basis for the whole composition from the first to the last moment. And I took out of it motives, and I broadened it. And then the prominent sixth and seventh, sometimes, which is also in this melody. I really did quite a deep research on this melody, and I took out of it some things for the continuing composition there, and then I had to use some Western techniques, of course, to harmonize it, to make the contrapuntal things. I did some before the very last chorale. I had some chorale variations, many kinds and many possibilities of harmonization and texture.

I tried to do some harmonic system out of these Indian scales, but it gave me only groups of three notes that could not make logic, no buildup of some original Indian harmonic tonality or harmonic functionality, so I went back to the Western system and it was satisfying, but with special connections and special modalities. The modal point comes into it, and Mediterranean maybe comes into it. I suppose that the local modal-minded conception that we have here, many of us Israeli composers, comes out somehow, it bursts out. Even if you don't know about it, it comes out somehow much more than things like superserialism. And if there is serialism in Israeli music, I suppose it would be impossible to cut it out of the local background. I go more to the roots of modal scales, including Arabic ones. I have very good relations with the concepts of Arabic music to be included in our musical culture. You can hear this in my song cycle *Girl-Butterfly-Girl*. It's something very natural to me. I know Arabic. It's not exotic for me, I'm just there. I'm there, you see. Many other composers still take it for themselves and take advantage of it. I work with it, I'm there somehow, and came into the area through my education, in Semitic philology, and I really work there. I don't take it somewhere else, but I come there and I work there. This work is typical for me. I already wrote two works, this is not the recent one. I have something even more recent, music for ballet, with the choreographer-dancer Ruth Eshel. She's very interesting, and she'll give an evening in the same hall as yesterday's concert in this Jaffa festival. It is on the sixth of July, in a few days. And then I have some music that is even later than the *Lamentation*.

I suppose the balance of Eastern and Western elements in my work is fifty-fifty. It cannot be good—the music cannot stand for itself and gain the reputation of artistic music—if it's not perfectly done technically, compositionally. That's only the result of what I know, what I learned. And I know music and I live as a Western musician, but I smell the Eastern, I suppose, more strongly than the other ones. I live it much more inclusively. But it's fifty-fifty. I know some composers who give such a strength to the Eastern and to the folklorist tunes, that it starts to be 80 percent, so it's not artistic anymore. And I know most of the other ones, that they're taking it, picking something of the East as something very exotic and rework it, and it does not function organically in the buildup of the piece. And this is the other side, that takes 80 percent of the West and only 20 of the East, and I suppose I'm in the middle. These, both East and West, are really organic with me. They don't live one without the other, very naturally.

I feel I must write Israeli music. I'm the one who is happy in Israel with whatever I do. The inspiration comes out of this area and the ideas and some very good audiences—and the students, who are the best audience for the future. Music teachers, for example, I teach them. So they are, for me, some very important personalities who will guide the musical life here, and the younger generations. I do a lot for contemporary music here in Israel to be more understandable for people here, for many audiences. So I say all of this in order to explain that I'm very happy as an Israeli composer. It's rare, I should say. I don't know if we have here ten composers who would say this. For me, I'm an Israeli composer first. Also, I must tell you that I'm looking for the idea to write a piece, a big piece, that deals with Judaism. But I hesitate. I haven't yet got to this stage, and still I suppose for one of my last works, I shall be dealing with my identity as a Jewish artist. Yet I am first of all an Israeli artist, but I live very, very sympathetically with my Jewish identity. I don't have any confrontations with this subject. I like many of the gestures that the Jewish religion already gave me from childhood.

So it's very natural to me. You can say, "She's a real Israeli composer. Whatever she writes—the subjects, the musical subjects, the influences, her identity as Israeli, and a healthy Israeli who is satisfied, who wants the musical life here to be richer, who doesn't complain about the situation that there is not very much money for big productions, that they still don't perform here too much Israeli music." Complaining is not my way. You have to fight—doing, yes. Doing positively. Build, do such work as I do. Our National Choir Rinat is now performing a big a cappella score of mine. It's called *Six Madrigals: Visions of Israel,* and from the standpoint of solfeggio, technical problems, it's more difficult than the *Lamentation.* Because I knew that this one would be first performed, not with the most professional choir. And they are doing it, and they're happy with it. Every madrigal is dedicated to another place in Israel, sung in Hebrew, to lyrics of some of our best poets. You see what my subjects are. So here, no problems of identity. And I suppose that if here there are no problems of identity as Israeli, so outside it's for me obvious that it would be even better. It will show even better my essence, and my creation will reflect what is going on here as something unique. It will be only better than here even, because it will be looked at with that special quality that it bears.

The music of Tsippi Fleischer has been performed in Israel, France, Germany, Belgium, the Netherlands, Finland, Spain, Yugoslavia, England, Japan, Canada, and, in the United States, in Alaska, California, Illinois, Minnesota, Washington, D.C., and New York.

Fleischer's tape pieces composed in 1988, *In the Gown of Night* (a collage of Bedouin children's voices) and *In the Mountains of Armenia* (for Armenian girls' voices, narrator, and clarinet), were selected by the Israeli Broadcasting Authority to represent Israel in the UNESCO

216

International Rostrum of Composers in Paris in 1989. Her *Oratorio 1492–1992*, based on the expulsion of Jews from Spain, was premiered in Israel in 1992 by the Haifa Symphony Orchestra and the National Choir Rinat (which jointly commissioned the work), with additional performers. The same year, Fleischer's *The Clock Wants to Sleep* (1981) for children's choir, based on a poem by Miriam Yalan-Shtekelis, received a prize from the Composers' League of Japan. Fleischer was named "First Career-Woman of Israel for 1993 in the Field of Music" by an Israeli newspaper, which similarly honored women in politics, art, engineering, architecture, industry, and academic life. In 1994, Fleischer participated in a seminar on "The Middle East as a Cultural Source" at the Kuopio Dance Festival in Finland.[10]

In June and July 1995, Fleischer was in residence at Villa Montalvo, an artist colony in Saratoga, California. In 1996 her compositional activities—including performances, lectures, and recording sessions (for two projected Vienna Modern Masters compact disks)— took her to the Netherlands, Italy, Germany, Poland, and the Czech Republic.[11] Tsippi Fleischer teaches at the Levinsky Institute and at Bar-Ilan University, where she earned a Ph.D. in musicology in 1995.

Gabriel Iranyi, photographed at the Samuel Rubin Israel Academy of Music (1986) by Robert Fleisher.

13

GABRIEL IRANYI

Gabriel Iranyi is the recipient of the Gaudeamus (1978), Rubinstein (1979), and Valentino Bucchi (1980) prizes in composition. His works have been performed at the Gaudeamus Music Week, the Steirischer Herbst in Graz, the ISCM World Music Days (1980 in Israel, 1985 in Holland), and the International Rostrum of Composers in Paris. Iranyi has taught at the Enesco Conservatory in his native Romania, and at the Rubin Academy of Music in Tel Aviv, the Gaton Studio for Music in the Galilee, and the Kfar Saba Conservatory. Since 1980 he has also been associated with the composers' organization Acoustic 7–11.[1]

Iranyi's music highlights texture and timbre, including the use of *Klangfarbenmelodie,* and he has employed graphic, proportional, and tablature notation. I heard a performance of Iranyi's *Metaphor* (1980) for flute in Jerusalem, and interviewed him on July 2, 1986, at the Samuel Rubin Israel Academy of Music in Tel Aviv.

―――――――

I was born in Romania in 1946. I came to Israel in 1977. I think two things in my musical training were very important. On one side, it was my teacher in composition, and today I think he should be considered a very important musicologist. He wrote a few books on Bach, unfortunately not translated yet into English. His name is Sigismund Todutza. He was a pupil of [Alfredo] Casella and [Virgilio]

Mortari at St. Cecelia in Rome when he was very young. In Romania he's a very important musician as a composer and teacher. I think mainly he is a very good musicologist and teacher. He taught us discipline. Maybe I am also influenced by him, because I do not write very much or very easily. So I look for details and I think very much before I write a piece. And I also like this. Why should I waste a lot of paper?

And the other thing was, that in those years also began the development of the avant-garde, all over the world. I mean in the late fifties, and then in the sixties and seventies, we could hear in Romania some avant-garde music. And later we even had live concerts and performances. I learned piano and I performed contemporary music. So these two things were very important.

I don't think my *Metaphor* for flute is "unconformist to the hilt, an angry, rebellious statement."[2] Maybe he's used to other kinds of contemporary music. Maybe there was too much new articulation in the piece for him, and this sounds unfamiliar, let's say. I wrote it in 1980, and I think basically I was very much impressed by nature in the area where I was living, in Tel Aviv. I was walking a lot and I heard many, many birds singing and also many insects. I heard these kind of asymmetric rhythmic patterns, and I couldn't not write a piece on this. I even wrote a piece for piano, which has no real melody. It is inspired by birds, by their rhythms. In April, May, and June there are a lot of birds in Israel, also in Europe. It's not at all like Messiaen, and also not in my piano piece. I was very glad when we had a concert with this piece, *Bird of Wonder,* and we also invited a composer from Frankfurt, Hans Ulrich Engelmann. He heard the piece and he said that it's not at all like Messiaen. It's something very obvious if you write a piece about birds—everybody associates you with Messiaen. They're not thinking about the piece. It's as though if you wrote a fugue today, and everybody would ask you about Bach maybe, or if you write a madrigal, then they ask you about the Renaissance.

Ornithologically, it doesn't matter what a bird is in my piece. I'm not interested to record something and to write it exactly as I heard it in nature on my walks. In my piano piece it is about an imaginary bird. Like the bird (*Pasarea Maiastra*) of Constantin Brancusi, the Romanian sculptor—I only translated the title. He has many sculptures with birds, but he just uses the shape, an abstract shape, and not each little detail. My music is much different from his work. He wants to have the whole world in three or four lines. My music is very colorful. I change registers and use all the keyboard, so it's completely different.

I think it cannot be otherwise that living here has changed my music. Even if you stay in the same place, you change. I have been here nine years already. But there are many things I can say about culture or even the ideological aspect. For instance, in Romania, suddenly everything is very open, you could have avant-garde theater, you could listen to everything, music with multiphonics, or based on twelve-tone method, I mean very free. And suddenly something happens, and after two or three years suddenly you see it's silence—nobody is writing anything interesting. And then it could change again. And this is very disturbing for creation. Of course, this is one difference in Israel.

What's interesting in Romania is you can have a very active musical life. We had two operas in the city where I was born, one was the Romanian Opera and the other the Hungarian Opera. And there was also a beautiful philharmonic orchestra, and ballet and theater—actually, two theaters and two ballets, and an Ars Nova ensemble. I was born in Cluj [Klausenburg], in Transylvania, and there was a big university. You could also buy very cheap scores there. I had a lot of scores. But I had also some from my family. Somebody from Germany, a cousin, sent me a lot of scores, a lot of Webern and Schoenberg, also Xenakis and Boulez.

We have a group here, directed by David Bloch,[3] that sometimes performs American music, for example by Charles Ives or John Cage, or George Crumb. I think I have to look at Ives's music, because Ligeti also told me that Ives could be interesting for me. I've heard very little music of his. And it seems this idea of having multimelodic things is very present there. But Ives was not the inspiration.

In my piece *Laudae,* I have Jewish music. The second movement contains three melodies of Jewish-Yemenite tradition, and one of three synagogue chants notated in the twelfth century by Obadya, the Norman proselyte. Obadya is very little known here, even though he was published by Israel Adler at the Jewish Music Research Centre in Jerusalem. It is a very small book, but I think it's very important for Jewish music. The second movement ends with prayer fragments from the first movement. For this I took a melody, "Praise the Lord" ("Barechu et Adonai"), from Idelsohn's book, for the Babylonian "High Holidays." I took this melody, but I thought of it in electronic music means. I cut it, like a loop, which comes and goes again. And I tried to build a harmonic structure for it, which is also modal. Sometimes there are no bar lines, and they can be rhythmically completely free.

This "Adon olam" is a very interesting melody. There are three melodies that are Yemenite in origin, and they have something in common, but they each have their own personality. They have the tetrachordal structure in common. And the other one, from the third century, is also tetrachordal. In the second movement, I have two, and then the three Yemenite melodies together. One of them is written in normal rhythmic values. To the second melody I added a dot to each note. By the third melody, in "Adon olam," I diminished the values. And then later on I even have four melodies together, like a chorale. I changed the original rhythms in order to have a multirhythmic texture. I also changed their original tonality. In *Laudae* I have not only polymelody, or polyphony, heterophony, but I have also multiharmony. For the end I chose the Hallelujah, which is originally divided between the cantor and the congregation. So I divided the melody for the two pianos antiphonally.

Am I an Israeli composer? I thought, "What can I say?" And then I thought, "OK, I know what I am not." I think I cannot say I am a Romanian composer. If you take Béla Bartók, even after he came to the States, he remained a Hungarian musician. I mean, he hated Hungary because of the fascism there, but he wrote Hungarian music, even in America, and he would have done it also in Australia—it doesn't matter. So to be a Romanian composer is to be connected with something that is Romanian. My teacher was trained in Italy and his mind was more oriented to Germany music—Bach and Beethoven, Brahms and Schoenberg. I think I never had really written Romanian music. In my works, it was always an international style.

But I think I am a Jewish and Israeli composer. Once our teacher, who was not pro-Israeli, of course, but also not anti-Semitic, said something to us—two Jewish students in the class—that was very much a surprise for me at the time. Today it is not. Now I know more about the subject than he. Then, he said that one of the most ancient layers of music is the Jewish music. And he explained that the Gregorian chant took the Hebrew cantillation and moved it to Europe. And later he made this connection between the Hebrew cantillation and the music of Bach, for which the Gregorian chant is such an important source.

So I think we are very, very important for all the older music. But one can never know enough about Jewish music. I'm interested also

222

in musicology. This music I quoted in *Laudae,* this twelfth-century melody by Obadya, I just found by accident, in a small book of about five pages, and it was fantastic. I thought this is in a way like finding a thesaurus, suddenly. There are three chants by Obadya, and I use only one here. They were found, I think, at the beginning of this century, in the *genizah*[4] of Cairo. And on two scrolls, somebody notated three chants. One is not complete.

And now there's a very interesting question—first of all, this is the first Jewish music written in neumatic notation in the twelfth century. There was never any before and not after, for hundreds of years. Nobody notated Jewish music, nobody, until the eighteenth century. So the question is, are these melodies his own compositions? Are they Jewish music? Or are they Christian music? Because Obadya was Christian. He saw many Jews killed by crusaders and therefore decided to become Jewish. So he moved here from Italy, and in the end decided to live in Cairo, in Egypt. So you see, it's very important, and this music is beautiful.

Laudae would never have been written had I not come to Israel and found these melodies. No, never. Only in Israel could this be possible, I am convinced. I think the Jewish music traditions have become important for my work. And I think this comes from my teacher, who was concerned with Romanian music—to keep the mind very clear and to try to separate what is really original. When you find a book, for instance, about folklore—the question is what is really original, and what could be more a combination of the different cultures when they meet together and produce something new.

So in Israel, for some historical reasons, I can say Yemenite music is maybe the most fascinating. It came from thousands of years ago, the original music. And also some Babylonian music is very interesting. And I also found in Idelsohn some German music from the synagogue, and Jewish music of the era of Beethoven, the eighteenth century. It's fantastic—Jewish music from Berlin, around 1750, the classical period. But I don't find it very interesting musically, as a composer.

Yemenite music doesn't have this very particular sound, which is more Arab and Turkish, but I think not properly Jewish—for instance, the augmented second. You can find it in Romanian and Bulgarian music, and it's the influence of the Turks. But I don't think it's Jewish. The Jewish character is more to be found in the Yemenite music. They have ancient scales, but also Mixolydian and other scales. And

223

the rhythmic patterns are small cells that are changing. You could have four, five, and seven, different patterns, tied very closely to pronunciation of the Jewish language, of Hebrew.

So it's very interesting, because the accents change very much. This kind of pattern is not even found in the Bulgarian folk music, for instance, where there's a lot of the irregular groupings like five or seven. But there it is all the time the same quantity, which in Yemenite music could change. I really think folklore could be very important for a composer today. I have other pieces. For example, this quintet, which hasn't yet been performed, is based on another song by Obadya. I think this could be very important for my music, maybe because it's connected with something very personal. I mean, in my mind, I think I'm more and more dialectic. As you say, there are very old and very new structures together. This is important for me, to have the contrast in my music.

Now I'm teaching at Kfar Saba Conservatory, near Tel Aviv. I teach theory of music. In Israel the conservatories are schools of music with very young students, not college age. They are learning only instruments, and theory. They asked me to establish a composition class. At the beginning there were twenty, and I had maybe three good students. I think it is a good beginning.

Iranyi received a grant from the Israel League of Composers in 1987 and from the Tel Aviv Council for Culture and Art in 1988. Since moving to Berlin in 1988, Iranyi has been a lecturer at the Leo Borchard School of Music and been involved in the organization of new-music concerts and festivals. One of several works that Iranyi completed in 1988, *Tempora* (three pieces for organ), was commissioned by the Rheinisches Musikfest in Düsseldorf. Since that time he has continued to compose chamber works, and his music has been performed in Israel, the United States, Germany, Holland, Iceland, Lithuania, Russia, the Ukraine, and his native Romania. Ensembles that have performed his work include the Ensemble Neue Musik–Düsseldorf,[5] Musica Nova, the Percussion Ensemble Berlin, Duo Contemporain, and the Drew Krause/Paul Marquardt Piano Duo.

In 1991, Iranyi's *The Severing of the Wings* was premiered during the First International Festival of Jewish Art Music in Vilnius (Lithuania), and in 1993 his *Laudae* (1984) for two pianos was performed during the Second International Festival of Jewish Art

Music, in Odessa (Ukraine). In 1994 several of Iranyi's compositions were performed in Germany, including *Bird of Wonder* (1981) and *Portraits of Bach* (1985), both for piano; *Scroll Fragments* for clarinet (1986); and *Triplum* for three percussionists. In Israel, soprano Eva Ben-Zvi and pianist Natasha Tadson premiered Iranyi's *The Hymns of Job* (1993).[6] In 1995 Gabriel Iranyi became deputy president of the Verein zur Förderung jüdischer Musik, established to organize the Forth International Festival of Jewish Art Music, in Berlin (1998).

Stephen Horenstein, photographed at his home in Jerusalem (1986) by Robert Fleisher.

14

STEPHEN HORENSTEIN

Stephen Horenstein is the only American-born composer included in this book. A performer of woodwind instruments, Horenstein combines in his compositions elements of jazz and improvisation with materials inspired by Jewish and Israeli sources. He has composed orchestral, chamber, solo, and computer music compositions, and views the performance environment as an integral component of his works. Horenstein was awarded grants from the National Endowment for the Arts in 1976 and again in 1980. Before immigrating to Israel, Horenstein earned a master's degree at the University of Wisconsin, was a member of the Judith Dunn/Bill Dixon Company from 1970 to 1973, and then a member of the faculty of Bennington College, teaching in both the music and dance departments.[1]

I interviewed Stephen Horenstein at Mishkenot Sha'ananim on June 17, 1986. Shortly thereafter, on July 2, his composition for solo harp, *Light and Motion*, was premiered at a new-music festival in Old Jaffa (near Tel Aviv) by Adina Har-Oz, a frequent performer of contemporary Israeli music.[2]

I was born in Winthrop, Massachusetts, February 24, 1948. My musical training was a mixed bag. I was after something. I started off as a performer, as a classical clarinetist. Then at a very early age I

227

decided I wanted to play the saxophone, so I continued sort of a dual career of playing the clarinet and the saxophone. And as there were no saxophones in symphony orchestras, I found myself playing all kinds of music. And then I continued to undergraduate school. I studied at Trinity College in Hartford, Connecticut, and the Hartt School of Music. I studied in a traditional music department. I had a B.A. in music, but that still wasn't what I wanted. Then I started flute at the age of eighteen. I decided then to look for my guru and I met Marcel Moyse, with whom I studied for a period of time, after which point I met a very great man who happened to be teaching at Bennington College—William Dixon, a composer.

And at that point I had to make a decision. I decided that I couldn't be both a performer and a composer, and I decided to go to the composition direction. And I started studying composition as his apprentice, and also in 1972 I went out to the University of Wisconsin and did an M.A. there, where Bill Dixon was a visiting professor for a year. I had two composition teachers, Dixon and Les Thimmig. Thimmig taught me some very interesting approaches to notation. Anyway, I got my master's at the University of Wisconsin, came back to the East Coast, and was appointed to the faculty of Bennington. I had been an assistant between 1970 and 1972, and in 1973 became a faculty member. I taught there until 1980. And that's my background.

I came to Israel in 1980. I was ready for a change. I'd been teaching at Bennington College for ten years and decided that it was time for me to advance my career in another way, creatively—to give up the cushy academic position and to enter into my own work. I've had opportunities here in Israel to do my work beyond my wildest dreams. I didn't imagine that in five years I would have achieved what I've achieved here. From the standpoint of creativity, I consider myself very lucky. I mean, not that it was without struggle, because it wasn't, just to survive on a day-to-day level. But what happened to me as a composer wouldn't have happened anywhere else.

There are two major projects. My last project, which is ongoing—I consider it ongoing research and an ongoing performance piece—is entitled *Agadot [Legends]*, and it's based on personal research, not academic research—research as a composer that I did into sound sources that were outlined in the Torah and the Talmud—the palette of sounds. In other words, just the way painters living in Greece can't ignore the quality of light, composers, as far as I'm concerned, living in this part of the world can't ignore the quality of sound that is part of the tradition. And to my mind, I'm the first composer that ever did this. In other words, I write with trumpets, a lot of plucked strings. I use the cymbal choir, an amplified cymbal choir put through various electronic devices—basically using the cymbal in not a dissimilar way to the way Stockhausen used the tam-tam. The trumpet was used. I use the shofar in several ways. I thought it would be too obvious to actually use a shofar. I did a piece where I recorded ten shofarot in a recording studio, and I used that as part of the fabric of the piece. I myself played all the wind instruments, including the alto and bass flute. I do a lot of bass flute, and I used the saxophone in a different sort of way, which is close to the shofar—I use a lot of harmonics and overblowing.

I believe that the future of composition lies, at least in my own work, in a physical presence, in my own physical presence in my music, or my physical nonpresence. Whether I choose to be in the piece or not in the piece determines to a great deal what the piece is about, the actual sound of the piece. That is, I have a series of performance pieces where I perform in an intimate relation with a group of musicians over a long period of time. We build a language that can be codified in traditional and nontraditional notation, verbal notation. This is one primary compositional direction, only possible through close and active collaboration with performers.

The second direction is more traditional: composing for any group of performers that might desire to play the music, anywhere in the world. For instance, I'm currently working on a piece for the Jerusalem Symphony Orchestra that was commissioned by the late Recha Freier for the next Testimonium. Her idea was to create commissions for contemporary composers, not necessarily Jewish, of pieces and works based on Jewish history, and for each cycle of pieces she chose a different theme. She chose the theme, she chose the text—all the pieces, actually, have texts associated with them. She would always do an opera or a mini-opera as part of the festival.

She commissioned a lot of very well known composers, who admitted that they wrote pieces they never would otherwise have written. Things that came out of these—Xenakis wrote several very beautiful pieces, very unlike Xenakis. Kagel wrote something. Stockhausen wrote several pieces, one of which, incidentally, is in one of his latest recordings—a massive volume, an opera. It's dedicated to her. The composers were mostly non-Israeli. Yet, she would always choose someone from this country, and in retrospect, she did choose some of the very established people.

229

But she also would give people, more or less young "dark horses," a chance. And about a year before she passed away, may her soul rest in peace, she went into her library and she brought out a text, and gave me the nod. It all started when I met her in 1983, when I was asked to perform in a piece by [Hans-]Joachim Hespos. I didn't care very much for the piece at the time. They brought me up to her house, and I met her. Through her gentle manner, she persuaded me to play in the piece. He was a composer in that Testimonium series.

We had a very beautiful relationship together. I started going to her every Tuesday at 4:00 and playing her excerpts of my latest pieces, and she would tell me if she liked them or didn't. And if she didn't, she would tell me why she didn't like them. She wasn't a trained musician, but she had a tremendous sense of intuition. She was the best composition teacher I ever had, I think. I used to go to her at 4:00 and play for her, just sit and talk. And we'd chat about everything under the sun. And I played for her, and I would tape everything. I have all the tapes of everything I played, and she would say this or that. Very often if she didn't like something, she would say to me "That's not you. You're trying to sound like the way you're supposed to sound, or the way of another composer." And that experience brought me tremendously close to who I was.

And then one day, after about two years of these meetings, she just gave me this poem by Uri Zvi Greenberg and said, "Listen, I want you to write a piece for the next Testimonium," and I nearly *plotzed* because it was the most cherished commission of contemporary music in this country. In Israel it's probably comparable to a Guggenheim fellowship, and for this country it's quite substantial a commission. It pays to compose for a year at least. There are many, many composers in line for that. And she said, "You'll be the only composer from this country." She said, "I'm writing to Berio to do a piece for double choir, I want to talk to Ligeti when he comes to this country, I have to invite Haubenstock-Ramati, because it's the anniversary of our starting this thing."[3] She went through all these composers and said, "I think it's going to be you and Berio on the same concert."

I then started to develop an idea for an orchestra piece.[4] At the same time I was preparing for *Agadot,* the piece that was premiered in last year's Israel Festival. I decided to use some of the same ideas for the commissioned orchestra piece. Yet I decided to stick to the theme of the poem. The poem is very specific. I'm using a choir of ten voices that will be offstage, but only as an instrumental color and not a choir—let's say an ensemble, not dissimilar to what Schoenberg did in *Moses und Aron* in using instrumental color. I told her right from the onset that the poem is very short, and that I probably wouldn't use the words, but I would use sort of the setting of the poem. It is about a man who leaves his shoes—he is walking in the desert and he leaves his shoes to journey in some other place, far, far away, a sort of mystic transformation.

After *Agadot,* I was in a tremendous state of exhaustion, because we rehearsed for six months. To put together a new-music ensemble in Israel is a near impossibility. I'm going to tell you something. The only way to do it is what we did. I found a group of musicians, like the percussionist Jeffery Kowalsky, who worked considerably with Lukas Foss. And I feel like I could be married to the guy! He's a beautiful musician, and I hope the relationship continues. We had a group, we had seven musicians and we rehearsed, we forced ourselves every weekend. And we had a kibbutz—a member of the group was a kibbutznik and we had the kibbutz every weekend, and rehearsed two or three days every week. Not only that, but we ate together, sometimes we'd sleep together in one room! People really ignore that kind of process. I'm very concerned with the process. Through this process we were able to do a piece of wide scope and tremendous length. And we got really good reviews. Someone from the university reviewed it and said that the festival "justified its existence," and it was the best piece. And some other people really came down on it, people who don't normally like new music. Anyway, that piece is continuing, we're trying to bring it to the States and to Europe. And we're rehearsing together, we're working as a trio now—the core members of that ensemble, Jeffery and I and another musician are working now to continue some of those ideas in a more chamber setting.

So now I'm working on a series of short pieces for solo musicians. I really became interested in the harp through the *Agadot,* and I want harp in my orchestra piece. First of all, we're talking about, in a most general sense, the quality of sound. I'm not interested in the harp the way most people have been writing for it. I'm trying to find my own way. And the sound of the strings in my orchestra piece won't be the traditional use of the harp, that's very clear. In *Agadot* I used a koto, amplified in a certain way. I had two harps made for me by a harp maker in Jerusalem, and I had another harp from Colombia, from South America. And I used the harps in a polymodal fashion, each one was tuned differently. I had everyone playing harps at one point or another in the piece. They played very simple parts, but put together I got a very interesting sound. Some of it was hocketlike texture, and some of it was very much done in unison, with the notation in hand patterns—motion up and down on the harp—with the positioning of the fingers in either fourths or thirds. I had all kinds of devices worked out to get the sounds I wanted, with a minimum of difficulty.

I was also very lucky in my first five years to be commissioned for a series of environmental works that weren't purely musical. I did a piece for the Tel Hai International Arts Festival, and one in the Israel Museum in which I collaborated with Isamu Noguchi in designing a sound environment for the Billy Rose Art Garden. He helped me especially on the placement of musicians and speakers, and how sounds would flow through the garden. The result was a mobilelike structure of seven interlocking sound environments, combined with many different performance events. And so, when either the commissions or the sources of inspiration for purely musical works became lacking, I always was able to meet artists outside of music who wanted some relationship—not in a multimedia or kitschy sense. I try to learn from other arts different approaches to my own work, and it's very exciting.

In Israel you have an established music community here that doesn't seem to welcome newcomers. There is a lot of behind-the-scenes politics always going on. I try not to be involved. Mordecai Seter chooses not to be involved. André Hajdu chooses not to be involved. And those are the people I respect in this country. As for many of the others, they are trying to outdo the other by trying to sound like a European composer better than the next. They don't know what's under their own feet, in terms of musical historical resources. Recha Freier knew this. The Greek painters know the essential beauty of the quality of light of their country, and the painters in this country also work with the shapes and forms in this country. And I respect André— in his way, he's tried to do that. I feel that when I'm listening to most pieces of new music in this country that I'm listening to people *doing* music and not people expressing something that's coming from inside them, and emanating from their environment. Yet I see the hope in some of the younger composers.

I'm a composer. I'm an American-born composer, living in Israel, who has declared himself a dual citizen, not by choice—well, by choice, but because it's required of people. And I consider myself very much a fabric of the society, but at the same time, an outsider and an observer, a documenter. I'm documenting in my work. I'm very affected by what I read in an essay by Albert Camus many years ago, where he said that the dilemma of the twentieth-century artist is how not to abandon his vision, the striving for beauty and perfection, while having to deal with the moral and political dilemmas of his time. Here I feel this dilemma even more. I'm in the middle of a tornado here, in the most volatile place in the world, and I feel it's a very vital place to be—the tension emanates from the day-to-day compression that one feels. I use these opposite extremes in my music. Thus, my work is very much rooted in collage, very much an extension of an Ivesian approach to the unity of opposite qualities of sound.

Schoenberg needed a system. Ives was more intuitive. I'm talking about the application of musical material and layered composition. For instance, shifting the layers of rhythm in a piece, or putting a brass band in the middle of a string orchestra. You would never call Ives a brass band composer! He chose to use that particular sound quality that came from an entirely different musical tradition—"out of the blue," so to speak. Like in Buñuel's film, *The Exterminating Angel,* where people are sitting in a very plush living room and suddenly a flock of sheep enters, or something—the whole sound of surprise. So I consider myself working out of that tradition.

It's the concept of time and the approach to the bar line and meter that interest me. First of all, in ancient Jewish music there were no bar lines. Obviously everything was related to the text, and to speech rhythm. If you look at Mt. Zion in Jerusalem, you see the electric wires and you also see two thousand years of history! There are two time experiences going on: the immediacy and the timelessness. I feel very comfortable in a kind of time that seems to have no end—over the horizon, so to speak. I use musical materials that are very stretched in time, contrasted by things that are very abrupt and of the moment.

I use in my work a lot of sustained sounds, a lot of percussive sounds. I use very unusual combinations in the orchestrations. For instance, very few composers have even the desire to use saxophones because they're afraid of what the connotation would be. I find in the saxophone, this glorious mongrel of an instrument, tremendous sound possibilities. Also, I was trained to be a flutist and a clarinetist and a saxophonist, so I know intimately all the nuances of quarter tones, and other polyphonic effects, on all the woodwinds, and I bring that to my work. I devise notation systems to translate them to the other musicians.

233

I like to use tonal resources; I don't consider myself an atonal composer. I like to work pantonally. I like the shifting layers of tonalities and the tensions that are created between them. So in that sense I'm not afraid of the Middle East tradition. I can deal with it, not often in a traditional melodic way—I use a lot of wide intervals— but I'm still using modality. But also I think I have a very Eastern sensibility. I don't know if it's exactly Eastern, because I think you find it in many other musics all over the world, where there's a tremendous respect for the players, for the musicians. I sometimes would rather write a piece for musicians I know than a paper piece for musicians I don't know, for instance. We're often dealing with things that cannot be expressed in traditional notation. I would even come from left field and say that Duke Ellington wrote for Harry Carney *on* baritone saxophone and not just *for* baritone saxophone. But I know there are many who would not consider Duke Ellington a composer, let alone a great composer. I would. I was taught in my various experiences, especially from Bill Dixon, to respect the player and write for the sound of the player.

But back to Israel. So where else in the world could I have a relationship with a symphony orchestra? That's one of the reasons I came to Jerusalem, where I could go to the first cellist and sing to him the way the part goes, or rewrite the part on the basis of how they play. I mean I couldn't do that with the Boston Symphony—I would be lucky if I had two or three rehearsals.

Creatively, it's better in some ways here. I have a commission from the Jerusalem Symphony. On the other hand, what I have to do to put food on the table! I'll tell you, I never thought of teaching children or young adults in the States. Yet, when I came to this country I saw there was a real need. I have a reputation in Jerusalem for working with problem kids from the age of twelve to eighteen—before the army—problems in the sense that they're extremely talented. They might have social problems, but they're willing to work hard. I work both privately and in ensembles. My dream is to start a small institute, in this country, of new music.

I am perfectly content to be a Jerusalem composer, and stay here, and work with the youth here. My last piece was done for the Jerusalem Foundation. It was a piece performed for [Jerusalem mayor] Teddy Kollek's birthday, composed for five trumpets, harp, and percussion, and performed two weeks ago. I was able to try some interesting things with the trumpets, within the tight rehearsal schedule. And I'm working in designing courses in music through the computer. Software basically, for export to the States. I'm working on a course in rhythm now.

My sense of time has to do with the relationship of the pulse— pulse and duration, which is nothing new—and the juxtaposition of various contrasting notational means, all for traditional orchestral instruments. I'm not afraid to use traditional notation at the same time as a nonspecific notation, but only on the condition I work with the players beforehand. I would never give a symphony player a series of pitches to play, without outlining a clear concept. I'm not afraid to go from the very general to absolutely the most specific—dynamics in ten shadings. I'll do that when it's compositionally necessary. But the audience never knows. If a player can play structurally from an experimental notation, that's fine with me. But I'll only do it for the player who has the experience or the desire. The disaster of a lot of contemporary composers—they throw all of this notation on the musicians. There was a scandal this last year, a piece by Bruno Maderna, with the Israeli Philharmonic. And there were players who sat there with newspapers—I mean, you know, like on strike. They refused to play. I mean, why would a composer want to do that, and why would musicians? I mean, you're dealing with an institution.

I really want to be more specific about this notation of time. I will relate to you an experience that I consider fundamental to my work. I engaged for the last three or four years in experiments in what I call supersaturation of texture, not unlike what Jackson Pollock did in his painting. Basically, to find out—I wrote a series of pieces, most in the lab, where I used all kinds of acoustic material, working with overdubbing, multitrack—to get to the point, to see how much material, or how much in a texture I could fill up before it became black. And what I found is that at the point just before it becomes black, there is a different time experience. I think that we're dealing with psychological time. There's something that happens before it goes black that is intrinsic to the notion of psychological time, and from the little bit of research I've done in the clinical sense, I've learned that our perception of time is determined by the amounts of inputs being channeled into our retina, and into our brain.

And I became fascinated by the saturation of texture and, juxta-posed, the very sparsest of textures. And also in terms of dynamics, from the most chaotic texture, to the most minimal. And I guess I deal in extremes in my work from that standpoint, and I find that the juxtaposition of the extremes creates different time senses. From this research I did a piece for the Tel Hai Festival, which is put on outdoors, in which I had a huge ten-foot speaker coming from a mountain— from about two hundred feet away—and I was on a field performing, surrounded by eight loudspeakers. I could send my sound, my live sound, to the mountain and play the echo. I had a recorded tape of high density playing. Thus, I was able to experiment with juxtaposition of extremes of texture and time. The piece is called *Chiasmus*.

I feel that this use of texture and time is fundamental to my concept, in addition to all the other things I mentioned—like the breaking down of the bar line, which we of course find in many ethnic traditions. The Western influence is in the choice of blocks of material that I use. Those materials reflect things around us on a day-to-day level. I don't think of it in East and West. I think of it just in terms of horizon and of parallax, of distant and close relationships and how the things move across a horizon line—as though you were traveling through a train in time. I see it all part of the same frame. But in the motion, things that are close to you are close to you.

Basically I'm trying to take what I learned from Ives and Varèse and people like that, and bring it to this part of the world. I don't know of anyone else who's even thought of it in those terms. And that's what my orchestra piece is about. Let's put it this way—that I'm not unaware of the overt use of scales and melodic contours from all those ethnic musics. I've listened to a lot of non-Western music—a lot of Indian music, a lot of Arabic music—I feel that it has become part of my blood. I don't feel the need to quote. I feel that every time I write or play a melody it's going to naturally possess certain influences, because of the sum total of my musical experience. And in fact, as a player, a lot of my work for bass flute now is really reflecting these kinds of melodic contours that are found—that is, using all the various tones between the tones, not being afraid. Also, I studied Japanese shakuhachi for a brief time, only to learn about the notational system, and I'm very taken by it.[5] I love Japanese flute playing, the use of all the nuances of tone and the timbre—the use of timbre—things that just can't be notated, and they don't need to be notated.

I had certain ideas in the States before I came, because I've always been a fan of Ives. And having a mixed upbringing, having to make a unity out of myself was enough work. Coming to this part of the world allowed those ideas to come to fruition in an unusual and, I think, unique way. Seeing fifty different cultures here, having something common tying them together—all within the most ancient and the most modern. It's a modern society, built on the most ancient soil— dealing with that paradox and having to come here and try to make some kind of sense out of it. I really consider artists as documentation, as documenters. I deal in violence in my work. One of my students committed suicide six months ago, something that caught us all by surprise. It was a few months before his army service. I'm writing a piece for him now that uses four percussionists and three saxophones and bass.

———

In 1987, Horenstein founded the Jerusalem New Music Ensemble and the Jerusalem Institute of Contemporary Music, which he directs. In 1990 his Quintet for winds was performed at the Jerusalem Van Leer Institute and at the Tel Aviv Museum. At the Merkin Concert Hall in New York City in June 1991, Horenstein led the Jerusalem New Music Ensemble in a performance of his *Agadot,* a composition in fifteen sections combining an eclectic array of instruments (including harps, alto flute, saxophones, trumpet, guitar, prepared piano, koto, darbukka, percussion, and synthesizer) and prerecorded tape. In 1993, during a tour of Russia and Finland with pianist Shai Bechar and percussionists Avi Yishay and Jeffery Kowalsky, Horenstein performed several of his newer works: *Between the Silences* (1994), *Zones* (1992–93), and *Metamorphosis* (1993).[6] His music has also been heard at international festivals in Austria, Germany, France, Italy, and Luxembourg.

The recipient of grants from the America-Israel Cultural Foundation and the Jerusalem Foundation, Horenstein has taught at the Jerusalem Rubin Academy of Music and Dance, Tel Aviv University, and the Bezalel School of Art and Design.[7] He serves as music director for the Jerusalem High School of the Performing Arts and Amit Experimental Religious High School.[8] Horenstein's recent research interests have concerned the interaction of computer and performer.[9] In 1996, Horenstein was preparing two new recordings of his music, and was named a Jerusalem Fellow by the Center for Advanced Professional Education.

Noa Guy, photographed in New York City (1995) by Michael H. Barker. Used with permission.

15

NOA GUY

Noa Guy's compositions include orchestral and electronic music, as well as works for theater and multimedia. She has also written choral and instrumental chamber works, including *Circles* (1986), a virtuosic composition for solo alto recorder, which includes a variety of extended performance techniques. During my visit, two of her compositions were performed by the Ankor Children's Choir.

Between 1972 and 1979, Guy worked as a calligrapher and music editor for Norsk Musikforlag (Norway), Nordiska Musikforlaget (Sweden), and Wilhelm Hansen Forlag (Denmark). From 1979 to 1984 she served as a calligrapher for composer Karlheinz Stockhausen, and from 1980 until 1987 she served as head of the string department for Matan, a music education program for Israeli youth.[1]

I interviewed Noa Guy on June 22, 1986, at Mishkenot Sha'ananim.

I was born in Jerusalem in 1949 and grew up here. I'm seventh generation in this country. My family came from Russia in the middle of the last century. I studied theory here in the Academy, because when I started here there was no composition at all. And they opened a theory class only once in two years, with five students. After theory, I had private composition lessons with Abel Ehrlich in Tel Aviv, and after studying with Ehrlich, I went to Berlin and studied with Boris Blacher. Later I had master classes with different people, including Milton Babbitt. He came here twice to give summer courses, and I managed to get private lessons with him. Also Stockhausen, Berio, [Erhard] Karkoschka. It was very strange, because when I studied here in the Academy I didn't know what I'd do with theory. And I went to Ehrlich just to study more music. And one day he said, "Why don't you write something?" That's the way I began, and I never stopped since then. So, it began just as a flower opens, suddenly, which has waited for that without knowing.

Being an Israeli composer is very hard, especially when one doesn't compromise. It's a very sensitive point, because—I'm surprised at myself saying it—I think I'm more a Jewish composer than an Israeli composer. There is no public here for contemporary music, and radio does not support it—musicians do not want to play the music. If I stay true to myself, if I don't compromise and I don't say, "Well, I'll make it less difficult for them to listen to"—well, that's my music and that's the way I write, and I don't compromise. And the result is that I'm played more and more abroad, and less and less here.

Just to give you an example, I wrote a big piece for a British singer, and we worked on this piece for a long time, about three years—a dream that became real. And now it's going to be performed at the Nettlefold festival in London, so I asked the foreign ministry here if they have support for artists, so I can be at the performance—because it's the only Israeli piece in a big festival. And they just told me: "We don't understand why you ask, because it's completely your private business." So, if it's my private business then I don't think of myself as an Israeli composer. You see, I live here, I was born here, OK—but I don't represent anything but myself. The radio is the same story, they don't want to play Israeli music now. They never did, actually, it was just to say they did. And it's not only the radio, it's the general education. I think it begins in kindergarten, in schools—they have absolutely no musical education at all. And all the wunderkinder that are here, it's up to the private effort of the parents. In Europe you have musical education in school. At least they know how to read music, they listen to music. They simply don't have anything here, it's unbelievable. And it begins there, because there is no public for that. Prokofiev is the most modern they can stand—they simply physically cannot stand it, it is too much for them. For example, they are not allowed to broadcast contemporary music during the morning hours. But that's the only radio you can get here, you don't have any other choice.

They have programs of contemporary music twice a week, that's true, and Israeli composers are fairly well represented. Once a week there is a mixed program of Israelis and others, but I don't believe that more than a hundred or two hundred people in the whole country listen to that program. And it's really a desert. It is, in a way, a very uncultured place. There is nobody to talk to because people are so closed, and physically also closed. I remember that once I had a concert—it wasn't a real concert, it was mixed. The first part was music proper and the second part was a sort of performance with actors, and more a music theater piece. It had an audience of only twenty people. That's not my experience in Europe.

I find myself detached from any institution now. I find that it's for the best for me to be on my own, and find my own way and my own connections. Also, pieces that I write lately are more personal, more for people I know. I wrote a piece for [oboist] Heinz Holliger, and a piece for Michael Barker, a Dutch-American recorder player who performs a lot of contemporary music, and this music theater piece for the English singer John Potter. So I have more and more personal contact with performers, and I also know every corner of their playing so I can really write for them. It's giving me much more than just writing in the air. The two choral pieces of mine that were performed last week, by the Ankor Choir—that's an exception. These two works aren't published. The third one is. But also, I don't know, did they sell? Because it's already two or three years, and they never bothered to inform me or anything, as if I didn't publish. Money and music don't go together in this place.

I don't use oriental or Middle Eastern sources. My only sources of Middle Eastern or Jewish origin are usually the texts. I write in Western, international styles, and I also try never to limit myself to the sounds, or choose to work, for example, with folk origins—anything like that is limiting. But it also doesn't appeal to me. The whole sound of the Middle East is far from me. There is a work that I wrote for a trio of flute, viola, and cello, which I call *The Echo of Stones*. The idea of the piece came to me when I sat in a place—you have in the mountains here, terraces of very old stones, becoming black—and I began to see things on the stones, and I made six little abstract drawings, very abstract things. And I wrote a piece in six little movements, after the drawings actually—so here was a work that was connected physically to the place where I live. But it doesn't necessarily have to be here—I mean it could have happened to me anywhere.

The sense of time—I feel like a foreigner here because everything goes so quickly, and is so tense. And I have many times been criticized for having too long pieces, like the choir piece that you heard. Many people here said it's too long. The public can't sit still and listen to a piece that's twelve minutes long. They lose their appetite or their interest, I don't know what. It's the same thing—look at how people walk here, how people work, and how people drive here. That's the way they sit in a concert. So I try to do the opposite. That's the whole way of life that we lead at home. We don't have television, we don't read newspapers. Everything is aimed at trying to be more relaxed. We listen to the radio once a day to hear the news, just to see if something happened. But I prefer good literature to newspapers. For me, its very hard to live here. I try to escape during writing, for example. I'm just with myself, or sounds, or people I want to write to.

This piece, *Angel's Solitude,* has both hurried and timeless qualities.[2] But, for example, *Who Knows the Secret*, the work written for this English singer, is based on different creation mythologies of different parts of the world—which is also a timeless subject. I wrote the text myself, and I didn't take any story as such. I just took a word from here, a sentence from there, and made my own set of events. It's in seven parts. The time conception of this piece is compound. On the one hand it feels static at some places, as if it does not move at all. On the other hand these thirty minutes are over so fast—at least that's the reaction of everybody who heard the piece. It is slow and fast, standing and running—at the same time. I find that writing for a solo instrument, five or seven minutes is a nice time. Bigger works need more time. In the last theater work that I've done, there is almost no acting at all onstage. There is lighting, and the one man onstage moves to seven stations, which are lighted differently, but he doesn't have to sing, it's all talk. The piece lasts thirty minutes.

During Hanukkah they're going to have a marathon of three days of Israeli music, and I'm the only one included who does mixed media. I'm doing things with painting and lighting. So I don't know where to put myself, but I know that I touch many areas that many composers don't. What I like to do is be involved also in the staging, not necessarily doing it all by myself but taking part at least—I think more in a wide sense. Many times when I write a piece I see also the staging. I would like, for example, the choir works to be performed differently—not just to stand like that and sing. For example the second one, *Colours*. It could be improved, they could move onstage and do things. It wouldn't do with this choir because they're so well behaved, but I can imagine it being done differently, more lively.

I haven't been to the United States, but I lived in Europe for six years—Germany and Norway, mostly Norway. For the first three years I didn't do anything but bring two children into the world. But many contacts, and most all of my connections now, are still from European days. Being in Norway especially, which is the absolute opposite of Israel—in the sense of society's behavior and how the things are run in the country—was a wonderful experience, it goes to the other extreme. It showed me that it's possible to live that way. We went to Germany in 1971, quite young, at the beginning of our twenties. I studied with Blacher, which was a very good thing for me. But we couldn't stay for more than one year. It was a hard experience, a difficult one for us. We came openhearted and we tried, but it didn't work. It's very personal—there are people who can, there are people who can't.

It's under the surface all the time—everything is alright, it looks like everything is OK, but it's not. And I remember taking a book from the library and it had this stamp with a swastika. Usually they put a black stamp on it so you can't see it. But you open the page and there it is, suddenly—in Bach chorale preludes for organ. It was from the time of the war, and it belonged to the library at that time—and it just stayed there. And for us to see it, it's shocking. You can say it's nothing—"They forgot, so what?"—but it's not. And there are many, many small things like that. But you can't really tell what makes it so unpleasant. I think I matured during this time, filled my batteries. Boris Blacher was a very special teacher, because he didn't try to influence the sense of style. But he worked very deeply into the sense of composition, to read a story into it, to see a picture and to analyze it—to hear music and analyze it. Your style is your own business, but compositionally it has to be done properly, and I learned a lot from this, because he never interfered in style. I was one of four pupils from four different countries, and we were really very different. He died in 1975, but there are other Israeli composers who have worked with him too, Noam Sheriff included. Blacher was born in China, but he's of Russian origin I think.

Our education, at the Music Academy—we learn Western music, harmony, and counterpoint. I believe we have almost basically the same education as you get. And for me to listen to oriental music is an effort, I have to listen to it. I believe I would react to folk, rock, and jazz the same way as I react to this kind of music. I grew up in a very, very unmusical family, and for me it was a revelation to hear music at all, at a fairly late age. I think I was fourteen when I heard, for the first time in my life, a ceremony in a church—Gregorian chant. And it was a new world for me, it was fascinating. And I used to run out of school on Sundays and go to listen, to different churches here in town. I also come from a very secular family. I'd never been in a synagogue until a very, very late age. So I hadn't any contact with music until very late. Then it came, with all its power and force.

It happened with my choir piece, *And Everyone an Earring of Gold (Impression from the Book of Job),* that Arnon Meroz, the children's choir conductor, asked me to write a piece on that subject. I had several suggestions, and at the end I found this one. But in other works, it's other contemporary poets or my own texts.[3] And the work with the mythologies, that is a subject that has fascinated me for a long time. I have a big collection that I collected over the years, of different stories, and I never knew what I was going to do with this until it came. I have Far Eastern, Middle Eastern, North American, South American Indians, Tibetan, Japanese, Hebrew, Mesopotamian stories. Really all kinds of stories. I have the text here—it's seven different sections, and I simply wrote seven poems. I wrote a score for a singer, he's my sound source for the tape. It's the singer and himself actually, except for two parts that combine the singer and synthesizer. He sings on top of the tape in the performance. The singer recorded the score I wrote line by line—there are sometimes eight voice parts—and I put it together on the tape. I manipulated the voice, changing its quality. The sixth part is built from the whispered text of the whole piece—recorded and then put on tape, multiplied twenty-four times. For the seventh part, the tape is created from a single note sung repeatedly, multiplied and changed. The singer is John Potter, he's doing a lot of contemporary music and music theater. The premiere is in October, and it's almost finished.

I have a few new works. One is a tape work and the other two are instrumental. I have a small studio at home, very limited. And this is a problem, because I couldn't make this voice tape anywhere here, I needed special equipment for working with voice. I looked for studios, and the Basel Academy gave me a grant for doing the tape, and they really have a wonderful studio there. So I was there for four weeks and worked many, many hours every day—it was wonderful. I had an advantage, because it was the middle of winter—it's so cold there, you don't want to go out. But that is a problem, studios, a problem always.

––––––

In 1987, Noa Guy was awarded a prize from the Israel Music Institute for her piano composition *Over Fallen Leaves* (1986) and was appointed head of the master class program of the Jerusalem Music Centre, in conjunction with which she was involved in the production of concerts, broadcasts, recordings, and videotapes. Responding to an inquiry concerning her compositional activities, Guy wrote in 1990:

> I think that basically not much has changed in terms of the society-composer relationship, but I myself have changed quite a lot. I complain less, I work more and I criticize less. I am played here and there. This summer I was teaching in a summer course in Switzerland (in Lenzburg) and there a new string quintet I wrote was played. Two weeks after I came back I was invited by surprise to England where the BBC singers performed my work on the Book of Job. Next Thursday a new work for voice and harpsichord is going to be premiered here in Jerusalem. It is not always that dense, but there is always something to look forward to.
>
> To make a living I work full-time in the Jerusalem Music Centre, where I produce a series of concerts for young musicians and I am the coordinator of the master classes. All that means that now composing takes place only in the darkness when the rest of the world is asleep, quite an experience.[4]

In 1990, *Over Fallen Leaves, At the Evening Tide* (for soprano and harpsichord), and *Angel's Solitude* (1981, tape alone) were all heard in live broadcasts, and the BBC Singers performed *And Everyone an Earring of Gold* in London. Performances in Israel in 1992 included *The Forbidden Fruit* (1991) for tuba and women's choir, and *At the Evening Tide*.[5] Several of Guy's works were also performed during the First International Seminar of Contemporary Chamber Music at the Hed Music Center in Yahud: *Sparkles* for solo voice (1989), *Movement for String Quartet* (1992), and *Inter-Stellar* for string quintet (1990).[6] Guy's *Du-Li-Ru* (text by the composer) for mezzo-soprano and piano was performed at the Hed Center in 1993, the same year she completed *Four Episodes for Orchestra*. In 1995 the Havana String Quartet performed Guy's *Movement for String Quartet* in Cordoba, Spain. This performance was later broadcast on Spanish national radio.[7]

In connection with her duties at the Jerusalem Music Centre, Noa Guy traveled to New York in the fall of 1993, where she sustained injuries in an automobile accident requiring intensive rehabilitation and recuperation. She began painting in 1994, and was able to begin composing again only in 1996.[8]

Haim Permont, photographed by the composer.

16

HAIM PERMONT

Haim Permont is one of the few Eastern European immigrant composers in this book. I had the opportunity to hear a performance of Permont's *From the Book of the Dead* at the Israel Festival. Much of our discussion, consequently, concerned this work. I interviewed Haim Permont on June 25, 1986, in his office at the Jerusalem Rubin Academy of Music and Dance, where he continues to teach and perform administrative duties.

————

I was born in the USSR in 1950 and came to Israel in 1956. I came to a kibbutz near the northern border, kibbutz Kfar Giladi, in the upper Galilee near Tel Hai, about a one-hour drive north from Tiberia. My whole family came. First, I studied music here in Jerusalem at the Academy, with Mark Kopytman. Then I went to the University of Pennsylvania after graduating from the Rubin Academy. I was there for four years, from 1981 to 1985. At Penn I studied with Richard Wernick and George Crumb and another person, a young and upcoming composer Jay Reese. He's going to have his name all over. I won some awards there, the Sharet, CBS, and ASCAP, and then this fellowship, and the Nitze-Hubbel Prize, and some others. This is my first full year of teaching and doing the other stuff, scheduling, pushing papers.

As an Israeli composer—first, it has national connotation, identity. And it's very hard to define an Israeli composer, because there are several periods of Israeli music. In the thirties it was the Bartók influence, which was artificial quotations and exotic modes and all that stuff. So then there were artificial quotations, which was done very nicely, influenced by Bartók, and then there was a second period, which was some kind of incorporating—serialism—Josef Tal's work and electronic music. And now we stand, I hope, at the beginning of a third era or whatever, which is the freedom from complexes, from all "isms," and this is what we would like ourselves to think, but of course, nobody is free. Yes, any material—yes, I would say so, whatever suits the content of the piece. And it can be anything combined, whatever, and we're very fortunate because of the time, where we stand in history. I had a talk with George Rochberg, and he said, "You guys don't have to go through the whole thing, you know—serialism, dodecaphony, then come back to tonality—you can just use everything." Pick and choose, and everything goes and everything works.

The "Israeli quality" is not an issue, and it is an issue. I mean it's hard to define an Israeli composer. An Israeli composer is a composer who lives in Israel and works here, and writes for the Israeli public about issues that concern the public, the nation, whatever. But such a composer can be successful outside Israel. I call it music that has some kind of definition, you know what it is about—not what it is, per se, but what it is about.

The subject I choose may be familiar to my audience, but I wouldn't say the musical language is familiar. Sometimes it's not, and sometimes nobody knows if it's Israeli or not. A colleague, Professor Jehoash Hirshberg, who is a musicologist here, did research, an experiment with Israeli music. And the audience, astonishingly enough, responds well. I mean, everybody guessed right, the majority guessed right. They could hear something in it was Israeli, and nobody knows exactly what. Again, we can use modes, and all that stuff, and quotations from prayers, but this is not the only thing. But it's hard to define, because it's so young.

I cannot say that I was influenced in terms of style from my teachers. And it was strange, but they did not try to impose on me any aesthetic rules or things like this. But they had their technical aspects of it, the way they see things that they did try to impose, like having control over what you write and so on. But that's OK, that's part of the whole thing, that you study with somebody.

250

The other thing that happened when I was in the States is that I searched in terms of material and inspiration—it's a bad word, but this is it, inspiration. I was looking for some kind of contact to what I am, in terms of my personality, where I belong, my identity and all that.

But this day and date, what I can say—maybe a year from now it will be different, because I'm here—but when I was absent, my connection, my contact, my identification with things that are Jewish and Middle Eastern, Israeli, was very strong. And also in terms of politics and philosophy, history and all that. In some kind of strange way, it intensified the whole thing, being absent in the States. I felt cut off, and then I made an effort to bridge the gap somehow. The evidence is I wrote a piece, two songs on poems by Henry Thoreau, dedicated to the Penn faculty. And you know, it's Henry Thoreau, and it's pastorale, North American pastorale, but the style is Middle Eastern. I got letters from my friends saying that nobody knew that Thoreau had a hiding place near the Dead Sea. Now they know it. Maybe it's a kind of escape, but I don't believe that I can, at this stage in my life, have some kind of universal message, to be cosmopolitan and so on. And I don't believe anybody can. Yes, people, especially Israelis, are very much involved in everything here—it's hard not to be. It's a small country, a very intense life here. Every day something happens, and it's hard to detach yourself from the whole thing, and it influences your music. Maybe nobody hears it, once it's finished. But I believe you do hear it, especially if you compare it to other people's music, if you are abroad. In some way, people write about different things.

Wernick uses subjects for his music, I mean in terms of content— his piece *Visions of Terror and Wonder,* and then the *A Prayer for Jerusalem.* And he relates himself, too, to the whole thing, even though it's different from the way Kopytman relates himself, or Josef Tal relates himself. But it's very hard to define Israeli music. It's a pluralistic society. I came here when I was very young, but I grew up in a kibbutz, the whole shtick, of folk songs and the dances. It's all artificial stuff, but it became folk songs, by force. It was forced into the folk. And this is what I grew up on. And then I played violin, too, and I had classical training and so on. And I felt like I have to find some way to combine it in an intelligent and artistic way, and I hope I can do it. But I'm still making the effort.

My Western musical training helps me to say what I want in my music, because it provides a means to deal with the whole. The techniques with which you incorporate whatever you have in yourself, or whatever you take from your environment and incorporate into your music, the means with which to do it is the traditional training. I very strongly believe in it. I don't believe in universal freedom and simplicity and to get detached from everything, and start fresh. I think that tradition, and continuity of tradition, and all that, is a very powerful and necessary means to do it. It's the way of communicating.

The work that was performed at the Israel Festival, *From the Book of the Dead,* was based on a poem by Lea Goldberg. She belongs to the other generation, the one before us. She was a poet and a researcher in literature. She was a professor of the Hebrew University, I think she was the head of the literature department. And what I liked about her is especially the fact that she was from the older generation, not from my generation. Our generation writes about how we "shoot and cry"—shooting and crying at the same time. Which means that we're a bit chauvinistic, we fight for our lives, and so on, but then we all try to show ourselves to ourselves as having nice souls and nice emotions, and so on.

And I myself am that way, too, we're all like that. But the generation before us was a bit different. They were still strongly attached to Europe, to the European background. And they made an enormous effort to become Israelis, to study Hebrew, they worked out the whole language, and the whole thing. And still the mentality is still Eastern European, especially with Lea Goldberg. But she was an immensely cultured woman and she wrote a lot, and I read a lot of what she wrote and I liked it. Her generation had less mercy upon themselves, they are less sorry for themselves than our generation is. We have more self-pity, we tend to have. They were more modest. This is what my feeling is, and these two elements are enough. And I think they had more vision, they were more creative. They were more cultural, I think. Our generation is very practical, pragmatic. We're disillusioned.

I felt like trying to impose our disillusions on their illusions. Although it's not an issue, the song is about death, about self—all kinds of things that belong to her own life. But nevertheless, the fact that I used it, I was happy about it. I decided to use it, to identify with the old generation in this particular piece. The poem is all symbolic, of course. It's about one who leaves the land of the living, and ascending a steep, cruel, landscaped hill, he reaches a wall. There he stumbles and remains lying on the earth, waiting for a sign, but is left in complete solitude, forgotten by nature and God. His loved one—she talks to him from the grave, saying that "for seven days and seven nights, you did not shed a tear, you did not dream about me, and you did not think about me—and therefore I should not rise from the dead." And you can twist it the way you want it, you can say many things; I didn't think about it in this way. You can say that to rise from the dead is the Israeli nation, to build a new society from what happened, from the ashes and so on. And because we detach ourselves from our tradition, from what we are, we shall not rise, and we shall not survive.

It's very pessimistic, and I believe our generation is pessimistic. And also the absolute despair and hopelessness. Nothing helps and she's left all by herself, and even the sky did not accept her prayer— "and no star was lighted in the sky"—I like that, and I'm a bit pessimistic—I was when I wrote it.

Of course, the number seven is symbolic in Judaism, not only in Judaism. The number seven is the seven days, seven nights, the days of the week, the days in which the world was created, the number seven is widely used. I'm not religious and all that—I don't believe there's magic in the numbers. But these are the numbers she used in the poem. And also, when somebody dies, after seven days, you have the first memorial, shivah. And, of course, that's why she used it.

I decided in this piece to use all the techniques I had in command, freely. One of them is to use the row, dodecaphonic. But the work is absolutely tonal. It's a modal piece, it's in B-flat, some kind of Phrygian mode. For instance, the beginning of the piano is a row, and the whole fast section, with the crowds, is a row. Because it's kind of neutral. And it can be, if you want, attached to the desert—being detached from everything else, which is what I think about serialism—no definition. It only fills spaces. It only gives you some kind of freedom to be totally abstract and detached from everything. You can say so. And then—the lyric parts are modal.

There is some chromatic descending, which is a little onomato-poeia, word painting. And it shows also that emotional curve, in the second movement, the second song, the second part, the solo cadenza, or the first solo of the singer. And this is also a mode, but it's slightly different, more Lydian.

I seem to go back to the modes every time, especially the Phrygian cadence and the Lydian tetrachord, the tritone. I like the major third and tritone—C, E, F-sharp—together. I like this sound for some reason. The principle is probably in tonality. For some reason, there's no escape from it. It didn't sound very tonal because they missed all the notes. But it goes back to B-flat. What I did use is, for instance, an open fifth, B-flat, F. And the filling of that fifth with a minor second, either on this side or the other side: B-flat, C-flat, F, or B-flat, F, and E. That's the way Hindemith used it. Not exactly this way, but Hindemith has a lot of fifths and fourths, and he filled them every time in a different way. That's nice, it's easy, and it works. It gives you a center, gives you direction, but you can color it the way you want. You can make it more dissonant, less dissonant.

In Jewish music, there is the famous mode, hijāz, which is Phrygian with augmented seconds: E, F, G-sharp, A, B, C, D-sharp. There are all kinds of such modes. But I am in general attached to modes, octatonic scales and stuff like this, in this piece. What happens in other pieces I wouldn't know yet. This is a recent piece. It's typical of my work in the States, the way I worked in the States. I feel very good with it. This is the main thing that I learned over there, that everything can be used, incorporated into the whole atmosphere—it doesn't matter, it can even be a row. And Penn is a very nice place for those things. They teach the freedom, they preach the freedom. It's very pluralistic. Well, first it was different, because I was an undergraduate here. I was a beginner here. And over there, the relationship was more collegial. Here I was more a student—Mark Kopytman felt responsible. And he taught you everything he could in a short time. I studied here six years. I never wrote music before, I just wanted to write music. I improvised on the piano, but I didn't write music. And he took care of you, your way of thinking and your way of looking upon music. And techniques, and he is very strong on tradition, on counterpoint in particular. And this was the kind of training.

Now when I came to the States, they regarded me more as a colleague in some way. And it was frightening in the beginning because I expected them to tell you what to do, so you can do it. But they did not, so you go home and write. So it was kind of like they throw you into the water, and you have to swim. And it was good, the way Americans think, which I like—in the land of a lot of freedom, you must make your own decisions.

And I cannot say they imposed on me anything whatsoever. In technical things, especially, Wernick would say "this sounds good" or not—orchestration—which is good, fine. But some of the students quit, they give up because of that. It might be cruel in a way, but I think it's very good.

A composer is somebody who makes decisions—many, many decisions. A pianist has to make decisions, too, but he still has a tradition behind him. When he plays Schumann, he knows the general direction, where the composer is left all by himself. It was good, and Penn was also very strong in analysis. The main thing about Penn was that I had to form my own opinion about music in general, and about pieces and styles in particular. And it wasn't required here, when I was an undergraduate.

The graduate program here is still very young. It's just beginning, and we can't say yet. Nobody graduated yet. I'm not talking about musicology, which is different. But at Penn, at the end of the program, I had an oral exam. They don't have orals anymore. But what I had, the whole exam was about opinions, sound opinions that you can base on something—subjective, but you had to base it upon something. You had to prove it and to argue with all those people, the faculty. And it was tough, but I liked it because I think this is what music is all about. For some reason they decided not to continue this. Now it is just a piece and a thesis. I had to do all three. For the orals, I studied serialism so I could form an opinion. This is my interpretation of it. Other people thought that the orals were about information, that you just have to know things.

There are two ways to describe the influence of Western and Middle Eastern elements in my work. One, there is a general difference between Western and Eastern music, or Middle Eastern, whatever. One is in the organization of time, time moves differently. This is one way. The other way is in terms of pitches—modes, augmented second, and so on. In terms of pitch, I don't see any big difference now in this day and date, the twentieth century—everybody is using everything.

But in terms of time there is, of course, a big difference. And the stasis that is found in Eastern music now is being incorporated into Western music, minimalism, and all that. And these are the general differences. Now I think the main difference is that everybody tends to write a lot of slow music, not fast music, that things are fluid. They just stand still, and because we listen to Eastern music with Western ears, no matter where we live, this is what gives us some kind of tension. This is one of the ways to create tension—things stand still and don't move, just creation of atmosphere and then it doesn't go anywhere. And this is one of the means—music that is in a way undirectional— that has as a general feature a certain atmosphere. And, of course, it starts from Debussy, he was very much influenced from the East. But I think the main thing is that music can be artistic, abstract, and good without marking time. *From the Book of the Dead* has meter and

255

pulse, but there are sections that are without meter. I mean, you need so little to get so much, to gain so much. You could say that both Western and Middle Eastern time senses are there. And in a way, it was always there. It's such an easy solution. You can create music, and be so simple at the same time. And, of course, this is the whole secret, if one can be simple and get the message across at the same time, that's quite an achievement. In a way Schoenberg was simplistic. Boulez didn't like that at all, of course. He was simplistic, and he used very well defined rhythms and meters, and rhythmic gestures. You know, he used good old Brahms.

I don't know how to characterize my work in the context of Israeli music. I was absent for years, I'm not familiar at all. I didn't hear much yet here in Israel. I'm familiar with Nami's [Yinam Leef's] music and Ari Ben-Shabetai's music. I'm familiar with most of Kopytman's music. As a student, his work was quite influential. It gave me some kind of easy way out in tough times. But later on, it's not, I would say. But his approach to the whole thing of composition is very influential, the way composition becomes research. But it's not his way, it's Schäffer's way, Bogusław Schäffer. He has a book that is called *The Fundamentals of Composition*. But the thing about it is that composition is research, and when you're going to write a piece, you first do the research about the medium, about the sound.

And I really do that. I go and listen to other people's pieces, I look at scores, which are in the same, or even a different medium, but which have something in common. And it's a whole process. Maybe I'll write two pieces before, two small pieces, and then a big piece that incorporates them. My big piece that incorporates everything I studied, up to date, *Leaden Sky*, wasn't performed yet. And I don't believe it will be, because it's a huge piece—orchestra, choir, and so forth. I hope it will get performed. It's also a vocal piece for choir, and because it's for choir one has to be very careful with what he does. Otherwise, it's messy. You have to compromise something, some technical aspect. And I'm very curious to hear it, I mean, to see if it works. But it needs three choirs, three of the good Israeli choirs to be put together, and then a large orchestra and some soloists. And the issue is, of course, the Holocaust. There was one of the ghettos, one of the concentration camps, it was at Theresienstadt [Terezín], and it was an example—the Germans held it as an example for the Red Cross and visitors. So people there, they had orchestras, they had culture, the children studied in classes with the best teachers that they could find, very good teachers. And there

256

are paintings that were left, and poems by children, one very famous poem—I know at least three composers who wrote pieces on poems by those children—"I never saw another butterfly."

So I chose four other poems and I wrote some kind of Mahleresque symphony, but not really, not exactly that. It's a symphony, it's a vocal symphony, not a song cycle or an oratorio. It has four movements, well defined. This piece as well incorporates a brass quintet that I wrote as a preparation for the big piece, so I could deal with brass. I remember consulting with George Crumb and with Wernick. I had to submit a portfolio for the master's at Penn.

I wrote a string trio, a song cycle, and an orchestra piece that was recorded by the Jerusalem Symphony, a large ensemble. And then the only thing that was left for the major piece, the doctoral piece, was something with brass. They wanted me to write something for solo flute, a solo instrument, in order to complete the portfolio. So I asked if I could write for a brass quintet and they said it's OK, because brass was the last section I had to deal with.

And I wrote a brass quintet and Wernick performed it. And I heard the performance, and it was fine, it was good. So I could start a big work. And it has everything in it, almost. It doesn't have quotations, but the techniques. And in the quintet I tried everything. I believe that every piece by a composer should have at least a big portion— I don't want to talk in numbers—that is experimental, that he tries something new, for himself. Yes, each work is a study. No work is a work, it's an exercise. Each work is an exercise. If it works and it becomes a work of art—fine, we're lucky.

The most important thing is to see whether you can do certain things. And then you see if you can do it, and it will help sometime in the future. But that's the reason I don't feel that I'm writing for eternity. Some people do. I don't feel that way. Every work is an experiment. Not entirely, of course—it has to sound, it has to be nice. You have to like it. But it's not, in other words, a masterpiece. I don't have sentiments to the notes, I can change things, after the third performance. If at a particular performance, for the flutist, some passages don't suit him, and it's difficult, I can change it, no problem. But what is important, and I don't change, is the general feeling, and the atmosphere, and then the content. This I cannot change.

For me, vocal music has become more important lately, artistically, I felt that it's time to write some vocal pieces. Until then, I wrote only instrumental pieces. I wrote some here and there, but I felt it's time to write a choir piece, some choir pieces. I am feeling now that I have to write for choir a cappella, songs. And for voice and piano, just songs—good, nice music that's good to hear.

And then I'll go again to instrumental music. I feel that somebody who writes vocal music, good for choir, when he goes back to instrumental music, it's different, it'll come differently. Vocal music is the kind of music that in some way exposes you. You can't hide behind many things, and it poses problems—it's the raw bones, whether or not you can sing. It's like the moment of truth.

Schoenberg, for instance, didn't write a lot for voice, although his idea for the voice of God in *Moses und Aron,* it's a beautiful idea. It's very powerful. I think the most powerful of Schoenberg's pieces are *A Survivor from Warsaw* and *Pierrot lunaire.* I made an homage to Schoenberg in the piece that I dedicated to Penn. It ends with the beginning of *Pierrot lunaire,* the piano motive, and then it stops.

And in *From the Book of the Dead,* for instance, I gave an homage to George Crumb, a very slow thing where the vibes have to do this note bending. But they didn't know how to do it, the guy didn't remember that you press the key with one mallet while striking it with the other. I have a recording from Penn, and it works. It strikes out, it stands out. And then in another piece, in the brass quintet, there is a place that, if I remember correctly, I did an homage to Wernick, a little motive from *Visions of Terror and Wonder,* that's his big piece.

I just came back and it's the first year here, and all I did, until now—I wrote three pieces for guitar. It's like therapy. A big piece that I'm planning to do, I haven't decided yet. And I'm now preparing a piece, a former piece of mine, and I'm making some minor changes, I hope for the Israel Sinfonietta Beer Sheva. It's an essay for orchestra, my first orchestra piece. It's dodecaphonic, and uses heterophony. It was performed once, by the Israel Chamber Ensemble in Tel Aviv, but that was six years ago, before I went to the States. That was my graduation piece from here.

The use of heterophony is the result of Kopytman's influence, but I don't use it that much anymore. I think it's a big thing, heterophony, but I used to use proportional notation and all that. Now I don't use it very much. I like everything to be in a strict, clear meter, even though it will not sound so. I use proportional notation only if something has to be repeated constantly.

In a 1991 letter, Permont described the experience of living through the Gulf War:

In particular, our neighborhood was hit by Iraqi missiles—although our house suffered no damage. Sadly enough, I am quite used to it—as I am from the very upper Galilee, where we have been shelled by the P.L.O. from Lebanon many times in the past (don't make any mistakes—one gets scared stiff when the siren goes on and everybody rushes to the "sealed" room to put on their gas-masks, while trying to comfort the little children and stop the big ones from running outside to watch the scuds fall and the Patriots chasing them). Apart from all this I also had to spend my annual 4-days reserve duty up north (thank God—not in the *intifada*), and did my best for the rest of the time to stay out of trouble and teach at the Rubin Academy.[1]

Haim Permont has since completed works commissioned by the Kibbutz Chamber Orchestra, the First International Guitar Festival in Chile, Musica Nova, the Rehovot Chamber Orchestra, the Kibbutz Artzi choir, and the Haifa Symphony Orchestra. His melodrama for piano four hands, string quartet, and narrator, *The Scroll of Fire* (text by Bialik), composed for the fortieth anniversary of the state of Israel, was performed by the Jerusalem Soloists' Ensemble at the Kfar Bloom summer chamber music festival. In 1993, Permont's works were performed by the National Choir Rinat and the Israel Philharmonic Orchestra, among other ensembles. His *Fantasy* for solo voice and children's choir (text by Lea Goldberg) was performed several times in Germany. During a tour of several Latin American countries, composer-guitarist Daniel Akiva performed Permont's *Para Guitarra*. Permont also received the ACUM prize in 1993 for his composition *Leaden Sky* (1985; rev. 1992), based on poems by children at the Theresienstadt (Terezín) concentration camp.[2] In 1994 the Har-Oz Duo performed his *Movements and Pauses*, for harp and trombone, in Washington, D.C., and Permont received "special mention from ACUM for the year's best achievement in the field of concert music."[3]

In 1995, Haim Permont received a commission from the New Israeli Opera and was one of three composers awarded the Prime Minister's Prize. He is a senior lecturer at the Jerusalem Rubin Academy of Music and Dance and has served as chair of the faculty of composition, conducting, and music education.[4]

Yinam Leef, photographed by Yoram Lehmann. Used with permission.

17

YINAM LEEF

Yinam Leef was the first of several Jerusalem Rubin Academy graduates to pursue graduate degrees in composition at the University of Pennsylvania, where he studied with Richard Wernick, George Rochberg, and George Crumb. Leef was a composition fellow at the Johnson Composers Conference in Vermont and the Yale Composers Seminar at Norfolk. He is the recipient of numerous prizes and awards, including America-Israel Cultural Foundation scholarships, a CBS Foundation fellowship, a Margaret Lee Crofts fellowship at Tanglewood (where he studied with Luciano Berio), and a resident fellowship at the MacDowell Colony in Peterborough, New Hampshire. His works have been performed in Israel, Europe, the United States, and the Far East. Leef's *A Place of Fire* (1985) was performed in Jerusalem during my visit, as part of the 1986 Israel Festival.

I interviewed Yinam Leef on June 29, 1986, at Mishkenot Sha'ananim.

———

I was born in Jerusalem in December of 1953. It was a musical home, and we always had music in the house. My mother was a vocal teacher, so one of my first memories is that I am falling asleep during one of the lessons of some tenor or baritone singing Leporello's aria or the stuff from *Così fan tutte,* and the like. Also Schoenberg, I have to say. She was a very good teacher. There was lots of chamber music in the house, and my father also played the violin. I studied piano for many years and violin for two years, but my first dealings with composition were in a different idiom.

I began playing jazz when I was about fourteen or fifteen and I was playing in a group. We toured many kibbutzim. We did lots of arrangements of quasi-exotic tunes. When I listen to some of the tapes, it's a joke. But as I look back, it was an important introduction to music making. So, apart from playing all kinds of jazz standards, I was actually composing little pieces, also jazz. It kept me in touch with harmony, very rigorously and closely.

During my military service, I started to study at the Rubin Academy. I was in my third year in the army and I was stationed in Jerusalem, so I was able to do it. Normally, Israelis lose a minimum of three years in the service before attending college, so I gained one year, starting to study when I was twenty rather than twenty-one. In a very funny way, I was in a position where I had some free time during my service, and I said, "OK, I'm going to the Academy, and I'm going to study music." Not because I thought I wanted to be a musician. I come from a typical Jewish family, where when you say you are a musician, people would say, "And what do you do for a living?" It's demoralizing, that sort of negative attitude that I really had to fight, even though my mother was a musician. But I said to myself, "I'm going to do it," because I wanted to know more about harmony, counterpoint, orchestration, and all that.

At that time, I didn't think about serious composition so much. But I felt I would never forgive myself for the rest of my life if I didn't do it. And, you know, the appetite came with the food— *l'appétit viens en mangeant*. And then it was very clear. I was doing very well at the Academy, and before the third year I had to choose between conducting and composition. I chose composition, to the disappointment of the conducting faculty member, who was Mendi Rodan. He thought I would go for conducting, but I just didn't. I chose composition, although I do conduct. I decided I wanted to go for the real thing. I started to write, and I started to write like hell during the third and fourth year—just writing one piece after another, three or four pieces a year.

My composition teacher was Kopytman, and my harmony and counterpoint teacher was Yizhak Sadai. Although Sadai was not teaching composition, by writing fugues and other style studies I learned a lot from him, too. And Kopytman, of course, was a very good teacher, he kept you going. He's very much admired and respected, and I share this feeling. I think that like every other teacher, nobody knows all the truth. Everybody knows the truth, nothing but the truth, but not all of it. And I think I learned a lot from him, as many people might say about the person who actually had introduced them into the world of composing. Here it is different from in the U.S, not only with composers, but also with voice or piano teachers. You know, some teachers can get very possessive about the students. I think that Kopytman set up a good program to begin with, very gradual, and it depends on the students also. But he was so much involved, that's one of the great things about it.

Kopytman would really get involved. It's very good, but it's also a lot of pressure. You know, I think that the pleasing of the teacher is wrong. I don't know if it's the case with Kopytman. Maybe there are some people who should never be composers, but they just went on because the pressure from the teachers was too great to resist. I have to say that, actually, when I arrived at the University of Pennsylvania I discovered, or acknowledged, that the kind of education here at Rubin was really very good. Maybe because it's a conservatory and not a university. I think that this is an asset.

In the U.S., some composition study is done in classes, and that's because you have to take lots of liberal arts, and that's understandable and definitely has its advantages. Because students at the Academy might end up lacking in other aspects of life, in terms of general knowledge. Here there are electives, but the attitude toward them is negative. I've taught undergraduates at Penn, and people who were music majors were taking courses in chemistry, for example, to get their brain juices going. So you get a spectrum of interests that you really don't find here, or only on very, very rare occasions.

Anyway, during the years I was here, I also continued to work as a freelancer, as a pianist and accompanist, to make a living. And I also had a children's show on Israeli television for two years, once every two weeks. We called it *Musical Chairs*. It was kind of semi-educational. So I was editing it, working on the production, and I was the host. It was a lot of fun. Two other friends were helping me with the research, and we drove all over the country looking for young ensembles in all the conservatories.

We would bring them to the studio, and this was a place that looked very homey. And we'd sit there and talk very superficially, and there would be a little classical music, a little bit of this and that. It was very nice to be in touch with kids who really tried to play. I didn't see anything on American television that was similar to that. The only context for bringing classical music was *Sesame Street,* which was nice, but that was it. But anyway, this was one more thing that I did while I was at the Academy, earning my artist's diploma, after the bachelor's degree.

I went to Penn in 1979, but I was a little bit resistant to go abroad. I remember saying, "No, I'm feeling OK here," but many teachers were encouraging me to go. I was the first of several students to go from here, and actually, I didn't consider Penn at first, because I didn't know about it. I applied to other places, including Eastman, because I knew Samuel Adler. He was here a few times, and I met him and he looked at my music. And I applied to other places as well, where people I knew had gone. Kopytman went to the U.S. during that year, went to Penn and met Richard Wernick. I knew some of George Crumb's music, but I didn't know Rochberg's, I had never heard his work. His music wasn't played here, and there were no records or scores available. And then I met with Jehoash Hirshberg. Kopytman could tell me about Wernick and about Crumb, and Hirshberg told me about the department in general, since he had done his Ph.D. there in musicology. And it sounded very attractive.

What I liked very much was the fact that you could rotate between the teachers. And that the program was quite rigid, yet very interesting, because you had a bunch of people there, the composers on the one hand, and then someone like Leonard Meyer on the other, an interdisciplinary person. So I applied, and finally that's the place that gave me a fellowship. You know what they say—you end up going to the place that gives you the most money. It sounds awful, but if you end up having to have three part-time jobs just to pay for your studies, you end up not composing at all.

I don't think I opened up a door, I don't know. I'm not going to take this responsibility myself. I was the first one to go there, I did well, I think that they respected my work. Then Haim Permont came, while I was still there. I think it also stemmed from the very warm relationship that had developed between Kopytman and Wernick and the other people there. And between Jehoash and Norman Smith, Gene Narmour, and others there. But I think there might be something dangerous in it for too many people go to the same place, although the place is very diverse and they have many approaches there. Because if all these people end up coming back and teaching at the Rubin Academy, or in other institutions in Israel, we're going to end up with an inbreeding. I mean Penn is a diverse place, you have people coming from many backgrounds. It's not a place for a guru and disciples. You have people who are taking analysis, theory, and composition, so it is pluralistic. But maybe it's good that we would have here in the future somebody who went to Yale, and somebody who went to Chicago.

Being an Israeli composer, I think, has positive and negative aspects, and I think it has certain objective aspects: the fact that I was born in Israel and my native tongue is Hebrew. This is what it means for me, that I am an Israeli. That I was born and raised here, and that's why I am an Israeli composer. That's the objective aspect of it. Just as a Finnish composer, a Swiss composer, a British composer, an Illinois composer, or an Atlanta composer. I think the negative aspect of it is that perhaps various things are attached to it that might not be there, or might imply things that don't necessarily have to go hand in hand with the definition. Because when we say a Finnish composer or a Swiss composer, it's just somebody's nationality. When we say an American composer, it doesn't mean anything, really, as far as the music goes. It means that somebody lives in America and works in America and is part of the artistic life in that particular place. But I think that as far as "Israeli composer"—certain musical values are maybe attached to it, or implied. Maybe they have to be there, and if they are not—it's part of our heritage as Israelis that we always have to carry some additional burden, something. I know that you approach it very objectively, but I'm faced with a question that is loaded with other meanings. And I really don't know if I can give what many people think an Israeli artist should or should not have.

I read an article a few years ago in a periodical called *Ariel*, which in English is called *Arts in Israel*. They had sort of a semi–art history, but more like a gossipy, article about the early thirties and the kind of struggles they had here between artists that were here since the twenties—the painters in Israel who founded Bezalel School, who came mainly from Poland, and the people who came here in the 1930s, after the Nuremburg laws, from Germany. Those who came from Germany were more influenced by German expressionism and were much more abstract, and there was a struggle here about—"What does it mean to be an artist in Israel? It has to mean something else." And in the whole period of the thirties and forties, and into the fifties, I think, in music also, the idea was to create a folklore. Then the second generation includes people like Tzvi Avni. Well, we're in a different position. I think we're in a position to benefit from being sort of the third generation of Israeli composers, that is to say, composers who were born here. I think that the decision to use any kind of folklorist elements is purely optional and highly personal.

I don't know if he would like what I'm saying or not, but I think Kopytman was, is still, similar to the Mediterranean school in concept—not in sound, of course, but in principle. Because he came from the Diaspora and tries to find roots. And I think that people who grew up here, the second generation, looked more westward, and I would say that these are the people who rebelled against the Mediterranean school. Electronic music, serialism—just look at Josef Tal, for example.

I think maybe my generation is less complex. Maybe we don't have to have the complex of feeling the responsibility to create something that belongs to here, because it was done already. We're one step further from this. And then not being ashamed, or not having to feel any guilt by taking from things that don't belong here in a sense. My God, you know, I'm talking, I'm hearing—it's the same kind of very typical apologetic attitude that we're so used to, you know what I mean? My training was definitely Western, I mean I was playing jazz. I used some reminiscences of quasi-folklore. What it is I don't know, I can't point it out. Well, the way I tend to rationalize these is that we all look for tunes or for some kind of pitch combinations that could mean something to us, and for me they are already taken out of context and become more abstract. I think they might seem more characteristic or more exotic to, let's say, American ears or audiences other than Israeli audiences, for example. Yes, I guess I do, I guess I try. I don't want to make generalizations, but I see it with some of my colleagues who are the same age. We may be trying to combine—not like Ben-Haim, who was in a way forcing Russian-German techniques on modal tunes, which is a highly stylized attitude toward folklore. Because he eliminated all the fine nuances of quarter tones.

The thing that really interests me is that what characterizes non-Western music cultures is the linear development, not a vertical approach toward music. What characterizes Western development is the vertical. Maybe I try in my music to find a combination, to use some material—some and *not* always—as a window into the past, and to try to find a combination—some kind of a modus vivendi, if you like—of a kind of melos like that, but with a highly controlled

266

approach to harmony. And this is something that I did learn mostly in America, I would say.

I think that I did learn how to control things vertically at Penn. I was harmonically oriented before, but it helped. My aesthetic did not really change, I think it solidified. If I look at people with whom I studied, I may explain this better: from Crumb, I learned about color and timing; from Wernick, controlling vertical entities, how to manipulate, how to really try to find a substitute for dominant/tonic relationships, and to have a feeling that besides the development and the gradual unfolding of material, there are really levels of importance, in terms of harmony.

The idea of a dissonance, for example—to hear, even with what is called, unjustifiably, but still called, an "atonal" idiom—that you really can get some kind of hierarchy going, a sense of a progression, resolution, something like that. To really look more deeply. And from Rochberg, although we had really great heated discussions about language and style, what I learned was to look ahead, and to plan, and to think formally on a large scale. In that sense, I think, I'm a Western-educated traditionalist, I would say.

I think Middle Eastern materials do appear quite consistently in a few pieces that I've written lately, the last four or five years. I have another song cycle, *The Invisible Carmel* [text: Zelda], the last song has a long English horn passage. And in my Violin Concerto, in the third movement—a theme and variations—the theme is a similar, long melody that also has small intervals and the sense of repetition.

If we really are to analyze the component of Middle Eastern material in this melting pot—Arabic, Yemenite—it is small intervals, repetition, very ornamented grace notes and a sort of weaving through the notes, and a slow pace. These are things that I think have absolute music values. Why is the so-called Polish school so accepted in Israel? Because they also deal with small intervals, microtones, repetition of elements. Their music is very influential—it speaks. There is a kind of a common bond, things that are shared—not mainly with the pitches, you know. Also with some of the Italian avant-garde—Berio, Donatoni, and others whose works also appeal to Israeli audiences and composers. Actually, it's the oriental approach to time, a non-Western approach to time. I don't go for that, particularly. Look, I know that in America, for example, some composers were looking for some roots—for some kind of exoticism, going for Indian folklore, the use of non-Western, Japanese, Chinese elements—looking for some kind of identity, something fresh. Israelis maybe have to carry the burden of having something to give in that respect.

———

Yinam Leef's music was chosen to represent Israel in international music festivals held in 1986 (Pittsburgh), 1988 (ISCM/Hong Kong), and 1990 (Oslo). His music has also been performed in Israel, Germany, Spain, Czechoslovakia, Poland, and Russia. Leef received the Israel Composers' League Prize for his a cappella choral work *Sounds, Shadows* . . . (1987), a citation of honor from the city of Haifa (1991) for *A Place of Fire* (1985), and the 1992 ACUM Prize for Publication for his Violin Concerto (1992). Leef was one of three recipients of the Prime Minister's Prize in 1993. The jury responsible for selecting the recipients wrote that Leef "draws from the best of all worlds—the cultural diversity of Israel, the schools imported from Europe, and his teachers in the United States."[1] In 1994, Leef's Symphony No. 1 was performed in a live broadcast by the Jerusalem Symphony Orchestra, and his *Scherzos and Serenades* was performed by the Israel Philharmonic Orchestra.[2] His *Visions of Stone City* (Symphony No. 2), commissioned by the Jerusalem Symphony Orchestra to celebrate "Jerusalem 3000," was premiered in 1995 under the baton of music director David Shallon.

Yinam Leef is a senior lecturer at the Jerusalem Rubin Academy of Music and Dance, and was named chair of the department of composition, conducting, and theory in 1995. He has also served for several years as a music consultant to the Israel Museum in Jerusalem, and as a member of the Public Council of Culture and Art. Since 1990, Leef has been a member of the Israel Composers' League Council and has taught at the Wizo High School for the Arts, in Haifa.[3]

Betty Olivero, photographed by Raffaello Majoni. Used with permission.

18

BETTY OLIVERO

Like other native Israeli composers, Betty Olivero received her early musical training in Israel. She later studied at Yale University. In 1982, Olivero received the Leonard Bernstein Fellowship at Tanglewood, where her teacher was Luciano Berio, with whom she continued to study in Italy through 1986. The same year, Olivero was awarded a Fromm Music Foundation commission.

Betty Olivero's music bears the imprint not only of her Jewish and Israeli upbringing, but also of Ladino, the language of her Sephardic ancestry, which she has set in several compositions.[1] In addition to the tradition of Western art music, Olivero finds "an infinite wealth of inspiration and source of enrichment in the music of the various Jewish communities," which provide her with "a dramatic stimulus." Rather than being quoted in their original form, these elements "undergo a thorough transformation, so profound as to make their original form unrecognizable yet their spirit and dramatic potential remain untouched." In describing her work, Olivero distinguishes between compositional process and materials: "I perceive my composition as a natural continuation of the music of the past. The process of composition is quite conventional and adheres to traditional techniques (counterpoint, harmonic and structural thought), but the material I use and the content of my work are contemporary. They are inspired, in the main, by my search for new sources of colour and by a different morphology of melody."[2]

I interviewed Betty Olivero on June 29, 1986, at Mishkenot Sha'ananim. Only a couple of months before our meeting, the New York Philharmonic performed her *Cantes Amargos* (*Songs of Bitterness*) during its New Horizons Festival. I was impressed with the evocative power of the recorded works Ms. Olivero played for me on that occasion, and by her colorful use of orchestration.

———

I was born in 1954 in Israel. I attended a music conservatory, where I received very elementary music training, music education plus private lessons that I took with a composer here for many years. I started writing music at a very early age, so I was referred to Yizhak Sadai, with whom I was working for about ten years on composition. He also introduced me to counterpoint. I did something like eight years of Palestrina counterpoint, harmony, Bach chorales, and so on. Yizhak Sadai is a fantastic musician and a great melodist. Later, in the Tel Aviv Academy, all of us were introduced to music at a very, very high level of craft. However, we were not introduced to music from an academic point of view. When I came to the States I was amazed at how untrained I was about writing papers, research, and all that. Sadai taught me theory and composition. I also studied with León Schidlowsky, a Chilean composer who immigrated to Israel. With him I did composition at the undergraduate level; with Sadai I mainly studied theory and harmony.

Then it was very complementary to come to the States and get the other, academic side. At Yale I studied with Jacob Druckman and Gilbert Amy, and for a while with Morton Subotnick and Earle Brown, who were visiting there. When I finished school I went to Tanglewood, and there I met Luciano Berio, who invited me to come to Italy to work with him. This was the summer of 1982. That summer I decided I must come back to Jerusalem for one year. I had to do that because I felt I was too far away from my own place. And I stayed here for one year, just composing and doing small jobs to maintain myself.

Then came this grant from the Italian government together with some commissions. At that time Berio was the artistic director of the Maggio Musicale, a big festival there. I was commissioned to do a piece, a big project that we did and we performed there, so it was like a job in Italy for one year plus a grant. I worked very well with Berio, he

272

was very helpful. And so I decided to stay, learn some more. I've been there almost three years. By now I really don't study with him. The first year was mostly like that, but by now I just meet him whenever he can and I show him whatever I do, and he might have some kind of criticism mostly, not really teaching. But it has been very good.

The piece that was just performed at the New Horizons Festival by the New York Philharmonic was the piece that was commissioned by the Maggio Musicale.[3] In fact, this was a piece that I had already started at Yale. I set to music texts in Ladino, which is the language of my parents, of my Spanish heritage. I collected lots of small bits of Ladino verses, from Ladino romances. I put them together and I wrote a first movement, and then the commission from Italy was in fact an extension of that first movement and became a trilogy of three movements connected to each other. And so it was performed at the New Horizons festival in New York, with mezzo-soprano Kim Wheeler, and Oliver Knussen conducted it. We didn't have much rehearsal time, but they are so good. It was strange, you know, I felt they could sight-read the piece. They are so good and they are so precise and everything is in place. But I felt there was a cultural gap that it wasn't possible to overcome in such little rehearsal time— or maybe it would never be possible to overcome. The singer was not such a problem, because I knew her for a long time and we could work together. But the orchestra was not as involved as the experience I had in Italy where Berio also conducted, I think because of cultural things. It was like there was something about this music that was much more near to people who come from Italy, from the Mediterranean, naturally. If you hear the piece you will understand immediately, but to put it in words, it's like there is a lot of oriental music in it. It's not quotation, there is nothing quoted there. It's just there, you know— where it comes from. It's not modes. It is very ornamented and it has the air of the Orient.

I felt they could play the notes and even played very musically, but the spirit was like a little bit untouched. They did it really very nicely and elegantly, but there was not this thing that I found in the performances in Italy. It was a very good experience because I'd never faced it before. It was like I always felt that what I'm writing is really perceivable immediately, naturally, and there it wasn't like that. There was so little time, and I didn't feel that I wanted to start talking. It wasn't very wise to do, and I don't think it would have good results.

But I think that if I would have to describe Israeli music today, I would say there is a lot of that in it. We all got a very Western training to start with. In our formal education we were never, never exposed to oriental music, not even on a formal level. We studied everything in the Western history of music. But the thing is that in the streets and all around us, some were more attracted or less attracted, but it was a reality that we were just there, you know. It's in the air, so it penetrated, at least in me, and I see it in lots of Israeli composers. It penetrates and it comes out in the music. On the other hand, in early works of composers who were here even before 1948, they consciously wanted to reflect oriental motives in their music. I mean there you feel a very academic and conscious effort. Somebody like Yehezkel Braun, you find it in his music, there you feel more of a conscious orientation. So it's very interesting.

I think the younger generation, at an early stage—we rebelled against it because we found in it something very pioneering, and somewhat artificial, and we were kind of saying, "Now we are part of this country, and we are not pioneers, ḥalutzim." As far as I am concerned, I wanted to be what I am without trying to do anything. When I came to the States, I realized that it's coming out, without even trying. It's like it is my personal touch, and need, not an academic or scientific way of working. You heard Yinam Leef's songs. There is a passage that is very conscious, kind of a Turkish melody. It's like a metaphor.

I feel I come from here, my music very much reflects the music that is going on here, very much so. It's like a crossroad of oriental music and Western music. Once Luciano Berio was giving a lecture somewhere, and it was before a concert where a piece of mine was performed, and he put it in a very funny way. And afterward he said, "Excuse me for putting it in such a simplistic way," because he was saying that somewhere my music symbolizes a peace, a wishful peace situation between the Arab world and the Jewish world, which is like the Western world. And it was simplifying, but I didn't have to forgive him because that was a very nice way of putting it, and very true. Of course, I wasn't conscious about that—I mean, I didn't mean to convey any political or nationalistic message, but I did feel this piece, and many other pieces of mine which I wrote later, manifested a mixture of cultures. Jewish music in itself is a mixture of so many cultures if you really think about it. Hasidic music—all kinds of Hasidic tunes, if you really listen—has Gypsy music elements in it, and at the same

274

time very oriental motives. These motives, as you were just saying, are oriental in a way, but it's also very Jewish.

I wouldn't be able to do it if I felt I was obliged to. I'll tell you, really, there was not a moment of choice or conscious decision when I started writing this particular music. I think there was a process of really finding that that's what I want to do, that that's what is really the music that I have inside me. Otherwise I don't see any other reason to compose. If I have to compose just from what I've learned, I don't see any reason in writing any music. But if it is to bring out something that I have inside me, the real thing, then I should do that.

It is very hard to describe, but I could, for instance, say that the thought of building up a piece of music—development, the whole conception of form—is very Western. I mean writing music in time, the conception and the way I realize it, is very Western. Maybe the time concept is Western, but it's a very complicated issue. Because content is not separable from the time conception. In general, I would say that the thought of the form and the development, or way of making decisions, is in a completely Western terminology, and the precise notation. At the same time, the harmony, the melody, the colors, the timbre—are derived from oriental music that I was surrounded by. I use a lot of heterophonic textures. I think Kopytman got it from the music that we have here. That's why you will meet a lot of people who use this and were not pupils of Kopytman, along with the use of quarter tones, ornaments, and so on. I don't mean any specific music. It's enough to walk through the Old City in Jerusalem.

I remember once on a very hot summer night, I walked with a friend somewhere around three o'clock in the morning and it was already almost sunrise, during the peak of the summer. And we went just above the Old City at a point above the quarter, the Wailing Wall. And there was a moment where from the left you heard the muezzin, when they start calling for prayer. From the other side we started hearing the voices of Jewish prayers starting to come from the quarter. This was just before Rosh Hashanah. They have a month of morning prayer, and you could clearly hear their voices. I heard the voices of the town, that is, just the animals around and the bells from the churches. All this together—that's heterophonic music, in a way, for me.

I don't think I even want to define or classify my work in the context of Israeli music. I don't yet have the perspective even of time. I feel also I'm not yet introduced in the musical scene here in Israel because I've been away for so many years, and maybe somebody else can do it. I am familiar with what the young people are writing here, but we don't have this personal exchange with the other generations as well, unfortunately.

My *Cantes Amargos* are based on three Ladino texts.[4] The second one says, "Very bitter songs I want to sing on the border of the sea. In the sea there was a tower. On top of the tower there was a window, and in the window there was a dove. Give me your hand, my dove." And the last one says, "Oh, Mama, I have never seen a bird with such green eyes! The keys to my palace were lost in foreign seas." You can think of many things, biblical symbols if you like, as well. In the Song of Songs there appears similar motives of the dove, representing beauty, for instance. These are excerpts from different Ladino verses that were orally transmitted from generation to generation. I just took quotations, different lines, and put them together into a structure of poetry that I thought was proper. So these verses serve like quotations. We all know them by heart because they were set to music with many different melodies, and we are very familiar with them. Some of them I knew as songs, as popular songs, some of them I just found in different anthologies. And so I thought it was nice just to take such well-known phrases from different poems and compose them into new poetry. No traditional melodies are quoted at all.

The thing that attracted me in these texts is that they carry within themselves a lot of history. They seem very naive and very beautiful, but since they were carried with the years, through history up to today, they also carry with them all the events that happened to the people who sang them. In the melodies you find there's a lot of pain, but with kind of a dreamy nostalgia—like the pain was transformed in dream, into something very different. But for somebody who doesn't know anything about it and just reads the text, it seems something very simplistic. I wanted to set it to music to give that other dimension. On one level, it is just very romantic verse—the usual romantic symbol of anything far away, beyond the sea, beyond the mountains. On a deeper layer, the last verse, where it says "the keys to my palace were lost in foreign water,"[5] for me it is like a descriptive metaphor of the Diaspora, of the loss of something very old, and something that we owned, and we just lost it in foreign water (ex. 19).

There are some places where the text is very literally portrayed in the music. I was told this by many people, but I honestly did not think about it at the time. It was absolutely not a conscious choice. It

276

Ex. 19

was a complete musical thought behind it but no illustration of the text, and I agree with you, because I hear that. I really did not do it consciously, it's interesting.

I found in that text, which is apparently so idyllic and peaceful, a lot of powerful moments, almost tragic. And I wanted to give the notion of that other side of it, like enlarging the meaning of it. Like opening the door into something that was there, that this text was carrying with it—that is covered, is unseen, is like a secret inside, beyond these symbols.

The title of my contrabass solo is *Batnún,* which is the Hebrew word for a very old stringed instrument. Mainly, today, it is the Hebrew word for double bass, but it's a very old word, not used at all in daily spoken Hebrew.

I used to write vocal music when I was a student. I wouldn't present these pieces anymore. They are more experimental for myself. Lately I just finished a piece for ten instruments that was commissioned by the Fromm Foundation. And I wrote a piece for twelve cellos and four double basses. It's called *Psalms*—in Hebrew, *Tehillim.* And I'm going to write now a piece for violin and piano that was commissioned by the first violinist of the Maggio Musicale Orchestra.

It's hard, it's very stressful. But here I would have to work very hard teaching. It's not like in America where you can live from grant to grant, year after year. That's the impression I got meeting with young composers who really would jump from one grant to another. Here it is very hard to find any teaching jobs as well.

We're not so few, women composers in Israel. It's not an issue to me, never. It started being an issue when people started asking me about that. Then I thought, maybe there's something about it, but I must say I've never felt there's any particular thing about being a woman composer—never, ever. I never had any problems about it from the people I had to work with. In fact, maybe, in my case anyway, this drew attention to my music a little bit more. That's true, because people are not used to it. We were just at the Women's Music Festival in Beer Sheva and I heard all kinds of complaints and claims about how discriminated against we are, but I don't believe it. I think it is self-indulgence. I think it's an excuse for many for not admitting certain things.

I don't think we are discriminated against in the contemporary music scene. I think contemporary music is discriminated against, and any male composer has exactly the same problems as we do. I really don't agree with that view. And the reason why I went to Beer Sheva to participate in this panel discussion is not because I identify with the ideas of the festival, but to be able to tell what I think about it, because I thought it was important. I do think that women should get some help. The problem we have is practical, because if I wanted to have children I would have an extra job. I would have to write music and take care of a family at the same time. So if we need to get help, it's not after we write our music, and to be promoted by different conductors, who would say, "Oh, women have to be promoted, so we will perform them more," because I don't think we have a problem there.

But the problem we have is that on a practical level, we have a lot of extra nonmusical work to do, which is time-consuming. I have the privilege to be able to write music. I mean, it's hard on us financially, but we chose to do that. So I think if I were by myself, I'd have to look for a stable teaching job. I would like to teach at a certain point, not now.

I don't know how long I'll stay in Italy, I hope not too long. As long as I can come here so often and I have this possibility, it doesn't really matter. I can come here whenever I like and work here. I have a home here and I have a home there.

———

Betty Olivero's music has been performed by the Juilliard Ensemble, the Chicago Symphony Orchestra, the Israel Philharmonic

Orchestra, the Royal Stockholm Philharmonic, the Berlin Radio Symphony Orchestra, the Munich Philharmonic, the Cologne Radio Symphony Orchestra, and the London Sinfonietta, and in such festivals as the Isem World Music Days 1994 (Stockholm), the Maggio Musicale Fiorentino (Florence), the Aspen Music Festival, the Gaudeamus Music Week (Amsterdam), and the Israel Festival.[6]

Ari Ben-Shabetai, photographed (1994) by Liora Ziv-Li. Used with permission.

19

ARI BEN-SHABETAI

Ari Ben-Shabetai is one of several graduates of the Jerusalem Rubin Academy of Music and Dance to have furthered his studies in composition at the University of Pennsylvania. I interviewed Ari Ben-Shabetai on June 15, 1986, and heard a recording of his *Harps and Horns: Five Love Songs from Egyptian Antiquity* (1985) at the Jerusalem Rubin Academy of Music and Dance.[1]

I was born in 1954 in Jerusalem, on January 22. I went to the army for six years—that was three compulsory years, and then three I signed on for—after which I went to London, at the age of twenty-four. I needed a break, and I took a one-year course at the Guildhall School of Music [and Drama]. This was specifically in composition, nothing else—various courses in composition, in writing for chamber groups, all sorts of aesthetics seminars, things like that. I was taking it as a trial sort of thing to see if I could be a composer or not. I wrote a few pieces during that year. This was just to see whether I wanted to be a composer, and I got out and said, "Yes, I do want to be one." So I enrolled at the Rubin Academy when I got back from London.

I had things that I had written. I studied piano, violin, various instruments as a child. I was brought up in a musical home, there was always music around. What sort of kicked off writing music for me was the Yom Kippur War, really. I was driving a tank at that time, and I was at the Suez Canal. I went through a considerable amount of hell, and it affected me. Looking back, I think that's one of the things that sort of gave the urge. It's not that my music expresses war or anything. It's just that I had to express what I'd gone through in some way, and it came out in music. I wrote several pieces, and looking back now I think they were very naive and very beginner. In London, I got in on the basis of the things I had written without a teacher, just by myself.

Then I came back here, got into the four-year program at the Rubin Academy, and studied with Kopytman, who is an outstanding composer and a really incredible teacher. I have never met a teacher who's that much devoted to his students. He would call me three times a week, four times a week, just to see how I'm doing, and tell me how I did with my harmony exercises and counterpoint, and really devoting individual attention to the students. I don't think anybody in the world does this, I'd be willing to bet on that. He just puts himself all out, it's amazing. And not only that, but he helps you with your career, and gets in touch with the right people in the radio, things like that.

I was about to finish my studies at the Academy and I got an ITT international fellowship that enabled me to study in the States, and I chose the University of Pennsylvania, because of the faculty composers—George Crumb, Richard Wernick, and George Rochberg. Unfortunately, by the time I got there, George Rochberg had retired. I was the third from here to go. Yinam [Leef] and I both went to the same kindergarten, the same school. We went to the same piano teacher as kids. He's one month older than me, one month and a day. We were in the same platoon in the army, sleeping in the same tent. And then when I signed on, he went to the Academy, so he got a few years in front of me. But we also went to Penn together, and it looks like we're going to be teaching at the Academy together. It's something, one and the same story. It's too incredible, but this is Israel, you know, it's very small, and things like that do happen. They just got a license from some sort of higher-education authority in the government to offer a master's degree in music, in composition as well. So they need more people for that, and they need people with Ph.D.s, so that's what made it available. And hopefully, I can tell you now, I'm probably going to come back. I have an offer, and I wanted to come back.

So I went to Penn and I studied with all the teachers there. It was a different mentality, after you're under the guidance of somebody like Kopytman, who's so protective and who just did not hide his compliments from you when he had them. You come to Penn, where you're an equal to other people—who are as good as you or maybe better, or maybe not, but everybody is sort of equal. The mentality is that if you're a student there, you're a student—good or bad. The teachers do not give compliments, even if you do deserve them. That's the situation now, it may have been different before. You're just on your own. You start to feel what it's like to be a composer outside, where you've got to struggle, and that's what they want you to get used to. It's OK, but it takes getting used to. The contrast is very sudden. But you are still going to an individual composition lesson, you bring in music and they tell you what they think.

I think it took time, but it did definitely affect me. I think that the works I came with were somewhat avant-garde for Penn, not for Rubin, and I was being labeled as eclectic and rather extreme. For Israel, I don't think I was particularly avant-garde, for Europe definitely not, and compared with you, what I was doing was like Beethoven. And I had a hard time with that because they didn't seem to accept it so easily. Some of the faculty seemed to object to aleatoric techniques and allowing freedom to play a role in music. So I think as a result, my music became more moderate and my style changed, which produced my song cycle *Harps and Horns,* for example. But that was also written in a sort of a spirit of "Let's have some fun, let's not do all this academic stuff all the time," like using the amplified autoharp with a short digital delay in the fifth song. I actually had to invent a whole new tuning system for the instrument so that it could produce the chords I wanted.

That whole song is an experimental thing, because it was pure coincidence that I heard this Brahms song on the radio, from opus 17. The first song in Brahms's cycle, "The Harp's Full Sound Rings," is scored only for one harp and a horn. The chorus part is this beautiful melody in the sopranos, with the other voices accompanying homophonically. I had four songs written for this cycle, and I was pretty much lost how I would end the whole thing. Suddenly I hear this Brahms song, and it has sopranos, a horn, and a harp, and this was part of the ensemble I was using, and I said, "That's it, that's what I need!" I went and got the music to it, and I decided what I would do would be to manipulate Brahms's tonal material in an atonal manner. In the first half of my song, I present atonal pitch gestures based on the rhythm, articulation, and general context of the

283

Brahms song. For example, the opening arpeggio fanfare call of the horn, with its simple rhythm, is translated into an atonal gesture. And then a short interlude leads to the second half, in which the complete original Brahms song is presented, arranged and adapted for the new ensemble, but interrupted every so often by the metallic autoharp arpeggios clashing against the natural, pure harp arpeggio sound. I changed a few notes of the harmony. And people said, "Why do you present the whole song, why not just a stanza?" And I say, "Why not? It's such a beautiful song—the hell with my music. Brahms is so great!"

I was going through a feeling of resentment of modern music altogether, because I feel that a lot of it is cold—it doesn't warm your heart like the classical masters do. It can, but very rarely does it do that. I do like contemporary music, don't get me wrong, but it's a frustration with the public not appreciating modern music, things like that. I think this is sort of a reactionary piece rather than something that's really me. There's a problem there, in myself. To me, new music is warm, you know. But, for example—what started this was that I went to see *Lulu* at the Metropolitan Opera, and I found that the pieces I liked most were the ones with the warm, romantic orchestration, and I said, "God, that's terrific!" But the other stuff I could do without, and it's made me think. And I think this is one of the things that happened to me in America, more than before—I always had tonal areas in my music, but now I find that I'm really going back to it heavily. I'm writing a cello concerto that has a lot of contemporary techniques of playing—cluster figurations and polytonality, polymodality—but also a lot of heterophony, and things you wouldn't hear in classical works. With that, I tried to base the first movement on sonata form pretty strictly, even with a false recapitulation. But the harmony is always tonal, although it's muffled with atonal notes and things like that. It's some sort of a "statistical" tonality—all twelve tones are there, but statistically the more prominent notes are the ones belonging to a certain diatonic scale or triadic structure. It's like having tonality on a background of atonality.

Heterophony is something that I got from Kopytman. He's definitely very into that technique, and he's approached it in depth in his music. It's more than a technique, it's a way of thinking about music relationships. It's Arabic tradition, essentially, Middle Eastern. I mean, if you look at the oriental or Arab orchestra, you see that they're all playing the same melody, but different bowings, for example—

that is heterophony. The heterophony that I use, or that Kopytman and others in this school here use, is sort of a mixture of what Boulez calls "heterophony of a chord," which he talks about in *On Music Today*, and also things that we hear in music here. Like in the synagogues, people will sing a song, and because they're very unmusical, actually, they'll really never be together, and the tonality will shift. If it goes too high for them, they'll just shift automatically in pitch and go lower, and then continue from there on as though it was that from the beginning. But this is something we grow up with, and even if you don't try to use it consciously it is definitely in the subconscious. I think it's something that just grows on you and you like it.

To my mind there's no such thing as Israeli music, you must have heard this before. The heterophony is just part of it. However, there are certain things about people who come from this area, and it doesn't have to be necessarily Israeli, I guess. If they write music that relates to Western contemporary music or even traditional music, there will be something that will affect them, because of the background sounds in this country, in this area. You wake up in the morning and you hear church bells and Arab muezzin calls, and it's this mixture—you feel you're in a crossroad junction, sort of, of East and West. And I think that's what comes out.

In my music I can say that many times I find there's a sort of ironic use of romantic music, where I'll write a romantic-style song but I'll insert, say, an augmented second somewhere instead of just having major seconds, going down. There will be something ironic in that. You're hearing a Schumann-style melody, and yet in the melody there's something invented, something that comes from here. I had an argument with George Rochberg. He didn't like that, he thought it ruins the song—but that's me. He said, "This doesn't sound right—it's wrong, it's not pure." But to me, that's what I want to say. What I want to say is Western people do not understand what the music of this area is like. Take, for example, Saint-Saëns's music from *Samson and Delilah*, or Richard Strauss's "Dance of the Seven Veils" from *Salomé*. It's totally biased by the romantics' impressions of this area. And when you live here, you know that it's not like that, and what on earth are they writing? Whose music are they presenting? Well, now I'm doing the opposite. I'm presenting what I could think of in the same light, that's why I'm saying it's ironic. If I did the same to romantic music as they did to oriental music, that's what it would sound like.

It took me a long time to realize that I was doing this. I mean, I'd always fought this, and then I realized that in my own music I was doing the same sort of thing. And this is something that I think is maybe Israeli, because it could only be in a place that's far enough from an all-Western music center. This mixture is what I believe to be the essence of what makes Israeli music. Because otherwise we are using Western notation, we learn Western theory. We do get lessons here as well in Arab music, there are courses in Arab music, Far Eastern music, and basically we're exposed to everything here. And it takes a toll. I think it shows, that's as much as I can say about Israeli music.

There's a school here of what they call Mediterranean style, these were the first European composers who arrived in then Palestine. Boskovitch, Ben-Haim, Lavry, Salomon, and people like that. Boskovitch, for example, was a student of Dukas in Paris. Well, oddly enough, it's something you find also in composers such as Milhaud, there's some sort of Mediterranean flavor—it's hard to explain. It's the orchestration, something that sounds a bit like an Italian town band—like they have in the little towns, marching bands, a sort of very rough sound. It's not the silken, northern European, German sound. It's a few people who are still doing that. It's really dead, I think. It's becoming more and more universal, international. We have so many visits of important European composers—you name them, they've come here. Less so American composers, it's further away. But Xenakis, Penderecki—I think Lutosławski has been here—Messiaen, Stockhausen, there's quite a stream always coming.

My orchestra piece is called *Elegy for Anne Frank*. But the next day after I visited her house, I traveled to Italy on a train, and it went through Germany. For the first time in my life I was actually over German territory, and with the whole question of the Holocaust so fresh in my mind from the Anne Frank house, you know, it was a terrible experience. You come to the border and you see this passport control officer come out, and he's dressed like in an S.S. uniform. And I just went into sort of a traumatic experience, where I was feeling like the earth was burning under me and the birds were screeching and things like that. I was actually hearing some sounds, sort of metallic sounds—and I scribbled something down in music notation, and it didn't come close. I couldn't get my mind fixed on what the sound was, it sounded like nothing in an orchestra. And when I got back to Israel a half a year later, this was with me. I was carrying this experience with me, and not knowing how I would do it. I finally sat down to write something, and I realized that I would have to build an instrument that could create these metallic sounds. With the help of a sculptor friend, Ran Morin, and of Professor Dalia Cohen's knowledge of acoustics, this was accomplished, and the piece enjoyed performances with three different orchestras in Israel. At the time I wrote the piece, this instrument did not exist at all. I wrote for an imaginary instrument.

In April 1987 at Northern Illinois University, Ari Ben-Shabetai's wife, pianist Liora Ziv-Li, performed the composer's *Three Romances* (1986) and Paul Ben-Haim's "Toccata."[2] In 1990, Ben-Shabetai received an ACUM Composition Prize for *Yehezkel* (1984), a work for violoncello and orchestra. In 1993 his composition *Bells, A Prayer for Peace* (1992) was performed the Eden-Tamir Piano Duo in Turkey, England, Russia, and Finland, and his *Visions of Time* (1983) for flute and percussion with digital delay was premiered by Stephen Horenstein and Jeffery Kowalsky.

The Israel Philharmonic Orchestra performed Ben-Shabetai's *Sinfonia Chromatica* (1993) during its 1994–95 season, including performances in Israel and on tour in the United States (in Boston, Washington, D.C., and New York City), Italy, France, and Germany.[3] The source of inspiration for this work is found in the music and aesthetic ideals of Alexander Scriabin.[4] Ben-Shabetai's approach was to unify this work through the use of motives emphasizing the chromatic scale, and highly coloristic treatment of timbres, including marked contrasts of register, dynamics, and articulation. A new symphonic composition, *Magréffa* (1995), commissioned by conductor Lorin Maazel and the Pittsburgh Symphony to jointly celebrate "Jerusalem 3000" and the centenary of the orchestra, was premiered in Pittsburgh in December 1995.[5]

As chairman of the Israel Composers' League in 1994 and 1995, Ari Ben-Shabetai was instrumental in establishing the Israeli Music Center, which publishes and records works by members of the League. In 1996 he was one of three composers awarded the Prime Minister's Prize. He currently serves as treasurer of ACUM, and resumes the position of ICL chairman in 1997. Ben-Shabetai is a lecturer at the Jerusalem Rubin Academy of Music and Dance, where he has taught since 1987.

*Oded Zehavi, photographed at the Northern Illinois University
School of Music (1987) by George Tarbay (NIU Art/Photo). Used
with permission.*

20

ODED ZEHAVI

Oded Zehavi, the youngest composer in this book, was, at the time of these interviews, completing his studies at the Jerusalem Rubin Academy. He subsequently earned a master's degree at the University of Pennsylvania, and a doctorate at the State University of New York at Stony Brook. He regards as his principal teachers the Israeli composer André Hajdu (in Israel) and George Crumb.[1]

I interviewed Oded Zehavi on June 29, 1986, at Mishkenot Sha'ananim. Among the works discussed is a score composed for the Kibbutz Dance Company premiered at the Israel Festival on May 28.

I was born in Israel in 1961. I'm finishing my studies at the Rubin Academy in Jerusalem. And I will go to the University of Pennsylvania this coming year. There is one thing you should know. While calculating our age according to our education, one should understand that we serve for three years in the army, a time when we are not able to make any formal studies. It was really a bad thing for me since I was a tank commander in the army, took part in the last war, and so on.

But in a way it has some benefits—for example, the fact that we come to the Academy for our studies a bit older, and have some very personal ideas about life, about what we want to say. When I saw the graduate students at Penn while I was visiting there, I got the impression that, really, they are just kids. And to compare us to them, it is strange. You know, one cannot say it is good or it is bad, you cannot judge it this way. This is the way we are here. But you know, it is really strange sometimes. I know it, for myself, from the opposite side, when speaking to young composers from other countries. They ask me, "What is your degree?" and I say, "I am a graduating senior." They ask, "How old are you?" So I just want to make it clear in a way. In a way I think it affects my music, it affects my attitude toward life. I don't think one can make a complete separation between our biographies and our music, of course not. But on the other side, I think most young Israeli composers are rather naive or cynical, because it is really difficult to leave behind such an experience like the army. And it's really strange, but I think every one of us up to the age of thirty-five has experienced war, a real war, and most of us have really fought in the first battle line. And it turns us into one of two extremes—either very naive and belief in God and people, and really wanting to build a new life in our young country—or the other way, out [of Israel] really.

I think this is one of the reasons, not the main one, that many of us try to find a way out of the country. Just the fact that you must do a reserve army duty for sixty days a year is really something. Most of us use the opportunity to learn, to complete, or to have some training abroad—and while studying abroad, we needn't do the reserve duty. And it is important to us also to see some other sorts of things. For me, it's a total benefit to be in Philadelphia, I just won't see the tanks. It affects.

I think we are the first generation of composers that served in the army. The old ones came to Israel too old to do it, or lived in the time that they needn't do it. I think, of the older composers who were born in Israel, the only one who served in the army was Tzvi Avni.[2] And maybe this is the reason I asked myself while working in the radio: Why is it that there are so few works that deal directly with our situation, with the way we live here? Especially, I mean, wars, immigration, all physical difficulties. And I came to the conclusion that most of the people who came as immigrants tried to regard Israel as an ideal place—not to deal with the real situation that was here, but tried to build some utopian life—and that was the reason why they spoke so much about ideology.

I don't know if you know about the oriental group, the oriental stream that was here in the first years of the country. For us, who were really born into the country, into the wars, into the army and into this situation—I think we are the first generation that could be regarded as real Israeli composers. And to compare my works to those of my friends, my young colleagues who are a bit older, to the age of forty, I can see that there are many things in common in a way. Now, while we are as young as I am, our works are a bit violent, I must say, not very introverted. But feeling, I think, the language of pain or sorrow, they become more and more introverted as the years pass. You learn how to express things in better ways.

But I think the main thing in common to our composers, and comparing it to other groups of young composers—I'm not very aware of what is going on in the States, but I'm very aware of what's going on in Europe—I think that we're a bit different, since I think there are very few works in Israel that you can say are decorative works. In every piece that I know—most of them, there are some exceptions—you can regard the fact that the composer has something very personal to say.

I can compare it most easily to some groups in the north countries—in Finland, in Iceland. I've got some new records of young composers from these countries, and I don't know—I didn't visit there—I cannot see much in common. But maybe there is, or maybe, after all, music is an international language. I don't know, I don't really believe it.

The best contrast I think is between our composers and the English composers. A work of mine was performed in London, and I used this opportunity to hear some concerts of young graduate students of the Royal Academy of Music. And you know, you can just imagine them with the nice eyes, blond hair, going to their nice houses, and there are some servants for you, and every five o'clock there is nice tea. I wouldn't regard them as little boxes, but they're very nice, educated, warm house composers. Maybe some of them are punks, I don't know. Maybe some of them are even not English, but it was so easy-going, very decorative. You know, the fact that the British now admire Tippett and almost ignore Britten says something about their priorities, and I must say they are very different than mine. Not that I have something against Tippett, but I think Britten was a much greater composer. It is interesting to compare. I know now that in Italy there are very fine composers. I do like to hear some of their work, especially the students of Berio and Donatoni—but again, I don't feel any similarity, personally, to this kind of music.

I think my idea of being a composer here is different from the music of people of my age in other parts of the world. What is it? I must say that this way of life is the only thing that I know. For example, the first time I was in New York, I had three nights of nightmares, just seeing these masses of people going this side and the other side and in front of me, like a Woody Allen movie. And for this reason, maybe—to be very, very nonsophisticated—you can say that there are so many empty spaces in my works. To turn it to the other side, one can understand Philip Glass's minimalism just while seeing people in New York, as I did in my nightmares, go da-da-da-da-da-da-da, no space—and in a way it is less emotional, less personal. And to be here means to be involved in everything emotionally—very, very highly. In Israel the composer, most of the time, is also the producer and the manager and the conductor and the parts copier and everything—and you are involved. And everyone has a great deal of knowledge about politics here, everyone argues. We are very personally involved, and in such a way we cannot create a Philip Glass piece—none of us, really—we just cannot. We can admire this kind of aesthetic, but it is difficult for us.

Now, I don't think there is a special oriental language that we developed here. It is mainly because we don't know—culturally— who we are, really. And I can say that this opinion is very similar to the opinions of most of the composers and artists who live here. On one side, we have pretensions to be Europeans. On the other side, our climate, our neighbors—let's say, our natural culture—is oriental, Levantine.

I don't know the real situation now in Greece, but some—maybe one regards them as popular composers—like Mikis Theodorakis, seem to be very close to the aesthetic language that had already developed here, that some of the less talented composers here tried to build with the decorative style elements of the oriental melos, like the quarter tones, and so on—all the quasi-Arabic music. I don't accept it, mainly because for me it is much more important to understand the context and not the output. Really, the output has a very strong linkage to the cultural life, and for me it is much more important, rather, to understand the cultural life or the habits in the Middle East.

Or what seems to be much more natural, to try to create something that will be an output of my cultural life. And if you ask me, "What is your cultural life?"—it is very complicated. From one side, I'm going to concerts—the other side, my neighbors hear some oriental music. And it is like in food, you can eat here gefilte fish and schnitzel, or the Arabs' food. It is just the same problem here, you know, in my stomach—there is something that might be regarded as unique—and the same in my head.

I cannot go into details, I cannot make the connection between— well, since I was born in Jerusalem, I use a lot of minor chords and the Phrygian cadence. Mentally, of course, I belong to the Western stream. We were educated to regard music according to [Heinrich] Schenker, [Charles] Rosen, and [Donald Francis] Tovey, all of these—it was classical music. I came from a very educated home, and I was playing the piano since the age of six. And then at the age of sixteen I became a composition student of Mark Kopytman. I'm speaking especially about the formal education. I don't think the Rubin Academy was the changing point in my life, it was a natural continuation of the way I worked before. But it was something formal, one should pass it. Here they are very nonflexible. You cannot finish your studies before the four years, maybe because they have so very few students and they want our money to be paid to them for the four years, I don't know.

But as I said before, most of us are very cynical, and I include myself in this group, not that I'm very happy about it. Sometimes I see my colleagues from other countries speaking about the protests they are making against air pollution and I say, OK, I wish I would come to their country, where my main problem would be air pollution. Of course, but we haven't the luxury to die from the pollution. We are dying in the wars, not at the age of eighty or ninety. The problem for us is not to die at the age of twenty-one. And it affects, maybe, the way we compose. And again, maybe this is one of the reasons that young composers here have so many problems with form. Maybe we are used to saying what we have to say, to come to the main idea and that's all— because we have no time, you know? We really don't have any time, not as young kids who know that they might die at the age of eighteen. For this reason I think that sex relations begin here much earlier than in other countries. That's the reason why we don't have much time, really, to be educated. Everything is very fast, very quick. Our colleges are very, very quick, and the first degree, the B.A., is very quick.

That's maybe one of the reasons that you can hear so many works—I hear many works of pupils—and say, OK, I could have developed these materials for another two hours. And sometimes, while hearing my pieces, it's just the same. The piece that you just heard now is A and B and C and D and E and F and—what kind of form is it after all? And now, just three months after hearing it, I know everything that is wrong with it—and I know that in a way it is something that is very, very much like me, to do the one thing after the other, after the other, to build it. OK, in the very foreground, it is well built, there are three parts, and so on. Inside, I could have used much of this material, much more. And I think that this is the thing that belongs to the way we are used to thinking here. It disturbs me to admire Messiaen and Debussy and all the French scores—really Messiaen, *Vingt regards [sur l'enfant-Jésus]*, two or three chords for five minutes, and I enjoyed every minute of it.[3] But I think that if Messiaen had happened to be Israeli, he couldn't do it, he couldn't afford to.

I don't know why I'm still in the position that I feel that my greatest piece is the next one. I hope I will have power to combine the things that I know and the things that I feel. And I think that the oriental temperament with the European knowledge can bring something, can create something very, very good—on the one side, not to lose my spontaneous way of thinking from here, and on the other, to learn every tool and everything that Western culture knows about how to design music, how to work in large and small forms.

And I think that it is just like small kids that sometimes become aware of what they are doing. They switch from the un-knowledge, from doing things intuitively, to doing things while knowing what they are doing. Playing is the main, really the most important point in the life of a composer, if you don't lose your temperament and start to create some Babbitt-like music—or in Israel, I call it Shambadal-like music—music with the highly mathematical ideas, with really no emotional meanings. And not to be just throwing on the paper the notes.

Well, there are some colleagues of mine who really succeeded in doing it, and I really admire them and hope they will continue composing in this way. Jan Radzynski is one of them. I think he's the most important young composer who works here in Israel. As a matter of fact, he is at Yale. And Betty Olivero is another very, very talented composer, and I really do like her works. She is very special. She is one who created a very special language, and it is very interesting for me that she chose to train in another Mediterranean country, in Italy. I think she created something very interesting. She is really a very good composer.

And other young composers in Israel—I think that, in a way, Nami [Yinam Leef] and Haim [Permont] are in a stage that one should see what is going to be out of them. I expect a great future, but it will be in the future. From the other young composers—there are not many that I am very curious to hear from. There are some good pieces that are created here.

The composers whose music I really admire, most of them are either communists or coming from very, very active situations—like Penderecki, the Polish composer; Berio, who is really involved in everything that goes on in the work emotionally; and Lutosławski, who again is Polish.

From the Americas, I think that I mostly admire George Crumb's music, but one must understand that in Israel we are not really aware of what is going on in the States. I don't know why, probably because our record connections are mainly in Europe. We have every Deutsche Grammophon record, EMI, Clavecin, and so on—even the contemporary records. But we don't know much about what is going on in the States. I think we are not that important to the record companies in the U.S., and that's the reason why. In my short visits in the States, I was really amazed to hear about many composers that I didn't know, and much good music that I wasn't aware of.

Again, I admire Messiaen. His religious music, his organ music. The *Catalog of Birds* is something really unique, and touches me.[4] I have some difficulty with Boulez and this group, but I think that Maderna and Nono in a way, and Blacher in a way—some of the works I know are quite close to me, I can feel a lot of sympathy toward them. I think, in a way, what is common to these works is that it's emotional music. Emotional music, I think, is a very wide definition, but in a way I can feel very good with it. Because I regard also Bartók's music as emotional music, and also Stravinsky's *Oedipus Rex* as emotional music.

But there is so much music that keeps you away in our century— and OK, for sometimes it is very good to be kept away. I can imagine a radio program that includes Tchaikovsky's *Romeo and Juliet,* and then a Schumann piano concerto, and then unemotional—I don't know whom, but some unemotional music—and I'll feel very good. Like you sometimes eat those tasteless ice creams—I don't know the English names—just to clean your mouth for the next course. It has some practical uses, but sometimes to hear this very extreme minimalism, or very non-emotional music, or those catalog effects of using the trombone—I'm not speaking now about Globokar, but his imitators who just "see what I can make out of the trombone," make it sound like an oboe. OK, for this reason just use the oboe. And all this aleatoric music that sometimes works and sometimes doesn't—and you can mainly be suspicious toward them—and all these electronic systems.

There's so many bad works in the century that really I think one of the most important people in our century is the radio editor, the lector, really. Hans Keller was, I think, much more important to the musical life in our century than some of the most important composers.[5] He was the Esterházy, in a way, of our time, because he made the first selection for the amateurs, and kept them away from all the garbage. You know, in a way, it is very dangerous also, because there are many good works that Hans Keller didn't like personally.

But in a way, I think every one of us should work in the media, so I plan my future as a composer and as a lector in the media. Because I think the only way to educate, and to bring a new audience to the concert halls of modern music, is to make the very unpleasant separation between good music and bad music. Just because one should be in the position to think about the whole picture, and not the personal and emotional relations.

And since we are so non–grown up here, mostly because you feel sorry for the people you do like, it's one of the reasons there are so many garbage works that are broadcasted and recorded and performed here. And I think the main thing Israel needs now is a good lector—a brave man, one who is very open minded and who would be able to produce or to broadcast also things that personally he wouldn't have written, but to make the real separation between good and bad music.

I am working at Kol Israel, but I don't put myself yet in the position to make the very sharp decisions, though the fact is I can do it because I am one of the two people who deal with Israeli music. The other one is in Tel Aviv, Joan Franks Williams. She is also a composer, a very good one, by the way. I don't feel myself yet baked enough to deal with it in the total meaning, just to cut. But I try, in a way, to promote the works I do appreciate, and there are some works I broadcast at least once every month, just so people will get used to it.

And I think that Gary Bertini, the musical director of the radio orchestra [Jerusalem Symphony Orchestra], was very brave in a way, to perform eight times, works by Kopytman, until the audience and orchestra got used to it. And now the last concert was really a great one, it was a great performance. It really, really shocked the audience, as it should. And if they wouldn't have wasted their time and money and power on another twelve unimportant works in the year, they could make such a benefit to many other works.

For me, it's the ideal thing I would like to see everywhere in the world. I want to see it as a world of lectors—of good, educated lectors. As a composer, I would be very glad to deal with lectors, with the audience, and with critics. In Israel we have no lectors, no audience for modern music. We have some critics, but they are not that important, their position here is not that important. I'll be very glad to deal with here Harold Schonberg, George Bernard Shaw, may he rest in paradise, and I don't know—the audience of the Penn Contemporary Music Players. I'd be very glad to deal with them in every work of mine, and if they would say that it is garbage, I'll go home and write another one. But I would like to be in a position that there is something I can trust, and not because of political things, or something—manipulations.

I think my works are good, but I would be very glad to be in a position or a situation where there would be a lector who will tell me, "Young man, it is not that good, please wait another two years." Nowadays, I think I don't trust most of the people who are acting like lectors here. I know for sure that some of them don't know how to read contemporary music. And I know for sure that some of them don't read at all the scores that they do have. And for this reason, there are a lot of problems. But in spite of these problems I'm very glad to say that there are some good performances of good Israeli works—for example, the Seter works, some Maayani works, some Avni works. Really, we have some records of good music here. But it's a matter of luck—we are lucky.

And this work of mine that was performed by the orchestra, and some works of mine were performed abroad by Israeli groups. Yes, I was lucky. In a way, I know how to sell my works, and it's probably because I'm young, and people want to discover the next great composer. And probably because my music, in a way, is communicative—and I do believe in communicative music. And maybe it is because of this, maybe it was just good fortune, I don't know. I just hope it will continue. I wish myself all the best.

Well, there are three works that are directly connected to the war. One of them is a quintet for flute, piano, and string trio called *Prophet,* which really deals with my feelings toward the war. It was much more of a psychiatric treatment than of creating music, just to deal with all these materials again. But it was interesting. It never imitates noises from the war—you cannot hear the bombs, and so on—but it deals with my personal feeling toward it in the time of pressure. It was something like going to a psychiatrist. I don't have one, but I'm writing music instead of it.

The other one is a piano sonata, which I wrote during the war itself. It was composed in the tank. And there you can find my idée fixe of those church bells ringing, you can hear the chimes—most of the work is based on it. We fought in Lebanon, and we attacked some churches. Though we fought for the Christians, it was a battle in a Christian country, and it was so strange for me. Really, my main memory of sounds is those of the churches there. We fought nearby the beach there—Tzor, Tzidon, Damur, and Beirut. There are a lot of churches, small and big, and every one has its special bells, and it really becomes such a kind of a musical idée fixe. It was interesting, and you can find it very much in my piano sonata.

And then there is a work of mine for children's choir, which is going to be performed next year, based on a medieval poem that is an elegy for the sponsor of the poet, who died. And for me, I reacted to it very, very emotionally and I composed it in memory of one of my friends—we were fighting together. He died and I stayed alive, and I dedicated it to his memory. I hope it is going to be performed. This is my best work, I think, and not performed here.

In the dance piece, the choreographer and I tried to deal a bit with some very primitive feelings, emotions. Everything there is around the accelerando and the ritardando, and the crescendo and the descrescendo—the melos is less important—and the density and space and all these things. And we tried to imitate something that's going on inside the head of one who is attacking or being attacked, or something like this. In a way, it was a bit aggressive.

The practical thing that they did onstage was not connected very much to the first ideas. The dance itself is decorative, there is something that is nice. There are handsome dancers and nice females with nice bodies, and you can really ignore everything that you don't want. It helps every one of your protective mechanisms, to protect you. You can enjoy the light, the bodies—you can even feel something erotic in it.

For this reason I much prefer it to be performed as a concert piece, and I think it is going to be performed here live next year. It will be very interesting to me, I'll be very curious to see the reactions of the people toward this work. They will have to see the conductor and the players—just the music, without dance. And I am very curious to see what reaction is going to be coming out of it.

I made a third version that is a bit shorter, a concert version—I'm very curious to see it. It was originally commissioned by the dance group. I took the opportunity to write a piece that I felt good with, and they cut it again. We all knew that it was going to work this way, that I would do my piece and they would dance my piece in their way.

The flute piece you heard was just a thing, something to write. I feel very bad about it, we'd better leave it. It's something that I thought was going to work in some other way. Suddenly, I really didn't feel good with it, and I left it. It shouldn't have been performed, maybe in some other way. I'm going to do some materials of it. The idea is good—to take one line, one bunch, and to separate it. I called it a composed folk music, which is another thing. I wrote it in two hours. It's really something that one shouldn't do.

The music of Oded Zehavi has been performed in Israel, Germany, France, Luxembourg, Belgium, and the United States.[6] Zehavi's orchestral works have been performed by the Israel Philharmonic under Leonard Slatkin, the Israel Chamber Orchestra under Shlomo Mintz, the Curtis Orchestra under Richard Wernick, the Rishon LeZion Symphony Orchestra under Noam Sheriff, and the Haifa Symphony under Stanley Sperber. Noted soloists who have performed his music include flutists Samuel Baron and Eugenia Zukerman.

Zehavi was founder and director of the composition department at Rodman Regional College at Tel Hai from 1992 to 1994, and currently heads the music division at the University of Haifa. In 1993 he was appointed composer-in-residence with the Haifa Symphony Orchestra, the first position of its kind in Israel.[7] In 1994, Zehavi received the ACUM Prize for chamber music. In 1995 he was one of three composers to receive the Prime Minister's Prize and was also awarded the Engel Prize.[8] In 1996 Zehavi received a Barlow Foundation commission and an ACUM award for his Violin Concerto.

CONCLUSION

Music has played an important role in the development of modern Israel, as a vehicle of social unification and as a link to the traditions and cultural histories of its many ethnic communities. The enthusiasm of Israeli audiences is well known to performers throughout the world, and one perceives it is due at least in part to the extramusical implications of a guest performance within the nation's borders. During the 1991 Gulf War, violinist Isaac Stern performed on an Israeli concert stage in the middle of an air raid before a sea of gas masks, and Israel Philharmonic Orchestra music director Zubin Mehta stepped through SCUD missile wreckage in a Tel Aviv neighborhood after canceling a scheduled appearance with the New York Philharmonic. Frank Pelleg, a prominent musician who immigrated to Palestine in 1936 from his native Czechoslovakia, described a similar episode from the dawn of the nation:

> I remember the day after the proclamation of the State of Israel. The unprepared and—then—defenceless citizens of Tel Aviv were exposed to incessant, murderous air raids, and the radio had announced the first casualties. But there was not a single empty seat at the regular subscription concert of the Philharmonic Orchestra. Earlier still, during the fighting on the border with Jaffa, a Bach recital had to wage a desperate battle with the clatter of the machineguns

301

around the Municipal Museum, and the large audience, ordered to wait for the "All clear" to disperse, were granted a repeat of the programme, item by item, as an encore.[1]

These scenes from the past attest to the special place of music and musicians in modern Israel. Soloists and ensembles from other countries continue to be very much in demand in Israel, just as in the 1920s, when the visits of such artists to British-mandate Palestine attracted considerable attention.[2]

For the Israeli composer, the environment has been somewhat less than propitious, and the contemporary art music of Israel has yet to find a place within its own society. Writing in 1963, Pelleg observed that Israelis did "not respond enthusiastically to local talent."[3] Elie Yarden has noted that Israeli audiences are generally more interested in the performance of music than in the music performed, a condition less than conducive to the reception of new works: "In the cult of celebrity which dominates the Israeli concert world, music is the unavoidable concomitant noise present in the significant experience of contact with the aura of the performer. Sounds which are not thoroughly familiar are an unwelcome disturbance of the valued audience-performer relationship. At best, music is the vehicle whereby the expectations generated by the performer's reputation are fulfilled."[4] Despite the historical importance of music and music education in Israel, many Israeli composers have responded to the allure of European and American cultural centers and educational institutions and pursued advanced training abroad, where many have also found greater chances of success and a livelihood than at home. Though music is everywhere in Israel, the wealth of contemporary music to which the nation has given rise remains largely unknown, even among its potentially most appreciative audience. Though the lack of enthusiasm of concertgoers for contemporary music is a phenomenon with which composers elsewhere are familiar, it may seem ironic, given the context that gave birth to this nation, that Israelis have been unreceptive to expressions of the new in the arts.

The special pressures that social and political circumstances have exerted on Israel's artistic community have challenged its composers perhaps above all others. The generalized local indifference to contemporary Israeli art music is contrasted by the significantly greater value that has been traditionally accorded writers and visual artists.[5] Benjamin Bar-Am has stated that the pioneering generations, "not blessed with a great understanding of musical values," considered the composer "strangely removed," while in the writer they saw "the personification of the spirit of the people."[6] Despite living and working in a country known for its love of music, Israeli composers have been increasingly active outside of Israel because of limited local opportunities for education, audiences, support, and professional advancement.[7] Many Israeli composers have felt isolated at home but continue to engage in a dialogue between self and society through the language of music, reflecting and representing their native or adopted culture in the outside world.

The time and place in which artists create form the cultural subtext of their individual expression. The myriad influences found in Israeli art music reflect the many ethnic and national origins of its population, as well as the impact of regional, Jewish, and Arabic musical traditions, and the international milieu of contemporary music. Awareness of the historical, social, and cultural contexts in which they live affects most Israeli composers deeply, including Ami Maayani, who remarked: "The mere fact of our being here, from the spiritual point of view, directs the trend of musical creativity. This creativity reflects the untiring search for typical expression of a people renewing its life and existence."[8] The arts and artists of Israel originate from and interact with those of other cultures. The interviews in this book, however, also suggest that the artistic output of Israel bears the imprint of this society's unique and complex social and cultural history. Tzvi Avni has observed that "what characterizes life in our time, in the spiritual sense, is that this is the age of questions, a generation that wonders and searches for ways."[9] Yinam Leef recently articulated other aspects of life in present-day Israel that influence its creative artists: "Our society and its needs bear little resemblance to that of the 1930's, 40's and 50's. But I live and create in a society still torn by contradictions. It embraces and rejects its heritage at the same time. It is ethnically diverse, but tensions overflow daily. A deeply rooted sense of personal responsibility is mixed with egotism, impatience and lack of tolerance. Unconsciously, these contradictions must find their way into my work."[10]

Some younger Israeli composers have continued, revived, or re-vised the focus on indigenous musical elements earlier associated with the Eastern Mediterranean school. Oded Zehavi described one of his recent works as having been composed "in a style which I consider neo-Mediterranean."[11] A recent work by Haim Permont that employed a traditional Middle Eastern drum known as a darbukka prompted one writer to describe some of the younger Israeli composers as "post-modernists" who "follow the paths along which their teachers have trodden." These composers, the writer suggested, seek "means for greater communicativity" rather than new idioms, having become "tired of being enclosed in a double 'ghetto': that of modernism and of Israel."[12] The continued interest of Israeli composers in Arabic musical traditions has also been reflected in a number of works. Early examples include works by Ben-Haim and Partos, as well as Orgad's *Taksim* and Ehrlich's *Bashrav.* Other composers whose works clearly reflect the influence of Arabic musical traditions are Betty Olivero, Ami Maayani, and Tsippi Fleischer. In Fleischer's compositions, especially, one also perceives extramusical dimensions to be consciously at work. With her training in theory and composition, Middle Eastern studies, and Hebrew and Arabic philology, Fleischer is committed to expressing Israeli and Jewish traits while evoking the drama of Arabic poetry, an aspect of the broader cultural environment of which she feels a part. The overall form of Roman Haubenstock-Ramati's *Berahot* ("Blessings") is articulated by reflections on a different musical tradition in each of its movements: "Prelude" is based on Indian raga, "Incantation" on the Arabic *maqām,* "Hallelujah" on Byzantine chant, and "Chorale" on Hebrew cantorial song.[13]

Philip Bohlman contends that neither a synthesis of East and West nor a national style has developed in contemporary Israeli music, noting that the younger composers prefer "international styles" to the musical traditions of the region in which they live. Rather, he observes, "Israeli composers continue to write in a number of styles, and their works continue to reflect the international character of the immigrant society that still prevails."[14] Though a single, unified national style has not taken root in modern Israel, and may never, Bohlman has also observed that the diverse musical culture of Israel has nonetheless produced a sizable body of national music: "However one defines 'national music,' whether as explicitly, implicitly, or accidentally referring to something 'Israeli,' the repertory of national music stretches across many genres."[15] The notion of "East-West synthesis" has continued to evolve, and is still discussed by Israeli composers. Peter Gradenwitz has drawn the distinction between the "genuine impact of Near Eastern music" and the use of "mannerisms" or "stylistic clichés."[16] Zvi Keren predicted three decades ago that "the former type of East-West synthesis in which Oriental music is 'Westernized' may well give way to a type in which Western music is 'Orientalized.' "[17] The aesthetics, techniques, and musical dialects associated with recent works suggest that individually integrated voices, rather than a synthetic national style, will emerge from the present environment, which is still more diverse than that fostered by the early Central European immigrant composers.

In the relative absence of the particular pressures that confronted their predecessors, the younger generation of Israeli composers may find more natural means by which to integrate the disparate elements of their social and cultural environment in a postnationalistic era. Freed of previous generations' concerns with ideology or aesthetic formula, the essential challenge of Israel's present and future composers will be to identify, select, and integrate those elements that represent their individual voices. It seems certain that elements and evocations of East and West will continue to play a role in Israeli culture and the arts, as in the daily life these reflect. What seems equally certain is that new possibilities of organizing sound in time will continually present themselves to composers in Israel, as elsewhere, and that as Israel's society and culture continue to develop, so too will the global and regional dialects of its musical language.

In recent years there appears to have been an awakening of interest among Israelis, and others, in this nation's established and growing art-music tradition. Israeli composers are also increasingly active abroad in ever-widening venues. With each generation, there is perhaps also a growing appreciation of contemporary Israeli music as a literature that documents and reflects the culture and history of its people. It was announced in 1994 that six streets in a new section of Beer Sheva would be named after Israeli composers Yedidya (Admon) Gorochov, Menahem Avidom, Paul Ben-Haim, Alexander U. Boskovitch, Marc Lavry, and Oedoen Partos.[18]

It is hoped that publications such as this one might help draw increased interest and attention, in Israel and elsewhere, to this vibrant and rapidly growing art-music culture, one that has persisted and developed despite an abundance of obstacles. In the twentieth century, art music in the Western world may have experienced both its most marginal and most essential role in the lives of the general public. The interactions and cross-pollinations linking musics of different cultures and subcultures, genres, styles, and eras in this period has been unprecedented. At the beginning of a new century and millennium, perhaps Israelis and others may discover new ways in which the time and place they live are uniquely reflected in music, as all other arts, from which these are inseparable.

APPENDIX

The following organizations are able to provide information and materials (scores, recordings, catalogs) concerning contemporary Israeli art music and composers. Street and post office box addresses are included below. In the telephone and fax numbers listed below, the prefix 2 represents the city code of Jerusalem; 3 is the code for Tel Aviv. When calling phone numbers in Israel from elsewhere, the country code (972) must precede the number. Callers from the United States must precede this country code with the international code (011).

1. Israel Composers' League (ICL)/Israeli Music Center (IMC/MALI)
    Ari Ben-Shabetai, Chairman; Irit Karmi, General Secretary
    7 Petach Tikva Road, Tel Aviv 66181, Israel
    P.O. Box 196, Tel Aviv 61001, Israel
    Tel: 3-5660905; Fax: 3-5660907

    Recordings produced by the Israeli Music Center (IMC/MALI) may be ordered by mail.

2. Israel Music Institute (IMI) and Israel Music Information Centre (IMIC)
    Paul Landau, Director; Miriam Morgan, Foreign Department
    144 Hayarkon Street, Tel Aviv 63451, Israel;
    P.O. Box 3004, Tel Aviv 61030, Israel
    Tel: 3-5246475, 3-5245275; Fax: 3-5245276

    Since 1991, the IMI has been represented in the United States, Canada, and Mexico, by Theodore Presser Co., Bryn Mawr, Pennsylvania 19010; Tel: (215) 525-3636 (rental and sales).

3. Israeli Music Publications (IMP)
    Sergey Khanukaev, Acting Manager
    25 Keren Hayesod Street, Jerusalem 91076, Israel
    P.O. Box 7681, Jerusalem 94188, Israel
    Tel: 2-6241377, 2-6251370; Fax: 2-6241378

4. Israel Broadcasting Authority (IBA), Kol Israel (Voice of Israel)
    Avi Hanani, Head of Music
    21 Helene Hamalka Street, Jerusalem 95101, Israel
    P.O. Box 1082, Jerusalem 91010, Israel
    Tel: 2-5302208; Fax: 2-6259861
    Tape duplication: Ms. Michal Issan; Tel. 2-5302255

    The IBA records and broadcasts music by Israeli composers, including many works for which recordings are not otherwise readily available. The IBA possesses recorded performances of works by all of the composers included in this book, and will make duplicate cassette tapes for a fee, provided blank tapes accompany such requests.

5. Several American libraries maintaining significant collections of contemporary Israeli music are listed in Alice Tischler's *Bibliography*. These include the Performing Arts Research Collection at Lincoln Center and the Donnell Media Center of the New York Public Library; the Library of Congress in Washington, D.C.; the School of Music Library at Indiana University, in Bloomington; and the Birnbaum Music Library at the Elaine Kaufman Cultural Center (formerly the Hebrew Arts Center) at Abraham Goodman House in New York City. The Edwin A. Fleisher Collection of Orchestral Music at the Free Library of Philadelphia also possesses a number of works by Israeli composers.

N O T E S

INTRODUCTION

1. Alexander L. Ringer, "Musical Composition in Modern Israel," in *Contemporary Music in Europe: A Comprehensive Survey*, ed. Paul Henry Lang and Nathan Broder (1965; reprint, New York: Norton, 1968), 282–97. The imperfect term "art music" (also called "serious" and "classical" music) may be unfamiliar even to many who enjoy one or more of its various repertories. The definition found in *Webster's Third New International Dictionary*—"music composed by the trained musician as contrasted with folk music and often with popular music"—serves in the present instance to denote professional musicians schooled in the art of musical composition through both private instruction and in conservatory environments, whose musical ideas are conveyed through notated scores which are interpreted by performers and conductors. The unprecedented cross-pollinations characterizing our musical world in the twentieth century have lessened the potency of such designations as "art," "folk," "traditional," or "popular" music, but terminology is less important here than the range of experience, aesthetics, objectives, and techniques which serve to unite the diverse creative musical artists profiled in this volume and distinguish them from other communities of musicians.

2. Ami Maayani, foreword to *Israeli Music, 1971–72* (Tel Aviv: League of Composers in Israel, 1972), 3.

3. In this book I use "Israel" in references to the modern state of Israel, which won its independence in 1948. In references to this region prior to Israeli statehood I use "Palestine," the political designation of the British mandate that succeeded Ottoman rule following World War I. Composers interviewed in this book employ the designation "Palestine" in the same context as above, but also use "Israel" and the symbolic, biblical designation "Eretz Israel" ("the land of Israel") in references to both periods.

4. For reasons to be discussed, the tradition of Israeli art-music composition is generally regarded to begin with the mass immigration, or *aliyah* ("ascent," or "rising up") to Palestine of Central Europeans who fled Nazism between 1933 and 1939. Western art music, however, was performed in Palestine more than a century ago, and the first community "orchestra," consisting of twenty-five to thirty performers (mostly woodwinds, with a few violins), was formed in 1895. Depending on the occasion, concerts of the Rishon LeZion Orchestra mixed "light classics" with anthems, folk songs, or religious songs of different ethnic populations. See Jehoash Hirshberg, *Music in the Jewish Community of Palestine, 1880–1948: A Social History* (New York: Oxford University Press, 1995), 25. Reviewed by this writer in *Middle East Journal* 50, no. 3 (Summer 1996): 437–38.

5. Peter Gradenwitz, "Israeli Composers," *Tempo* 20 (Summer 1951): 31.

6. Bernard Holland, review of *Agadot,* by Stephen Horenstein, *New York Times,* 18 June 1991. It would be interesting to learn where Mr. Holland would locate the "visceral center" of modern America, and which composer he would credit for turning it into "important music."

7. These distinctions are the subject of a chapter in Robert K. Merton, *The Sociology of Science: Theoretical and Empirical Investigations,* ed. Norman W. Storer (Chicago: University of Chicago Press, 1973), 99–136.

8. According to Jehoash Hirshberg, in *Music in the Jewish Community,* the term *Yishuv* ("settlement") refers to the "autonomous Jewish community in Palestine from 1840 to the establishment of the State of Israel in 1948" (2). Hirshberg also distinguishes between the Old *Yishuv* and New *Yishuv,* the former denoting the religious, mostly Sephardic, population and "traditional way of life" established in Palestine before World War I, the latter referring to the more nationalistic and secular European immigrant population, arriving in a series of immigration waves, or *aliyahs.*

9. Philip V. Bohlman, *"The Land Where Two Streams Flow": Music in the German-Jewish Community of Israel* (Urbana and Chicago: University of Illinois Press, 1989). One chapter is devoted to the experience of immigrant composers, and another to the World Centre for Jewish Music in Palestine, the latter more fully treated in Bohlman's *The World Centre for Jewish Music in Palestine, 1936–1940: Jewish Musical Life on the Eve of World War II* (New York: Oxford University Press, 1992). See also his foreword and afterword to *Israeli Folk Music: Songs of the Early Pioneers,* ed. Hans Nathan, Recent Researches in the Oral Traditions of Music, vol. 4 (Madison, Wis.: A-R Editions, 1994), ix–x, 39–55.

10. Alice Tischler, *A Descriptive Bibliography of Art Music by Israeli Composers* (Warren, Mich.: Harmonie Park Press, 1988). Tischler's bibliography includes all first- and second-generation composers represented in the present volume. Of the younger composers presented in Part III, only Aharon Harlap and Gabriel Iranyi are included. Another recent publication is Anat Feinberg, ed., *Kultur in Israel: Eine Einführung* (Stuttgart: Bleicher Verlag, 1993), a collection of essays including Oded Assaf's "Israeli Music: An Invitation into High Tension." An English translation is forthcoming of the late Yehuda W. Cohen's *The Heirs of the Psalmists: Israel's New Music* (Tel Aviv: Am Oved, 1990).

11. Mark Slobin, "Ten Paradoxes and Four Dilemmas of Studying Jewish Music," *World of Music* 37, no. 1 (1995): 20.

12. Bruno Nettl, "The Concept of Preservation," in *Proceedings of the World*

Congress on Jewish Music—Jerusalem, 1978, ed. Judith Cohen (Tel Aviv: The Institute for the Translation of Hebrew Literature, 1982), 55.

13. David N. Baker, Lida M. Belt, and Herman C. Hudson, eds., *The Black Composer Speaks* (Metuchen, N.J., and London: Scarecrow, for the Afro-American Arts Institute, Indiana University, 1978); William Duckworth, *Talking Music: Conversations with John Cage, Philip Glass, Laurie Anderson, and Five Generations of American Experimental Composers* (New York: Simon & Schuster Macmillan, Schirmer Books, 1995; London: Prentice-Hall International, 1995); Cole Gagne and Tracy Caras, *Soundpieces: Interviews with American Composers* (Metuchen, N.J., and London: Scarecrow Press, 1982); Paul Griffiths, *New Sounds, New Personalities: British Composers of the 1980s in Conversation* (London and Boston: Faber, 1985); Helen F. Samson, *Contemporary Filipino Composers: Biographical Interviews* (Quezon City, Philippines: Manlapaz, 1976); R. Murray Schafer, *British Composers in Interview* (London: Faber, 1963); and Edward Strickland, *American Composers: Dialogues on Contemporary Music* (Bloomington and Indianapolis: Indiana University Press, 1991).

14. The word "sabra" denotes a fruit with a rough, prickly exterior, but which is tender and juicy within—a metaphor for the "typical" Israeli.

15. "Sephardic" in the strict sense refers to descendants of Jews expelled from Spain in 1492, who were dispersed throughout Europe, Africa, and the Middle East. The term is also used to refer to "oriental" Jews (*mizrahim*) who have lived in Arabic regions, only some of whom are descended from families once living in Spain. For a discussion of some of the complexities involved in such designations identifying sectors of Israel's population, and their ramifications concerning definitions of culture, see Virginia R. Domínguez, *People as Subject, People as Object: Selfhood and Peoplehood in Contemporary Israel* (Madison: University of Wisconsin Press, 1989), 6–8, 101–7.

16. Alan P. Merriam, *The Anthropology of Music* (Evanston: Northwestern University Press, 1964), 6.

17. Four composers' interviews were omitted, for different reasons: one refused to permit his remarks to be published; another never responded to my requests to secure his permission; a third never provided a corrected draft; and a fourth abandoned an attempt to edit his remarks, which he considered insufficiently clear.

18. These include the Sinai War in 1956, the Six-Day War in 1967, the 1973 Yom Kippur War, Israel's invasion of Lebanon in 1982, and the 1991 Gulf War.

19. Some writers divide the population of modern Israel into four generations: "The first generation was firmly based on its European roots; the second generation was rooted in its experiences in Erez Israel, especially those connected with *aliyah* and the kibbutz movement; the third generation, emerging around the 1948 War of Independence, was dominated by the sabra with his newly found self-confidence; while the fourth generation (or the second sabra generation) has been the most universalistic and outward looking, seeing Israeli culture as one expression of contemporary world culture" (Geoffrey Wigoder, "Israel, State of [Cultural Life]: Music and Dance," *Encyclopaedia Judaica,* 2d ed., 1971). I have encountered no specific references to four generations of composers in Israel. The designations of first and second generation composers, used in this book, are commonly employed among Israeli composers. Some Israelis would refer to the second- and third-generation composers instead as those of the "middle generation" and "younger generation."

20. The occasion of these interviews was that of my first visit to Israel, and as

noted elsewhere, my first meeting with each of the composers. In this respect (i.e., as a non-Israeli and a first-time visitor), my "outsider" status was clear, and the composers I interviewed tended not to assume that I had direct knowledge of many things Israeli. Indeed, after reviewing a draft of this manuscript, Noa Guy characterized it as "a very balanced and comprehensive survey that only an objective, knowledgeable outsider could give" (letter to the author, 22 August 1995). On the other hand, given my status as an American composer and educator of Jewish ancestry, there were many instances that suggested that I was considered an "insider." Such presumptions led some composers to assume that I was more informed than I was concerning aspects of Jewish history, literature, or religion.

21. The last one of these core questions almost consistently failed to yield direct responses. However, since many composers reframed this question as an invitation to comment on contemporary Israeli music in general, it elicited some interesting perspectives and analyses concerning the musical culture of which these composers are a part.

22. I also respected the expressed wishes of some composers to delete remarks that, on reflection, they felt would be inappropriate to publish.

23. Joseph Cohen, *Voices of Israel: Essays on and Interviews with Yehuda Amichai, A. B. Yehoshua, T. Carmi, Aharon Appelfeld, and Amos Oz* (Albany: State University of New York Press, 1990).

24. I stipulate "Jewish and Israeli" in this context for the simple reason that while Israel is the only nation in which Jews are in the majority (82 percent, according to official population statistics for 1987), its population also includes Moslems (13.9 percent) and Christians (2.3 percent), as well as "Druze and others" (1.7 percent) (Domínguez, *People as Subject,* 196). Indeed, earlier publications concerning contemporary music in Israel discussed the work of Habib Touma (b. 1934), an Arab Israeli who resettled in Germany in the 1960s (see Ringer, "Musical Composition," 296–97, and Zvi Keren, *Contemporary Israeli Music: Its Sources and Stylistic Development* [Ramat Gan: Bar Ilan University Press, 1980], 25, 89). Touma studied with Alexander U. Boskovitch in Israel, and with Stockhausen, Messiaen, and other composers in Europe. Also a musicologist, he has contributed to the study of Arabic musical theory, and is the author of *The Music of the Arabs* (Portland, Ore.: Amadeus, 1996). See Peter Gradenwitz, "Touma, Habib," in *New Grove Dictionary of Music and Musicians,* 1980.

25. Hirshberg, *Music in the Jewish Community,* vi.

26. Bohlman, afterword to *Israeli Folk Music,* 54.

27. A relatively recent phenomenon in Israeli popular culture, "cassette" music includes "traditional ethnic music" of a "liturgical or semi-liturgical" nature and *musika mizrahit* ("Eastern music"), "a form of oriental (eastern) Jewish popular music, incorporating Arabic, Kurdish, Greek, Yemenite, Turkish, etc., 'colouration' in a standardized format based mainly on western music" (Pamela Squires-Kidron, "Multi-Coloured Musicians," *Ariel* 73 [1988]: 63).

28. As the immigrant composer Karel Salomon (b. 1897, Germany; imm. 1933; d. 1974) observed: "European music is exotic to young Israelis; Oriental music is not exotic to young Israelis" (Keren, *Contemporary Israeli Music,* 81).

29. Though few Israeli composers have consistently employed the twelve-tone, or "dodecaphonic," method of composition developed by the twentieth-century composer Arnold Schoenberg (1874–1951) and extended by his pupils Anton

Webern (1883–1945) and Alban Berg (1885–1935), the impact and influence of this compositional approach, and of post-Schoenbergian "serialism"—the application of Schoenberg's pitch-based method to other musical "parameters" (including durations, dynamics, register, articulation, and instrumentation)—is evident in the frequency with which related concepts or terms are cited by composers in these interviews. The method employed by Schoenberg and his followers begins with the composition of a "series," or "row," which arranges all twelve tones of the chromatic scale in a particular fashion, and serves to unify the melodic and harmonic vocabulary of a single work. Up to forty-eight (though generally far fewer) variants, or forms, of the tone row are then selected and used by the composer, these made possible by its twelve potential transpositions and four basic dispositions (original, inversion, retrograde, retrograde-inversion).

30. See Keren, *Contemporary Israeli Music,* 12–15.

31. Ben-Zion Orgad noted in 1959 that in Israel choral works outnumbered those of any other genre (Keren, *Contemporary Israeli Music,* 78). The emphasis on solo string writing has been attributed by Ringer to the influence of "Near-Eastern monophonic and heterophonic music" ("Musical Composition," 294).

32. Tsippi Fleischer informed me of a cycle of compositions in which she is setting to music texts in a variety of ancient Semitic languages (letter to the author, December 1995).

33. Angela Levine, "Musical Instruments in the Bible," *Ariel* 93 (1993): 79–87; Hirshberg, *Music in the Jewish Community,* 9.

34. See Nancy Uscher, "A 20th-Century Approach to Heterphony: Mark Kopytman's *Cantus II," Tempo* 156 (March 1986): 19–22. In a development resembling the shift of perspective from the homophonic and polyphonic textures of European music to the more transparent exoticism of heterophony, some immigrant painters in Israel abandoned perspective and three dimensions for the "flat modeling of two-dimensionality" associated with Asian and Persian traditions (Alfred Werner, "Pioneers of Israeli Art," *Jewish Frontier* 35, no. 1 [January 1968]: 15).

35. See Ringer, "Musical Composition," 286, and Keren, *Contemporary Israeli Music,* 18. The designation "oriental" bears a multiplicity of meanings, informed by demographic and ethnic perspective. Edward W. Said is quite right in noting that Americans tend not to associate the Middle East with this term (*Orientalism* [New York: Random House, Pantheon, 1978; reprinted, with a new afterword, New York: Random House, Vintage, 1994], p. 1). During my visit to Israel in 1986, I was at first surprised to hear Israelis refer to their region as the "Orient." For Israeli composers, the broad range of meanings of the term "oriental" encompasses music, customs, or influences ranging from *mizrahi* (Middle Eastern) to Arabic to Sephardic to Asian. Israeli composers and scholars seem to use the term inclusively, in references to music and culture associated with Jewish and Arabic (including Muslim and Christian) populations. Among artists, one tends to find interest in the theory, techniques, or styles of other traditions or cultures less often conjoined to presumptions of the superiority of one in relation to the "other." This should perhaps not be surprising toward the end of a century that has seen an unprecedented degree of cross-cultural collaboration and reciprocal influence.

36. Works by some of the composers in this book have been the subject of doctoral dissertations and articles written both in and outside of Israel.

37. Zecharia Plavin, "What's Behind Avni's and Kopytman's Sevenths?" *IMI News* 1995, no. 1: 3.

38. The membership of the Israel Composers' League has been approximately 160 for the past two decades. See Gideon Lefen, "Israeli Art Music: How Often Is It Performed?" *IMI News* 1995, no. 1: 8.

39. Of those listed, all except Lakner, Seroussi, and Weidberg are included in Tischler, *Bibliography*, which also includes many Israeli composers no longer living. Concerning Lakner, see Alfred Zimmerlin, "Audio-Visual Time Structures (AVTS) by Yehoshua Lakner," *IMI News* 1994, no. 2: 5–8. The only American-born composer in Tischler's book is Joan Franks Williams, who, according to Noa Guy, has since returned to the United States. While in Israel she was a program director for the Israel Broadcasting Authority and a tireless organizer of contemporary music concerts and festivals.

40. Information presented in the individual introductions and updates has either been provided by the composers themselves or appeared in the *IMI News* or other sources.

41. See Eric Hobsbawm and Terence Ranger, eds., *The Invention of Tradition* (Cambridge: Cambridge University Press, 1983); Bohlman, afterword to *Israeli Folk Music*, 41–44; and Hirshberg, *Music in the Jewish Community*, 146–56.

42. Both under Ottoman rule and, subsequently, under British control, Jewish society in Palestine was largely autonomous, particularly in matters of culture and education (Hirshberg, *Music in the Jewish Community*, v). European Jewish immigrants to Palestine, beginning with the first nationalistic immigration, or *aliyah*, of 1882, joined two other Jewish populations in Palestine. One demographic group, "in which mystical religious practices had sustained Judaism," predated and survived the four centuries of Ottoman rule that ended with World War I. The "oriental" community included both Jews who had lived in Muslim lands and Sephardim whose Spanish ancestral roots were severed by their expulsion in 1492 (Bohlman, afterword to *Israeli Folk Music*, 45).

43. Though the name ACUM (Agudat Compositorim Umehabrim) has been in use since 1934, the organization was officially inaugurated two years later (Hirshberg, *Music in the Jewish Community*, 170).

44. The trilingual programming of the Palestine Broadcasting Service, established by the British-mandate administration, helped to acquaint speakers of Hebrew, English, and Arabic with the musical traditions of each community (Peter Gradenwitz, *The Music of Israel: Its Rise and Growth through Five Thousand Years* [New York: Norton, 1949], 262). A second edition, revised and expanded, was published in 1996 by Amadeus Press (Portland, Oregon), with the subtitle *From the Biblical Era to Modern Times*. According to Hirshberg, some of the institutions and resources that have contributed to the development of modern Israeli culture were initially viewed with skepticism and fear. By the time sound film reached British-mandate Palestine, three years after its unveiling in New York in 1927, many working musicians who performed in the growing number of cinemas were convinced, as were their British counterparts, that the "Atlantic deluge" would signal the end of their employment. Similarly, the establishment in 1936 of the Palestine Broadcasting Service by the mandate administration was seen by many musicians as a threat, rather than a boost, to their future careers (*Music in the Jewish Community*, 63–64).

45. Due to its affiliation with the Israel Broadcasting Authority, the abbreviation IBA is sometimes added as a suffix to the name of the Jerusalem Symphony Orchestra, a practice not observed in this book.

46. Benjamin Bar-Am, "The League of Composers in Israel: Its Contribution to the Musical Scene in Israel," in *Twenty Years of Israeli Music: Articles and Interviews*, ed. Bar-Am (Tel Aviv: National Council for Culture and Art/League of Composers in Israel, 1968), 76. The IMI is sponsored by the Ministry of Education and Culture.

47. In *IMI News* 1993, no. 1: 15. This initiative of the ICL stemmed from the dissatisfaction of many Israeli composers with existing publishing opportunities.

48. See William Y. Elias, *IMI Comprehensive List of Works, A to Z, 1961–1989* (Tel Aviv: Israel Music Institute, 1989), a catalog listing 1,400 works by 160 composers, musicologists, and librettists, selected from 6,000 submitted during the first 27 years of its operation. IMI director Paul Landau noted that while financial circumstances necessitate the rejection of two-thirds of the scores it receives, the organization publishes approximately fifty works annually ("Enough Said," *IMI News* 1992, nos. 2–3: 25).

49. Elias, *IMI Comprehensive List*, 3. The IMIC is a member organization of the International Music Information Centres network and is affiliated with the International Association of Music Libraries, Archives and Documentation Centres (IAML).

50. In addition to the publication of works by Israeli composers, the IMP has published Schubert's "Tov l'hodos," Schoenberg's "De profundis," and works by Grieg, Britten, Milhaud, Hovhaness, and A. W. Binder. According to Olya Silberman, the IMP published approximately five hundred scores in its first twenty years ("Positive and Negative Aspects in the Integration of Israeli Works into the Local Musical Scene," in Bar-Am, ed., *Twenty Years of Israeli Music*, 67).

51. Since its founding in 1920, the Histadrut has been a potent force in labor relations, education, and culture. Through its cultural center, Merkaz LeTarbut, Hebrew-language folk songs for schoolchildren and choral works for kibbutz and community choirs have been published and disseminated. The cultural center is now known as Culture and Education Enterprises.

52. One writer notes that "undue importance attributed to publication, though it encourages Israeli composers to develop a productive relationship with the world outside, is but another symptom of alienation from the milieu" (Elie Yarden, "The Israeli Composer and His Milieu," *Perspectives of New Music* 4, no. 2 [Spring–Summer 1966]: 135).

53. In *IMI News* 1990, no. 4: 11. Nineteen recordings in this series had been issued as of 1996, and several new compact disks were in preparation. The America-Israel Cultural Foundation recently joined this cooperative enterprise.

54. Partos (b. 1907, Hungary; imm. 1938; d. 1977), a pupil of Kodály, was principal violist of the Palestine Orchestra, a member of the Israel Quartet, and later director of the Academy of Music in Tel Aviv. For a biography of the composer (in Hebrew), see Avner Bahat, *Oedoen Partos: His Life and Works* (Tel Aviv: Am Oved, 1984). The first comprehensive biography of an Israeli composer (first published in Hebrew in 1983) is Jehoash Hirshberg's *Paul Ben-Haim: His Life and Works*, trans. Nathan Friedgut, ed. Bathja Bayer (Jerusalem: Israeli Music Publications, 1990), reviewed by this writer in *Notes* 49, no. 3 (March 1993): 1045–47. Ben-Haim (b. 1897,

Munich; imm. 1933; d. 1984), born Paul Frankenburger, adopted the Hebraized last name (meaning "son of Haim") shortly after his arrival in Palestine as opportunities to perform as a pianist arose, and his tourist visa explicitly prohibited employment (101–5). Menahem Avidom (originally Mendel Mahler-Kalkstein, b. 1908, Galicia; imm. 1925; d. 1995) was for many years chairman of the ICL. Representative works by all three composers are listed in Tischler, *Bibliography.*

55. Until composers' groups persuaded governmental authorities to support creative work in music, this prize was awarded annually only to writers.

56. Several articles concerning the late Recha Freier (1892–1984) and the six Testimonium festivals that occurred between 1968 and 1983 appear in the double issue of *IMI News* 1991, no. 4/1992, no. 1: 1–11. There have been no further Testimonium festivals since Recha Freier's death in 1984.

57. The international choral festival, Zimriya, was established in 1952; the seventeenth Zimriya took place in Jerusalem, 7–17 August 1995. The International Harp Contest has been held in Israel every three years since its founding in 1959.

58. See Harai Golomb, "Rinat: Time for Harvest," *IMI News* 1993, nos. 2–3: 8–9; see also "The Cameran Singers: Chronicle," *IMI News* 1991, no. 4/1992, no. 1: 15–16.

59. According to a recent article, Musica Nova devotes approximately 40 percent of its programming to this repertoire, while the more recently established Music Now is unique in its apparently total dedication to contemporary Israeli works (Lefen, "Israeli Art Music," 9).

60. Ibid., 10.

61. Founded in 1988, the latter orchestra is supported by the municipality for which it is named (it is also known as the Israel Symphony Orchestra, Rishon LeZion). Two developments were announced for the 1995–96 season: the replacement of composer Noam Sheriff as music director by Asher Fish (*IMI News* 1995, no. 1: 18) and the merger of the orchestra with the Tel Aviv Symphony Orchestra (*IMI News* 1995, no. 2: 23).

62. Yaacov Mishori, "Are There Any 'Representative' Israeli Compositions?" *Philharmonia,* June 1991, reprinted in *IMI News* 1991, no. 2: 18. IPO archivist Ephraim Mittelmann has estimated that in the several following seasons, "about 20 works of some 15 new/young Israeli composers" were performed (letter to the author, 28 November 1995).

63. Olya Silberman stated in 1966 that in addition to having given "little encouragement to Israeli composition," the IPO "has had little to do with present-day music" and has devoted insufficient attention to music by Jewish composers ("The Philharmonic Orchestra and Israeli Composition," *Sixth Annual Conference—Israeli Music Week: December 19, 1965–January 1, 1966* [Tel Aviv: League of Composers in Israel, 1966], 86). Elsewhere ("Positive and Negative Aspects," 69–70) Silberman noted that the IPO "took years to perform all of the ten works it had commissioned for its world tour." Between its founding in 1936 as the Palestine Orchestra (renamed in 1948), and 1947, only 4.1 percent of the repertoire of the IPO was devoted to composers living within the country (Hirshberg, *Music in the Jewish Community,* 137). According to information collected in 1981, the IPO performed fewer Israeli works (between 3 and 4 percent of the total programming) in the two prior seasons than any of the six other orchestras studied (see Lefen, "Israeli Art Music," 9).

64. Ben-Haim's work was only performed in the United States (Ephraim Mittelmann, Israel Philharmonic Orchestra archivist, letter to the author, 7 October 1991).

65. The IPO, in association with the IMI, announced in 1995 a competition for a symphonic work to be performed in conjunction with the orchestra's sixtieth anniversary (*IMI News* 1995, no. 2: 23).

66. In *IMI News* 1994, no. 1: 16. The company produced a new opera by an Israeli composer in 1993, in collaboration with the Rishon LeZion Symphony Orchestra. Richard Farber's *The Quest to Polyphonia*, described as an "opera for the whole family," received its premiere in Stuttgart in 1990. On the occasion of its Israeli premiere, critics applauded the effort but had few kind words for the composition; see *IMI News* 1993, nos. 2–3: 11–12. For a brief historical account of earlier attempts to establish an operatic tradition in Palestine and Israel, see Shabtai Ben-Aroyo, "Pioneers of the Opera in Eretz Israel," *IMI News* 1995, no. 2: 9–12.

67. For a synopsis of Israel's complex legalistic struggles with this definition, see Domínguez, *People as Subject*, 169–78.

68. Eric Salzman, *Twentieth-Century Music: An Introduction*, 3d ed. (Englewood Cliffs, N.J.: Prentice-Hall, 1988), 90. As Salzman notes, the composer was "born in Switzerland, studied in Belgium, lived in Paris and—after 1916—in the United States." His music reflected elements associated with Debussy, Strauss, Mahler, Honegger, and Kodály, and he "was a strong eclectic with an extremely various and uneven production that remains difficult to pigeon hole."

69. Hirshberg, *Music in The Jewish Community*, 230. *Halel* also took a strong position against the sound-film, the advent of which had become clear in the Palestine of the 1930s, with significant economic ramifications for working musicians.

70. Bohlman, *"The Land Where Two Streams Flow,"* 133.

71. Bohlman, afterword to *Israeli Folk Music*, 54.

72. Philip V. Bohlman and Mark Slobin, eds., introduction to *Music in the Ethnic Communities of Israel*, Special issue of *Asian Music* 17, no. 2 (Spring–Summer 1986): 4.

73. Ibid.

74. Ibid. While the authors acknowledge that "casting East and West in monolithic terms usually tends, of course, toward oversimplifications," they stress that such conceptualizations represent "a cultural consciousness that pervades Israeli life" with "political, social, religious, and artistic" ramifications (5).

75. See Hermann Swet, "By Way of Introduction," in *Musica Hebraica* (Jerusalem: World Centre for Jewish Music in Palestine, 1938), 1–2; see also Max Brod, *Israel's Music*, trans. Toni Volcani (Tel Aviv: WIZO Zionist Education Department/Sefer Press Ltd., 1951), 5.

76. Kurt List, "What Jewish Music Means to Me," *Jewish Music Forum Bulletin* 9–10 (January 1956): 19.

77. In Jehoash Hirshberg, "Alexander U. Boskovitch and the Quest for an Israeli National Musical Style," in *Modern Jews and Their Musical Agendas*, ed. Ezra Mendelssohn (New York: Oxford University Press, 1993), 96. Alexander (Sandor) Uriyah Boskovitch (1907–64), whose name appears frequently in this book, was a pupil of Nadia Boulanger and Paul Dukas. Boskovitch (also Boscovich and Boskovich) immigrated to Palestine in 1938 and was among the founders of the Tel Aviv Music Academy. His late works evince his developing sense of affinities between European serial procedures of composition and the modal (*maqām*) basis of traditional Middle

Eastern music. The composer's own writings ("The Problems of Original Music in Israel" and "On Original Israeli Music") appear in Herzl Shmueli and Jehoash Hirshberg, *Alexander Uriyah Boskovich: His Life, His Work and His Thought* (Jerusalem: Carmel, 1994), in Hebrew.

78. Brod, *Israel's Music*, 8. Brod acknowledged "degrees of 'Jewishness' " in works by non-Jewish composers—citing, for example, the "profound understanding which gives rise to the 'Samuel Goldenberg and Schmyle' [sic] episode of Moussorgsky's 'Pictures at an Exhibition' with its deep insights into the conflicting aspects of Jewish folk character" (9–10).

79. Ibid., 43. It may be viewed by some as ironic that, considering Brod's promotion of the Eastern Mediterranean movement, he also remarked: "May Heaven guard us from one thing: nationalistic Kitsch" (62).

80. Mark Slobin, "Ten Paradoxes and Four Dilemmas," 22.

81. Kay Kaufman Shelemay, "Mythologies and Realities in the Study of Jewish Music," *World of Music* 37, no. 1 (1995): 24–26.

82. Ibid., 34.

83. Amnon Shiloah, "Revival and Renewal: Can Jewish Ethnic Tradition Survive the Melting Pot?" *Musica Judaica* 10, no. 1 (1987–88): 65.

84. Jehoash Hirshberg and David Sagiv, "The 'Israeli' in Israeli Music: The Audience Responds," *Israel Studies in Musicology* 1 (1978): 159.

85. Jehoash Hirshberg, "The Emergence of Israeli Art Music," in *Aspects of Music in Israel,* ed. Benjamin Bar-Am (Tel Aviv: Israel Composers' League/National Council for Culture and Art, 1980), 15.

86. Artur Holde, *Jews in Music: From the Age of Enlightenment to the Present* (New York: Philosophical Library, 1959), 339.

87. This designation was coined by the immigrant composer A. U. Boskovitch, based on Nietzsche's distinction between "southern" and "northern" music, as exemplified, respectively, by the music of Bizet and Wagner (Don Harrán, "Israel, Art Music," in *New Grove Dictionary of Music and Musicians,* 1980). Eastern Mediterraneanism's focus on "oriental" (i.e., Middle Eastern) musical traditions has thus been compared to the "Western Mediterraneanism" of Bizet's *Carmen,* and to works by Debussy and Ravel similarly inspired by the music of Spain (Keren, *Contemporary Israeli Music,* 71). Peter Gradenwitz formalized this term in the 1950s when he distinguished composers of "Eastern Mediterraneanism" from those of the "Eastern European School" and the "Central European School" (*Music and Musicians in Israel* [Tel Aviv: Israeli Music Publications, 1959]). Gradenwitz also listed composers of "The Younger Generation" (including profiles of Mordecai Seter, Haim Alexander, and Ben-Zion Orgad) and "Composers in Search of New Ways" (which included Abel Ehrlich). In most of the interviews included in the present volume, composers prefer the term "Mediterranean" to "Eastern Mediterranean."

88. Yohanan Boehm, "Music in Modern Erez Israel," *Encyclopaedia Judaica,* 2d ed., 1971. Boehm served as music editor and critic for the *Jerusalem Post* for thirty years, until his death in August 1986. Shortly before, he received the "Distinguished Citizen of Jerusalem" award honoring his many years of devoted service to the municipal youth bands, which he founded in 1939 (Tischler, *Bibliography,* 46). It was my pleasure to meet Mr. Boehm at a concert in the Old City of Jerusalem which included a performance of one of his works.

89. Bohlman, *"The Land Where Two Streams Flow,"* 198–200.

90. Alexander L. Ringer, moderator, "Composers' Round Table," in *Proceedings of the World Congress on Jewish Music—Jerusalem 1978,* ed. Judith Cohen (Tel Aviv: The Institute for the Translation of Hebrew Literature, 1982), 236.

91. Ibid., 241.

92. Ibid., 236.

93. Ibid., 242.

94. Yarden, "Milieu," 137.

95. My decision to interview Stephen Horenstein (b. 1949), a composer who immigrated to Israel from the United States six years earlier in 1980, was questioned by another musician who did not regard Mr. Horenstein as an Israeli composer.

96. Keren, *Contemporary Israeli Music,* 69.

97. In Michal Smoira-Cohn, "Music Here and Now—What Does it Mean?" *Music in Time* (1988–89): 25–26.

98. Ibid., 20.

99. Ibid., 20. Zehavi added that while studying in the United States, "my awareness of this environmental influence and its absence in my life now have become a major problem that I have to handle."

100. Tzvi Avni, "Yet the Sea Is Not Full: Currents in Contemporary Israeli Music," *Music in Time* (1986–87): 28. An earlier version of this article appeared as "Currents in Contemporary Israeli Music," trans. Judith Cooper-Weill, in *Ariel* 68 (1987): 82–91.

101. Peter Gradenwitz, *Music and Musicians in Israel,* 3d ed., rev. and enl. (Tel Aviv: Israeli Music Publications, 1978), 25.

PART I: THE FIRST GENERATION

1. [Peter] E. Gradenwitz, "Music in Israel," *Jewish Frontier* 33 (December 1966, sec. 2): 24.

2. Ibid.

3. Hirshberg, *Music in the Jewish Community,* 146. The kibbutz ("assembly" or "gathering"), the most widely known social institution of modern Israel, is largely the creation of Eastern European immigrants, who have always constituted a majority population in these settlements. But whereas music in the urban community of Central European immigrants in Israel has continued to thrive, musical life in the communal-agricultural kibbutzim has tended to decline since Israel achieved independence (Bohlman, *"The Land Where Two Streams Flow,"* 159–61).

4. Arieh Sachs, "Chamber Music in Israel: Changes in Concept," in Bar-Am, ed., *Twenty Years of Israeli Music,* 28.

5. Harrán, "Israel, Art Music."

6. Hirshberg, *Music in the Jewish Community,* 147.

7. Ibid., 146.

8. Avni, "Currents," 24.

9. Shiloah, "Revival and Renewal," 62.

10. Avni, "Currents," 18.

11. Shiloah, "Revival and Renewal," 62. The monumental ten-volume *Hebräisch-orientalischer Melodienschatz* (Leipzig: Breitkopf and Härtel, 1914–33), compiled by the Latvian immigrant musician Abraham Zvi Idelsohn (1882–1938),

319

was a resource of immense importance to immigrant composers of the pre-state period. See Hirshberg, *Music in the Jewish Community,* 11–22. Zephira (also Zefira), who died in April 1990, worked closely with many immigrant composers, commissioning new works based on the oriental Jewish melodies to which she introduced them. See Gila Flam, "Beracha Zephira—A Case Study of Acculturation in Israeli Song," *Music in the Ethnic Communities of Israel,* Special issue of *Asian Music* 17, no. 2 (Spring–Summer 1986): 108–25.

12. Bohlman, *"The Land Where Two Streams Flow,"* 189.

13. Amnon Shiloah, *Jewish Musical Traditions* (Detroit: Wayne State University Press, 1992), 231.

14. Keren, *Contemporary Israeli Music,* 81.

15. Shiloah, *Jewish Musical Traditions,* 231. Shiloah recounts the similar experience of the acclaimed Yemenite dancer-choreographer (and Israel Prize winner) Sara Levi-Tanai, founder and director of the dance group Inbal, established in 1949. According to Shiloah, Levi-Tanai was tremendously successful until her previously traditional (if stylized) dances yielded to a more "sophisticated form," albeit one still based on these traditions.

16. Ibid.

17. Bohlman, afterword to *Israeli Folk Music,* 47.

18. Ringer, "Musical Composition," 283. As Ringer notes, the orthodox Jewish religious community enforced severe limitations on musical expression, which continues to this day. See also Hirshberg, *Music in the Jewish Community,* 9–10.

19. Ringer, "Musical Composition," 283.

20. Hirshberg, "Emergence," 5–6. Stefan Wolpe (1902–72) immigrated to Palestine in 1933 but resettled in the United States by 1938. Wolpe found local conditions inhospitable for his avant-garde compositional interests. See also Hirshberg, *Music in the Jewish Community,* 176–83.

21. Hirshberg, "Emergence," 6.

22. Hirshberg, "Alexander U. Boskovitch," 92.

23. Wigoder, "Israel, State of (Cultural Life)."

24. Hirshberg, "Emergence," 5.

25. Ibid.

26. Erich Walter Sternberg, "The Twelve Tribes of Israel," *Musica Hebraica* 1–2 (1938): 24.

27. Hirshberg, *Music in the Jewish Community,* 274–75.

28. Bohlman, *"The Land Where Two Streams Flow,"* 184.

29. Harrán, "Israel, Art Music."

30. Keren, *Contemporary Israeli Music,* 75; among those Israeli composers against "self conscious nationalism in art," Keren cites Tal, Sadai, Jonel Patin, Sternberg, Alexander, and Artur Gelbrun, who, he states, don't "try" to write Israeli music: "They allow themselves to be influenced by musical folklore, but do not feel compelled to use either the style or specific melodies."

31. Ibid., 74. Keren cites as an example of archaism the *massechet* ("web" or "texture"), a musical form rooted in the collectivism of kibbutz life. The term "American Wave" was coined by musicologist H. Wiley Hitchcock.

32. Bohlman, afterword to *Israeli Folk Music,* 47.

33. Avni, "Currents," 16.

34. Ibid.

35. Nathan Mishori, "A Critic Looks at His Generation," in Bar-Am, ed., *Aspects of Music in Israel,* 17.

36. Ringer, "Musical Composition," 282–83.

37. This is Hirshberg's description of the opening cello passage from "The Mountains of Judea," the first of *Two Landscape Pictures* for cello and piano composed by Ben-Haim in 1938 (Hirshberg, *Paul Ben-Haim,* 159).

38. Werner, "Pioneers of Israeli Art," 15. French language and culture were also potent factors in the emerging society of Palestine, owing to the influence of such figures as the Baron Edmond de Rothschild (1845–1934), a French-Jewish banker and philanthropist who financially supported Jewish settlements (see Hirshberg, *Music in the Jewish Community,* 23–30). From the beginning of this century, Palestine's music and visual arts communities were by no means isolated from one another. Bezalel (founded in 1906) was one of several schools where the influential musician and scholar A. Z. Idelsohn was a teacher (ibid., 12). A concert in Jerusalem sponsored by the Violin of Zion Society (founded in 1904) featured a "virtuoso performance by four students of Bezalel art school who competed in drawing and painting to the rhythm of rapid piano-playing" (ibid., 32).

39. See Hirshberg, *Paul Ben-Haim,* 149–59. Hirshberg distinguishes between musical influences, dominated by the impressionism of Ravel and Debussy, and extramusical influences, especially acclimation to the Hebrew language and its ramifications for rhythmic and phrase organization (152–53). Among the musical influences on Eastern Mediterraneanism frequently attributed to French impressionist composers is the parallel motion of melodic lines, especially in fourths and fifths. This phenomenon has, however, also been described in the liturgical services of Yemenite Jews by Uri Sharvit in "Jewish Musical Culture—Past and Present," *World of Music* 37, no. 1 (1995): 3.

40. Ben-Haim's "impressionistic" *Variations on a Hebrew Theme* (1939), a piano trio he composed six years after settling in Palestine, is based on a melody of Arabic origin "which occupies a special place in the Israeli repertoire" (Hirshberg, *Paul Ben-Haim,* 155).

41. Elaine Brody, *Paris: The Musical Kaleidoscope, 1870–1925* (New York: George Braziller, 1987), 68. This perspective is evident in Victor Hugo's preface to *Orientales* (1828), his collection of lyrics inspired by themes of the visionary East: "Spain is still the Orient, it's half African and Africa is half asiatic" (69). One of the texts from *Orientales,* "Adieux de l'hôtesse arabe," was set by Bizet, whose opera *Carmen* (1873–74) initiated a fruitful repertory of music by French composers, inspired by images and echoes of Spain. As Brody notes (79–92), the Paris Expositions Universelles of 1867 and 1889 were influential in bringing art and artifacts of this broadly conceived "oriental" world to the attention of the French.

42. In Ringer, "Composers' Round Table," 237. After 1936, Arabic music could be heard daily on the radio (Palestine Broadcasting Service). As in the exposure of immigrant composers to oriental Jewish musical styles, certain individuals also promoted the awareness of Arabic music and culture within the Jewish community. See Hirshberg, *Music in the Jewish Community,* 198–203.

43. Herbert Fromm, *On Jewish Music: A Composer's View* (New York: Bloch, 1978), 86.

44. Peter Gradenwitz, "Israeli Composers—A Link between Orient and Occident," *Chesterian* 25, no. 165 (1951): 70.

45. Bohlman, *"The Land Where Two Streams Flow,"* 189.

46. Fromm, *On Jewish Music,* 85.

47. Stefan Wolpe criticized the artificiality of "the country's musical mannerisms," expressing puzzlement with "those idealists who believe that a national style should be deliberately created along the lines of a chemical formula" ("Music, Old and New, in Palestine," *Modern Music* 16, no. 3 [March–April 1939]: 158).

48. Perhaps at the other end of the spectrum from Wolpe was the musician and theorist Mordecai Sandberg, who rejected Western musical and technological influences. The founder of the Institute for Contemporary Music in 1927, he published articles promoting the use of microtones and discouraging performances of Western music. Although Sandberg's views "led to no viable musical results," his ideas continued to influence later critical and journalistic writings (Hirshberg, "Emergence," 5).

49. Yuval Shaked, "On Ehrlich's Personal Way in Music," *IMI News* 1990, no. 2: 1.

50. Bohlman, *"The Land Where Two Streams Flow,"* 191.

51. Ibid., 206–7.

52. Keren, *Contemporary Israeli Music,* 92.

53. Avni, "Currents," 24. Avni specifically refers, in this regard, to Seter's *Jerusalem* Symphony, discussed by the composer and illustrated in chap. 5.

CHAPTER 1: HANOCH JACOBY

1. Jacoby was a member of the IPO from 1958 until 1974. The late Allan D. Cisco, whose photograph of Jacoby appears in this chapter, was a cellist with the IPO from 1965 until 1972 and a close friend of the composer. This photograph previously appeared on the cover page of the IPO *Newsletter* 45 (June 1990).

2. Bohlman, *"The Land Where Two Streams Flow,"* 200.

3. Ibid., 201.

4. Ibid.

5. The last work of Jacoby's listed in Tischler's bibliography is *Mutatio No. 2,* a chamber composition for nine instruments, composed in 1977.

6. See David Chen, "In Memoriam Hanoch Jacoby," *IMI News* 1990, no. 4: 3–4.

7. Born in Hungary, Hauser immigrated to Palestine in 1932 and founded the Palestine Music Conservatory the following year. Within months, he recognized and realized the potential of the institution, whose promise of both employment and study for European Jews facilitated the rescue of many from Germany and Poland. The enrollment (including Arabs, European Christians, and Jews, and students from Egypt, Syria, and Turkey) and faculty rapidly expanded. So too did the curricular offerings, which included instruction in eurythmics, guitar, recorder, teacher training, and Arabic music as well as dance and drama. By 1944 the Conservatory had spawned academies for advanced students in Jerusalem and Tel Aviv. Jacoby served as director of the Jerusalem Music Academy from 1954 to 1958, and as principal violist with the Kol Israel Orchestra for over twenty years, before joining the IPO. See Hirshberg,

Music in the Jewish Community, 172–75; and Bohlman, *"The Land Where Two Streams Flow,"* 148–50.

8. Hanoch Jacoby, *Mutatio No. 1* for Symphony Orchestra (Tel Aviv: Israel Music Institute, 1975). The catalog number is IMI 6665.

9. See chap. 3.

10. Jacoby interrupted his text here to say, "That I learned later only."

11. The term "homophony" normally connotes a musical texture of melody and accompaniment, whereas "monophony" describes a one-voice or unison texture of pure melody, unaccompanied and uncombined with other (vocal or instrumental) parts.

12. Reprinted with permission of the Israel Philharmonic Orchestra, which performed *Mutatio* on nine subscription concerts in Tel Aviv, Haifa, and Jerusalem between 28 December 1980 and 8 January 1981, Charles Dutoit conducting (Ephraim Mittelmann, letter to the author, 28 November 1995). The original text has been edited slightly, for clarity.

13. After authorizing publication, Jacoby subsequently stipulated that portions of a previously published interview be incorporated into the text of his remarks. The preceding passage enclosed in curly brackets, slightly edited, appeared in Uri E. Toeplitz, "The Progressive Reactionary," Israel Philharmonic Orchestra program booklet, 18 March 1972 (used with permission). A flutist and member of the IPO from its start in 1936, Toeplitz is also the author of *The History of the Israel Philharmonic Orchestra Researched and Remembered* (Tel Aviv: Sifriat Poalim, 1992); in Hebrew.

14. In *IMI News,* passim.

CHAPTER 2: JOSEF TAL

1. Oskar Gottlieb Blarr, "Homage to Josef Tal: On the Occasion of His Winning the Johann Wenzel Stamitz Prize (Mannheim, Germany, March 28, 1995)," *IMI News* 1995, no. 2: 12.

2. Ringer, "Musical Composition," 288–89.

3. Alexander L. Ringer, "Tal, Josef," in *New Grove Dictionary of Music and Musicians,* 1980.

4. Bohlman, *"The Land Where Two Streams Flow,"* 203, 207.

5. William Y. Elias, "Josef Tal—80th Anniversary," *IMI News* 1990, no. 1: 1–2. The Israel Music Institute compiled a catalog of Tal's works in 1989 as part of its "Mini-Monograph" series.

6. Josef Tal, *Der Sohn des Rabbiners* (Darmstadt: Kuadriger Verlag, 1985).

7. Tal's birthplace, Pinne, near Posen, was an eastern province of Germany rather than a part of Europe that became East Germany.

8. Letter to the author, 30 May 1990.

9. Letter to the author, 17 May 1991. See Habakuk Traber, "Thoughts on Josef Tal's Symphony No. 5," *IMI News* 1992, no. 4: 3–5.

10. See *IMI News* 1995, no. 2: 1–8 for several related articles, including Josef Tal, "The Opera in the Life of the Composer." *Josef* is the fifth operatic collaboration between Tal and librettist Israel Eliraz, with whom he has created several additional works.

11. In *IMI News* 1995, no. 1: 19. See also Blarr, "Homage to Josef Tal," 12–13.

CHAPTER 3: HAIM ALEXANDER

1. The unpublished collection of Jewish and oriental songs, "deciphered" by Alexander at the Hebrew University during the years 1969–73, is in the possession of the IMI (letter to the author, 3 November 1995).

2. Michael Wolpe, "Profile of Composer Haim Alexander," *Music in Time* (1988–89): 54. Portions of this article were reprinted, with a biographical sketch, in *IMI News* 1993, no. 1: 1–3.

3. After authorizing publication, Haim Alexander stipulated that portions of a previously published interview be incorporated into the text. The passages enclosed in curly brackets, slightly edited, originally appeared in Wolpe, "Profile," and are reprinted with permission of *Music in Time*.

4. In a footnote, Wolpe explains that "Yekke" is "German for jacket, signifying the formal dress worn by the immigrants from Germany even at the height of the Middle Eastern summer." For further ramifications of this term see Bohlman, *"The Land Where Two Streams Flow,"* 19–21.

5. The Deutscher Akademisher Austauschdienst (German Academic Exchange Service) provides grants to individuals wishing to study in Germany.

6. Haim Alexander, *Improvisation am Klavier* (Mainz: B. Schott's Söhne, 1986), a two-volume text with two accompanying cassettes; the catalog number is ED 7536.

7. Pelleg (originally Pollack; 1910–68) was a noted harpsichordist, pianist, writer, lecturer, educator, and composer who counted among his teachers Alexander von Zemlinsky.

8. In *IMI News,* passim. In a June 19, 1986 concert given by Soprano Cilla Grossmeyer and organist Elisabeth Roloff, I heard Alexander's *De profundis* for organ and the premiere of his Psalm 146.

CHAPTER 4: ABEL EHRLICH

1. Letter to the author, 4 November 1996.

2. In the excerpt reproduced in this chapter, the last pitch in measure 12 is played three-quarters of a tone lower than G-natural; the first two pitches in measure 14 and the first pitch in measure 15 are all lowered a quarter tone.

3. Shaked, "Ehrlich's Personal Way," 3.

4. Ibid. Shaked also notes that Ehrlich was one of the founders of the Jerusalem Academy of Music, among the first teachers at the Academy of Music in Tel Aviv, and a senior lecturer at the Oranim Seminary for Music Teachers (1).

5. Ibid., 2.

6. Abel Ehrlich, *Bashrav* (Jerusalem: Israeli Music Publications, 1959). The catalog number for the original solo violin version, composed in 1953, is IMP 155. Later versions, also published by IMP, include a 1956 arrangement for solo violin and a choir of violins, and a 1958 arrangement for orchestra.

7. Philip Bohlman notes that "bashrav" traditionally connotes a kind of suite form in Turkish and Arabic classical music.

8. Simha Arom is an ethnomusicologist based in Paris.

9. The organizations referred to here are the International Society for Contemporary Music (ISCM) and the Israel Composers' League (ICL).

10. Ehrlich's reference is to the defacement and burning of bus stop shelters by orthodox Israeli Jews, in 1986, angered by their posted advertisements displaying attractive young women in bathing suits.

11. The program included world premieres of two works composed by Ehrlich in 1986: *Death of Dan Pagis,* for piano, performed by Prof. William Goldenberg of the School of Music faculty; and *The Dream about Strange Terrors,* for two flutes, performed by graduate students Betsy Brightbill and Deanna Mathews. Mr. Ehrlich's wife, Lea, also attended.

12. Letter to the author, 30 December 1986.

13. Letter to the author, 28 December 1990.

14. "IMI Composers' Reactions to the Gulf War," in *IMI News* 1991, no. 1: 4.

15. In *IMI News* 1995, no. 1: 18. A special Hebrew issue of the *IMI News* devoted to Ehrlich and distributed to the audience at this concert is expected to be issued in an English translation.

CHAPTER 5: MORDECAI SETER

1. William Y. Elias has written: "Seeing himself as an artist who writes according to his spiritual impulse, Seter has refused to accept commissions (including an opera, incidental music, orchestral music and educational works) since the mid-1960s, as he found himself drawn only to the writing of chamber music" ("Seter, Mordecai," in *New Grove Dictionary of Music and Musicians,* 1980).

2. Paul Landau, "Mordecai Seter: From the Collective to the Intimate," *IMI News* 1990, no. 3: 4–5.

3. See Ido Abravaya, "In Memoriam Mordecai Seter," *IMI News* 1994, no. 3–4: 24–25. A comprehensive list of Seter's compositions is available from the IMI, which also produced a special Hebrew edition of the *IMI News* in conjunction with a memorial concert held in March 1995, arranged jointly by the Tel Aviv Rubin Academy and the Feher Jewish Music Centre, Beth Hatefutsoth, Museum of the Jewish Diaspora. It is expected that the memorial issue will also be made available in English translation.

4. Ringer, "Musical Composition," 291.

5. Landau, "Mordecai Seter," 3.

6. Quoted in ibid., 5.

7. See "Mordecai Seter and His Music: On the Occasion of the 75th Birthday of the Composer," *IMI News* 1991, no. 2: 1.

8. Joachim Stutschewsky (b. Ukraine, 1891; imm. 1938; d. Israel, 1982) was a composer and cellist who collaborated with Hermann Swet and Salli Levi in directing the activities of the World Centre for Jewish Music in Palestine. Founder of the Society for the Development of Jewish Music in Vienna and member of the Kolisch (later Vienna String) Quartet, Stutschewsky became director of music in the cultural section of the Jewish National Council in Palestine until 1948. He collected and edited Hasidic melodies and incorporated many of these in his works.

9. The reference is to A. Z. Idelsohn's *Thesaurus.* The influential Jewish music scholar died in August 1938.

10. Emanuel Amiran-Pougatchov (1909–93), who supervised the Music Education Department of the Ministry of Culture from 1949 to 1975, was a prolific

composer of songs written mostly prior to statehood but known to most Israelis. See Alex Doron, "In Memoriam Emanuel Amiran," *IMI News* 1994, no. 1: 17–18.

11. Admon was born in the Ukraine in 1894, immigrated to Israel in 1906, and died there in 1982. He earned a baccalaureate degree at Johns Hopkins University (1923–27) and studied with Nadia Boulanger (1930–39). A composer of light and popular music, he received the Israel Prize in 1974. See Michal Smoira, "Homage to Yedidya Admon," *IMI News* 1992, nos. 2–3: 8–9.

12. Mordecai Seter, *Jerusalem,* Symphony for Mixed Choir, Brass, and Strings (Tel Aviv: Israel Music Institute, 1970). Seter's three-movement work (based on texts from Lamentations, Isaiah, and Psalm 137) is scored for SATB choir, brass, and strings. I am unable to reconcile the composer's stated inspiration (the Six-Day War, which began in June 1967) with the completion date of December 1966 cited in the score; Seter revised this work in 1979. The mode upon which this work is based, constructed of the four pentachords illustrated in ex. 4, is described by the composer as including all twelve tones of the chromatic scale, "as well as some enharmonics (G sharp–A flat, etc.), which are functionally independent" (163). This mode is used without transposition, according to Keren, *Contemporary Israeli Music,* 90.

13. I believe Mr. Seter's reference was again to the score of *Jerusalem.*

PART II: THE SECOND GENERATION

1. Holde, *Jews in Music,* 310–11.

2. Joseph Cohen, *Voices of Israel,* 1.

3. Aron Marko Rothmüller, *The Music of the Jews: An Historical Appreciation,* new and rev. ed., trans. H. S. Stevens (London and South Brunswick, N.Y.: Yoseloff, 1967), 250.

4. Sachs, "Chamber Music," 30.

5. Yarden, "Milieu," 136–37.

6. Mishori, "A Critic Looks at His Generation," 21.

7. Avni, "Currents," 22.

8. Keren, *Contemporary Israeli Music,* 89.

9. I am thankful to Alex Wasserman for suggesting this point. Though parallels have previously been cited between composers of the Eastern Mediterranean movement and those of the "American Wave," who were their contemporaries, the second-generation Israeli composers (despite many claims to their immunity from such concerns) were also searching for ways to represent their time and place in music. It is thus not unreasonable to suggest that just as American composers learned to write "American music" in France, Israel's first two generations of composers sought similar guidance from mentors in the United States and Germany, where universities and summer courses exposed them to composers and trends from many other countries.

10. Bohlman, *"The Land Where Two Streams Flow,"* 189.

11. Ibid. Peter Gradenwitz has cited several works exemplary of the Mediterranean style. In the *Song of Praise* (Concerto for Viola and Orchestra, No. 1, 1949) by Partos, "the way of scoring and combining orchestral colours" reflects "the instrumental playing of oriental musicians"; the orchestration, as well as "melodic and rhythmic invention" in the second movement of Ben-Haim's Piano Concerto (1949), achieves "a true 'Mediterranean' atmosphere." The concerto's last movement

is described as "a typical oriental dance, with the movement gaining in momentum and tempo towards the end and concluding in frenetic ecstasy." Boskovitch's Oboe Concerto (1942; rev. 1960) and *Semitic Suite* (1945–60) are also cited (Gradenwitz, "Israeli Composers—A Link between Orient and Occident," 70–71).

12. Keren, *Contemporary Israeli Music,* 75.

13. Ibid., 81. Keren observed that younger Israeli composers also looked beyond indigenous Middle Eastern traditions to Asian musical cultures for inspiration and influence (82).

14. Ibid., 102. Except for the final chapter ("After 1960," added in 1973), this doctoral thesis was completed nearly two decades prior to its publication.

15. Ami Maayani, "The Music of Israel, 1983–1985," *New Music in Israel, 1983–1985* (Tel Aviv: Israel Composers' League, 1985), 16.

16. Avni, "Currents," 26.

17. Keren, *Contemporary Israeli Music,* 84.

18. Shiloah, "Revival and Renewal," 59.

19. Brod, *Israel's Music,* 7–8.

20. Keren, *Contemporary Israeli Music,* 102.

21. Harrán, "Israel, Art Music."

22. Holde, *Jews in Music,* 346. The author was describing the broad range of common experiences that he felt would come to characterize Israel's new music.

23. Avni, "Currents," 27.

24. In Ringer, "Composers' Round Table," 241.

CHAPTER 6: BEN-ZION ORGAD

1. The IMI compiled a catalog of Orgad's works in 1981 as part of its "Mini-Monograph" series.

2. Ben-Zion Orgad, *Colmontage,* trans. Avi Jacobson and Sharon Ne'eman (Tel Aviv: Privately printed, 1989). The book is subtitled "A Partita for Solo Voice."

3. Boehm, "Music in Modern Erez Israel."

4. Ringer, "Musical Composition," 294. In conjunction with the 1978 World Congress on Jewish Music, Orgad prepared a monograph on the subject, *The Musical Potential of the Hebrew Language and Its Manifestations in Artistic Music,* trans. Avi Jacobson (Jerusalem: Privately printed, Summer 1978).

5. Ben-Zion Orgad, "Questions of Art and Faith," *Ariel* 39 (1975): 85.

6. Mâche, of the University of Strasbourg, is the author of *Music, Myth, and Nature, or The Dolphins of Arion* (1993) and the editor of *Music, Society, and Imagination in Contemporary France* (1994), both published by Harwood Academic Publishers (London).

7. During the 1991 Gulf War, Orgad was in New York City for a premiere of his *Filigrees No. 1* (1989–90) for clarinet and string quartet at the Mannes College of Music. Shortly thereafter, at Northern Illinois University, guest pianist Nadia Nehama Weintraub performed the composer's *Seven Variations on C* (1961), and the NIU Wind Ensemble, conducted by Stephen Squires, performed his *Two Movements for Wind Orchestra* (*Elul and Sheva*), completed in 1985.

8. In *IMI News,* passim.

9. This program also featured works by Tzvi Avni and Josef Tal. Avni and Orgad offered remarks concerning their works.

CHAPTER 7: TZVI AVNI

1. The IMI compiled a catalog of Avni's works in 1978 as part of its "Mini-Monograph" series.

2. In his *Harmonielehre (Theory of Harmony)*, originally published in 1911, the composer Arnold Schoenberg lamented the historical neglect of tone color (or timbre) as a compositional tool. He employed the term *Klangfarbenmelodie* ("tone color melody") to suggest a technique by which composers could control the linear development of timbre in ways comparable to the manner in which the tones of a melody or the chords in a harmonic progression normally succeed one another in tonal music.

3. A controversial Hasidic leader active in the Ukraine, Nachman of Bratzlav (1772–1811) was "the foremost narrator of Tales which Hassidism has produced" (Hirshberg, *Paul Ben-Haim,* 335).

4. Tzvi Avni, *Epitaph* (Piano Sonata No. 2) (Tel Aviv: Israel Music Institute, 1984). The catalog number is IMI 6287. This one-movement work, inspired by "The Story of the Seven Beggars," was composed during the years 1974–79 and received the ACUM Publication Prize in 1981 (p. 4). It is also examined in Aviva Espiedra, "A Critical Study of Four Piano Sonatas by Israeli Composers, 1950–1979," (Ph.D. diss., Peabody Institute of the Johns Hopkins University, 1992).

5. Avni's *Capriccio* for piano was performed at Northern Illinois University in April 1987 by Prof. William Koehler.

6. Zubin Mehta conducted an IPO performance of Avni's *Desert Scenes* (1987–91)—which, the composer noted, has "nothing to do with the war—it's the Biblical desert" (letter to the author, 22 March 1992). According to Benjamin Bar-Am, *Desert Scenes* "signifies a remarkable old-new development in Israeli music. There is a clear rebuttal of eccentric, cosmopolitan modernism in favor of a re-discovery of our Near-Eastern, regional and ancient Jewish roots. The symphony can almost be labelled 'neo-Mediterranean,' harking back to our music of the 1940s, the 1950s and the early 1960s, with its pastoral, landscape-inspired and dance-like connotations" (*Jerusalem Post,* 31 October 1991; in *IMI News* 1991, no. 4/1992, no. 1: 18).

7. This program also featured works by Ben-Zion Orgad and Josef Tal. Avni and Orgad also offered remarks concerning their works.

8. In Boston, where Avni was a guest lecturer at Northeastern University during his 1993–94 sabbatical leave, performances included his *Psalm Canticles* for choir a cappella, *Leda and the Swan* for soprano and clarinet, and *Three Songs from Song of Songs*. Avni visited the Northern Illinois University School of Music in April 1994, where Prof. William Koehler again performed his *Capriccio* for piano and graduate student Karen Cardon performed his *Elegy* for violoncello. In May 1995, "An Afternoon with Tzvi Avni" was presented at the Bruno Walter Auditorium at Lincoln Center in New York, which included performances of works composed by Avni between 1957 and 1995.

CHAPTER 8: AMI MAAYANI

1. Interview with Uri Toeplitz, in a 1969 IPO program booklet in conjunction with the orchestra's performance of Maayani's *Regalim*. Used with permission.

2. Benjamin Bar-Am, review, *Jerusalem Post*, 11 April 1990; in *IMI News* 1990, no. 2: 7.

3. Laya Harbater Silber, "Ami Maayani and the Yiddish Art Song (Part II)," *Musica Judaica* 9, no. 1 (1986–87): 64.

4. Maayani, "The Music of Israel," 17.

5. Yoel Engel (1868–1927), Joseph Achron (1886–1943), Moses Milner (1886–1953), Solomon Rosowsky (1878–1962), and Michael Gnessin (1883–1957) were composers associated with the St. Petersburg Society for Jewish Folk Music, formed in 1908. Following World War I, its members dispersed, to other parts of Europe, British-mandate Palestine, and the United States, influencing the formation of similar organizations devoted to the study and promotion of Jewish music (Irene Heskes, *Passport to Jewish Music: Its History, Traditions, and Culture*, Contributions to the Study of Music and Dance, no. 33 [Westport, Conn., and London: Greenwood Press, 1994], 23–24).

6. The shamisen and the koto are two of the most common instruments of traditional Japanese music. The shamisen has three strings and is roughly comparable to the Western banjo; the koto is a thirteen-string zither.

7. Maayani served for many years as chairman of the Israeli Composers' League.

8. Ruth Maayani, the composer's sister, is a harpist who frequently performs his work. She and flutist Betsy Brightbill performed Maayani's *Arabesque No. 2* (1973) at Northern Illinois University in April 1987.

9. In *IMI News*, passim.

10. Ami Maayani, *Richard Wagner: A Monograph* (Jerusalem: Fons Music Foundation/IMP, 1995). Maayani's massive study (1050 pp.) occupied him for twenty-one years.

11. Letter to the author, 15 October 1995. Maayani noted that the promotional booklet accompanying his letter lists his complete output—"all of it, as I stop[ped] writing music before this book was issued!"

PART III: THE THIRD GENERATION

1. Avni, "Currents," 26. Avni also describes other elements of change in Israeli musical culture: "Folk songs have developed in a way indicating the change in atmosphere which has taken place. Herdsmen's songs and pastorality are passé, paeans to prowess have gone the way of the recitals of immigration, brave defense and homeland, and even of the search for an authentic Israeli style. The songs popular here during the last two decades have come closer to the various international streams in the entertainment genre, with themes ranging from romance to protest in the spirit of today, just as they are being written everywhere else. Alongside these flourish what are called 'cassette tracks,' produced by popular singers reared in Mediterranean orientalism with strains of Greek, Turkish and Arab music" (27–28).

2. The generational groups of composers included in this book portray a process of continually increased exposure to "outside" influence. Among the first-generation composers, Alexander, Ehrlich, and Tal traveled to summer courses in Germany. The second-generation composers attended summer courses but also spent a couple of years in the United States, where Orgad earned a master's degree. Among the third-generation composers, several (Ben-Shabetai, Leef, Permont, and Zehavi) earned

doctorates in the United States, while Betty Olivero followed her graduate study at Yale with a summer at Tanglewood and four years of apprenticeship with Luciano Berio in Italy.

3. Israeli composers of Shulamit Ran's generation professionally active outside of Israel include Jan Radzynski (b. 1950, Poland), now teaching at Ohio State University, Ofer Ben-Amots (b. 1955, Israel), teaching at Colorado College, Amnon Wolman (b. 1955, Israel), a computer music composer teaching at Northwestern University, and Chaya Czernowin (b. 1957, Israel), who joined the music faulty of the University of California at San Diego in 1997, as well as Betty Olivero and Gabriel Iranyi. Other composers, once professionally active in Israel, who resettled in the United States and Europe include Herbert Brün, Issachar Miron, Roman Haubenstock-Ramati, Peter Jona Korn, Yehoshua Lakner, and Peter Feuchtwanger (Keren, *Contemporary Israeli Music*, 100).

4. Smoira-Cohn, "Music Here and Now," 17–18.

5. Haim Permont's interview appears in chap. 16. Works "encompassing all the possible musical styles and sounds" are produced by some of the younger composers, according to Maayani ("The Music of Israel," 17).

6. In Smoira-Cohn, "Music Here and Now," 25.

7. Maayani, "The Music of Israel," 16.

8. Keren, *Contemporary Israeli Music*, 81.

9. Yinam Leef, "On Traditions and Contradictions," *IMI News* 1990, no. 2: 6.

10. Ibid., 5.

11. Ibid., 6.

12. In Smoira-Cohn, "Music Here and Now," 20.

13. Max Stern, "In Search of a Sacred Ethos: Contexts and Contradictions," *New Music in Israel, 1985–1987* (Tel Aviv: Israel Composers' League, 1988), 17.

14. See Ringer, "Musical Composition," 285–88.

15. Keren, *Contemporary Israeli Music*, 91. A number of recent immigrant composers from the former USSR are profiled by Marina Ritsarev in "Let Me Introduce," *IMI News* 1991, no. 2: 3–5.

CHAPTER 9: AHARON HARLAP

1. For a list of compositions by Harlap, see Tischler, *Bibliography*, 122–24.

2. One who observes the traditions of the Jewish Sabbath, or the day of rest. Among these conventions are the prohibitions against cooking and driving.

3. "Nami" is a nickname, referring to Yinam Leef, whose interview appears in chap. 17.

4. Mary Even-Or was born in 1939 and died in 1989.

5. In *IMI News*, passim. See Michael Ajzenstadt, "The Two Faces of Aharon Harlap—The Composer as Conductor," and accompanying career summary in the *IMI News* 1994, nos. 3–4: 1–4.

CHAPTER 10: ARIK SHAPIRA

1. Shapira's reference is to the influential French composer Olivier Messiaen (1908–92), whose music is known for its eclectic palette of birdsong, Indian rhythms,

symmetrical "modes of limited transposition," and the influence of Christian mysticism. Messiaen visited Israel in 1983 to accept the Wolff Foundation Prize (shared with Vladimir Horowitz and Josef Tal) and to attend a concert of the Jerusalem Symphony Orchestra devoted to his works. He returned shortly before his death for performances of his *Turangalîla Symphony* by the Israel Philharmonic Orchestra, conducted by Zubin Mehta. See André Hajdu, "In Memoriam Olivier Messiaen: Messiaen as a Teacher," and Gilah Yaron, "Olivier Messiaen: A Personal Memoir," *IMI News* 1992, no. 4: 9–10.

2. Arik Shapira, *Missa Viva for Symphony Orchestra,* composed in 1978 (Tel Aviv: Israel Music Institute, 1982). The catalog number is IMI 6336.

3. Arik Shapira, *Off Piano* (1984). This work was performed by Israeli pianist Michal Tal at Northern Illinois University in April 1987. The program note Shapira submitted for that "New Music from Israel" concert reads: "In this piece I tried to find a new piano sound—restrained, hermit-like, obsessive, anti-virtuoso, and above all a piano piece in which the pianist is deeply involved in—in brief: off piano."

4. Letter to the author, 29 June 1989.

5. The first performance was in April 1991 in a Music Now concert in Tel Aviv; see *IMI News* 1991, no. 2: 10.

6. The first performance of this work, by the Rishon LeZion Symphony Orchestra, is listed under the title *Jingle 83* (*IMI News* 1990, no. 4: 5).

7. The first performance of this work, listed as *The Mad Man of Culture,* was in July 1991 in Tel Aviv (*IMI News* 1991, no. 3: 9).

8. See *IMI News* 1994, no. 2.

9. "Arguments of the Jury" (Prof. Shay Burstyn, Chairman; Dr. David Alexander; Joseph Mar-Haim; Roni Somek; Rema Samsonov), in *IMI News* 1994, no. 2: 18.

10. It was reported that when Shapira was awarded the Prime Minister's Prize in 1986, then Prime Minister Yitzhak Shamir refused to shake his hand due to the criticism of contemporary Zionism in his work *Upon Thy Ruins Ophra* (*IMI News* 1994, no. 2: 20).

11. D. Orstav, *Yedioth Ahronot,* 27 January 1994; reprinted in *IMI News* 1994, no. 2: 20.

12. Ami Maayani, *Jerusalem Post,* 25 April 1994; reprinted in *IMI News* 1994, no. 2: 23.

13. H. Ron, *Ha'ir,* 4 February 1994; reprinted in *IMI News* 1994, no. 2: 21.

14. E. Rigbi, *Kol Ha'ir,* 11 February 1994; reprinted in *IMI News* 1994, no. 2: 22.

15. O. Assaf, in *Ha'ir,* 11 February 1994; reprinted in *IMI News* 1994, no. 2: 21.

16. Yuval Shaked, "All or Nothing at All: Correspondence with Arik Shapira," *IMI News* 1994, no. 2: 1.

17. Ibid., 2.

18. Shabtai Petrushka, letter to the editor, 6 August 1994, in *IMI News* 1994, nos. 3–4: 26.

19. Jehoash Hirshberg, letter, 6 November 1994, in *IMI News* 1994, nos. 3–4: 26.

20. Letter to the author, 5 October 1994.

21. Letter to the author, 26 July 1995.

22. Letter to the author, 6 March 1996.

Chapter 11: Daniel Galay

1. Daniel Galay, *Tzu Singen un Tzu Sogen* (Holon: Israel Brass-Woodwind Publications, 1983).
2. In *IMI News*, passim.
3. Letter to the author, 5 November 1995.

Chapter 12: Tsippi Fleischer

1. Tsippi Fleischer, "History of Hebrew Song: An Anthology" (Ramat Gan: Bar-Ilan University Department of Musicology, 1985; internal publication), 2 vols., 160 pp.
2. Ora Binur-Schmit, "Tsippi Fleischer—A Concert at the Zionist Confederation House, Jerusalem," *Ma'ariv*, 6 November 1988.
3. Jehoash Hirshberg, "Tsippi Fleischer: Musician between East and West," *Ariel* 76 (1989): 47, 49. *Girl-Butterfly-Girl* is published by the IMI.
4. Fleischer's *Lamentation* (1985) is published by Peer Musikverlag (Hamburg). Fleischer received the Marc Lavry Award for this work from the Haifa municipality in 1990. It was commissioned by the International Women's Music Festival, Beer Sheva, where it was premiered on 23 June 1986.
5. Lasker-Schüler (1869–1945) immigrated to Palestine in the 1930s.
6. From Else Lasker-Schüler, *Sämtliche Gedichte*. Copyright 1984 by Kösel Verlag (München). All rights reserved by Suhrkamp Verlag (Frankfurt am Main). Used with permission.
7. From Else Lasker-Schüler, *Gedichte*, Hebrew trans. Yehuda Amichai (Tel Aviv: Eked Publishing House, 1969), 17. Used with the permission of Eked Publishing House and the estate of Else Lasker-Schüler (P. A. Alsberg, administrator).
8. English translation by Gila Abrahamson; used with permission.
9. Fleischer's reference was to a review of the performance by Eli Karev, "Tsippi Fleischer's 'Lament' Opens Women's Music Festival," *Jerusalem Post*, 25 June 1986.
10. In *IMI News*, passim. The double issue, *IMI News* 1991, no. 4/1992, no. 1, features a biographical sketch of Fleischer, and her "Notes about My *1992-Oratorio*" (14–15).
11. Letter to the author, 5 January 1996.

Chapter 13: Gabriel Iranyi

1. For a list of compositions by Iranyi, see Tischler, *Bibliography*, 130–32.
2. Iranyi's remark responds to a review by Eli Karev (n.p., 1986).
3. Bloch is director of the Group for New Music and a member of the musicology faculty at Tel Aviv University. He is married to the mezzo-soprano Emilie Berendsen, who is also devoted to the performance of contemporary and Israeli music.
4. The term denotes a secret archival storeroom in a synagogue; the *genizah* of Cairo contained an important collection of Hebrew manuscripts which was discovered in 1896.
5. Letter to the author, 20 March 1990.
6. In *IMI News*, passim.

CHAPTER 14: STEPHEN HORENSTEIN

1. Stephen Horenstein, *Agadot* (1985), Merkin Concert Hall, New York, 16–17 June 1991, program note.

2. This composition, originally titled *Arbres de joi*, was selected to represent Israel in the 1987 International Harp Congress, held in Vienna (ibid.).

3. The Polish-born composer and teacher lived in Israel from 1950–57, thereafter settling in Vienna; he died in March 1994 at the age of seventy-five. See Peter Gradenwitz, "In Memoriam: Roman Haubenstock-Ramati," *IMI News* 1994, no. 2: 19.

4. The orchestral work commissioned for the Testimonium festival is still in progress according to Horenstein, who hoped "to have it finished by 1997." Horenstein also reported that he was "finishing a string quartet commissioned by the late Shalhevit Freier and Dr. Tzipora H. Jochsberger, based on Jewish thematic material." Shalheveth Freier was the daughter of Recha Freier. Letter to the author, 23 December 1995.

5. A bamboo flute common in traditional Japanese music.

6. In *IMI News*, passim.

7. Horenstein, *Agadot*, program note.

8. Letter to the author, 23 December 1995.

9. Horenstein wrote in 1995: "I am currently working on a series of pieces exploring interaction between computer and performer. My latest work for saxophone and interactive MIDI environment is entitled *Angels and Ladders*. I am now working on a similar work for saxophone, multi-percussion and computer" (e-mail letter to the author, 6 November 1995).

CHAPTER 15: NOA GUY

1. Information provided by the composer.

2. Ms. Guy later provided the following additional remarks concerning this work: "The text is from 'The Scroll of Fire' by Bialik. The subject is ancient—the destruction of the temple, of which the eternal flame is saved and hope and love were kept alive. This subject is ancient and actual and might be interpreted in essence as the destiny of the Jewish people. I start the piece with a roar of electronic music, but when the voices enter, they are treated in strict counterpoint technique— the new against the old. It ends with a very thin hopeful sound that goes upward" (letter to the author, 22 August 1995). Chaim Nachman Bialik (1873–1934) settled in Palestine in 1924, by which time, according to Jehoash Hirshberg, he was regarded as "the greatest living Jewish poet" (*Music in the Jewish Community*, 68).

3. Ms. Guy later provided the following additional remarks concerning this work: "The text is a 'panorama' of the Book of Job. I took roughly a sentence from each chapter of the book and managed to re-create the story in a 'shorter' version. This enabled me to concentrate on the atmosphere in the music" (letter to the author, 22 August 1995). This work received the European Broadcasting Union Prize in 1986.

4. Letter to the author, 15 December 1990.

5. *The Forbidden Fruit* was commissioned by Roger Bobo of the Los Angeles Philharmonic, and *At the Evening Tide* was commissioned by the Israel Broadcasting Authority; both works employ texts by the composer.

6. In *IMI News,* passim.

7. Information provided by the composer.

8. Letter to the author, 1 November 1995.

CHAPTER 16: HAIM PERMONT

1. Letter to the author, 26 March 1991.

2. The prize sponsored a recording of this work, for later release, performed by alto Mira Zakai, the Kibbutz Artzi Choir, and the Tel Aviv Symphony, Avner Itai conducting.

3. In *IMI News* 1994, nos. 3–4: 23.

4. Letter to the author, 29 November 1995.

CHAPTER 17: YINAM LEEF

1. Liner notes, Yinam Leef, *Symphony No. 1/Violin Concerto* (Jerusalem Symphony Orchestra, IBA), Music in Israel (MII-CD-16). This was the first instance, since the inception of the award in 1983, in which more than one composer was named a recipient, a practice that has since continued.

2. In *IMI News,* passim. Leef's thoughtful essay "On Traditions and Contradictions" is accompanied by a biographical sketch in *IMI News* 1990, no. 2: 5–6. See also his "Four Questions, Three Answers, and a Reaction," *IMI News* 1991, no. 2: 6–7, for further remarks concerning Israeli music.

3. Letter to the author, 8 October 1995.

CHAPTER 18: BETTY OLIVERO

1. The composer provided a summary of her family history: "My mother was born in Greece—Thessaloniki, to a Sephardic Jewish family that immigrated to Greece back in 1492. My father was born in north of Greece, in a town called Comotini where there was a quite important Sephardic community that arrived there also after 1492. My father's family immigrated to Israel in 1932. My mother's family, unfortunately were deported by the Germans, probably to Auschwitz, and never came back (grandparents, parents, and a six-year-old brother). My mother and her other brother managed to escape on time to Athens, and shortly after the war was over she immigrated to Israel" (letter to the author, 5 January 1996).

2. Betty Olivero, "Sources of Inspiration," *IMI News* 1990, no. 3: 12.

3. Olivero's reference is to her *Cantes Amargos (Songs of Bitterness).* Another work commissioned by the Maggio Musicale festival is the composer's *Pan* for five flutists (1984–88).

4. Betty Olivero, *Cantes Amargos (Songs of Bitterness): Three Ladino Romances for Female Voice and Chamber Orchestra* (Tel Aviv: Israel Music Institute, 1983). The catalog number is IMI 6401.

5. During a performance by the Jewish music ensemble Voice of the Turtle (2 December 1995, Fermilab, Batavia, Illinois), director Judith Wachs explained the reference to keys found in many Ladino poems and songs: when they were expelled from Spain, many Jewish families retained the large door keys, which they were certain they would again need upon their return.

6. Letter to the author, 27 November 1995.

CHAPTER 19: ARI BEN-SHABETAI

1. This work is scored for soprano, English horn, French horn, double bass, and harp.

2. This movement is the last of Ben-Haim's *Five Pieces for Piano,* op. 34 (1943), premiered by the composer on the Palestine Broadcasting Service on 17 April 1944 (Hirshberg, *Paul Ben-Haim,* 408).

3. In *IMI News,* passim. Conductors of these performances included Zubin Mehta, Hans Graf, and Gary Bertini. The performances were the outcome of a composition contest sponsored by the Israel Philharmonic Orchestra and the IMI, in which Ben-Shabetai was awarded first prize.

4. In a program note accompanying recent performances of the work, Ben-Shabetai explained: "I decided to attempt, in my own way, to pick up where Scriabin left off and to continue his ideas about the representation of tonal and harmonic sonorities by means of color timbres and shades (*chroma* in Greek), and about the use of extended chromaticism" (Ari Ben-Shabetai, program note, *Stagebill* [New York: Lincoln Center, February 1995], 19). The dual meaning of Ben-Shabetai's title is reflected in his titles of the three movements: "Magenta," "Aquamarine," and "White Light."

5. The Pittsburgh premiere performances, conducted by Kirk Muspratt, were on 8–10 December 1995. A performance in Jerusalem, conducted by Lorin Maazel, took place on 13 February 1996.

CHAPTER 20: ODED ZEHAVI

1. Information provided by the composer.

2. According to Tzvi Avni (letter to the author, June 1995), this is incorrect.

3. Oliver Messiaen's work for piano was composed in 1944.

4. Oliver Messiaen's monumental *Catalogue d'oiseaux,* for piano, was composed in 1958.

5. The Austrian-born music critic, scholar, and educator Hans Keller (1919–1985) was affiliated with the BBC music division for two decades.

6. His works have been performed in New York at the Merkin Concert Hall, the Brooklyn Academy of Music, and most recently, at the Greenwich House Music School. While at the University of Pennsylvania, Zehavi won the Helen Weiss Award for his composition *Wire* (1986), a setting of the poem "Strange Brightness" by Haya Shenhav. Premiered at the Annenberg Center in Philadelphia in December 1986, *Wire* was also included in the "New Music from Israel" concert at Northern Illinois University in April 1987, in a performance conducted by H. Stephen Wright and featuring the composer as pianist. The work was also performed during the 1987 Israel Festival.

7. The appointment of Ukrainian immigrant composer Mark Kopytman to a similar post with the Rehovot Chamber Orchestra was noted in the *IMI News* 1993, no. 4: 27.

8. Letter to the author, 5 January 1996.

CONCLUSION

1. Frank Pelleg, "Listening to Music in Israel," *Ariel* 6 (1963): 24–25.

2. Writing to Joachim Stutschewsky in 1929, the Russian-immigrant pianist and educator David Schor lamented that the country had become "a centre of attraction" for European performers, rather than a "centrifugal force" that would "send its own artists, especially musicians, to the world" (Hirshberg, *Music in the Jewish Community,* 107).

3. Pelleg, "Listening," 25. Pelleg was a vigorous advocate of "local talent," performing and recording many works by Israeli composers ("Frank Pelleg Plays Works by Israeli Composers," CBS-72821, LP; "Frank Pelleg Plays Bach, Couperin, Tal, and Stravinsky," Hed Artzi BAN 14190/1/2, LP); additional recordings are preserved in the Israel Broadcasting Authority archives.

4. Yarden, "Milieu," 134.

5. This is reflected, for example, in the content of *Ariel,* a quarterly journal of the arts in Israel published since 1962, which includes occasional music reviews and articles but primarily focuses on literature and the visual arts.

6. Bar-Am, "The League of Composers in Israel," 75.

7. Government support of writers and other artists has been disproportionately greater than that of musicians. See Max Stern, "The Israel Composers' League," *New Music in Israel, 1988–1990* (Tel Aviv: Israel Composers' League, 1991), 15.

8. Ami Maayani, introduction to *Israeli Music, 1972–73* (Tel Aviv: Israel Composers' League, 1973), 3.

9. Tzvi Avni, "The Performer in the Age of Change," *Music in Time* (1983–84): 55.

10. Leef, "On Traditions and Contradictions," 6.

11. Zehavi was referring to his composition for double children's choir, *Thy Mornings I Shall Seek* (1994), based on a text by Shlomo Ibn Gabirol and commissioned by the Ministry of Education and Culture (*IMI News* 1994, no. 2: 18).

12. The writer reviewing Permont's *A Return to the South* (text: Abba Kovner) wonders: "Are we witnessing the emergence of a young generation of old composers?" (I. Abravaya, *Ha'aretz,* 14 November 1993, in *IMI News* 1993, no. 4: 19).

13. Gradenwitz, "Music in Israel," 27.

14. Bohlman, *"The Land Where Two Streams Flow,"* 190.

15. Bohlman, afterword to *Israeli Folk Music,* 54.

16. Gradenwitz, "Music in Israel," 26.

17. Keren, *Contemporary Israeli Music,* 81. Twelve years later, in 1973, Keren stated that despite all attempts by Israeli composers to create such a synthesis, "the overall sound of their music in unmistakably Western" (107).

18. In *IMI News* 1994, no. 2: 19. Another street was to be named for Israeli cellist and music educator Thelma Yellin.

SELECTED DISCOGRAPHY

The twenty composers profiled in this book are listed alphabetically below, with the publisher(s) of their music identified, and a list of selected recordings that are arranged, as closely as possible, in the order in which they were issued.

Music by composers in this book is published by firms located in Israel and elsewhere. Israeli music publishers cited below include Israel Music Institute (IMI/Tel Aviv); Israeli Music Publications (IMP/Jerusalem); Israeli Music Center (IMC/Tel Aviv), affiliated with the Israel League of Composers; Ministry of Education and Culture, General Federation of Labor, Music Division, Merkaz LeTarbut (MLT/Tel Aviv); Israel Brass and Woodwind Publications (IBWP/Holon); Or-Tav (Tel Aviv); Jerusalem Institute of Contemporary Music (JICM/Jerusalem); and Midona (Givatayim).

Recordings of works by composers in this book are available in various formats. Earlier works by composers whose interviews appear in Parts I and II of this book were originally issued on long-playing (LP) records, some of which have been reissued in compact disk (CD) format. Most recent recordings have been issued in CD and occasionally cassette (CS) format. Where complete details concerning each listed recording are known, the following information is given in order: titles of individual compositions by the listed composer, with year of completion; title of recording; featured soloists, ensembles, conductor; recording label and catalog number; recording format and year issued.

Abbreviations: sop/soprano; mez/mezzo; alt/alto; ten/tenor; bar/baritone; bas/bass; nar/narrator; fl/flute; pic/piccolo; ob/oboe; cl/clarinet; bn/bassoon; sax/saxophone; hn/French horn; tpt/trumpet, trb/trombone; pno/piano; kbds/keyboards; org/organ; hp/harp; gtr/guitar; hpd/harpsichord; perc/percussion; vn/violin; va/viola; vc/violoncello; cond/conductor.

Haim Alexander
[Publishers: IMI, IMP]

De profundis (1972)
Organ Landscape Jerusalem
Elisabeth Roloff, org
Musikproduktion Darbinghaus und Grimm
MDG 319 0538-2 (CD, 1994)

If I forget thee, Oh Jerusalem (original title: *Variations;* 1947)
Anthology of Israeli Piano Music
Allan Sternfield, pno
Israeli Music Center IMC/MALI (CD, 1997)

Sonata for Piano (1994)
Anthology of Israeli Piano Music
Yuval Admoni, pno
Israeli Music Center IMC/MALI (CD, 1997)

Tzvi Avni
[Publishers: IMI, IMP, MLT]

Vocalise (1964)
Electronic Music
Pnina Avni, sop
Turnabout TV-34004S/TV 4004 (LP, 1965)

Meditations on a Drama (1966)
Israel Chamber Ensemble, Gary Bertini, cond
CBS S-72578 (LP, 1968)

Piyutim Le'Shabat (*Sabbath Devotional Songs*) (1962)
Cameran Singers; Avner Itai, cond
Israel Ministry of Culture and Art (LP, 1981)

Lyric Episodes for oboe and tape (1972)
Israeli Electroacoustic Music
Eliahu Thorner, ob
Folkways FSS-33878 (LP, 1981)

Elegy for Cello Solo (1970)
Uzi Wiesel, vc
RCA Red Seal RL 83032 (LP, 1983)

Five Pantomimes (1968)
Israel Sinfonietta Beer Sheva; Mendi Rodan, cond
Jerusalem/Music in Israel (ATD 8301) (LP, 1983)

Two Psalms for oboe and strings (1975)
Oded Pintus, ob; Israel Chamber Orchestra; Yoav Talmi, cond
Music in Israel MII-CD-C6 (CD, 1987)

Psalms (1967); *On Mercy* (1973)
Choral Music from Israel
Cameran Singers; Avner Itai, cond
Music in Israel MII-CD-12 (CD, 1989)

Programme Music 1980 (1980)
Israel Philharmonic Orchestra; Zubin Mehta, cond
Inak/in-akustik CD 9005 (CD, 1991)
[reissue of Jerusalem MII-S-2 (ATD-8402A) (LP, 1984)]

Beside the Depths of a River (1969/75), *Collage* (1967), *Leda and the Swan* (1976), *A Monk Observes a Skull* (1981), *Love Under a Different Sun* (1982)
Tzvi Avni—Love Under a Different Sun: Vocal Works
Emilie Berendsen, mez-sop; Members of the Group for New Music and guest artists; David Bloch, pno and cond
Symposium 1110 (CD, 1992)

Odecha Ki Anitani (Variations on a Sephardic Tune) (1991)
Renanim Recorder Ensemble, Ephraim Marcus, cond
Renanim (limited issue) (CD, 1994)

Summer Strings (String Quartet No. 1) (1962)
New Israel String Quartet (Alexander Tal, Raphael Markus, vn; Zeev Steinberg, va; Yaacov Menze, vc)
Music in Israel MII-CD-18 (CD, 1995)
[reissue of RCA Israel ISZ-0013 (LP, 1970)]

Piano Sonata No. 1 (1961)
Pnina Salzman Plays Mediterranean Piano Music
Pnina Salzman, pno
Music in Israel MII-CD-19 (CD, 1996)

Five Variations for Mr. "K" (for Percussionist and Tape) (1983)
Oron Schwartz, perc
Jerusalem Music Centre (CD, 1996)

Capriccio (1955)
Anthology of Israeli Piano Music
Allan Sternfield, pno
Israel Music Center IMC/MALI (CD, 1997)

Epitaph (Piano Sonata No. 2) (1974/1979)
Anthology of Israeli Piano Music
Astrit Balzan, pno
Israeli Music Center IMC/MALI (CD, 1997)

Ari Ben-Shabetai
[Publishers: IMI, IMC]

Three Songs in the Romantic Style (1977, 1982, 1985)
Anthology of Israeli Art Song
Eva Ben-Zvi, sop; Natasha Tadson, pno
Israeli Music Center IMC/MALI (CD, 1997)

Three Romances (1986)
Anthology of Israeli Piano Music
Natasha Tadson, pno
Israeli Music Center IMC/MALI (CD, 1997)

Abel Ehrlich
[Publishers: Breitkopf and Härtel, IMI, IMP, Or-Tav]

The Writing of Hezekia (1962; rev. 1970), *Bashrav* (1953), *Be Ye Not As Your Fathers*
(1964)
Rachel Adonailo, sop; Alexander Tal, vn; Israel Chamber Ensemble; National Choir
Rinat; Gary Bertini, cond
CBS S-72837 (LP, 1970)

Be Ye Not as Your Fathers (1964)
Rinat: Recordings from the Years 1956–1972
Rinat Israel Chamber Choir; Gary Bertini, cond
NMC 1032-2 (CD, 1993)

Will It Work? (1985)
Guitar Masterpieces of the Twentieth Century
Ruben Seroussi, gtr
Icarus Nuova Era 7255 (CD, 1994)

May There Be Abundant Peace (1994)
Kaprisma Ensemble
Gadi Abadi, va; Hanan Feinstein, gtr
Kaprisma (CD, 1995)

I Hear (1986)
Ankor Children's Choir; Dafna Ben-Yohanan, cond
Thorofon CTH 2306 (CD, 1996)

Nudi Harkhèm Tsipor (1979), *You Do Not Know* (1986), *The Book of the Sign* (1992),
Music for Symphony Orchestra (1990)
Soloists of the Jerusalem Symphony Orchestra; Paul Mefano, cond; Ankor Children's
Choir; Arnon Meroz, cond; Ensemble Oriol, Berlin; Rishon LeZion Symphony Or-
chestra; Noam Sheriff, cond
Music in Israel MII-CD-21 (CD, 1997)

Selected Discography

Furious Rondo (1953)
Anthology of Israeli Piano Music
Ora Rotem-Nelken, pno
Israeli Music Center IMC/MALI (CD, 1997)

Ludi III (1993)
Anthology of Israeli Piano Music
Yuval Admoni, pno
Israeli Music Center IMC/MALI (CD, 1997)

Piano Trio (1986)
Jewish Musical Heritage
Israel Piano Trio (Alexander Volkov, pno; Menahem Breuer, vn; Marcel Bregman, vc)
Museum of the Jewish Diaspora, Beth Hatefutsoth, BTR 9504 (CD, 1997)

Bashrav (1953)
Israeli Compositions for Solo Violin
Nitai Tsori, vn
Moetsa LeTarbut/Ministry of Education and Culture (CD, 1997)

Tsippi Fleischer
[Publishers: IMI, IMP, IMC, Peer Verlag]

Daughters of Eve
Compositions and arrangements conducted by Tsippi Fleischer
Various performers
Hed-Arzi BAN 14372 (LP, 1973)

Girl-Butterfly-Girl (1977), *To The Fruit of My Land* (1981), *Ten Fragments for Oboe, Clarinet, and Bassoon* (1984), *Resuscitation: Five Miniatures for Cello Solo* (1980)
Tsippi Fleischer: Music for Small Ensembles
Robin Weisel-Capsouto, Marina Levit, sop; Nissim Daqwar, oriental vn; Taysir Elias, oud; Amir Sela, fl; Miri Zamir-Capsouto, pno; Uriel Atlas, gtr; Michael Amit, ob; Eric Drucker, cl; Hillary Milne, bn; Alexander Kaganovsky, vc
Hataklit DD 35362 (LP/CS, 1986)

A Girl Named Limonad (1977)
Jerusalem Symphony Orchestra; Shalom Ronly-Riklis, cond
Music from Six Continents series
Vienna Modern Masters VMM 3004 (CD, 1991)

Lamentation (1985), *In The Mountains of Armenia* (1988), *The Gown of Night* (1988), *Girl-Butterfly-Girl* (1977/84), *The Clock Wants to Sleep* (1980), *Scenes of Israel* (Six Madrigals; 1981–83)
Tsippi Fleischer: Vocal Music
Various performers, including Cilla Grossmeyer, sop; Neve Shir Choir; N. Margalit, cond; National Choir Rinat; Stanley Sperber, cond
Opus One CD-158 (CD, 1992)

341

Oratorio 1492–1992 (1991)
National Choir Rinat; Maayan Chamber Choir; Israel Shfeya Mandolin Ensemble;
Guitar Ensemble of the Music Education Centre (Hadera); Haifa Symphony Orches-
tra; Stanley Sperber, cond
Music from Six Continents series
Vienna Modern Masters VMM 3013 (CD, 1992)

"A Girl Dreamed She Was a Butterfly" from *Girl-Butterfly-Girl* (1977/84), *Ballad of
Expected Death in Cairo* (1987), *CANTATA: Like Two Branches* (1989)
Arabische Texturen: Art Music Settings of Arabic Poetry by Tsippi Fleischer
Isabelle Ganz, mez-sop; various instrumentalists; Cameran Singers, Israel Kibbutz
Choir; Gérard Wilgowicz, Avner Itai, cond
Koch Schwann AULOS 3-1420-2 (CD, 1993)

In a Chromatic Mood (1986)
Anthology of Israeli Piano Music
Michal Tal, pno
Israeli Music Center IMC/MALI (CD, 1997)

Daniel Galay
[Publishers: IMI, Rimon, Dorn, Needham, Edipan Edizioni Musicali]

Noa Guy
[Publishers: IMI, IMP]

Lost Hope (1982)
Israeli Vocal and Instrumental Music
Emilie Berendsen, mez-sop; various performers
Folkways FTS 37466 (LP, 1985)

Over Fallen Leaves (1986)
Anthology of Israeli Piano Music
Michal Tal, pno
Israeli Music Center IMC/MALI (CD, 1997)

Aharon Harlap
[Publishers: IBWP, IMI, IMP, MLT, Or-Tav]

The Sacrifice of Isaac (1977)
National Choir Rinat; Stanley Sperber, cond
RCA RL 83031 (LP, 1981)
MU 181 (France) (LP, 1981)

Scenes of Jerusalem (1979)
Flute Sounds from Jerusalem
Raanan Eylon, fl; Yaacov Shilo, pno
EMI F668.763 (LP, 1985)

Sichot (*Conversations*) (1984)
Music by Israeli and Jewish Composers
Raanan Eylon, fl; Yaacov Shilo, pno
EMI F669.295 (LP, 1985)

O Sing Unto the Lord (1979)
Tel Aviv Philharmonic Choir; Michael Shani, cond
Isradisc SI 31172 (LP, 1986)

Jephtha's Daughter
Meir Rimon, hn; Kibbutz Artzi Choir; Aharon Harlap, cond
CDI (CD, 1988)

Beterem (*Before*) (1983–84)
Jerusalem Rubin Conservatory of Music and Dance
Ankor Children's Choir; Dafna Ben-Yohanan, cond
ISRC-DE-C29-9630601 bis 18 (CD, 1996)

Symphony No. 2 (*L'Oiseau de la Guerre*) (1992)
Sivan Rotem, sop; Haifa Symphony Orchestra; Stanley Sperber, cond
Music in Israel MII (CD, 1997)

Stephen Horenstein
[Publisher: JICM]

Breaking the Walls (1985), *Chiasmus* (1985), *Piece for Large Ensemble* (1985), *Meditation on a Line* (1984), *Seven Faces of a Garden* (1981)
Stephen Horenstein: Collages
Various performers, including featured soloists Yuval Mesner, Roman Kunsman, Jerry
Garval, Eli Magen, Morton Kam, Stephen Horenstein
Black Saint/Soul Note SN 1099 IREC (LP, 1986)

The Cave (1995), *Gorky Park* (1995), *Between the Silences* (1994), *Alta Alta* (1995),
Journey Tale (1994–95)
Stephen Horenstein: Between the Silences
Performers include Jeffery Kowalsky, Avi Yishay, perc; Shai Bechar, kbds; Stephen
Horenstein, sax, alt fl
Jerusalem Institute of Contemporary Music JICM (CD, 1995)

Gabriel Iranyi
[Publishers: IMI, IMC, IMP, Bèrben, Edizioni musicali]

Quatuor pour Flutes (1987), *Bird of Wonder* (1981), *Scroll Fragments I* (1986), *Laudae*
(1984), *Five Haiku* (1994–95)
Portrait Gabriel Iranyi: Kammermusik
Arcadie Flute Quartet; Yoriko Ikeya, pno; Christian Peters, sop sax; Piano Duo Beer-
Sheva; Modern Art Sextet (Berlin)
Pool (CD, 1997)

Two Pieces for Chamber Ensemble (1988)
Musica Nova; Itai Talgam, cond
Music in Israel MII (CD, 1997)

The Hymns of Job (1993)
Anthology of Israeli Art Song
Eva Ben-Zvi, sop; Natasha Tadson, pno
Israeli Music Center IMC/MALI (CD, 1997)

Hanoch Jacoby
[Publishers: IMI]

Judean Hill Dance: Hora Variations (1952)
Orchestral version
Pro-Prius 25-04-02-0006 (LP, 1955)

Quintet for Flute, Oboe, Clarinet, Horn, and Bassoon (1946)
Israeli Woodwind Quintet (U. Shoham, fl; E. Thorner, ob; G. Marton, cl; P. Delvescovo, hn; M. Rechtman, bn)
RCA ISZ-1019 (LP, 1967)

Hora Dance
Renanim Recorder Ensemble, Ephraim Marcus, cond
Private issue (CD, 1994)

Seven Miniatures (1944)
Anthology of Israeli Piano Music
Liora Ziv-Li, pno
Israeli Music Center IMC/MALI (CD, 1997)

Yinam Leef
[Publishers: IMI, IMC, IMP, Thedore Presser]

Symphony No. 1 (1981/92), *Violin Concerto* (1983)
Bat-Sheva Svaldi-Kohlberg, vn; Jerusalem Symphony Orchestra; David Shallon, Shalom Ronly-Riklis, cond
Music in Israel MII-CD-16 (CD, 1995)

How Far East, How Further West? (Canaanite Fantasy No. 2) (1987)
Anthology of Israeli Piano Music
Natasha Tadson, pno
Israeli Music Center IMC/MALI (CD, 1997)

The Invisible Carmel (1982)
Michal Shamir, Sop; Musica Nova; Itai Talgam, cond
Music in Israel MII (CD, 1997)

Ami Maayani
[Publishers: Lyra, IMP]

Trio for Flute, Viola, and Harp (1966; rev. 1975)
Kathleen Alister, hp; Lucien Grujon, fl; Walter Mony, va
Westminster Gold WGS-8196 (LP, 1972)

Concerto for Eight Winds and Percussion (1966); *Deux Impromptus for Piano* (1974, 1976)
U. Toeplitz, fl; E. Thorner, ob; G. Marton, cl; M. Rechtman, bn; P. Delvescovo, hn; R. Pennig, tpt; R. Parness, trb; G. Steiner, perc; Sara Fuxon-Heyman, pno; Ami Maayani, cond
Isradisc SI-31153 (LP, 1976)

Concerto for Violin and Orchestra (1967); *Concerto for Violoncello and Orchestra* (1967)
L. Mordkovitch, vn; U. Wiesel, vc; Jerusalem Symphony Orchestra; Mendi Rodan, cond
Isradisc SI-31147 (LP, 1977)

Arabesque (No. 2) for flute and harp (1973)
Amir Sella, fl; Ruth Maayani, hp
SACEM ELF 20-881 (LP, 1984)

Symphony No. 4 (Sinfonietta on Popular Hebraic Themes) (1982)
Israel Sinfonietta Beer Sheva; Mendi Rodan, cond
Music in Israel MII-CD-9 (CD, 1988)

Toccata for Harp (1961; rev. 1969)
Susanna Mildonian, hp; Musidisc 16002 (LP, 1971)
Susann McDonald, hp; Klavier KS507 (LP, 1972)
Chantal Mathieu, hp; Eurodisc 202181-366 (CD, 1988)

Ouverture Solenelle (1982)
Israel Philharmonic Orchestra; Zubin Mehta, cond
Inak/in-akustik CD 9005 (CD, 1991)
[reissue of Jerusalem MII-S-2 (ATD-8402A) (LP, 1984)]

Sonata for Harp No. 1 (1979)
Grace Wong, hp; Isradisc SI 31165 (LP, 1982)
Naoko Yoshino, hp; CBS/Sony 30 DC 5311 (CD, 1993)

Toccata (1961/1969), *Maqamat/Arabesque No. 1* (1961/1984), *Passacaglia dans le Style Oriental* (1975), *Sonata No. 1* (1979), *Sonata No. 2* (1990), *Five Easy Pieces* (1974)
Ami Maayani: Music for Harp
Naoko Yoshino, hp
IMP Digital 02-9420 (CD, 1995)

Sonata for Violin (1978), *Sonata for Violoncello* (1979), *Sonatina for Guitar* (1979), *Sonatine en trio for Violin, Cello, and Piano* (1988)
Ami Maayani: Baroque Sonatas

Orit Wolf, pno; Bing Jing Yu, vn; Natalia Khoma, vc; Tali Roth, gtr
IMP Digital 01-2096 (CD, 1996)

Concerto for Percussion (Percussion and Two-Piano Version, 1993), *Three Preludes for Percussion Ensemble, Avant-Propos* (Two Preludes for Piano, 1958), *Deux Impromptus pour Piano* (1974, 1976)
Ami Maayani: Music for Piano and Percussion
Orit Wolf, Aviram Reichert, Josef Reshef, Gil Shohat, pno; Chen Zimbalista, perc; Samuel Rubin Israel Academy of Music Percussion Ensemble; Alon Bor, cond
IMP Digital 02-2096 (CD, 1996)

Betty Olivero
[Publisher: IMI, Ricordi]

Cantigas Sepharadies (1982)
Israeli Vocal and Instrumental Music, Volume Two
Bonita Hyman, mez-sop; Yale University Contemporary Ensemble; Gisele Buka, cond
Folkways FTS 37466 (LP, 1985)

Makamat (1988)
Five mideastern folk songs for female voice and nine players
Ensemble Musica '900; Maurizio Dini Ciacci, cond
Ricordi CRMCD 1009 (CD, 1989)

Juego de siempre (1991)
The Never-ending Game: Jewish-Spanish Traditional Songs
Esti Kenan-Ofri, mez-sop; Michael Meltzer, fl/pic; Adina Har-Oz, hp; Ilan Schul, cl/bas-cl; Chen Zimbalista, perc; Yaron Prenski, vn; Irit Livne, va; Emmanuel Gruber, vc; Israel Idelson, cond
Museum of the Jewish Diaspora, Beth Hatefutsoth, BTR 9201 (CD, 1992)

Mode Ani (1995) (transcription of a Jewish Prayer)
Giora Feidman, cl; North German Radio Choir
Pläne CD 8874 (CD, 1995)

Bakashot (1996)
Giora Feidman, cl; North German Radio Choir and Symphony Orchestra; Lior Shambadal, cond
Koch (CD, 1996)

Endings (1991)
Anthology of Israeli Piano Music
Michal Tal, pno
Israeli Music Center IMC/MALI (CD, 1997)

Ben-Zion Orgad
[Publishers: IMI, IMP, Peters]

Yedidot (1966)
Israel Kibbutz Choir; Avner Itai, cond
Kibbutz KRC S002 (LP)

Dialogues on the First Scroll (1975)
The Contemporary Chamber Players; Ralph Shapey, cond
Grenadilla GS-1045 (LP, 1977)

Sha'ar Sha'ar (1977)
Elaine Bonazzi, mez-sop; The Cantilena Chamber Players (Edna Michell, vn; Harry Zaratzian, va; Steven Thomas, vc; Frank Glazer, pno)
Grenadilla GS-1029/30 (LP, 1979)

Reshuyoth (Options) (1978)
Arie Vardi, pno
RCA-YJRL 10004 (LP, 1981)

Individuations I (1981)
Erik Druckman, cl; Israel Sinfonietta Beer Sheva; Mendi Rodan, cond
Music in Israel MII-CD-9 (CD, 1988)

Mizmorim (Psalms; 1966–68), *Hallel (Song of Praise;* 1979)
Zimra Ornatt, sop; Miriam Laron, mez-sop; Rema Samsanov, alt; Neil Jenkins, ten; Willy Haparnas, bar; Israel Chamber Ensemble, Jerusalem Symphony Orchestra; Gary Bertini, cond
Music in Israel MII-CD-14 (CD, 1993)

Filigrees No. 1 (1989–90)
Eli Heifetz, cl; Shiran Quartet (O. Shiran, C. Leiman, vn; M. Kugel, va; F. Nemirovsky, vc)
Music in Israel MII-CD-15 (CD, 1994)

Two Preludes in an Impressionistic Mood (1960)
Anthology of Israeli Piano Music
Ora Rotem-Nelken, pno
Israeli Music Center IMC/MALI (CD, 1997)

Reshuyot (Options) (1978)
Anthology of Israeli Piano Music
Astrit Balzan, pno
Israeli Music Center IMC/MALI (CD, 1997)

Haim Permont
[Publishers: IMI, IMP]

A Return to the South (1988)
Mira Zakai, alt; Israel Kibbutz Chamber Orchestra; Lior Shambadal, cond
Network Medien LC-6759 (CD, 1991)

Fantasy (1990)
Amakim-Mizra Girls' Choir; Rachel Bartenstein, cond
Municipality of the Jezreel Valley (CD, 1991)

Symphonette for Symphony Orchestra (1992)
Symphonette Orchestra Raanana, Yeruham Scharovsky, cond
Private issue (CD, 1992)

Romanza for Guitar Solo (1990)
Daniel Akiva, gtr
ACUM RAP CD-100 (CD, 1992)

Suite (1982)
Anthology of Israeli Piano Music
Michal Tal, pno
Israeli Music Center IMC/MALI (CD, 1997)

For Oboe (1986)
Musica Nova; Itai Talgam, cond
Music in Israel MII (CD, 1997)

Mordecai Seter
[Publishers: IMI, MLT]

Midnight Vigil (1961)
Ovadia Touvia, bar; Moshe Hovav, nar; Israel Broadcasting Authority Symphony
Orchestra and Choir; Gary Bertini, cond
CBS/Israel S-72564 (LP, 1962)

Yemenite Suite (1966)
Rema Samsonov, mez-sop; Israel Chamber Ensemble; Gary Bertini, cond
CBS S-72838 (LP, 1972)

Sine Nomine (1973)
Arie Vardi, pno
RCA-YJRL 10004 (LP, 1981)

The Daughter of Jephtah (1965)
Israel Sinfonietta Beer Sheva; Mendi Rodan, cond
Jerusalem/Music in Israel MII-S-1 (ATD 8301) (LP, 1983)

Trio for Violin, Cello, and Piano (1973)
The Yuval Trio
Jonathan Zak, pno; Uri Pianka, vn; Simcha Heled, vc
Music in Israel MII-CD-8 (CD, 1988)

Midnight Vigil (1961; rev. 1978), *String Quartet No. 1* (1975)
Mira Zakai, alt; Cameran Singers, National Choir Rinat, Kibbutz Artzi Choir, Jerusa-
lem Symphony Orchestra; Gary Bertini, cond; Tel Aviv Quartet
Capriccio 10 368 WDR (CD, 1990)

Dialogues (1983), *Piano Preludes to . . .* (1982), *Music* (1982), *Piano Cycle* (1982),
Sonata (1982)
Mordecai Seter: Piano Works, 1982–83
Ora Rotem, pno
Music in Israel MII-CD-13 (CD, 1993)

Four Festive Songs (1945–49), *Two Motets* (1951)
Rinat: Recordings from the Years 1956–1972
Rinat Israel Chamber Choir; Gary Bertini, cond
NMC 1032-2 (CD, 1993)

Opposites Unified (1984), *Improvisation* (1983), *Triptiques I–III* (1985), *Presence*
(1986)
Mordecai Seter: Piano Works, 1983–86
Ora Rotem-Nelken, pno
Private issue; CDI (CD, 1995)

Ricercar for string quartet (1962)
New Israel String Quartet (Alexander Tal, Raphael Markus, vn; Zeev Steinberg, va;
Yaacov Menze, vc)
Music in Israel MII-CD-18 (CD, 1995)
[reissue of RCA ISZ-0013 (LP, 1966)]

Chaconne and Scherzo (1955)
Pnina Salzman plays Mediterranean Piano Music
Pnina Salzman, pno
Music in Israel MII-CD-19 (CD, 1996)

Chaconne and Scherzo (1955)
Anthology of Israeli Piano Music
Ora Rotem-Nelken, pno
Israeli Music Center IMC/MALI (CD, 1997)

Arik Shapira
[Publishers: IMI, MIDONA]

The Kastner Trial: Electronic Opera in Thirteen Scenes (1991–94)
Private issue (AS-001) (CD, 1992)

Post Piano for piano and magnetic tape (1991)
Jeffrey Burns, pno
Pool 76033 (CD, 1994)

Upon Thy Ruins Ophra (1990); *Lament for Lotan* (1987); *Exchanges* (with Raviv Gazit;
1988)

Raviv Gazit/Arie Shapira: Electronic Compositions
ACUM (CD, 1995)

Off Piano (1985)
Anthology of Israeli Piano Music
Michal Tal, pno
Israeli Music Center IMC/MALI (CD, 1997)

Josef Tal
[Publishers: IMI, IMP]

String Quartet No. 1 (1959)
New Israel String Quartet (Alexander Tal, Raphael Markus, vn; Zeev Steinberg, va;
Yaacov Menze, vc)
RCA Israel ISZ-0011 (LP)

Concerto for Violoncello and Strings (1961)
Uzi Wiesel, vc; Israel Chamber Ensemble; Gary Bertini, cond
CBS S-72578 (LP)

Ma'amar (Treatise; 1973)
Uzi Wiesel, vc
RCA Red Seal RL 83032 (LP, 1983)

Concerto for Harpsichord and Electronics (1964)
Frank Pelleg plays Bach, Couperin, Tal, and Stravinsky
Frank Pelleg, hpd
Hed-Arzi BAN 14190/1/2 (LP, 1972)

Shape for Chamber Orchestra (1975)
Contemporary Chamber Players; Ralph Shapey, cond
Grenadilla GS-1044 (LP, 1977)

Concerto No. 6 for Piano and Electronics (1970)
Electroacoustic Music from Israel
Jonathan Zak, pno
Folkways FSS 33878 (LP, 1981)

Symphony No. 2 (1960)
Israel Philharmonic Orchestra; Zubin Mehta, cond
Inak/in-akustik CD 9005 (CD, 1991)
[reissue of Jerusalem MII-S-2 (ATD-8402A) (LP, 1984)]

Concerto for Harp and Electronics (1971; rev. 1980)
Israeli Music for Harp
Adina Har-Oz, hp
Jerusalem MII-S-4; ATD-8505 Digital (LP, 1985)

In Memoriam of a Dear Friend (1985)
Israeli and French Contemporary Cello Music
Ina Joost, vc
IMI 20005 (CS, 1988)

Sus Ha'ets (The Wooden Horse) (1976)
Choral Music from Israel
Cameran Singers; Avner Itai, cond
Music in Israel MII-CD-12 (CD, 1989)

Else-Homage (1975); *Essays I-III* for piano (1986/1988/1989)
Catherine Geyer, sop; J. Bliese, nar; H. Ganz, va; G. Teutsch, vc; N. Hauptmann, hn;
K. Helwig, pno; Josef Tal, cond; Jeffrey Burns, pno
Akademie der Künste Berlin (ACADEMY/edel company ACA 8506-2) (CD, 1992)

Symphony No. 2 (1960)
Jeunesses Musicales World Orchestra; Ronald Zollman, cond
Rainer Maillard Musikproduktion RMM 21692 (CS/CD, 1992)

Concerto No. 6 for Piano and Electronics (1970)
Jeffrey Burns, pno
Pool 76033 (CD, 1994)

Salve venia (1983)
Organ Landscape Jerusalem
Elisabeth Roloff, org
Musikproduktion Darbinghaus und Grimm
MDG 319 0538-2 (CD, 1995)

String Quartet No. 2 (1964)
New Israel String Quartet (Alexander Tal, Raphael Markus, vn; Zeev Steinberg, va;
Yaacov Menze, vc)
Music in Israel MII-CD-18 (CD, 1995)
[reissue of RCA Israel ISZ-0013 (LP, 1966)]

Sonata for Piano (1952)
Anthology of Israeli Piano Music
Allan Sternfield, pno
Israeli Music Center IMC/MALI (CD, 1997)

Five Densities (1975)
Anthology of Israeli Piano Music
Herut Israeli, pno
Israeli Music Center IMC/MALI (CD, 1997)

Essay 2 (1988)
Anthology of Israeli Piano Music
Natasha Tadson, pno
Israeli Music Center IMC/MALI (CD, 1997)

Oded Zehavi
[Publisher: IMI]

Juego de Siempre (The Never-Ending Game): Jewish-Spanish Traditional Songs
Esti Kenan-Ofri, mez-sop; various instrumentalists; Oded Zehavi, cond
Museum of the Jewish Diaspora, Beth Hatefutsoth BTR 9201 (CD, 1992)

L.H.M.—Israeli War Requiem (1986–91)
T. Tal, sop; E. Kenan-Ofri, alt; Rishon LeZion Symphony Orchestra; Ankor Children's
Choir; New Israeli Opera Choir; Noam Sheriff, cond
Isteldisc/Phonokol 410003 (CD, 1993)

SELECTED BIBLIOGRAPHY

Appleby, Bertram H. "Is There an Israeli Music?" *Congress Weekly* 24, no. 18 (20 May 1957): 8–9.

Avenary, Hanoch. "The Experience of Nature and Scenery in Israeli Song." In *Israeli Music, 1974–1975,* 35–40. Tel Aviv: Israel Composers' League, 1975.

Avni, Tzvi. "Music in the Eighties—Onward or Backwards?" *Music in Time* (1988–89): 34–38.

———. "Yet the Sea Is Not Yet Full: Currents in Contemporary Israeli Music," *Music in Time* (1986–87): 14–30.

Bar-Am, Benjamin, ed. *Aspects of Music in Israel.* Tel Aviv: Israel Composers' League/National Council for Culture and Art, 1980.

———. *Twenty Years of Israeli Music: Articles and Interviews.* Tel Aviv: National Council for Culture and Art/League of Composers in Israel, 1968.

Boehm, Yohanan. "Music in Modern Erez Israel, Composers." *Encyclopaedia Judaica.* 2d ed. 1971.

Bohlman, Philip V. Foreword and afterword to *Israeli Folk Music: Songs of the Early Pioneers,* edited by Hans Nathan, ix–x, 39–55. Recent Researches in the Oral Traditions of Music, vol. 4. Madison: A-R Editions, 1994.

———. *"The Land Where Two Streams Flow": Music in the German-Jewish Community of Israel.* Urbana and Chicago: University of Illinois Press, 1989.

———. *The World Centre for Jewish Music in Palestine, 1936–1940: Jewish Musical Life on the Eve of World War II.* New York: Oxford University Press, 1992.

Bohlman, Philip V., and Mark Slobin, eds. *Music in the Ethnic Communities of Israel.* Special issue of *Asian Music* 17, no. 2 (Spring–Summer 1986).

Brod, Max. *Israel's Music.* Translated by Toni Volcani. Tel Aviv: WIZO Zionist Education Department/Sefer Press Ltd., 1951.

353

Cohen, Joseph. *Voices of Israel: Essays on and Interviews with Yehuda Amichai, A. B. Yehoshua, T. Carmi, Aharon Appelfeld, and Amos Oz.* Albany: State University of New York Press, 1990.

Cohen, Judith, ed. *Proceedings of the World Congress on Jewish Music—Jerusalem, 1978.* Tel Aviv: Institute for the Translation of Hebrew Literature, 1982.

Domínguez, Virginia R. *People as Subject, People as Object: Selfhood and Peoplehood in Contemporary Israel.* Madison: University of Wisconsin Press, 1989.

Elias, William Y., ed. *IMI Comprehensive List of Works, A to Z 1961–1989.* Tel Aviv: Israel Music Institute, 1989.

————. "Josef Tal—80th Anniversary." *IMI News* 1990, no. 1: 1–2.

————. "Seter, Mordecai." In *New Grove Dictionary of Music and Musicians.* 1980.

————. "What Makes a Composer in Israel Write?" In *Israel Music Weeks,* edited by Benjamin Bar-Am, 17–24. Tel Aviv: League of Composers in Israel, 1971.

Fromm, Herbert. *On Jewish Music: A Composer's View.* New York: Bloch, 1978.

Gilbert, Felix, and Stephen R. Graubard, eds., *Historical Studies Today.* New York: Norton, 1971; Toronto: George J. McLeod, 1971.

Gradenwitz, [Peter] E. "Music in Israel." *Jewish Frontier* 33 (December 1966, sec. 2): 24–28.

Gradenwitz, Peter. "Israeli Composers." *Tempo* 20 (Summer 1951): 30–34, 38.

————. "Israeli Composers—A Link between Orient and Occident." *Chesterian* 25, no. 165 (1951): 69–72.

————. *Music and Musicians in Israel.* 3d ed., rev. and enl. Tel Aviv: Israel Music Publications, 1978.

————. *The Music of Israel: Its Rise and Growth through Five Thousand Years.* New York: Norton, 1949.

————. "Touma, Habib." In *New Grove Dictionary of Music and Musicians.* 1980.

Harrán, Don. "Israel, Art Music." In *New Grove Dictionary of Music and Musicians.* 1980.

Heskes, Irene. *Passport to Jewish Music: Its History, Traditions, and Culture.* Contributions to the Study of Music and Dance, no. 33. Westport, Conn., and London: Greenwood Press, 1994.

Hirshberg, Jehoash. "Alexander U. Boskovitch and the Quest for an Israeli National Musical Style." In *Modern Jews and their Musical Agendas,* ed. Ezra Mendelsohn, 92–109. New York: Oxford University Press, 1993.

————. *Music in the Jewish Community of Palestine, 1880–1948: A Social History.* New York: Oxford University Press, 1995.

————. *Paul Ben-Haim: His Life and Works.* Translated by Nathan Friedgut. Edited by Bathja Bayer. Jerusalem: Israel Music Publications, 1990.

————. "Tsippi Fleischer: Musician between East and West." *Ariel* 76 (1989): 46–54.

Hirshberg, Jehoash, and David Sagiv. "The 'Israeli' in Israeli Music: The Audience Responds." *Israel Studies in Musicology* 1 (1978): 159–73.

Hobshawm, Eric, and Terence Ranger, eds. *The Invention of Tradition.* Cambridge: Cambridge University Press, 1983.

Holde, Artur. *Jews in Music: From the Age of Enlightenment to the Present.* New York: Philosophical Library, 1959.

Idelsohn, A. Z. *Hebräisch-orientalischer Melodienschatz.* 10 vols. Leipzig: Breitkopf and Härtel, 1914–33.

———. *Jewish Music in Its Historical Development.* 1929; rpt. New York: Schocken, 1967.

Kenny, Herbert A. *Israel and the Arts.* Boston: Quinlan Press, 1988.

Keren, Zvi. *Contemporary Israeli Music: Its Sources and Stylistic Development.* Ramat Gan: Bar-Ilan University Press, 1980.

Landau, Paul. "Mordecai Seter: From the Collective to the Intimate." *IMI News* 1990, no. 3: 3–5.

Leef, Yinam. "Four Questions, Three Answers, and a Reaction." *IMI News* 1991, no. 2: 6–7.

———. "On Traditions and Contradictions." *IMI News* 1990, no. 2: 5–6.

Lefen, Gideon. "Israeli Art Music: How Often Is It Performed?" *IMI News* 1995, no. 1: 8–11.

Levine, Angela. "Musical Instruments in the Bible." *Ariel* 93 (1993): 79–87.

Levy, Emanuel. *The Habima—Israel's National Theater, 1917–1977: A Study in Cultural Nationalism.* New York: Columbia University Press, 1979.

List, Kurt. "What Jewish Music Means to Me." *Jewish Music Forum Bulletin* 10 (January 1956): 19.

Maayani, Ami. "The Music of Israel 1983–1985." *New Music in Israel 1983–1985,* 13–17. Additions and commentary by Dr. Eliyahu Schleifer. Tel Aviv: Israel Composers' League, 1985.

Olivero, Betty. "Sources of Inspiration." *IMI News* 1990, no. 3: 12.

Orgad, Ben-Zion. *Colmontage.* Translated by Avi Jacobson and Sharon Ne'eman. Tel Aviv: Privately printed, March 1989.

———. *The Musical Potential of the Hebrew Language and its Manifestations in Artistic Music.* Translated by Avi Jacobson. Jerusalem: Privately printed, Summer 1978.

———. "Questions of Art and Faith." *Ariel* 39 (1975): 85–95.

Pelleg, Frank. "Listening to Music in Israel." *Ariel* 6 (1963): 23–29.

Prins, Gwyn. "Oral History." In *New Perspectives in Historical Writing,* edited by Peter Burke, 114–39. London: Polity, 1991; University Park: Pennsylvania State University Press, 1992.

Ringer, Alexander L. "Musical Composition in Modern Israel." In *Contemporary Music in Europe: A Comprehensive Survey,* edited by Paul Henry Lang and Nathan Broder, 282–97. 1965. New York: Norton, 1968.

———. "Tal, Josef." In *New Grove Dictionary of Music and Musicians.* 1980.

Rothe, Friede F. "Music in Israel." *Tempo* 17 (Autumn 1950): 28–32.

Rothmüller, Aron Marko. *The Music of The Jews: An Historical Appreciation.* New and revised edition. Translated by H. S. Stevens. New York: Yoseloff, 1967.

Sabaneev, Leonid. "The Jewish National School in Music." Translated by S. W. Pring. *Musical Quarterly* 15 (1929): 448–68.

Said, Edward W., *Orientalism.* New York: Random House, Pantheon, 1978; rpt., with a new afterword, New York: Random House, Vintage, 1994.

Shaked, Yuval. "On Ehrlich's Personal Way in Music." *IMI News* 1990, no. 2: 1–3.

———. "All or Nothing at All: Correspondence with Arik Shapira," *IMI News* 1994, no. 2: 1–3.

Sharvit, Uri, guest ed. *Jewish Musical Culture—Past and Present.* Special issue of *World of Music* 37, no. 1 (1995).

Shelemay, Kay Kaufman. "Mythologies and Realities in the Study of Jewish Music." *World of Music* 37, no. 1 (1995): 24–38.

Shiloah, Amnon. "Eastern Sources in Israeli Music." Edited by Jay Shir. *Ariel* 88 (1992): 4–19.

———. *Jewish Musical Traditions.* Detroit: Wayne State University Press, 1992.

———. "Revival and Renewal: Can Jewish Ethnic Tradition Survive the Melting Pot?" *Musica Judaica* 10, no. 1 (1987–88): 59–69.

Silber, Laya Harbater. "Ami Maayani and the Yiddish Art Song (Part I)." *Musica Judaica* 8, no. 1 (1985–86): 75–86.

———. "Ami Maayani and the Yiddish Art Song (Part II)." *Musica Judaica* 9, no. 1 (1986–87): 47–64.

Silberman, Ulya. "The Philharmonic Orchestra and Israeli Composition." In *Sixth Annual Conference—Israeli Music Week: December 19, 1965–January 1, 1966,* 79–86. Tel Aviv: League of Composers in Israel, 1966.

Slobin, Mark. "Ten Paradoxes and Four Dilemmas of Studying Jewish Music." *World of Music* 37, no. 1 (1995): 18–23.

Smoira-Cohn, Michal. "Music Here and Now—What Does It Mean?" *Music in Time* (1988–89): 17–33.

Sowden, Dora. "Israel Music." *Musical Opinion* 91 (July 1968): 545–49.

Squires-Kidron, Pamela. "Multi-Coloured Musicians." *Ariel* 73 (1988): 63–67.

Stern, Max. "In Search of a Sacred Ethos." *New Music in Israel, 1985–1987,* 16–20. Tel Aviv: Israel Composers' League, 1988.

———. "The Israel Composers' League." *New Music in Israel, 1988–1990,* 12–17. Tel Aviv: Israel Composers' League, 1991.

Swet, Hermann, ed. *Musica Hebraica.* 2 vols. Jerusalem: World Centre for Jewish Music in Palestine, 1938.

Tischler, Alice. *A Descriptive Bibliography of Art Music by Israeli Composers.* Warren, Mich.: Harmonie Park Press, 1988.

Toeplitz, Uri. "The Progressive Reactionary." Israel Philharmonic Orchestra concert program, 18 March 1972, n.p.

———. Israel Philharmonic Orchestra concert program, 1969, n.p.

Weisser, Albert. *The Modern Renaissance of Jewish Music, Events, and Figures: Eastern Europe and America.* New York: Bloch, 1954.

Werner, Alfred. "Pioneers of Israeli Art." *Jewish Frontier* 35, no. 1 (January 1968): 13–17.

Wigoder, Geoffrey. "Israel, State of (Cultural Life): Music and Dance." *Encyclopaedia Judaica.* 2d ed. 1971.

Wolpe, Michael. "Profile of Composer Haim Alexander." *Music in Time* (1989–89): 39–72.

Wolpe, Stefan. "Music, Old and New, in Palestine." *Modern Music* 16, no. 3 (March–April 1939): 156–59.

Yarden, Elie. "The Israeli Composer and His Milieu." *Perspectives of New Music* 4, no. 2 (Spring–Summer 1966): 130–39.

INDEX

357

Tal, Josef (*cont.*)
68; commissions, 67–68, 71, 77–78;
correspondence, 77, 323 nn. 8–9;
diversity, stylistic, 68; education,
68, 76–77; electronic music, 54,
67, 70–71, 75, 117, 250, 266; and
Eliraz, 323 n.10; and Galay, 197;
Germany, returning to, 76; at Hebrew
University, 70; notation, electronic
music, 70–71, 77; IMI catalog,
323 n.5; Israeli composer, being
an, 72–75; immigration, 68–69; on
Jewish and Israeli music, 40; Keren
on, 54; on Mahler, 75–76; on national
music, 72–75; operas, 71; and
Orgad, 126; Palestine Conservatory
and Academy of Music, 69–70;
Palestine Broadcasting Service, 69;
performances, 36, 68, 69, 71, 77–78;
photography, 68–69; Ringer on,
67–68; on Schoenberg, 76; Seter
on, 117–18; *Der Sohn des Rabbiners*
(autobiography), 68; on Stockhausen,
70, 73; as teacher, 167; on teaching,
71–72; on young composers, 73.
Works: *Ashmedai*, 67–68; Fourth
Symphony, 77; Fifth Symphony, 77,
323 n.9; *Josef*, 78, 323 n.10; *Masada*,
71; Piano Quartet, 77; Second Piano
Concerto, 74; Second Symphony, 36,
67; Sixth Symphony, 78; *The Tower*, 77
Talmud, 228
Tanglewood, Berkshire Music Center at:
Avni at, 140–41, 143; Leef at, 261;
Olivero at, 271, 272, 329–30 n.2;
Orgad at, 129, 131
Taqsīm, 30, 123. *See also* Arabic music
Targ, Fanny and Max, 35
Tchernichovsky, Saul, 190
Technion, 152; Symphony Orchestra,
61, 62
Tel Aviv Council for Culture and Art,
224
Tel Aviv Foundation for Literature and
the Arts, 34, 135, 151
Tel Aviv Museum, 189, 237
Tel Aviv Philharmonic Choir, 177

Tel Aviv Symphony Orchestra, 316 n.61,
334 n.2
Tel Hai International Arts Festival, 232,
236
Tempo, 129, 141, 255, 267
Testimonium, 35, 229–30, 316 n.56
Tetrachords, 151, 222; Lydian, 253
Texts, biblical, 88, 172, 173, 178, 189,
326 n.12; Psalms, 51, 88, 115, 134,
277, 326 n.12; Song of Songs, 88, 276,
328 n.8; Torah, 113, 228
Texture, musical. *See* Heterophony;
Homophony, Monophony; Polyphony
Theodorakis, Mikis, 292
Theresienstadt (Terezín), concentration
camp at, 256–57, 259
Thimmig, Les, 228
Third-generation composers, 24–25,
26, 41–42, 163–68; compared to
earlier generations, 163–65, 252–53,
265–66; and diversity, stylistic,
167–68; and immigration, 167;
and internationalism, 163–65; and
Jewish identification, 166–67; and
Mediterranean style, 167; and oriental
influences, 164–65, 167; Permont
on, 252–53, 253; and pluralism,
cultural, 166–68; Seter on, 117–18;
and independence, Israeli, 26, 163,
164, 309 n.3; study abroad, 163–64;
and synthesis, East-West, 165, 166–67
Thoreau, Henry David, 251
Tiessen, Heinz, 67
Time: in poetry of Celan, 133–34; in
Hindu philosophy, 134; Hume, in
philosophy of, 134; in Israeli culture,
293–94, 242; in music, 134, 233,
235–36, 255–56, 267, 275; Nachman
of Bratzlav, in legend of Rabbi, 145;
oriental approach to, 267
Tippett, Michael, 291
Tischler, Alice, 22, 24, 314 n.39; on
Boehm, 318 n.88; first-generation
composers in, 54, 310 n.10, 322 n.5;
Harlap in, 330 n.1; Iranyi in, 332 n.1;
second-generation composers in, 126,